Manhattan Review®

Test Prep & Admissions Consulting

Turbocharge your GMAT: Quantitative Question Bank

part of the 6th Edition Series

April 20th, 2016

- ☐ *Complete & Challenging Training Set*
  - *Problem Solving - 250 Questions*
  - *Data Sufficiency - 250 Questions*
- ☐ *Questions mapped according to the scope of the GMAT*
- ☐ *Over 100 questions with Alternate Approaches*
- ☐ *Text-cum-graphic explanations*

www.manhattanreview.com

Copyright and Terms of Use

Copyright and Trademark

Terms of Use

No Warranties

Limitation on Liability

10-Digit International Standard Book Number: (ISBN: 1-62926-066-5)
13-Digit International Standard Book Number: (ISBN: 978-1-62926-066-2)

Last updated on April 20th, 2016.

Manhattan Review, 275 Madison Avenue, Suite 1429, New York, NY 10016.
Phone: +1 (212) 316-2000. E-Mail: info@manhattanreview.com. Web: www.manhattanreview.com

About the Turbocharge your GMAT Series

The Turbocharge Your GMAT Series is carefully designed to be clear, comprehensive, and content-driven. Long regarded as the gold standard in GMAT prep worldwide, Manhattan Review's GMAT prep books offer professional GMAT instruction for dramatic score improvement. Now in its updated 6th edition, the full series is designed to provide GMAT test-takers with complete guidance for highly successful outcomes. As many students have discovered, Manhattan Review's GMAT books break down the different test sections in a coherent, concise, and accessible manner. We delve deeply into the content of every single testing area and zero in on exactly what you need to know to raise your score. The full series is comprised of 16 guides that cover concepts in mathematics and grammar from the most basic through the most advanced levels, making them a great study resource for all stages of GMAT preparation. Students who work through all of our books benefit from a substantial boost to their GMAT knowledge and develop a thorough and strategic approach to taking the GMAT.

- ☐ **GMAT Math Essentials (ISBN: 978-1-62926-057-0)**
- ☐ **GMAT Number Properties Guide (ISBN: 978-1-62926-058-7)**
- ☐ **GMAT Arithmetics Guide (ISBN: 978-1-62926-059-4)**
- ☐ **GMAT Algebra Guide (ISBN: 978-1-62926-060-0)**
- ☐ **GMAT Geometry Guide (ISBN: 978-1-62926-061-7)**
- ☐ **GMAT Word Problems Guide (ISBN: 978-1-62926-062-4)**
- ☐ **GMAT Sets & Statistics Guide (ISBN: 978-1-62926-063-1)**
- ☐ **GMAT Combinatorics & Probability Guide (ISBN: 978-1-62926-064-8)**
- ☐ **GMAT Data Sufficiency Guide (ISBN: 978-1-62926-065-5**
- ■ **GMAT Quantitative Question Bank (ISBN: 978-1-62926-066-2**
- ☐ **GMAT Sentence Correction Guide (ISBN: 978-1-62926-067-9)**
- ☐ **GMAT Critical Reasoning Guide (ISBN: 978-1-62926-068-6)**
- ☐ **GMAT Reading Comprehension Guide (ISBN: 978-1-62926-069-3)**
- ☐ **GMAT Integrated Reasoning Guide (ISBN: 978-1-62926-070-9)**
- ☐ **GMAT Analytical Writing Guide (ISBN: 978-1-62926-071-6)**
- ☐ **GMAT Vocabulary Builder (ISBN: 978-1-62926-072-3)**

About the Company

Manhattan Review's origin can be traced directly back to an Ivy League MBA classroom in 1999. While teaching advanced quantitative subjects to MBAs at Columbia Business School in New York City, Professor Dr. Joern Meissner developed a reputation for explaining complicated concepts in an understandable way. Remembering their own less-than-optimal experiences preparing for the GMAT, Prof. Meissner's students challenged him to assist their friends, who were frustrated with conventional GMAT preparation options. In response, Prof. Meissner created original lectures that focused on presenting GMAT content in a simplified and intelligible manner, a method vastly different from the voluminous memorization and so-called tricks commonly offered by others. The new approach immediately proved highly popular with GMAT students, inspiring the birth of Manhattan Review.

Since its founding, Manhattan Review has grown into a multi-national educational services firm, focusing on GMAT preparation, MBA admissions consulting, and application advisory services, with thousands of highly satisfied students all over the world. The original lectures have been continuously expanded and updated by the Manhattan Review team, an enthusiastic group of master GMAT professionals and senior academics. Our team ensures that Manhattan Review offers the most time-efficient and cost-effective preparation available for the GMAT. Please visit www.ManhattanReview.com for further details.

About the Founder

Professor Dr. Joern Meissner has more than 25 years of teaching experience at the graduate and undergraduate levels. He is the founder of Manhattan Review, a worldwide leader in test prep services, and he created the original lectures for its first GMAT preparation class. Prof. Meissner is a graduate of Columbia Business School in New York City, where he received a PhD in Management Science. He has since served on the faculties of prestigious business schools in the United Kingdom and Germany. He is a recognized authority in the areas of supply chain management, logistics, and pricing strategy. Prof. Meissner thoroughly enjoys his research, but he believes that grasping an idea is only half of the fun. Conveying knowledge to others is even more fulfilling. This philosophy was crucial to the establishment of Manhattan Review, and remains its most cherished principle.

The Advantages of Using Manhattan Review

- **Time efficiency and cost effectiveness.**
  - For most people, the most limiting factor of test preparation is time.
  - It takes significantly more teaching experience to prepare a student in less time.
  - Our test preparation approach is tailored for busy professionals. We will teach you what you need to know in the least amount of time.
- **Our high-quality and dedicated instructors are committed to helping every student reach her/his goals.**

International Phone Numbers and Official Manhattan Review Websites

Manhattan Headquarters	+1-212-316-2000	www.manhattanreview.com
USA & Canada	+1-800-246-4600	www.manhattanreview.com
Argentina	+1-212-316-2000	www.review.com.ar
Australia	+61-3-9001-6618	www.manhattanreview.com
Austria	+43-720-115-549	www.review.at
Belgium	+32-2-808-5163	www.manhattanreview.be
Brazil	+1-212-316-2000	www.manhattanreview.com.br
Chile	+1-212-316-2000	www.manhattanreview.cl
China	+86-20-2910-1913	www.manhattanreview.cn
Czech Republic	+1-212-316-2000	www.review.cz
France	+33-1-8488-4204	www.review.fr
Germany	+49-89-3803-8856	www.review.de
Greece	+1-212-316-2000	www.review.com.gr
Hong Kong	+852-5808-2704	www.review.hk
Hungary	+1-212-316-2000	www.review.co.hu
India	+1-212-316-2000	www.review.in
Indonesia	+1-212-316-2000	www.manhattanreview.id
Ireland	+1-212-316-2000	www.gmat.ie
Italy	+39-06-9338-7617	www.manhattanreview.it
Japan	+81-3-4589-5125	www.manhattanreview.jp
Malaysia	+1-212-316-2000	www.review.my
Netherlands	+31-20-808-4399	www.manhattanreview.nl
New Zealand	+1-212-316-2000	www.review.co.nz
Philippines	+1-212-316-2000	www.review.ph
Poland	+1-212-316-2000	www.review.pl
Portugal	+1-212-316-2000	www.review.pt
Qatar	+1-212-316-2000	www.review.qa
Russia	+1-212-316-2000	www.manhattanreview.ru
Singapore	+65-3158-2571	www.gmat.sg
South Africa	+1-212-316-2000	www.manhattanreview.co.za
South Korea	+1-212-316-2000	www.manhattanreview.kr
Sweden	+1-212-316-2000	www.gmat.se
Spain	+34-911-876-504	www.review.es
Switzerland	+41-435-080-991	www.review.ch
Taiwan	+1-212-316-2000	www.gmat.tw
Thailand	+66-6-0003-5529	www.manhattanreview.com
Turkey	+1-212-316-2000	www.review.com.tr
United Arab Emirates	+1-212-316-2000	www.manhattanreview.ae
United Kingdom	+44-20-7060-9800	www.manhattanreview.co.uk
Rest of World	+1-212-316-2000	www.manhattanreview.com

Contents

Chapter 1

Welcome

Dear Students,

Here at Manhattan Review, we constantly strive to provide you the best educational content for standardized test preparation. We make a tremendous effort to keep making things better and better for you. This is especially important with respect to an examination such as the GMAT. A typical GMAT aspirant is confused with so many test-prep options available. Your challenge is to choose a book or a tutor that prepares you for attaining your goal. We cannot say that we are one of the best, it is you who has to be the judge.

There are umpteen numbers of books on Quantitative Ability for GMAT preparation. What is so different about this book? The answer lies in its approach to deal with the questions. Solution of each question is dealt with in detail. There are over hundred questions that have been solved through Alternate Approaches. You will also find a couple of questions that have been solved through as many as four approaches. The objective is to understand questions from multiple aspects. Few seemingly scary questions have been solved through Logical Deduction or through Intuitive approach.

The has a great collection of 500 GMAT-like questions: 250 PS and 250 DS.

Apart from books on 'Word Problem', 'Algebra', 'Arithmetic', 'Geometry', 'Permutation and Combination', and 'Sets and Statistics' which are solely dedicated on GMAT-QA-PS & DS, the book on 'Fundamentals of GMAT math' is solely dedicated to develop your math fundamentals. We recommend that you go through it before attempting questions from 'GMAT Quantitative Ability Question Bank.'

The Manhattan Review's 'GMAT Quantitative Ability Question Bank' book is holistic and comprehensive in all respects. Should you have any queries, please feel free to write to me at info@manhattanreview.com.

Happy Learning!

Professor Dr. Joern Meissner
& The Manhattan Review Team

Chapter 2

Problem Solving Question Bank

2.1 Number properties

1. $99999^2 - 1^2 =$

   (A) $10^{10} - 2$
   (B) $(10^5 - 2)^2$
   (C) $10^4(10^5 - 2)$
   (D) $10^5(10^4 - 2)$
   (E) $10^5(10^5 - 2)$

2. If the greatest integer k for which 3^k is a factor of $n!$ is 8, what is the largest possible value of p so that 5^p is a factor of $n!$?

   (A) 2
   (B) 3
   (C) 4
   (D) 5
   (E) 6

3. If $r = 0.345$, $s = (0.345)^2$ and $t = \sqrt{0.345}$, which of the following is the correct ordering of r, s and t?

   (A) $r < s < t$
   (B) $r < t < s$
   (C) $s < t < r$
   (D) $s < r < t$
   (E) $t < r < s$

4. If s is the product of the integers from 100 to 200, inclusive, and t is the product of the integers from 100 to 201, inclusive, what is $\left(\frac{1}{s} + \frac{1}{t}\right)$ in terms of t?

   (A) $\frac{(201)^2}{t}$
   (B) $\frac{(201)(202)}{t}$
   (C) $\frac{201}{t}$
   (D) $\frac{202}{t}$
   (E) $\frac{(201)(202)}{t^2}$

5. If s is the sum of all integers from 1 to 30, inclusive, what is the sum of all the factors of s?

   (A) 303
   (B) 613
   (C) 675
   (D) 737

(E) 768

6. If s is the sum of the reciprocals of the consecutive integers from 91 to 100, inclusive, which of the following is less than s?

   I. $\frac{1}{8}$

   II. $\frac{1}{9}$

   III. $\frac{1}{10}$

   (A) Only I
   (B) Only II
   (C) Only III
   (D) Only II and III
   (E) I, II and III

7. If the number $5m15n$, where m and n represent the thousands' and unit digits, is divisible by 36, what is the maximum value of $|m - n|$?

   (A) 1
   (B) 3
   (C) 5
   (D) 6
   (E) 8

8. A positive integer n is said to be "prime-saturated" if the product of all the different positive prime factors of n is less than the square root of n. What is the greatest two-digit prime-saturated integer?

   (A) 99
   (B) 98
   (C) 97
   (D) 96
   (E) 95

9. A set of numbers has the property that for any number t in the set, $(t + 2)$ is also in the set. If -1 is in the set, which of the following is also in the set?

   I. -3

   II. 1

   III. 5

   (A) Only I
   (B) Only II
   (C) Only I and II
   (D) Only II and III

(E) I, II and III

10. If the sequence $x_1, x_2, x_3, \ldots x_n$, is such that $x_1 = 3$ and $x_{n+1} = 2x_n - 1$ for $n \geq 1$, then $x_{20} - x_{19} =$

(A) 2^{19}
(B) $2^{20} - 1$
(C) 2^{20}
(D) $2^{21} - 1$
(E) 2^{21}

11. If w, x, y and z are integers such that $1 < w \leq x \leq y \leq z$ and $w * x * y * z = 924$, then how many possible values exist for z?

(A) Three
(B) Four
(C) Five
(D) Six
(E) Seven

12. If $0 < x < 1$ and $y > 1$, $(\sqrt{x + y - 2\sqrt{xy}} + \sqrt{x + y + 2\sqrt{xy}}) =$

(A) $\sqrt{x}$
(B) $2\sqrt{x}$
(C) $\sqrt{y} + \sqrt{x}$
(D) $\sqrt{y}$
(E) $2\sqrt{y}$

13. If $x \geq 0.9$, which of the following could be the value of $\left(\frac{1}{\sqrt{x}}\right)$?

(A) 1.02
(B) 1.12
(C) 1.23
(D) 1.45
(E) 2.10

14. If x and y are positive integers and $180x = y^3$, which of the following must be an integer?

I. $\frac{x}{2^2 * 3 * 5}$
II. $\frac{x}{2 * 3^2 * 5}$
III. $\frac{x}{2 * 3 * 5^2}$

(A) Only I
(B) Only II
(C) Only III

(D) Only I and II

(E) I, II and III

15. In the correctly worked addition problem shown below, where the sum of the two-digit positive integers *AB* and *BA* is the three-digit integer *AAC*, and *A*, *B*, and *C* are different digits, what is the unit digit of the integer *AAC*?

$$\begin{array}{r} A\ B \\ +\ B\ A \\ \hline A\ A\ C \\ \hline \end{array}$$

(A) 9
(B) 6
(C) 3
(D) 2
(E) 0

16. In the first week of the year, Nancy saved \$1. In each of the next 51 weeks, she saved \$1 more than she had saved in the previous week. What was the total amount that Nancy saved during the 52 weeks?

(A) \$1326
(B) \$1352
(C) \$1378
(D) \$2652
(E) \$2756

2.2 Percents

17. A certain pair of used shoes can be repaired for $12.50 and will last for one year. A pair of the same kind of shoes can be purchased new for $28.00 and will last for two years. The average cost per year of the new shoes is what percent greater than the cost of repairing the used shoes?

 (A) 3%
 (B) 5%
 (C) 12%
 (D) 15%
 (E) 24%

18. A certain state has a sales tax of 5 percent on the portion of a purchase price that is greater than $100. If a customer paid a sales tax of $4 on a particular item, what was the purchase price of the item?

 (A) $120
 (B) $124
 (C) $180
 (D) $184
 (E) $220

19. A certain sales tax rate is $0.82 per $50. What is the rate, as a percent, which is thrice as much as the rate mentioned?

 (A) 492%
 (B) 49.2%
 (C) 4.92%
 (D) 1.23%
 (E) 0.055%

20. A certain telescope X increases the visual range of a particular location from 90 kilometers to 270 kilometers. Another telescope Y increases the visual range of another location from 45 kilometers to 180 kilometers. By what percent is the percent increase in visual range using Y more than that obtained using X?

 (A) 33
 (B) 50
 (C) 75
 (D) 100
 (E) 150

21. The population of a certain country X is 120,108,000 and its land area is 2,998,000 square kilometers. The population of another country Y is 200,323,000 and its land area is 7,899,000 square kilometers. The population density is defined as the population per square kilometer of land area. The population density of country X is approximately what percent greater or lesser than that of country Y?

 (A) 60%

(B) 50%

(C) 45%

(D) 37%

(E) 15%

22. A coat's original price of \$112 was reduced by 20 percent for a sale. If the sale price was then increased by 20 percent, which of the following, expresses the single percent change, which when applied to the original price of the coat, would result in the same final price of the coat now?

(A) $100(1-0.2)^2$

(B) $100\,(1-0.4)$

(C) $100(1-0.4)^2$

(D) $100\,(1-0.8)$

(E) $100\,(1-0.96)$

23. A doctor prescribed 18 cubic centimeters of a certain drug to a patient whose body weight was 120 pounds. If the typical dosage is 2 cubic centimeters per 15 pounds of body weight, by what percent should the prescribed dosage be reduced to bring it down to the typical dosage?

(A) 7.5

(B) 9.0

(C) 11.1

(D) 12.5

(E) 14.8

24. A factory that employs 100 assembly-line workers pays each of these workers \$5 per hour for the first 40 hours worked during a week and $1\frac{1}{2}$ times that rate for hours worked in excess of 40. What was the total payroll for the assembly-line workers for a week in which 30 percent of them worked 20 hours, 50 percent worked 40 hours, and the rest worked 50 hours?

(A) \$18000

(B) \$18500

(C) \$19000

(D) \$20000

(E) \$20500

25. A pharmaceutical company received \$3 million in royalties on the first \$20 million in sales of the generic equivalent of one of its products and then \$9 million in royalties on the next \$108 million in sales. By approximately what percent did the ratio of royalties to sales decrease from the first \$20 million in sales to the next \$108 million in sales?

(A) 8%

(B) 15%

(C) 44%

(D) 52%

(E) 56%

26. A salesperson received 6 percent commission on the amount of total sales up to and including \$10,000, and r percent commission on the amount of total sales above \$10,000. If the salesperson received a total commission of \$920 on total sales of \$14,000, what was the value of r?

(A) 3.2

(B) 4.3

(C) 6.6

(D) 8.0

(E) 9.2

27. A shipment of 1,500 heads of cabbage, each of which was approximately the same size, was purchased for \$600. The day the shipment arrived, $\frac{2}{3}$ of the heads were sold, each at 25 percent above the cost per head. The following day the rest were sold at a price per head equal to 10 percent less than the cost per head. What was the percent profit on this shipment?

(A) 7.5%

(B) 13.3%

(C) 17.5%

(D) 22.5%

(E) 25.0%

28. Due to a 25% increase in the price of diesel, a person got 10 liters less quantity for \$50 than he was getting before the increase. What was the initial price per liter of diesel?

(A) \$1.00

(B) \$1.50

(C) \$2.25

(D) \$2.50

(E) \$3.00

29. Company K has an annual budget for a certain project, and $\frac{1}{5}$ of this budget was spent during the first quarter of the year. If $\frac{1}{8}$ of the remainder of the budget was spent during the second quarter, by what percent is the budget that was left at the end of the second quarter more than that spent in the previous two quarters?

(A) 80.0%

(B) 120.0%

(C) 125.0%

(D) 133.3%

(E) 250.0%

30. Dick and Jane each saved \$3,000 in 2006. In 2007 Dick saved 8 percent more than he did in 2006, and together he and Jane saved a total of \$5,000. Approximately, what percent less did Jane save in 2007 than he did in 2006?

(A) 8%

(B) 25%
(C) 41%
(D) 59%
(E) 70%

31. The price of each share of stock K, when traded at a certain stock exchange, first goes up by p percent and then falls down by p percent every alternate day. After one such up-down cycle, the price of the stock fell by \$2. If, after another such up-down cycle, the price per share of stock K comes to \$196.02, what was the original price per share of stock K?

(A) \$300
(B) \$270
(C) \$250
(D) \$200
(E) \$150

32. Based on this year's costs, an orchard grower budgets p dollars for planting n new trees. If the average cost of planting each tree were to increase 25 percent from this year's cost, then the number of trees that the orchard grower could plant next year using $2p$ dollars would be

(A) 12% less than n
(B) 20% less than n
(C) 33% greater than n
(D) 60% greater than n
(E) 75% greater than n

33. Before a certain tire is used, 40 percent of its total weight consists of tread. If during a lifetime of use, 50 percent, by weight, of the tire's tread is lost and no other parts of the tire is lost, what per cent of the tire's total remaining weight consists of the remaining tread?

(A) 55%
(B) 35%
(C) 30%
(D) 25%
(E) 20%

34. A nut mix contains, by weight, 20 percent peanuts and 80 percent cashews. If this mixture costs 10 percent more than the cost of an equal quantity of pure peanuts, by what percent are cashews more expensive than peanuts?

(A) 10.0%
(B) 12.5%
(C) 15.0%
(D) 22.5%
(E) 25.0%

35. At Company X, senior sales representatives visit the home office once every 30 days, and junior sales representatives visit the home office once every 20 days. The number of visits that a junior sales representative makes in a 2-year period is approximately what percent greater than the number of visits that a senior representative makes in the same period?

(A) 10%

(B) 25%

(C) 33%

(D) 50%

(E) 67%

36. Anne bought a computer for $2,000 and then paid a 5 percent sales tax, and Henry bought a computer for $1,800 and then paid a 12 percent sales tax. The total amount that Henry paid, including sales tax, was what percent less than the total amount Anne paid, including sales tax?

(A) 3%

(B) 4%

(C) 7%

(D) 10%

(E) 12%

37. In a corporation, 50 percent of the male employees and 40 percent of the female employees are at least 35 years old. If 42 percent of all the employees are at least 35 years old, what fraction of the employees in the corporation are females?

(A) $\frac{3}{5}$

(B) $\frac{2}{3}$

(C) $\frac{3}{4}$

(D) $\frac{4}{5}$

(E) $\frac{5}{6}$

38. In a recent election, Ms. Robbins received 8,000 votes cast by independent voters, that is, voters not registered with a specific political party. She also received 10 percent of the votes cast by those voters registered with a political party. If N is the total number of votes cast in the election and 40 percent of the votes were cast by independent voters, which of the following represents the number of votes that Ms. Robbins received?

(A) $0.06N + 3200$

(B) $0.1N + 7200$

(C) $0.4N + 7200$

(D) $0.06N + 8000$

(E) $0.1N + 8000$

39. In Company X, 30 percent of the employees live over ten miles from work and 60 percent of the employees who live over ten miles from work use car pools. If 40 percent of the employees of Company X use car pools, what percent of the employees of Company X live ten miles or less from work and use car pools?

(A) 12%

(B) 20%

(C) 22%

(D) 28%

(E) 32%

40. A total of 30 percent of the geese included in a certain migration study were male. If some of the geese migrated during the study and 20 percent of the migrating geese were male, what was the ratio of the migration rate for the male geese to the migration rate for the female geese?

(A) $\frac{1}{4}$

(B) $\frac{7}{12}$

(C) $\frac{2}{3}$

(D) $\frac{7}{8}$

(E) $\frac{8}{9}$

41. In 2006, the book value of a certain car was $\frac{2}{3}$ of the original purchase price, and in 2008 its book value was $\frac{1}{2}$ of the original purchase price. By what percent did the book value of this car decrease from 2006 to 2008?

(A) 16.6%

(B) 25.0%

(C) 33.3%

(D) 50.0%

(E) 75.0%

42. In a certain city, 60 percent of the registered voters are Democrats and the rest are Republicans. In a mayoral race, if 75 percent of the registered voters who are Democrats and 20 percent of the registered voters who are Republicans are expected to vote for Candidate A, what percent of the registered voters are expected to vote for Candidate A?

(A) 50%

(B) 53%

(C) 54%

(D) 55%

(E) 57%

43. In 2005, 45 percent of a document storage facility's 60 customers were banks, and in 2007, 25 percent of its 144 customers were banks. What was the simple annual percent growth rate in the number of bank customers the facility had?

(A) 11.1%

(B) 16.6%

(C) 25.0%

(D) 33.3%

(E) 58.3%

44. In 2006, the book value of a certain car was $\frac{2}{3}$ of the original purchase price, and in 2008 its book value was $\frac{1}{2}$ of the original purchase price. By what percent did the book value of this car decrease from 2006 to 2008?

(A) 16.6%
(B) 25.0%
(C) 33.3%
(D) 50.0%
(E) 75.0%

45. In a certain city, 60 percent of the registered voters are Democrats and the rest are Republicans. In a mayoral race, if 75 percent of the registered voters who are Democrats and 20 percent of the registered voters who are Republicans are expected to vote for Candidate A, what percent of the registered voters are expected to vote for Candidate A?

(A) 50%
(B) 53%
(C) 54%
(D) 55%
(E) 57%

2.3 Profit & Loss

46. A collection of books went on sale, and $\frac{2}{3}$ of them were sold for \$2.50 each. If none of the 36 remaining books were sold, what was the total amount received for the books that were sold?

(A) \$180
(B) \$135
(C) \$90
(D) \$60
(E) \$54

47. A farmer produced 750 bushels of a certain crop at a cost of \$20 per bushel. If the farmer sold $\frac{2}{3}$ of the bushels for double their production cost and sold the remaining bushels at 25 percent above their production cost, what was the farmer's gross profit on the sale of the crop?

(A) \$11250
(B) \$13375
(C) \$15000
(D) \$18750
(E) \$26250

48. A furniture store sells only two models of desks, model A and model B. The selling price of a model A desk is \$120, which is 30 percent of the selling price of a model B desk. If the furniture store sells 2,000 desks, $\frac{3}{4}$ of which are model B, what is the furniture store's total revenue from the sale of desks?

(A) \$114000
(B) \$186000
(C) \$294000
(D) \$380000
(E) \$660000

49. A retailer bought a machine at a wholesale price of \$90 and later on sold it for 10% less than the suggested retail price. If the retailer made a profit equivalent to 20% of the wholesale price, what is the suggested retail price of the machine?

(A) \$81
(B) \$100
(C) \$120
(D) \$135
(E) \$160

50. A small business invests \$9,900 in equipment to produce a product. Each unit of the product costs \$0.65 to produce and is sold for \$1.20. How many units of the product must be sold before the revenue received equals the total expense of production, including the initial investment in equipment?

(A) 12000
(B) 14500
(C) 15230
(D) 18000
(E) 20000

51. A store's selling price for a certain computer would yield a profit of 40 percent of the store's cost for the computer. If the price were increased by $200, it would yield a profit of 50 percent of the computer's cost. What was the initial selling price of the computer?

(A) $2000
(B) $2400
(C) $2800
(D) $3000
(E) $3500

52. Company C produces toy trucks at a cost of $5.00 each for the first 100 trucks and $3.50 for each additional truck. If 500 toy trucks were produced by Company C and sold for $10.00 each, what was Company C's gross profit?

(A) $2250
(B) $2500
(C) $3100
(D) $3250
(E) $3500

53. A toy store's gross profit on a computer game was 10 percent of the cost of the game. If the store increased the selling price of the game from $44 to $46 and the cost of the game remained the same, then the store's gross profit on the game after the price increase was what percent of the cost of the game?

(A) 10.5%
(B) 11.0%
(C) 12.5%
(D) 13.0%
(E) 15.0%

54. A wholesaler bought 1200 radios for $18 each. He then sold 60 percent of the radios for $30 each and the rest for $15 each. What was the wholesaler's average (arithmetic mean) profit per radio?

(A) $2
(B) $3
(C) $4
(D) $5
(E) $6

55. A man sold an article at k percent profit after offering k percent discount on the listed price. Had he sold the article at $(k + 15)$ percent discount on the listed price, his profit would have been $(k - 20)$ percent. What would have been his percent profit had he sold the article without offering any discount?

(A) 5.0%

(B) 10.0%

(C) 25.0%

(D) 33.3%

(E) 38.0%

2.4 Averages

56. A certain college has a student-to-teacher ratio of 11 to 1. The average (arithmetic mean) annual salary for teachers is \$52,000. If the college pays a total of \$6,760,000 in annual salaries to its teachers, how many students does the college have?

(A) 130
(B) 169
(C) 1300
(D) 1430
(E) 1560

57. A club sold an average (arithmetic mean) of 92 raffle tickets per member. Among the female members, average number sold was 84, and among the male members, the average number sold was 96. What was the ratio of the number of male members to the number of female members in the club?

(A) 1 : 1
(B) 1 : 2
(C) 1 : 3
(D) 2 : 1
(E) 3 : 1

58. A college chemistry course is divided into two sections. In section A, the average score in the final examination was 92. In section B, the average score in the final examination was 84. If the average score of all 40 students in the course was 89, how many students are in section A?

(A) 15
(B) 18
(C) 20
(D) 22
(E) 25

59. A grocer has 400 pounds of coffee in stock, 20 percent of which is decaffeinated. If the grocer buys another 100 pounds of coffee of which 60 percent is decaffeinated, what percent, by weight, of the grocer's stock of coffee is decaffeinated?

(A) 28%
(B) 30%
(C) 32%
(D) 34%
(E) 40%

60. A class has 4 sections P, Q, R and S and the average weights of the students in the sections are 45lb, 50lb, 55lb and 65lb respectively. What is the maximum possible number of students in section R if there are 40 students in all sections combined and the average weight of the all students across all the sections is 55lb? It is known that each section has at least one student.

(A) 18

(B) 20

(C) 25

(D) 35

(E) 37

61. A set S consists of the integers $\{1,\ 2,\ 3,\ 4\ldots(2n+1)\}$, where n is a positive integer. If X is the average of the odd integers in set S and Y is the average of the even integers in set S, what is the value of $(X - Y)$?

(A) 0

(B) $\frac{1}{2}$

(C) 1

(D) $\frac{3}{2}$

(E) 2

62. The average of seven numbers is 20. The average of the first four numbers is 19 and that of the last four is 24. What is the value of the fourth number?

(A) 23

(B) 25

(C) 32

(D) 43

(E) 63

63. Box W and Box V each contain several blue sticks and red sticks, and all of the red sticks have the same length. The length of each red stick is 18 inches less than the average length of the sticks in Box Wand 6 inches greater than the average length of the sticks in Box V. What is the difference between average (arithmetic mean) length, in inches, of the sticks in Box W and of the sticks in Box V?

(A) 3

(B) 6

(C) 12

(D) 18

(E) 24

64. At a certain company, the average (arithmetic mean) salary of 10 of the employees is \$30,000, the average salary of 30 other employees is \$40,000, and the average salary of the remaining 20 employees is \$60,000. What is the average salary of the 60 employees at the company?

(A) \$40,000

(B) \$43,000

(C) \$45,000

(D) \$50,000

(E) \$55,000

65. At a certain food stand, the price of each apple is 40 cents and the price of each orange is 60 cents. Mary selects a total of 10 apples and oranges from the food stand, and the average (arithmetic mean) price of the 10 pieces of fruit comes to 56 cents. How many oranges must Mary put back so that the average price of the pieces of fruit that she keeps with her is 52 cents?

(A) 1

(B) 2

(C) 3

(D) 4

(E) 5

66. A student's average (arithmetic mean) test score on four tests is 78. If each test is scored out of 100, which of the following can be the student's score on the fifth test so that the student's average score on the five tests increases by an integer value?

(A) 82

(B) 87

(C) 89

(D) 93

(E) 95

67. A teacher gave the same test to three history classes: A, B, and C. The average (arithmetic mean) scores for the three classes were 65, 80, and 77, respectively. The ratio of the numbers of students in each class who took the test was 4 : 6 : 5, respectively. What was the average score for the three classes combined?

(A) 74

(B) 75

(C) 76

(D) 77

(E) 78

68. A total of 22 men and 26 women were at a party. The average (arithmetic mean) age of all of the people at the party was exactly 35 years. If the average age of the men was exactly 38 years, which of the following was closest to the average age, in years, of the women?

(A) 31.0

(B) 31.5

(C) 32.0

(D) 32.5

(E) 33.0

69. This is a modified question of the above question.

A total of 22 men and 26 women were at a party. The average (arithmetic mean) age of all of the people at the party was exactly 66.74 years. If the average age of the men was exactly 69.74 years, which of the following was closest to the average age, in years, of the women?

(A) 61.24

(B) 63.74

(C) 64.24

(D) 64.74

(E) 69.24

2.5 Ratio & Proportion

70. The total expenses of organizing a party has a fixed expense of \$250 as the rent of the place where the party is to be organized and a variable expense depending on the number of guests attending the party. For 10 guests the total expense was estimated to be \$650. What is the estimated total expense for 20 guests?

(A) \$800

(B) \$900

(C) \$1050

(D) \$1250

(E) \$1300

71. A glass was filled with 10 ounces of water and spirit mixture with the components in the ratio 2 : 3 respectively. If 1 percent of the initial quantity of water and 3 percent of the initial quantity of spirit evaporated each day during a twenty-day period, what percent of the original amount of mixture evaporated during this period?

(A) 4.4%

(B) 24.4%

(C) 44.0%

(D) 50.0%

(E) 80.0%

72. In Diana's stamp collection, $\frac{4}{5}$ of the stamps are Canadian, and $\frac{3}{7}$ of the Canadian stamps were issued before 1940. If 192 stamps in Diana's collection are Canadian stamps that were issued in 1940 or later, how many stamps in her collection are not Canadian?

(A) 84

(B) 88

(C) 96

(D) 104

(E) 112

73. The ratio of the ages of A and B is 7 : 11. Which of the following cannot be the ratio of their ages after 5 years?

(A) 1 : 3

(B) 9 : 20

(C) 4 : 15

(D) 3 : 5

(E) 2 : 3

74. Company S produces two kinds of stereos: basic and deluxe. Of the stereos produced by Company S last month, $\frac{2}{3}$ were basic and the rest were deluxe. If it takes $\frac{7}{5}$ as many hours to produce a deluxe stereo as it does to produce a basic stereo, then the number of hours it took to produce the deluxe stereos last month was what fraction of the total number of hours it took to produce all the stereos?

(A) $\frac{7}{17}$

(B) $\frac{14}{31}$

(C) $\frac{7}{15}$

(D) $\frac{17}{35}$

(E) $\frac{1}{2}$

75. At a certain school, the ratio of the number of second graders to the number of fourth graders is 8 to 5, and the ratio of the number of first graders to the number of second graders is 3 to 4. If the ratio of the number of third graders to the number of fourth graders is 3 to 2, what is the ratio of the number of first graders to the number of third graders?

(A) 5 to 4

(B) 9 to 5

(C) 16 to 15

(D) 4 to 5

(E) 5 to 16

76. At a monthly meeting, $\frac{2}{5}$ of the attendees were males and $\frac{7}{8}$ of the male attendees arrived on time. If $\frac{9}{10}$ of the female attendees arrived on time, what fraction of the attendees at the monthly meeting who did not arrive on time are males?

(A) $\frac{11}{100}$

(B) $\frac{3}{25}$

(C) $\frac{11}{50}$

(D) $\frac{9}{20}$

(E) $\frac{5}{11}$

77. Ann, Carol, and Judy paid a total of \$45 for their dinner at a restaurant. If Ann paid $\frac{2}{5}$ of what Judy paid, Carol paid \$17 and Judy paid the rest, what fraction of the total amount did Judy pay?

(A) $\frac{2}{9}$

(B) $\frac{14}{45}$

(C) $\frac{1}{3}$

(D) $\frac{2}{5}$

(E) $\frac{4}{9}$

78. A total of n trucks and cars are parked in a lot. If the number of cars is $\frac{1}{4}$ the number of trucks, and $\frac{2}{3}$ of the trucks are pickups, how many pickups, in terms of n, are parked in the lot?

(A) $\frac{n}{12}$

(B) $\frac{n}{6}$

(C) $\frac{5n}{12}$

(D) $\frac{8n}{15}$

(E) $\frac{11n}{12}$

79. A wire that weighs 20 pounds is cut into two pieces so that one of the pieces weighs 16 pounds and is 36 feet long. If the weight of each piece is directly proportional to the square of its length, how many feet long is the other piece of wire?

(A) 9

(B) 12

(C) 18

(D) 24

(E) 27

80. A sum of money was divided between John and Bob so that the ratio of John's share to Bob's share was $5 : 3$. If John's share exceeded $\frac{5}{9}$ of the total sum of money by \$50, what was Bob's share?

(A) \$180

(B) \$270

(C) \$340

(D) \$450

(E) \$720

81. In a certain English class, $\frac{1}{4}$ of the number of girls is equal to $\frac{1}{6}$ of the total number of students. What is the ratio of the number of boys to the number of girls in the class?

(A) $1 : 4$

(B) $1 : 3$

(C) $1 : 2$

(D) $2 : 3$

(E) $2 : 1$

82. In a certain quiz that consists of 10 questions, each question after the first is worth 4 points more than the preceding question. If the 10 questions on the quiz are worth a total of 360 points, how many points is the third question worth?

(A) 18

(B) 24
(C) 26
(D) 32
(E) 44

83. In a certain school, 40 more than $\frac{1}{3}$ of all the students are taking a science course and $\frac{1}{4}$ of those taking a science course are taking physics. If $\frac{1}{8}$ of all the students in the school are taking physics, how many students are in the school?

(A) 240
(B) 300
(C) 480
(D) 720
(E) 960

84. In a certain class containing 36 students, some boys and some girls, exactly $\frac{1}{3}$ of the boys and exactly $\frac{1}{4}$ of the girls walk to school. What is the greatest possible number of students in this class who walk to school?

(A) 9
(B) 10
(C) 11
(D) 12
(E) 13

85. In a certain English class, $\frac{1}{4}$ of the number of girls is equal to $\frac{1}{6}$ of the total number of students. What is the ratio of the number of boys to the number of girls in the class?

(A) 1 : 4
(B) 1 : 3
(C) 1 : 2
(D) 2 : 3
(E) 2 : 1

86. In a certain shipment, there are 30 boxes which weigh either 10 pounds or 20 pounds, and the average (arithmetic mean) weight of the boxes in the shipment is 18 pounds. If the average weight of the boxes in the shipment is to be reduced to 16 pounds by including few extra 10-pound boxes, how many extra 10-pound boxes must be included?

(A) 4
(B) 6
(C) 10
(D) 20
(E) 24

87. How many liters of pure alcohol must be added to a 90-liter solution that is 20 percent alcohol in order to produce a solution that is 25 percent alcohol?

(A) 4.5

(B) 5.0

(C) 5.5

(D) 6.0

(E) 6.5

2.6 Speed, Time, & Distance

88. A bus trip of 450 miles would have taken one hour less if the average speed S for the trip had been greater by five miles per hour. What was the average speed S, in miles per hour, for the trip?

(A) 10

(B) 40

(C) 45

(D) 50

(E) 55

89. A car traveled 462 miles per full tank of gasoline on the highway and 336 miles per full tank of gasoline in the city. If the car traveled six fewer miles per gallon in the city than on the highway, how many miles per gallon did the car travel in the city?

(A) 14

(B) 16

(C) 21

(D) 22

(E) 27

90. A car traveling at a certain constant speed takes two seconds longer to travel one kilometer than it would take to travel one kilometer at 75 kilometers per hour. At what speed, in kilometers per hour, is the car traveling?

(A) 71.5

(B) 72

(C) 72.5

(D) 73

(E) 73.5

91. A certain car increased its average speed by 5 miles per hour in each successive 5-minute interval after the first interval. If in the first 5-minute interval, its average speed was 20 miles per hour, how many miles did the car travel in the third 5-minute interval?

(A) 1.0

(B) 1.5

(C) 2.0

(D) 2.5

(E) 3.0

92. A certain pilot flew 400 miles to City K at an average speed of 350 miles per hour with the wind and made the trip back at an average speed of 250 miles per hour against the wind. Which of the following is closest to the pilot's average speed, in miles per hour, for the round-trip?

(A) 280

(B) 290

(C) 300

(D) 310

(E) 320

93. A driver completed the first 20 miles of a 40-mile trip at an average speed of 50 miles per hour. At what average speed (in miles per hour) did the driver complete the remaining 20 miles to achieve an average speed of 60 miles per hour for the entire 40-mile trip? It is known that the driver did not make any stops during the 40-mile trip.

(A) 65

(B) 68

(C) 70

(D) 75

(E) 80

94. A hiker walked for two days. On the second day the hiker walked at an average speed of 1 mile per hour faster than he walked on the first day. If during the two days he walked a total of 64 miles and spent a total of 18 hours walking, which of the following could be his average speed (in miles per hour) on the first day?

(A) 2

(B) 3

(C) 4

(D) 5

(E) 6

95. If two trains are 120 miles apart and are traveling toward each other on parallel tracks at constant rates of 30 miles per hour and 40 miles per hour, how far apart will they be one hour before they meet?

(A) 10

(B) 30

(C) 40

(D) 50

(E) 70

96. Because of construction, the speed limit along an 8-mile section of highway is reduced from 55 miles per hour to 35 miles per hour. Approximately how many minutes more will it take to travel along this section of highway at the new speed limit than it would have taken at the old speed limit?

(A) 5

(B) 8

(C) 10

(D) 15

(E) 24

97. Cars X and Y traveled the same 80-mile route. If car X took 2 hours and car Y traveled at an average speed which was 50 percent faster than the average speed of car X, how many hours did it take car Y to travel the route?

(A) $\frac{2}{3}$

(B) 1

(C) $1\frac{1}{3}$

(D) $1\frac{3}{5}$

(E) 3

98. Joe drives five times farther in 50 minutes than what Bob drives in 40 minutes. If Joe drives at a speed of 36 miles per hour, at what speed, in miles per hour, does Bob drive?

(A) 6.0

(B) 9.0

(C) 20.0

(D) 32.5

(E) 64.8

99. A train left a station P at 6 am and reached another station Q at 11 am. Another train left station Q at 7 am and reached P at 10 am. At what time did the two trains pass one another?

(A) 7:50 am

(B) 8:13 am

(C) 8:30 am

(D) 8:42 am

(E) 9:03 am

2.7 Time & Work

100. A certain machine produces 1,000 units of product P per hour. Working 12 hours each day, another machine, twice as efficient, will produce how many units of product P in seven days?

(A) 7,000
(B) 24,000
(C) 40,000
(D) 100,000
(E) 168,000

101. A pump started filling an empty pool with water and continued at a constant rate until the pool was full. At noon, the pool was $\frac{1}{3}$ full, and $1\frac{1}{4}$ hours later, it was $\frac{3}{4}$ full. What would be the total number of hours that another pump thrice as efficient would take to completely fill a pool twice as large?

(A) 2
(B) $2\frac{2}{3}$
(C) 3
(D) $3\frac{1}{2}$
(E) $3\frac{2}{3}$

102. Two taps can fill a cistern in 20 minutes and 30 minutes. The first tap was opened initially for x minutes after which the second tap was opened. If it took a total of 15 minutes for the tank to be filled, what is the value of x?

(A) 5.0
(B) 7.5
(C) 9.0
(D) 10.0
(E) 12.5

103. An empty swimming pool with a capacity of 5,760 gallons is filled by a pipe at the rate of 12 gallons per minute. There is an emptying pipe which can empty the pool which is $\frac{3}{4}$ full in 9 hours. How many hours does it take to fill the entire pool which is already half filled, if both pipes are kept open?

(A) 6
(B) 12
(C) 24
(D) 36
(E) 72

104. Machine A produces parts twice as fast as machine B does. Machine B produces 100 parts of product X in 40 minutes. If each machine produces parts at a constant rate, how many parts of product Y does machine A produce in 6 minutes, if each part of product Y takes $\frac{3}{2}$ times of the time taken to produce each part of product X?

(A) 45
(B) 30
(C) 25
(D) 20
(E) 15

105. Machine A, operating alone at its constant rate, produces 500 feet of a particular fiber in 2 hours. Machine B, operating alone at its constant rate, produces 500 feet of the same fiber in 3 hours. Machine C, operating alone at its constant rate, produces 500 feet of the same fiber in 6 hours. How many hours will it take machines A, B, and C, operating together at their respective constant rates, to produce 1,000 feet of the fiber?

(A) 1.0
(B) 1.5
(C) 2.0
(D) 2.5
(E) 3.0

106. On a 3-day fishing trip, 4 adults consumed food costing \$60. If it is known that one child consumes half the amount of food consumed by an adult in the same time, for the same food costs per person per day, what would be the cost of food consumed by 6 adults and 3 children during a 4-day fishing trip?

(A) \$180
(B) \$150
(C) \$125
(D) \$90
(E) \$75

107. Mark and Kate individually take 12 hours more and 27 hours more, respectively, to complete a certain project than what they would have taken to complete the same project working together. How many hours do Mark and Kate take to complete the project, working together?

(A) 12
(B) 16
(C) 18
(D) 24
(E) 39

2.8 Computational

108. A certain liquid leaks out of a container at the rate of k liters for every x hours. If the liquid costs 6 dollars per liter, what is the cost, in dollars, of the amount of the liquid that will leak out in y hours?

(A) $\frac{ky}{6x}$

(B) $\frac{6x}{ky}$

(C) $\frac{6k}{xy}$

(D) $\frac{6ky}{x}$

(E) $\frac{6xy}{k}$

109. A certain quantity is measured on two different scales, the R-scale and the S-scale, that are related linearly. Measurements on the R-scale of 6 and 24 correspond to measurements on the S-scale of 30 and 60, respectively. What measurement on the R-scale corresponds to a measurement of 100 on the S-scale?

(A) 20

(B) 36

(C) 48

(D) 60

(E) 84

110. If Jack had twice the amount of money that he has, he would have exactly the amount necessary to buy three hamburgers at \$0.96 a piece and two milk shakes at \$1.28 a piece. How much money does Jack have?

(A) \$1.60

(B) \$2.24

(C) \$2.72

(D) \$3.36

(E) \$5.44

111. The population of a certain country increases at the rate of 30,000 people every month. The population of the country in 2012 was 360 million. In which year would the population of the country be 378 million?

(A) 2060

(B) 2061

(C) 2062

(D) 2063

(E) 2064

112. A restaurant buys fruit in cans, each containing $3\frac{1}{2}$ cups of fruit. If the restaurant uses $\frac{1}{2}$ cup of the fruit in each serving of its fruit compote, what is the least number of cans needed to prepare 60 servings of the compote?

(A) 7

(B) 8

(C) 9

(D) 10

(E) 12

113. Coins are to be put into 7 pockets so that each pocket contains at least one coin. At most 3 of the pockets are to contain the same number of coins, and no two of the remaining pockets are to contain an equal number of coins. What is the least possible number of coins needed for the pockets?

(A) 7

(B) 13

(C) 17

(D) 22

(E) 28

114. During a spring season, a certain glacier surged at the rate of $\frac{1}{4}$ mile per 25 days. How many hours does it take the glacier to cover one foot? (1 mile = 5,280 feet)

(A) $\frac{5}{264}$

(B) $\frac{6}{25}$

(C) $\frac{5}{11}$

(D) $\frac{11}{5}$

(E) $\frac{25}{6}$

115. At a certain carpet factory, if carpeting of width 10 feet is moving continuously through a dryer at a constant speed of 2160 feet per hour, how many SECONDS does it take for an area of 1 square foot of carpeting to move through the dryer?

(A) $\frac{1}{6}$

(B) $\frac{1}{3}$

(C) 6

(D) 36

(E) 60

116. At a certain company, each employee has a salary grade s that is at least 1 and at most 5. Each employee receives an hourly wage p, in dollars, determined by the formula $p = 950+0.25(s-1)$. An employee with a salary grade of 5 receives how many more dollars per hour than an employee with a salary grade of 1?

(A) \$0.50
(B) \$1.00
(C) \$1.25
(D) \$1.50
(E) \$1.75

117. At a garage sale, the prices of all the items sold were different. The items sold were radios and DVD players. If the price of a radio sold at the garage sale was the 15th highest price as well as the 20th lowest price among the prices of the radios sold, and the price of a DVD player sold was the 29th highest price as well as the 37th lowest price among all the prices of all the items sold, how many DVD players were sold at the garage sale?

(A) 30
(B) 31
(C) 32
(D) 64
(E) 65

118. An author received \$0.80 in royalties for each of the first 100,000 copies of her book sold, and \$0.60 in royalties for each additional copy sold. If she received a total of \$260,000 in royalties, how many copies of her book were sold?

(A) 130,000
(B) 300,000
(C) 380,000
(D) 400,000
(E) 420,000

119. A tourist purchased a total of \$1,500 worth of traveler's checks in \$10 and \$50 denominations. During the trip, the tourist cashed only seven checks and then lost all the rest. If the number of \$10 checks cashed was one more or one less than the number of \$50 checks cashed, what is the minimum possible value of the checks that were lost?

(A) \$1430
(B) \$1310
(C) \$1290
(D) \$1270
(E) \$1150

2.9 Interest

120. A sum of money invested under simple interest, amounts to \$1200 in three years and \$1500 in five years. What is the rate at which the sum of money was invested?

(A) 10%

(B) 15%

(C) 20%

(D) 25%

(E) 45%

121. The difference, after two years, between compound interest and simple interest on a certain sum of money invested at the same rate of interest, is \$18. If the simple interest accumulated on the sum after two years is \$180, what is the rate of interest at which the sum of money was invested?

(A) 36%

(B) 30%

(C) 25%

(D) 20%

(E) 10%

122. Andrew borrows equal sums of money under simple interest at 5% and 4% rate of interest. He finds that if he repays the former sum on a certain date six months before the latter, he will have to pay the same amount of \$1100 in each case. What is the total sum that he had borrowed?

(A) \$750

(B) \$1000

(C) \$1500

(D) \$2000

(E) \$4000

123. A total of \$10,000 was invested in two certificates of deposit at simple annual interest rates of 6 percent and 8 percent, respectively. If the total interest on the two certificates was \$720 at the end of one year, what fractional part of the 10,000 was invested at the higher rate?

(A) $\frac{3}{8}$

(B) $\frac{2}{5}$

(C) $\frac{1}{2}$

(D) $\frac{3}{5}$

(E) $\frac{3}{4}$

124. In 2005, 45 percent of a document storage facility's 60 customers were banks, and in 2007, 25 percent of its 144 customers were banks. What was the simple annual percent growth rate in the number of bank customers the facility had?

(A) 11.1%

(B) 16.6%

(C) 25.0%

(D) 33.3%

(E) 58.3%

125. A basket contains five apples, of which one is spoiled and the rest are good. If Henry is to select two apples from the basket simultaneously and at random, what is the probability that the two apples selected will include the spoiled apple?

(A) $\frac{1}{20}$

(B) $\frac{1}{10}$

(C) $\frac{1}{5}$

(D) $\frac{2}{5}$

(E) $\frac{3}{5}$

126. At the start of an experiment, a certain population consisted of x organisms. At the end of each month after the start of the experiment, the population size increased by twice of its size at the beginning of that month. If the total population at the end of five months is greater than 1000, what is the minimum possible value of x?

(A) 2

(B) 3

(C) 4

(D) 5

(E) 6

127. At the end of each year, the value of a certain antique watch is c percent more than its value one year earlier, where c has the same value each year. If the value of the watch was k dollars on January 1, 1992, and m dollars on January 1, 1994, then in terms of m and k, what was the value of the watch, in dollars, on January 1, 1995?

(A) $m + \frac{1}{2}(m - k)$

(B) $m + \frac{1}{2}\left(\frac{m-k}{k}\right)m$

(C) $\frac{m\sqrt{m}}{\sqrt{k}}$

(D) $\frac{m^2}{2k}$

(E) km^2

128. Alex deposited x dollars into a new account that earned 8 percent annual interest compounded annually. One year later Alex deposited additional x dollars in the account. If there were no other transactions and if the account contained w dollars at the end of the two years, which of the following expresses x in terms of w?

(A) $\frac{w}{1 + 1.08}$

(B) $\frac{w}{1.08 + 1.16}$

(C) $\frac{w}{1.16 + 1.24}$

(D) $\frac{w}{1.08 + 1.08^2}$

(E) $\frac{w}{1.08^2 + 1.08^3}$

129. The compound interest on a certain sum of money invested at a certain rate of interest in the 2nd year and in the 3rd year was \$600 and \$720 respectively. What was the rate of interest at which the sum of money was invested?

(A) 12.0%

(B) 12.5%

(C) 15.0%

(D) 20.0%

(E) 25.0%

2.10 Functions

130. If the function f is defined by $f(x) = x^2 + \frac{1}{x^2}$ for all non-zero numbers x, then $\left(f\left(-\frac{1}{\sqrt{x}}\right)\right)^2 =$

(A) $\frac{2}{f(x^2)}$

(B) $\left(\frac{1}{f(\sqrt{x})}\right)^2$

(C) $1 - (f(\sqrt{x}))^2$

(D) $f(x) - 2$

(E) $f(x) + 2$

131. The function f is defined by $f(x) = -\frac{1}{x}$ for all non-zero numbers x. If $f(a) = -\frac{1}{2}$ and $f(ab) = \frac{1}{6}$, then $b =$

(A) 3

(B) $\frac{1}{3}$

(C) $-\frac{1}{3}$

(D) -3

(E) -12

132. The function f is defined by $f(x) = \sqrt{x} - 10$ for all positive numbers x. If $u = f(t)$ for some positive numbers t and u, what is t in terms of u?

(A) $\sqrt{u + 10}$

(B) $(\sqrt{u} + 10)^2$

(C) $\sqrt{u^2 + 10}$

(D) $(u + 10)^2$

(E) $(u^2 + 10)^2$

133. The function f is defined for each positive three-digit integer n by $f(n) = 2^x 3^y 5^z$, where x, y and z are the hundreds', tens and unit digits of n, respectively. If m and v are three-digit positive integers such that $f(m) = 9f(v)$, then $m - v =$

(A) 8

(B) 9

(C) 18

(D) 20

(E) 80

134. For which of the following functions f, is $f(x) = f(1 - x)$ for all x?

(A) $f(x) = 1 - x$

(B) $f(x) = 1 - x^2$

(C) $f(x) = x^2 - (1 - x)^2$

(D) $f(x) = x^2(1 - x)^2$

(E) $f(x) = \frac{x}{1 - x}$

135. If $f(x) = \frac{1}{x}$ and $g(x) = \frac{x}{x^2 + 1}$, for all $x > 0$, what is the minimum value of $f(g(x))$?

(A) 0

(B) $\frac{1}{2}$

(C) 1

(D) $\frac{3}{2}$

(E) 2

136. If $P(r) = \frac{8r}{1 - r}$, for what value of r does $P(r) = \frac{1}{2}P(3)$?

(A) 6

(B) 3

(C) 0

(D) −3

(E) −6

137. If $3f(x) + 2f(-x) = 5x - 10$, what is the value of $f(1)$?

(A) 0

(B) 1

(C) 2

(D) 3

(E) 4

2.11 Permutation & Combination & Probability

138. $C_n^m = \dfrac{m!}{(m-n)!.n!}$ for non-negative integers m and n, $m \geq n$. If $C_3^5 = C_x^5$ and $x \neq 3$, what is the value of x?

(A) 0

(B) 1

(C) 2

(D) 4

(E) 5

139. A "code" is defined as a sequence of three dots arranged in a row. Each dot is colored either "yellow" or "blue". How many distinct codes can be formed?

(A) 3

(B) 5

(C) 6

(D) 8

(E) 9

140. A certain office supply store stocks two sizes of self-stick notepads, each in four colors: blue, green, yellow and pink. The store packs the notepads in packages that contain either three notepads of the same size and the same color or three notepads of the same size and of three different colors. If the order in which the colors are packed is not considered, how many different packages of the types described above are possible?

(A) 6

(B) 8

(C) 16

(D) 24

(E) 32

141. A certain restaurant offers six kinds of cheese and two kinds of fruit for its dessert platter. If each dessert platter contains an equal number of kinds of cheese and an equal number of kinds of fruits, how many different dessert platters could the restaurant offer?

(A) 8

(B) 12

(C) 15

(D) 21

(E) 27

142. A certain stock exchange designates each stock with a one, two or three-letter code, where each letter is selected from the 26 letters of the alphabet. If the letters may be repeated and if the same letters used in a different order constitute a different code, how many different stocks is it possible to uniquely designate with these codes?

(A) 2951

(B) 8125
(C) 15600
(D) 16302
(E) 18278

143. A certain university will select one of seven candidates eligible to fill a position in the Mathematics department and two of ten candidates eligible to fill two identical positions in the Computer Science department. If none of the candidates is eligible for a position in both departments, how many different sets of three candidates are there to fill the three positions?

(A) 42
(B) 70
(C) 140
(D) 165
(E) 315

144. A company has assigned a distinct three-digit code number to each of its 330 employees. Each code number was formed from the digits 2, 3, 4, 5, 6, 7, 8, 9 and no digit appears more than once in any one code number. How many unassigned code numbers are there?

(A) 6
(B) 58
(C) 174
(D) 182
(E) 399

145. A company plans to assign identification numbers to its employees. Each number is to consist of four different digits from 0 to 9, inclusive, except that the first digit cannot be 0. If any digit can be repeated any number of times in a particular code, how many different identification numbers are possible that are odd numbers?

(A) 2520
(B) 2268
(C) 3240
(D) 4500
(E) 9000

146. A fast-food company plans to build four new restaurants. If there are six sites A, B, C, D, E and F, that satisfy the company's criteria for location of the new restaurants, in how many different ways can the company select the four sites if the order of selection does not matter, given that both the sites A and B cannot be selected simultaneously?

(A) 4
(B) 5
(C) 6
(D) 9
(E) 15

147. A photographer wants to arrange 6 men of 6 different heights for a photograph by placing them in two rows of three so that each man in the first row is standing in front of someone in the second row. The heights of the men within each row must increase from left to right, and each man in the second row must be taller than the man standing in front of him. How many such arrangements of the 6 men are possible?

(A) 5
(B) 6
(C) 9
(D) 24
(E) 36

148. A researcher plans to identify each participant in a certain medical experiment with a code consisting of either a single letter or a pair of distinct letters written in alphabetic order. What is the least number of letters that can be used if there are 12 participants, and each participant is to receive a different code?

(A) 4
(B) 5
(C) 6
(D) 7
(E) 8

149. Departments A, B, and C have 10 employees each, and department D has 20 employees. Departments A, B, C, and D have no employees in common. A task force is to be formed by selecting 1 employee from each of departments A, B, and C and 2 employees from department D. How many different task forces are possible?

(A) 19,000
(B) 40,000
(C) 100,000
(D) 190,000
(E) 400,000

150. An analyst will recommend a combination of 3 industrial stocks, 2 transportation stocks, and 2 utility stocks. If the analyst can choose from 5 industrial stocks, 4 transportation stocks, and 3 utility stocks, how many different combinations of 7 stocks are possible?

(A) 12
(B) 19
(C) 60
(D) 180
(E) 720

151. In a meeting of 3 representatives from each of 6 different companies, each representative shook hands with every person other than those from his or her own company. How many handshakes took place in the meeting?

(A) 45

(B) 135

(C) 144

(D) 270

(E) 288

152. A three-digit code for certain logs uses the digits 0, 1, 2, 3, 4, 5, 6, 7, 8 and 9 according to the following constraints: the first digit cannot be 0 or 1, the second digit must be 0 or 1, and the second and third digits cannot both be 0 in the same code. If the digits may be repeated in the same code, how many different codes are possible?

(A) 144

(B) 152

(C) 160

(D) 168

(E) 176

153. A box contains exactly 24 balls, of which 12 are red and 12 are blue. If two balls are to be picked from this box at random and without replacement, what is the probability that both balls will be red?

(A) $\frac{11}{46}$

(B) $\frac{1}{4}$

(C) $\frac{5}{12}$

(D) $\frac{17}{40}$

(E) $\frac{19}{40}$

154. A certain basket contains 10 apples, seven of which are red and three of which are green. If three different apples are to be selected at random from the basket, what is the probability that two of the apples selected will be red and one will be green?

(A) $\frac{7}{40}$

(B) $\frac{7}{20}$

(C) $\frac{49}{100}$

(D) $\frac{21}{40}$

(E) $\frac{7}{10}$

155. A certain characteristic in a large population has a distribution that is symmetric about the mean m. If 68 percent of the distribution lies within one standard deviation d of the mean, what percent of the distribution is less than $(m + d)$?

(A) 16%

(B) 32%

(C) 48
(D) 84%
(E) 92%

156. A certain club has 20 members. What is the ratio of number of 5-member committees that can be formed from the members of the club to the number of 4-member committees that can be formed from the members of the club?

(A) 16 to 1
(B) 15 to 1
(C) 16 to 5
(D) 15 to 6
(E) 5 to 4

157. A certain company assigns employees to offices in such a way that some of the offices can be empty and more than one employee can be assigned to an office. In how many ways can the company assign three employees to two different offices?

(A) 5
(B) 6
(C) 7
(D) 8
(E) 9

158. A certain company employs six senior officers and four junior officers. If a committee is to be created that is made up of three senior officers and one junior officer, how many different committees are possible?

(A) 8
(B) 24
(C) 58
(D) 80
(E) 210

159. A certain company expects quarterly earnings of \$0.80 per share of stock, half of which will be distributed as dividends to shareholders while the rest will be used for research and development. If earnings are greater than expected, shareholders will receive an additional \$0.04 per share for each additional \$0.10 of per share earnings. If quarterly earnings are \$1.10 per share, what will be the dividend paid to a person who owns 200 shares of the company's stock?

(A) \$92
(B) \$96
(C) \$104
(D) \$120
(E) \$240

160. A certain company sold 800 units of its product for \$8 each and 1,000 units of its product for \$5 each. If the company's cost of producing each unit of its product was \$6, what was the company's profit or loss on the 1,800 units of its product?

(A) $1,600
(B) $600 loss
(C) No profit or loss
(D) $600 profit
(E) $1,600 profit

161. A certain company that sells only cars and trucks reported that revenues from car sales in 1997 were down 11 percent from 1996 and revenues from truck sales in 1997 were up 7 percent from 1996. If total revenues from car sales and truck sales in 1997 were up 1 percent from 1996, what is the ratio of revenue from car sales in 1996 to revenue from truck sales in 1996?

(A) 1:2
(B) 4:5
(C) 1:1
(D) 3:2
(E) 5:3

162. A certain company's profit in 1996 was 15 percent greater than its profit in 1995, and its profit in 1997 was 20 percent greater than its profit in 1996. The company's profit in 1997 was what percent greater than its profit in 1995?

(A) 5%
(B) 18%
(C) 33%
(D) 35%
(E) 38%

163. A certain computer program generates a sequence of numbers $a_1, a_2, \dots a_n$ such that $a_1 = a_2 = 1$ and $a_k = a_{(k-1)} + 2a_{(k-2)}$ for all integers k such that $3 \le k \le n$. If $n > 6$, then $a_7 =$

(A) 32
(B) 43
(C) 64
(D) 100
(E) 128

164. If the probability that stock A will increase in value during the next month is 0.54 and the probability that stock B will increase in value during the next month is 0.38, what is the approximate probability that exactly one of stock A and stock B would increase in value during the next month? It is known that price fluctuations of stock A in no way affect the price fluctuations of stock B.

(A) 0.21
(B) 0.29
(C) 0.51
(D) 0.73
(E) 0.92

165. A coin that is tossed will land heads or tails, and each outcome has equal probability. What is the probability that the coin will land heads at least once on two tosses?

(A) $\frac{1}{4}$

(B) $\frac{1}{3}$

(C) $\frac{1}{2}$

(D) $\frac{2}{3}$

(E) $\frac{3}{4}$

166. A contest will consist of n questions, each of which is to be answered either "True" or "False." Anyone who answers all n questions correctly will be a winner. What is the least value of n for which the probability is less than $\frac{1}{1000}$, that a person who randomly guesses the answer to each question will be a winner?

(A) 5

(B) 10

(C) 50

(D) 100

(E) 1000

167. A gum ball dispenser has 24 gum balls – 12 white and 12 black, which are dispensed at random. If the first three gum balls dispensed are black, what is the probability that the next two gum balls dispensed will also be black?

(A) $\frac{6}{35}$

(B) $\frac{1}{3}$

(C) $\frac{4}{15}$

(D) $\frac{3}{7}$

(E) $\frac{1}{2}$

168. A jar contains 16 marbles, of which 4 are red, 3 are blue, and the rest are yellow. If 2 marbles are to be selected at random from the jar, one at a time without being replaced, what is the probability that one marble selected will be red and the other marble selected will be blue?

(A) $\frac{3}{64}$

(B) $\frac{1}{20}$

(C) $\frac{1}{10}$

(D) $\frac{1}{8}$

(E) $\frac{1}{6}$

169. A shipment of eight television sets contains two LCD sets and six LED sets. If two television sets are to be chosen at random from this shipment, what is the probability that at least one of the two sets chosen will be a LCD set?

(A) $\frac{1}{7}$

(B) $\frac{1}{4}$

(C) $\frac{5}{14}$

(D) $\frac{13}{28}$

(E) $\frac{15}{28}$

170. In a stack of cards, 9 cards are blue and the rest are red. If 2 cards are to be chosen at random from the stack without replacement, the probability that the cards chosen will both be blue is $\frac{6}{11}$. What is the number of cards in the stack?

(A) 10

(B) 11

(C) 12

(D) 15

(E) 18

171. A string of 10 light bulbs is wired in such a way that if any individual light bulb fails, the entire string fails. If for each individual light bulb the probability of failing during time period T is 0.06, what is the probability that the string of light bulbs will fail during time period T?

(A) 0.06^{10}

(B) 0.06

(C) $1 - 0.94^{10}$

(D) 0.94^{10}

(E) $1 - 0.06^{10}$

172. In a box of 12 pens, a total of 3 are defective. If a customer buys 2 pens, selected at random from the box, what is the probability that neither pen will be defective?

(A) $\frac{1}{6}$

(B) $\frac{2}{9}$

(C) $\frac{6}{11}$

(D) $\frac{9}{16}$

(E) $\frac{3}{4}$

173. In a box of 12 pens, a total of 3 are defective. If a customer buys 2 pens, selected at random from the box, what is the probability that neither pen will be defective?

(A) $\frac{1}{6}$

(B) $\frac{2}{9}$

(C) $\frac{6}{11}$

(D) $\frac{9}{16}$

(E) $\frac{3}{4}$

2.12 Sets

174. A club with a total membership of 30 has formed committees, M, S, and R, which have 8, 12, and 5 members, respectively. If no member of the committee M is on either of the other two committees, what is the greatest possible number of members in the club who are on none of the committees?

(A) 5

(B) 7

(C) 8

(D) 10

(E) 12

175. In each production lot for a certain toy, 25 percent of the toys are red and 75 percent of the toys are blue. Half the toys are size A and half are size B. If 10 out of a lot of 100 toys are red and size A, how many of the toys are blue and size B?

(A) 15

(B) 25

(C) 30

(D) 35

(E) 40

176. In an isosceles triangle PQR, if the measure of angle P is 80°, which of the following could be the measure of angle R ?

I. 20°

II. 50°

III. 80°

(A) Only I

(B) Only III

(C) Only I and II

(D) Only II and III

(E) I, II and III

177. According to a survey, 7 percent of teenagers have not used a computer to play games, 11 percent have not used a computer to write reports, and 95 percent have used a computer for at least one of the above purposes. What percent of the teenagers in the survey have used a computer both to play games and to write reports?

(A) 13%

(B) 56%

(C) 77%

(D) 87%

(E) 91%

178. In a survey, 2000 executives were each asked whether they read newsletter A or newsletter B. According to the survey, 55 percent of the executives read newsletter A,

62 percent read newsletter B, and 37 percent read both newsletter A and newsletter B. How many of the executives surveyed read at most one among newsletter A and newsletter B?

(A) 1600

(B) 1260

(C) 900

(D) 860

(E) 760

179. In a certain region, the number of children who have been vaccinated against rubella is twice the number of children who have been vaccinated against mumps. The number of children who have been vaccinated against both is twice the number of children who have been vaccinated only against mumps. If 5,000 have been vaccinated against both, how many have been vaccinated only against rubella?

(A) 2500

(B) 7500

(C) 10000

(D) 15000

(E) 17500

2.13 Statistics & Data Interpretation

180. 150, 200, 250, n: (not in order)

Which of the following could be the median of the four integers listed above (not in order)?

I. 175
II. 215
III. 235

(A) I only
(B) II only
(C) I and II only
(D) II and III only
(E) All of them

181. 40, 45, 50, 55, 60, 75, 75, 100, 100, 100

The list above shows the scores of ten schoolchildren on a certain test. If the standard deviation of the ten scores is 22.4, rounded to the nearest tenth, how many of the scores are more than 1 standard deviation below the mean of the ten scores?

(A) One
(B) Two
(C) Three
(D) Four
(E) Five

182. A certain list consists of 21 different numbers. If n is a number in the list and is four times the average (arithmetic mean) of the other 20 numbers in the list, then n is what fraction of the sum of the 21 numbers in the list?

(A) $\frac{1}{20}$
(B) $\frac{1}{6}$
(C) $\frac{4}{21}$
(D) $\frac{1}{5}$
(E) $\frac{5}{21}$

183. If the average (arithmetic mean) of 3, 8 and w is greater than or equal to w and smaller than or equal to $3w$, how many integer values of w exist?

(A) 5
(B) 4
(C) 3

(D) 2
(E) 1

184. If the average (arithmetic mean) of five distinct positive integers is 10, what is the least possible value of the greatest of the five numbers?

(A) 11
(B) 12
(C) 24
(D) 40
(E) 46

185. If the average (arithmetic mean) of x, y and 20 is 10 greater than the average of x, y, 20 and 30, what is the average of x and y?

(A) 40
(B) 45
(C) 60
(D) 75
(E) 95

186. A set of 15 different integers has a median of 30 and a range of 30. What is the greatest possible integer that could be in this set?

(A) 42
(B) 47
(C) 50
(D) 53
(E) 60

187. The mean of the set of the positive integers $\{4, 4, 5, 5, 6, x\}$ is $\frac{x^2}{2}$. What is the range of the above set of integers?

(A) 1
(B) 2
(C) 3
(D) 4
(E) 5

188. Company A has a total of n employees, where n is an odd integer, and no two employees have the same annual salary. The annual salaries of the n employees are listed in increasing order, and the 16th salary in the list is the median of the annual salaries. If the sum of the annual salaries of Company A's employees is \$942,400, what is the average (arithmetic mean) of the annual salaries of Company A's employees?

(A) \$29450
(B) \$30400
(C) \$32500

(D) $47120

(E) $58900

189.

Time	Amount of bacteria
1:00 pm	10.0 grams
4:00 pm	x grams
7:00 pm	14.4 grams

Data for a certain biology experiment are given in the table above. If the amount of bacteria present increased by the same fraction during each of the two 3-hour periods shown, how many grams of bacteria were present at 4:00 pm?

(A) 12.0

(B) 12.1

(C) 12.2

(D) 12.3

(E) 12.4

190. According to the table given below, the number of fellows was approximately what percent of the total membership of organization X?

Membership of an Organization X, 2008	
Honorary members	78
Fellows	9209
Members	35509
Associate members	27909
Affiliates	2372

(A) 9%

(B) 12%

(C) 18%

(D) 25%

(E) 35%

191. According to the table below, what was the approximate average number of watts of electricity used per hour per appliance in the household on May 1?

Electricity usage in a certain household on May 1		
Appliance	Number of hours in use	Number of watts of electricity used per hour
TV	4	145
Computer	3	155
VCR	2	45
Stereo	2	109

(A) 31

(B) 74

(C) 123

(D) 281

(E) 338

2.14 Linear Equations

192. A cashier mentally reversed the digits of one customer's correct amount of change and thus gave the customer an incorrect amount of change. If the cash register contained 45 cents more than it should have as a result of this error, which of the following could have been the correct amount of change in cents?

(A) 14

(B) 45

(C) 54

(D) 65

(E) 83

193. A certain business produced x rakes each month from November through February and shipped $\frac{x}{2}$ rakes at the beginning of each month from March through October. The business paid no storage costs for the rakes from November through February, but it paid storage costs of \$0.10 per rake each month from March through October for the rakes that had not been shipped. In terms of x, what was the total storage cost, in dollars, that the business paid for the rakes for the 12 months from November through October?

(A) $0.4x$

(B) $1.2x$

(C) $1.4x$

(D) $1.6x$

(E) $3.2x$

194. A certain fruit stand sold apples for \$0.70 each and bananas for \$0.50 each. If a customer purchased both apples and bananas from the stand for a total of \$6.30, what is the total number of apples and bananas did the customer purchase? The customer purchased at least one of both the fruits.

(A) 10

(B) 11

(C) 12

(D) 13

(E) 14

195. If $x + y + z = 2$, and $x + 2y + 3z = 6$ and $y \neq 0$, then what is the value of $\left(\frac{x}{y}\right)$?

(A) $-\frac{1}{2}$

(B) $-\frac{1}{3}$

(C) $-\frac{1}{6}$

(D) $\frac{1}{3}$

(E) $\frac{1}{2}$

196. An optometrist charges \$150 per pair for soft contact lenses and \$85 per pair for hard contact lenses. Last week she sold five more pairs of soft lenses than hard lenses. If her total sales for pairs of contact lenses last week were \$1690, what was the total number of pairs of contact lenses that she sold?

(A) 11

(B) 13

(C) 15

(D) 17

(E) 19

2.15 Quadratic Equations & Polynomials

197. If $x \geq 0$ and $x = \sqrt{8xy - 16y^2}$, then in terms of y, $x =$

(A) $-4y$

(B) $\frac{y}{4}$

(C) y

(D) $4y$

(E) $4y^2$

198. What is the difference between the maximum and the minimum value of $\left(\frac{x}{y}\right)$ for which $(x-2)^2 = 9$ and $(y-3)^2 = 25$?

(A) $-\frac{15}{8}$

(B) $\frac{3}{4}$

(C) $\frac{9}{8}$

(D) $\frac{19}{8}$

(E) $\frac{25}{8}$

199. If x and y are positive integers and $2x + 3y + xy = 12$, what is the value of $(x + y)$?

(A) 2

(B) 4

(C) 5

(D) 6

(E) 8

200. An object thrown directly upward is at a height of h feet, t seconds after it was thrown, where $h = -16(t-3)^2 + 150$. What is the height of the object now once it reached its maximum height and descended for 2 seconds?

(A) 6 feet

(B) 86 feet

(C) 134 feet

(D) 150 feet

(E) 214 feet

201. According to a certain estimate, the depth $N(t)$, in centimeters, of the water in a certain tank at t hours past 2:00 in the morning is given by $N(t) = -20(t-5)^2 + 500$, for $0 \leq t \leq 10$. According to this estimate, at what time in the morning does the depth of the water in the tank reach its maximum?

(A) 5:30

(B) 7:00

(C) 7:30

(D) 8:00

(E) 9:00

2.16 Inequalities

202. Bill's school is 10 miles from his home. He travels 4 miles from school to football practice, and then 2 miles to a friend's house. If he is then x miles from home, what is the range of possible values for x?

(A) $2 \leq x \leq 10$

(B) $4 \leq x \leq 10$

(C) $4 \leq x \leq 12$

(D) $4 \leq x \leq 16$

(E) $6 \leq x \leq 16$

203. $2x + y = 12$ $|y| \leq 12$

For how many ordered pairs (x, y) that are solutions of the above system such that x and y both are integers?

(A) 7

(B) 10

(C) 12

(D) 13

(E) 14

204. If the cost of 12 eggs varies between \$0.90 and \$1.20, and the cost of 5 sandwiches varies between \$10 and \$15, then the cost of 4 eggs and 3 sandwiches varies between

(A) \$2.15 and \$3.20

(B) \$2.30 and \$3.40

(C) \$6.40 and \$9.30

(D) \$6.30 and \$9.40

(E) \$9.30 and \$12.40

205. If $x < 0$ and $0 < y < 1$, which of the following has the greatest value?

(A) x^2

(B) $(xy)^2$

(C) $\left(\frac{x}{y}\right)^2$

(D) $\frac{x^2}{y}$

(E) x^2y

206. Anne traveled from City A to City B in 4 hours, and her speed was between 25 miles per hour and 45 miles per hour. John also traveled from City A to City B along the same route in 2 hours, and his speed was between 45 miles per hour and 60 miles per hour. Which of the following could be the distance, in miles, from City A to City B?

(A) 95

(B) 115

(C) 125

(D) 160

(E) 180

2.17 Geometry–Lines & Triangles

207. If each of the two lines l and m are parallel to line n, which of the following MUST be correct?

I. Lines l, m and n lie in the same plane.

II. Lines l and m are parallel to one another.

III. Line l is the same as line m.

(A) Only I
(B) Only II
(C) Only III
(D) Only I and II
(E) Only II and III

208. On the line segment AD shown below, AB $= \frac{1}{2}$CD and BD $= \frac{3}{2}$AC. If BC = 24, then AD =

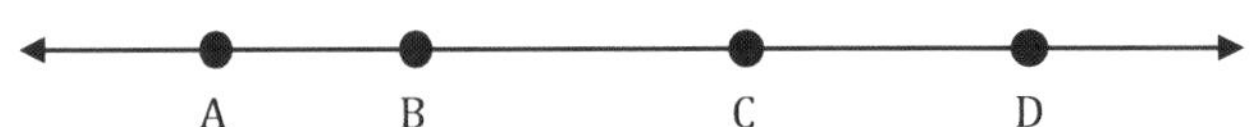

(A) 24
(B) 48
(C) 72
(D) 96
(E) 120

209. R, S, T, and U are points on a line, and U is the midpoint of line segment ST. If the lengths of line segments RS, RT, and ST are 20, 4, and 16, respectively, what is the length of line segment RU?

(A) 6
(B) 8
(C) 12
(D) 14
(E) 16

210. A cash register in a certain clothing store is the same distance from two dressing rooms in the store. The distance between the two dressing rooms is 16 feet, which of the following could be the distance between the cash register and either dressing room?

I. 6 feet

II. 12 feet

III. 24 feet

(A) I only
(B) II only
(C) III only

(D) I and II

(E) II and III

211. A certain right triangle has sides of length x, y and z, where $x < y < z$. If the area of this triangular region is 1, which of the following indicates all of the possible values of y?

(A) $y > \sqrt{2}$

(B) $\frac{\sqrt{3}}{2} < y < \sqrt{2}$

(C) $\frac{\sqrt{2}}{3} < y < \frac{\sqrt{3}}{2}$

(D) $\frac{\sqrt{3}}{4} < y < \frac{\sqrt{2}}{3}$

(E) $y < \frac{\sqrt{3}}{4}$

212. A certain right triangle has sides of length x, y and z, where $x < y < z$. If the area of this triangular region is 1, which of the following indicates all of the possible values of z?

(A) $z > 2$

(B) $\sqrt{2} < z < 2$

(C) $\sqrt{2} < z < \sqrt{3}$

(D) $1 < z < \sqrt{2}$

(E) $z < 1$

213. In the figure below, DA = DB = DC. What is the value of x?

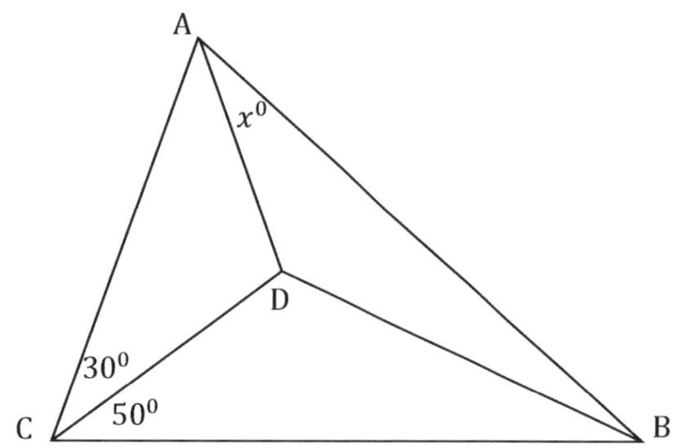

(A) 10

(B) 20

(C) 30

(D) 40

(E) 50

214. In the figure below, each side of square ABCD has length 1, the length of line segment CE is 1, and the length of line segment BE is equal to the length of line segment DE. What is the area of the triangular region BCE?

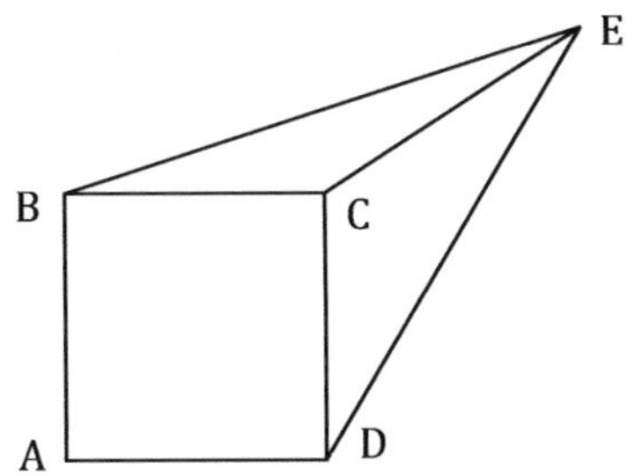

(A) $\frac{1}{3}$

(B) $\frac{\sqrt{2}}{4}$

(C) $\frac{1}{2}$

(D) $\frac{\sqrt{2}}{2}$

(E) $\frac{3}{4}$

215. In the figure shown below, what is the value of x?

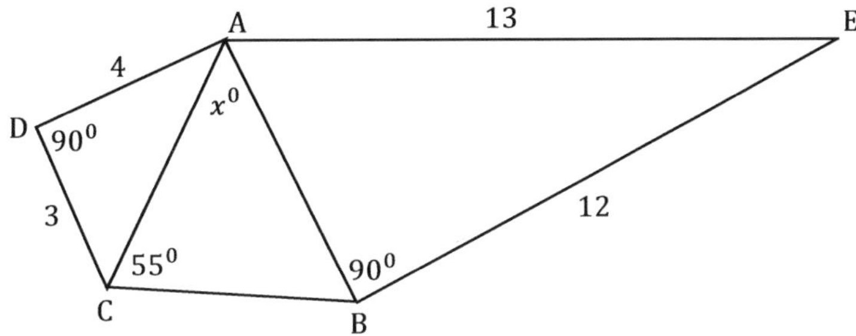

(A) 55

(B) 60

(C) 65

(D) 70

(E) 75

216. In the figure below, what is the perimeter of triangle BCD?

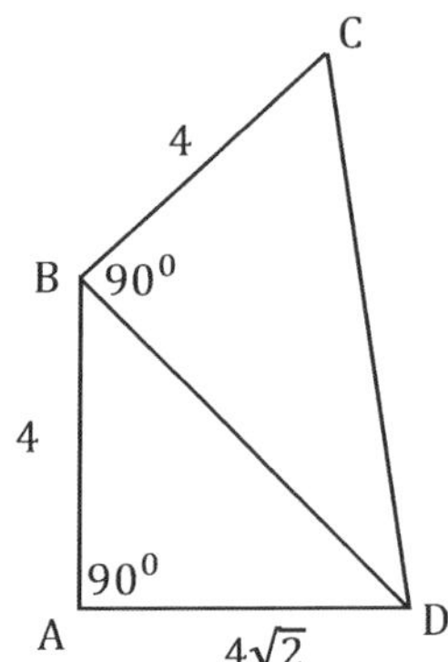

(A) $4 + 4\sqrt{3}$

(B) 12

(C) $12 + 4\sqrt{3}$

(D) $8 + 8\sqrt{3}$

(E) $16\sqrt{2}$

2.18 Geometry–Circles

217. If the circle below has centre O and length of the arc RST is 18π, what is the perimeter of the region RSTU?

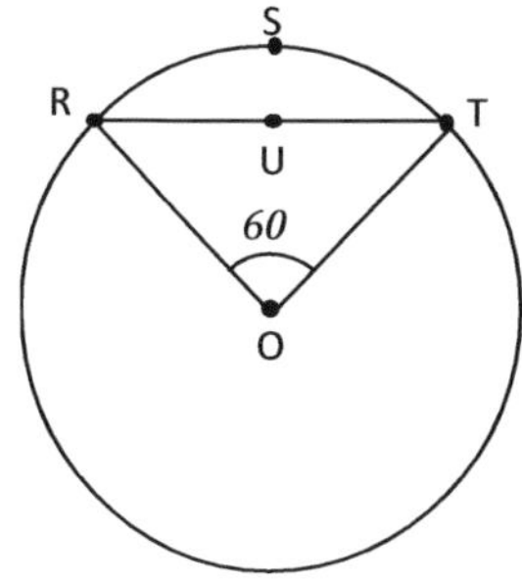

(A) $12\pi + 18$

(B) $12\pi + 27$

(C) $18\pi + 27$

(D) $18\pi + 54$

(E) $18\pi + 108$

218. In the figure below, O is the center of the circle. If the area of the sector containing the angle x^o is 2π, what is the value of x?

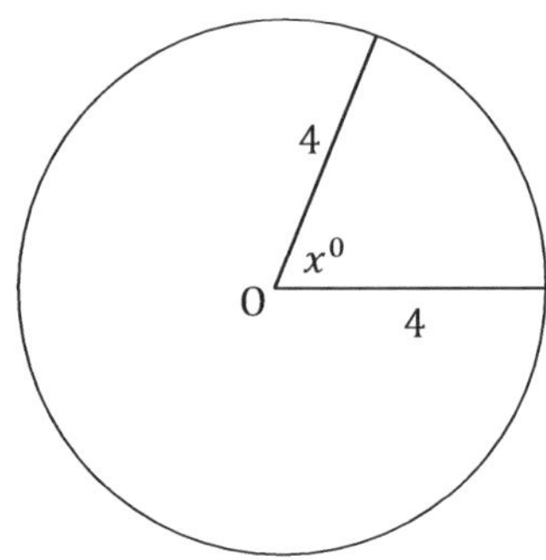

(A) 22.5

(B) 30.0

(C) 45.0

(D) 60.0

(E) 90.0

219. In the figure shown below, if the area of the shaded region is 3 times the area of the smaller circular region, then the circumference of the larger circle is how many times the circumference of the smaller circle?

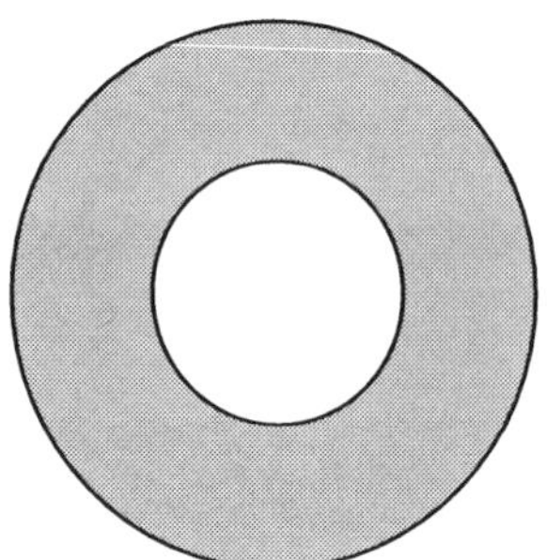

(A) 4

(B) 3

(C) 2

(D) $\sqrt{3}$

(E) $\sqrt{2}$

220. In the figure shown below, line segments QS and RT are diameters of the circle. If the distance between Q and R is $\frac{8}{\sqrt{2}}$, what is the area of the circle?

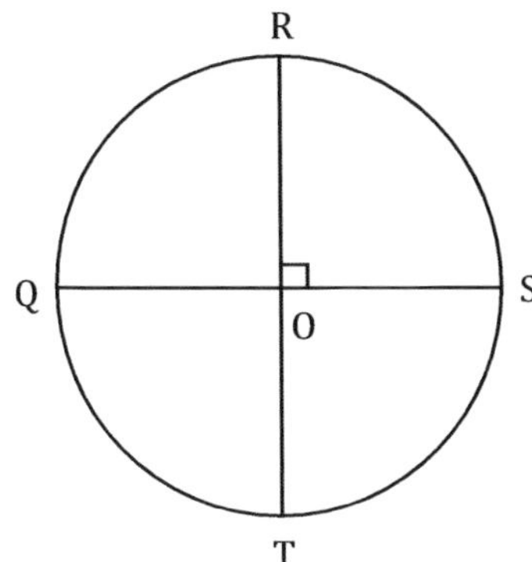

(A) 4π

(B) 8π

(C) 16π

(D) 32π

(E) 64π

221. In the figure shown below, the triangle ABC is inscribed in a semicircle. If the length of line segment AB is 8 and the length of line segment BC is 6, what is the length of arc ABC?

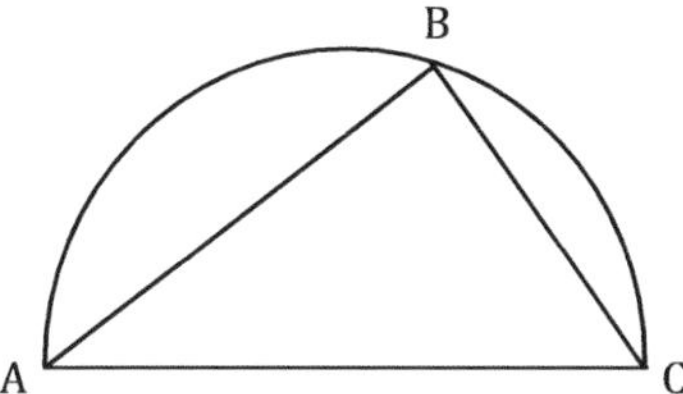

(A) 15π

(B) 12π

(C) 10π

(D) 7π

(E) 5π

222. An equilateral triangle that has an area of $9\sqrt{3}$ is inscribed in a circle. What is the area of the circle?

(A) 6π

(B) 9π

(C) 12π

(D) $9\sqrt{3}\pi$

(E) $18\sqrt{3}\pi$

2.19 Geometry–Polygon

223. A circular mat with diameter 20 inches is placed on a square tabletop, having its sides equal to 24 inches. Which of the following is closest to the fraction of the tabletop NOT covered by the mat?

(A) $\frac{1}{2}$

(B) $\frac{3}{5}$

(C) $\frac{2}{3}$

(D) $\frac{1}{4}$

(E) $\frac{9}{20}$

224. Rectangular floors having perimeter of 16 meters are to be covered with carpet squares that measure 1 meter by 1 meter each, costing $6 apiece. What is the maximum possible cost for the number of carpet squares needed to cover any such rectangular floor if the sides of the floors are integers?

(A) $42

(B) $72

(C) $90

(D) $96

(E) $120

225. A rectangular photograph is surrounded by a border that is 1 inch wide on each side. The total area of the photograph and the border is m square inches. If the border had been 2 inches wide on each side, the total area would have been $(m + 52)$ square inches. What is the perimeter of the photograph, in inches?

(A) 34

(B) 36

(C) 38

(D) 40

(E) 42

226. A rectangular picture is surrounded by a border, as shown in the figure below. Without the border, the length of the picture is twice its width. If the area of the border is 196 square inches, what is the length, in inches, of the picture, excluding the border?

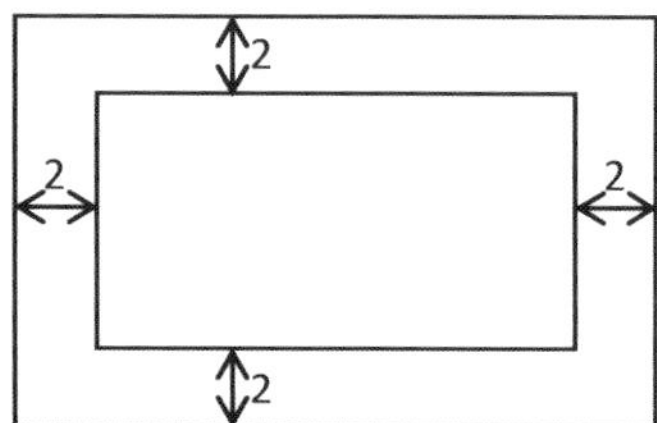

(A) 10

(B) 15

(C) 30

(D) 40

(E) 60

227. Two brothers inherited a rectangular field of dimension 80 feet by 120 feet. If they decide to split the land into two equal rectangles, then what is the minimum cost required to fence one such half at the rate of $2 per feet?

(A) $240

(B) $280

(C) $320

(D) $560

(E) $640

228. A rectangular park has a perimeter of 560 feet and a diagonal measurement of 200 feet. What is its area, in square feet?

(A) 19200

(B) 19600

(C) 20000

(D) 20400

(E) 20800

229. A solid yellow stripe is to be painted in the middle of a certain highway. If 1 gallon of paint covers an area of p square feet of highway, how many gallons of paint will be needed to paint a stripe t inches wide on a stretch of highway m miles long? (1 mile = 5,280 feet, and 1 foot = 12 inches)

(A) $\frac{5280mt}{12p}$

(B) $\frac{5280pt}{12m}$

(C) $\frac{5280mpt}{12}$

(D) $\frac{5280 * 12m}{pt}$

(E) $\frac{5280 * 12p}{mt}$

230. In the parallelogram PQRS shown below, if PQ = 4 and QR = 6, what is the area of PQRS?

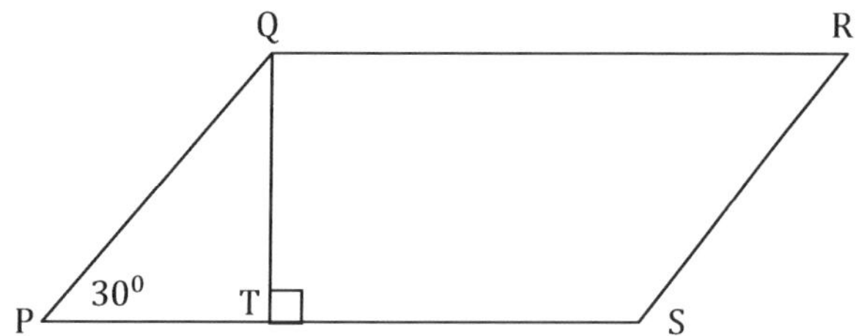

(A) 8

(B) 12

(C) 24

(D) $8\sqrt{3}$

(E) $12\sqrt{3}$

231.

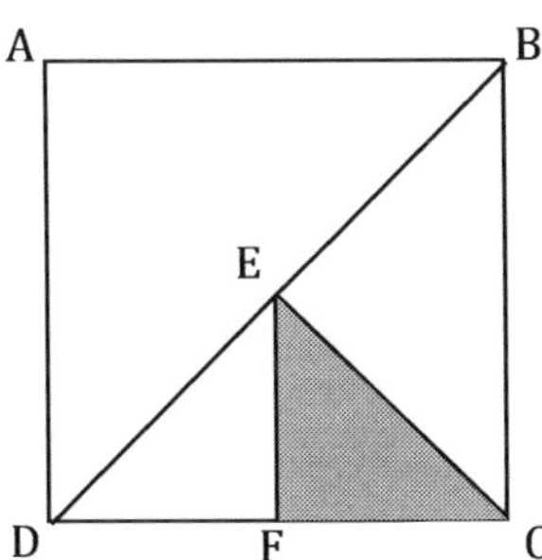

In square ABCD above, if DE = EB and DF = FC, then the area of the shaded region is what fraction of the area of square region ABCD?

(A) $\frac{1}{16}$

(B) $\frac{1}{8}$

(C) $\frac{1}{6}$

(D) $\frac{1}{4}$

(E) $\frac{1}{3}$

232. In the figure shown below, the area of square region PRTV is 81, and the ratio of the area of square region XSTU to the area of square region PQXW is 1 to 4. What is the length of segment RS?

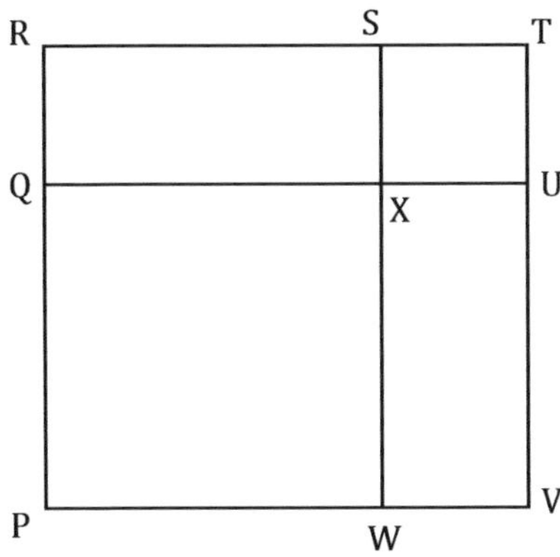

(A) 5.0

(B) 5.5

(C) 6.0

(D) 6.5

(E) 7.0

233.

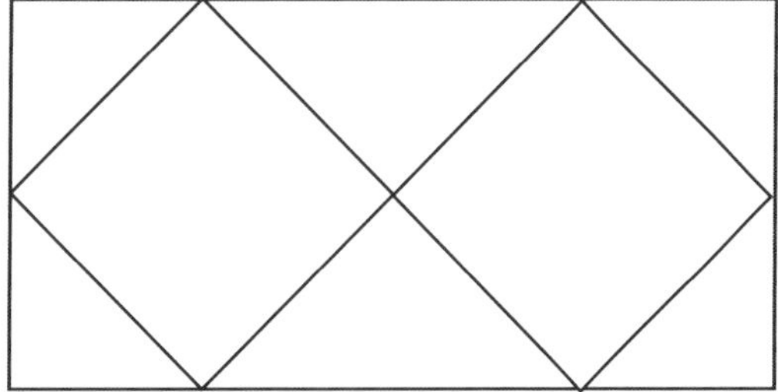

In the figure above, two identical squares are inscribed in the rectangle. If the perimeter of the rectangle is $18\sqrt{2}$, then what is the perimeter of each square?

(A) $8\sqrt{2}$

(B) 12

(C) 16

(D) $12\sqrt{2}$

(E) 18

234. A certain number of desks and bookshelves, at least one each, are to be placed along a library wall that is 16 meters long. Each desk is 2 meters long, and each bookshelf is 1.5 meters long. If the maximum possible number of desks and bookshelves are to be placed along the wall, then the space along the wall that is left over will be how many meters long?

(A) 0.5

(B) 1.0

(C) 1.5

(D) 2.0

(E) 3.0

235. A thin piece of wire 40 meters long is cut into two pieces. One piece is used to form a circle with radius r, and the other is used to form a square. If no wire is left over, which of the following represents the total area, in square meters, of the circular and the square regions in terms of r?

(A) πr^2

(B) $\pi r^2 + 10$

(C) $\pi r^2 + \frac{1}{4}\pi^2 r^2$

(D) $\pi r^2 + (40 - 2\pi r)^2$

(E) $\pi r^2 + \left(10 - \frac{1}{2}\pi r\right)^2$

2.20 Geometry–3 Dimensional

236. A certain right circular cylinder has a radius of 5 inches. A certain quantity of liquid fills this cylinder to a height of 9 inches. When all of this liquid is poured into a second right circular cylinder, the liquid fills the second cylinder to a height of 4 inches. What is the radius of the second cylinder, in inches?

(A) 6.0
(B) 6.5
(C) 7.0
(D) 7.5
(E) 8.0

237. A circular rim 28 inches in diameter rotates the same number of inches per second as a circular rim 35 inches in diameter. If the smaller rim makes x revolutions per second, how many revolutions per minute does the larger rim make in terms of x?

(A) $\frac{48\pi}{x}$
(B) $75x$
(C) $48x$
(D) $24x$
(E) $\frac{x}{75\pi}$

238. In the rectangular solid below, the three faces shown have areas 12, 15, and 20. What is the volume of the solid?

(A) 60
(B) 120
(C) 450
(D) 1800
(E) 3600

239. The interior of a rectangular carton is designed by a certain manufacturer to have a volume of x cubic feet and a ratio of length to width to height of 3 : 2 : 2. In terms of x, which of the following equals the height of the carton, in feet?

(A) $\sqrt[3]{x}$
(B) $\sqrt[3]{\frac{2}{3}x}$
(C) $\sqrt[3]{\frac{3}{2}x}$

(D) $\frac{2}{3}\sqrt[3]{x}$

(E) $\frac{3}{2}\sqrt[3]{x}$

240. Two oil cans, X and Y, are right circular cylinders, and the height and the radius of Y are each twice those of X. If the oil in can X, which is filled to capacity, sells for $2, then at the same rate, how much does the oil in can Y sell for, if Y is filled to only half its capacity?

(A) $1

(B) $2

(C) $4

(D) $8

(E) $16

241. For the cube shown below, what is the degree measure of ∠PQR?

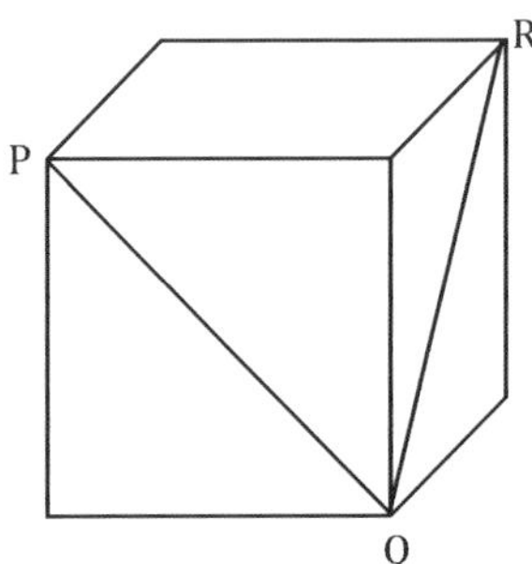

(A) 30°

(B) 45°

(C) 60°

(D) 75°

(E) 90°

242. A solid cube is placed in a cylindrical container. Which of the following percent values COULD possibly represent the ratio of the volume of the cylinder not occupied by the cube to the volume of the cylinder? (Assume the value of π to be 3)

(A) 16%

(B) 25%

(C) 28%

(D) 32%

(E) 36%

2.21 Co-ordinate geometry

243. In the coordinate plane, a diameter of a circle has the end points $(-3, -6)$ and $(5, 0)$. What is the area of the circle?

(A) 5π

(B) $10\sqrt{2}\pi$

(C) 25π

(D) 50π

(E) 100π

244. A straight line in the XY-plane has a slope of 2 and a Y-intercept of 2. On this line, what is the X-coordinate of the point whose Y-coordinate is 500?

(A) 249

(B) 498

(C) 676

(D) 823

(E) 1002

245. In the XY-plane, a line n passes through the origin and has a slope 4. If points $(1, c)$ and $(d, 2)$ are on the line n, what is the value of $\frac{c}{d}$?

(A) $\frac{1}{4}$

(B) $\frac{1}{2}$

(C) 2

(D) 4

(E) 8

246. In the XY-plane, the point $(-2, -3)$ is the center of a circle. The point $(-2, 1)$ lies inside the circle and the point $(4, -3)$ lies outside the circle. If the radius of the circle is an integer, then what is the value of r?

(A) 6

(B) 5

(C) 4

(D) 3

(E) 2

247. In the XY-plane, the points (c, d), $(c, -d)$ and $(-c, -d)$ are three vertices of a certain square. If $c < 0$ and $d > 0$, which of the following points is in the same quadrant as the fourth vertex of the square?

(A) $(-5, -3)$

(B) $(-5, 3)$

(C) $(5, -3)$

(D) $(3, -5)$

(E) $(3, 5)$

248. In the XY-plane, the vertices of a triangle have coordinates $(0, 0)$, $(3, 3)$ and $(7, 0)$. What is the perimeter of the triangle?

(A) $\sqrt{34}$

(B) $\sqrt{43}$

(C) 13

(D) $7 + 6\sqrt{2}$

(E) $12 + 3\sqrt{2}$

249. If the points $(a, 0)$, $(0, b)$ and $(1, 1)$ are collinear, what is the value of $\left(\frac{1}{a} + \frac{1}{b}\right)$?

(A) -1

(B) 0

(C) 1

(D) 2

(E) 3

250. In the XY-plane, what is the area of the triangle formed by the line $3y - 4x = 24$ and the X and Y axes?

(A) 6

(B) 14

(C) 24

(D) 36

(E) 48

Chapter 3

Data Sufficiency Question Bank

Data Sufficiency

For most of you, Data Sufficiency (DS) may be a new format. The DS format is very unique to the GMAT exam. The format is as follows: There is a question stem followed by two statements, labeled statement (1) and statement (2). These statements contain additional information.

Your task is to use the additional information from each statement alone to answer the question. If none of the statements alone helps you answer the question, you must use the information from both the statements together. There may be questions which cannot be answered even after combining the additional information given in both the statements. Based on this, the question always follows standard five options which are always in a fixed order.

(A) Statement (1) ALONE is sufficient, but statement (2) ALONE is not sufficient to answer the question asked.

(B) Statement (2) ALONE is sufficient, but statement (1) ALONE is not sufficient to answer the question asked.

(C) BOTH statements (1) and (2) TOGETHER are sufficient to answer the question asked, but NEITHER statement ALONE is sufficient to answer the question asked.

(D) EACH statement ALONE is sufficient to answer the question asked.

(E) Statements (1) and (2) TOGETHER are NOT sufficient to answer the question asked, and additional data specific to the problem are needed.

3.1 Numbers

251. For any positive integer x, the 2-height of x is defined to be the greatest non-negative integer n such that 2^n is factor of x. For example, the 2-height of 24 is 3 as 3 is the greatest exponent of 2 which is also a factor of 24. If k and m are positive integers, is the 2-height of k greater than the 2-height of m?

(1) $k > m$

(2) $\frac{k}{m}$ is an even integer

252. For each positive integer n, the integer $n^\#$ is defined by $n^\# = n^2 + 1$. What is the value of the positive integer k?

(1) When k is divided by 4, the remainder is 1

(2) $18 \le k^\# \le 36$

253. Harvey teaches a certain number of biology students in two classes, K and L. He can divide the students in class K into seven groups of n students each. However, if he divides the students in class L into six groups of p students each; one student will be left over. How many students are in class L?

(1) $n = p$

(2) There are five more students in class K than in class L

254. How many different positive factors does the integer n have?

(1) $n = a^4b^3$, where a and b are different positive prime numbers.

(2) The only positive prime numbers that are factors of n are 5 and 7.

255. If $\sqrt{x}$ is an integer, what is the value of $\sqrt{x}$?

(1) $11 < x < 17$

(2) $2 < \sqrt{x} < 5$

256. If $xy^{\left(\frac{4}{3}\right)} = \sqrt[3]{432}$, is $x + y = 5$?

(1) y is a positive integer.

(2) x is an integer.

257. If $xy \neq 0$, what is the value of $\frac{25x^2}{y^2}$?

(1) $x = 3$

(2) $5x - 2y = 0$

258. If $|m + 4| = 2$, what is the value of m?

(1) $m < 0$

(2) $m^2 + 8m + 12 = 0$

259. If $|n + 5| = 5$, what is the value of n?

(1) $n^2 \neq 0$

(2) $n^2 + 10n = 0$

260. If $1 < d < 2$, is the tenth's digit of the decimal representation of d equal to 9?

(1) $d + 0.01 < 2$

(2) $d + 0.05 > 2$

261. If a and b are integers, is b even?

(1) $3a + 4b$ is even.

(2) $3a + 5b$ is even.

262. If a, b, k and m are positive integers, is a^k a factor of b^m?

(1) a is a factor of b.

(2) $k \leq m$

263. If four of the five integers in a list are 10, −2, −8, and 0, what is the fifth integer?

(1) The product of the five integers is 0.

(2) The sum of the given four integers divided by the fifth integer is 0.

264. If J, S and V are points on the number line, what is the distance between S and V?

(1) The distance between J and S is 20.

(2) The distance between J and V is 25.

265. If k is a positive integer, what is the remainder when 2^k is divided by 10?

(1) k is divisible by 10.

(2) k is divisible by 4.

266. If k, m, and p are integers, is $(k - m - p)$ odd?

(1) k and m are even and p is odd.

(2) k, m and p are consecutive integers.

267. If k, m and t are positive integers and $\frac{k}{6} + \frac{m}{4} = \frac{t}{12}$, do t and 12 have a common factor greater than 1?

(1) k is a multiple of 3.

(2) m is a multiple of 3.

268. If m and v are integers, what is the value of $(m + v)$?

(1) $mv = 6$

(2) $(m + v)^2 = 25$

269. If m is a positive integer, then what is the number of digits of m^3?

(1) m has three digits.

(2) m^2 has five digits.

270. If m, p and t are positive integers and $m < p < t$, is the product mpt an even integer?

(1) $t - p = p - m$

(2) $t - m = 16$

271. If $n = 3k$, is k an integer?

(1) n is an integer.

(2) $\frac{n}{6}$ is an integer.

272. If n and k are positive integers, is $\frac{n}{k}$ an even integer?

(1) n is divisible by 8.

(2) k is divisible by 4.

273. If n and k are positive integers, is n divisible by 6?

(1) $n = k(k+1)(k-1)$

(2) $(k-1)$ is a multiple of 3.

274. If n is a positive integer and r is the remainder when $(n-1)(n+1)$ is divided by 24, what is the value of r?

(1) 2 is not a factor of n.

(2) 3 is not a factor of n.

275. If n is a positive integer, is $(n^3 - n)$ divisible by 4?

(1) $n = 2k + 1$, where k is an integer.

(2) $(n^2 + n)$ is divisible by 6.

276. If n is a positive integer, is n odd?

(1) $3n$ is odd.

(2) $(n + 3)$ is even.

277. If n is a positive integer, what is the value of n?

(1) When n is divided by 3, the remainder is 2.

(2) When n^2 is divided by 3, the remainder is 1.

278. If n is a positive integer, what is the value of the hundreds' digit of 30^n?

(1) $30^n > 1000$.

(2) n is a multiple of 3.

279. If n is an integer and $100 < n < 200$, what is the value of n?

(1) $\frac{n}{36}$ is an odd integer.

(2) $\frac{n}{45}$ is an even integer.

280. If n is an integer and $2 < n < 6$, what is the value of n?

(1) n is a factor of 15.

(2) n is a factor of 21.

281. If n is an integer and $x^n - x^{-n} = 0$, what is the value of x?

(1) x is an integer.

(2) $n \neq 0$

282. If n is an integer between 10 and 99, is $n < 80$?

(1) The sum of the two digits of n is a prime number.

(2) Each of the two digits of n is a prime number.

283. If n is an integer, is $\frac{n}{7}$ an integer?

(1) $\frac{3n}{7}$ is an integer.

(2) $\frac{5n}{7}$ is an integer.

284. If n is an integer, is $10^n \leq 0.001$?

(1) $n \leq -2$

(2) $n > -5$

285. If p, r, s and t are non-zero integers, is $\frac{p}{r} = \frac{s}{t}$?

(1) $s = 3p$ and $t = 3r$

(2) $3p = 2r$ and $3s = 2t$

286. If p, s and t are positive prime numbers, what is the value of $p^3s^3t^3$?

(1) $p^3st = 728$

(2) $t = 13$

287. If the positive integer x is a multiple of 12 and the positive integer y is a multiple of 10, is x^2y a multiple of 216?

(1) x is a multiple of 8.

(2) y is a multiple of 6.

288. If q is a positive integer less than 17 and r is the remainder when 17 is divided by q, what is the value of r?

(1) $q > 10$

(2) $q = 2^k$, where k is a positive integer.

289. If $r > 0$, is $rs > 0$?

(1) $s \leq r$

(2) $s \geq r$

290. If r and s are integers, is r divisible by 7?

(1) The product rs is divisible by 49.

(2) s is divisible by 7.

291. If r and s are non-zero integers, is $\frac{r}{s}$ an integer?

(1) $r - 1 = (s + 1)(s - 1)$

(2) $r - s = 20$

292. If r and t are integers, what is the value of t?

(1) $t^{r-1} = 1$

(2) $r \neq 1$

293. If p is a constant and $a_{n-1} + a_n = pn(n - 1)$ for all positive integers n, what is the value of ?

(1) $a_{31} - a_{29} = 120$

(2) $a_2 = 6$

294. If R, S, $\&T$ are numbers on the number line, not necessarily in that order, is the value of $|R - T|$ at least 9?

(1) $|R - S| = 50$.

(2) $|S - T| = 41$.

295. If r, s, $\&t$ are positive integers, is $(r + s + t)$ even?

(1) $(r + s)$ is even.

(2) $(s + t)$ is even.

296. If r, s, w are positive numbers such that $w = 60r + 80s$ and $r + s = 1$, is $w > 70$?

(1) $r > \frac{1}{2}$

(2) $r > s$

297. If S is a set of 10 consecutive integers, is the integer 5 present in S?

(1) The integer -3 is present in S.

(2) The integer 4 is present in S.

298. If the sequence S has 250 terms, what is the 243rd term of S?

(1) The 242nd term of S is -494.

(2) The first term of S is -12 and each term of S after the first term is 2 less than the preceding term.

299. If the digit h is the hundredths' digit in the decimal $d = 0.2h6$, what is the value of d rounded to the nearest tenth?

(1) $d < \frac{1}{4}$

(2) $h < 5$

300. If the integer n is greater than 1, is n equal to 2?

(1) n has exactly two distinct positive factors.

(2) The difference of any two distinct positive factors of n is odd.

301. If the product of the digits of the two-digit positive integer n is 12, what is the value of n?

(1) n can be expressed as the sum of two perfect squares in exactly one way.

(2) n is smaller than 40.

302. If the sum of three integers is even, is the product of the three integers a multiple of 4?

(1) All three integers are equal.

(2) All three integers are not even.

303. If the tens digit of the three-digit positive number k is non-zero, what is the tens' digit of k?

(1) The tens' digit of $(k + 9)$ is 3

(2) The tens' digit of $(k + 4)$ is 2

304. If v and w are different integers, does $v = 0$?

(1) $vw = v^2$

(2) $w = 0$

305. If $vmt \neq 0$, is $v^2m^3t^4 > 0$?

(1) $m > v^2$

(2) $m > t^3$

306. If x and y are integers, is y an even integer?

(1) $2y - x = x^2 - y^2$

(2) x is an odd integer.

307. If x and y are integers, what is the value of $(2x^{6y} - 4)$?

(1) $x^{2y} = 16$

(2) $xy = 4$

308. If x and y are positive integers and 18 is a multiple of xy^2, what is the value of y?

(1) x is a factor of 54 and is less than half of 54.

(2) y is a multiple of 3.

309. If x and y are positive integers and $x^y = x^{2y-3}$, what is the value of y^x?

(1) $x = 2$

(2) $x^2 < 9$

310. If x and y belong to the set {2, 4}, and $x^{ky} = x^{(ly^2-8)}$, is $kl > 2$?

(1) $k = -6$

(2) $3l - k = 3$

311. If x and y are non-zero integers, what is the value of $(x^{2y} - 1)$?

(1) $|x| + |y| = 5$, where $1 < |x| < y$

(2) $|x^2 - 4| + |y - 3| = 0$

312. If x and y are positive integers and r is the remainder when $(3^{4x+2} + y)$ is divided by 10, what is the value of r?

(1) $x = 25$

(2) $y = 1$

313. If x and y are positive integers, what is the value of $(x + y)^2$?

(1) $x = y - 3$

(2) x and y are prime numbers.

314. If x and y are positive integers, what is the value of x?

(1) $3^x + 5^y = 134$

(2) $y = 3$

315. If x and y are distinct positive integers, is $|x - y|$ a factor of 12?

(1) $x^2 - 6x + y^2 - 4y = 0$

(2) $x = 1$

316. If x and z are positive integers, is at least one of them a prime number?

(1) $x^2 = 15 + z^2$

(2) $(x - z)$ is a prime number.

317. If x is a positive integer, does the remainder, when $(7^x + 1)$ is divided by 100, have 0 as the tens digit?

(1) $x = 4n + 2$, where n is a positive integer.

(2) $x > 5$

318. If x, y and z are positive integers, is xz even?

(1) $(2xy - x)$ is even

(2) $(x^2 + xz)$ is even

319. If x, y and z are positive integers, is $y > x$?

(1) $y^2 = xz$

(2) $z - x > 0$

320. If z is positive, is $|x - y| > 0$?

(1) $xy + 2z = z$

(2) $x^2 - 2x = 0$

321. If y is an integer and $y = |x| + x^3$, is $y = 0$?

(1) $x < 0$

(2) $y < 1$

322. In the decimal representation of x, where $0 < x < 1$,is the tenths' digit of x non-zero?

(1) $16x$ is an integer.

(2) $8x$ is an integer.

323. In the sequence of non-zero numbers $t_1, t_2, t_3, \ldots t_n, \ldots$, the value of $t_{(n+1)} = \frac{t_n}{2}$, for all positive integers n. What is the value of t_5?

(1) $t_3 = \frac{1}{4}$

(2) $t_1 - t_5 = \frac{15}{16}$

324. Is 2^x greater than 100?

(1) $2^{\sqrt{x}} = 8$

(2) $\frac{1}{2^x} < 0.01$

325. Is $|x| < 1$?

(1) $|x + 1| = 2|x - 1|$

(2) $|x - 3| \neq 0$

326. Is $\sqrt{(x-5)^2} = (5 - x)$?

(1) $- - x|x| > 0$

(2) $5 - x > 0$

327. Is $\frac{x}{y} < xy$?

(1) $xy > 0$

(2) $y < -1$

3.2 Percents

328. An attorney charged a fee for estate planning services for a certain estate. The attorney's fee was what percent of the assessed value of the estate?

(1) The assessed value of the estate was \$1.2 million.

(2) The attorney charged \$2,400 for the estate planning services.

329. Are at least 10 percent of Country X's citizens who are 65 years old or older employed?

(1) In Country X, 11.3 percent of the population is 65 years old or older.

(2) In Country X, of the population 65 years old or older, 20 percent of the men and 10 percent of the women are employed.

330. By what percent was the price of a certain candy bar increased?

(1) The price of the candy bar was increased by 5 cents.

(2) The price of the candy bar after the increase was 45 cents.

331. Did Sally pay less than x dollars, including sales tax, for her bicycle?

(1) The price Sally paid for her bicycle was $0.9x$ dollars, excluding the 10 percent sales tax

(2) The price Sally paid for her bicycle was \$170, excluding the 10 percent sales tax

332. Does Joe weigh more than Tim?

(1) Tim's weight is 80 percent of Joe's weight.

(2) Joe's weight is 125 percent of Tim's weight.

333. Each week a certain salesman is paid a fixed amount equal to \$300 plus a commission equal to 5 percent of the amount of total sales that week over \$1,000. What was the total amount paid to the salesman last week?

(1) The total amount the salesman was paid last week is equal to 10 percent of the amount of total sales last week.

(2) The salesman's total sales last week was \$5,000

334. Each week Connie receives a base salary of \$500, plus a 20 percent commission on the total amount of her sales that week in excess of \$1,500. What was the total amount of Connie's sales last week?

(1) Last week Connie's base salary and commission totaled $\$1,200$

(2) Last week Connie's commission was \$700

335. For a certain car repair, the total charge consisted of a charge for parts, a charge for labor, and a 6 percent sales tax on both the charge for parts and the charge for labor. If the charge for parts, excluding sales tax, was \$50.00, what was the total charge for the repair?

(1) The sales tax on the charge for labor was \$9.60

(2) The total sales tax was \$12.60

336. For what percent of those tested for a certain infection was the test accurate; that is, positive for those who had the infection and negative for those who did not have the infection?

(1) Of those who tested positive for the infection, 8 did not have the infection.

(2) Of those tested for the infection, 90 percent tested negative.

337. From 1985 to 1994, what was the percent increase in total trade of the United States?

(1) Total trade of the United States in 1985 was 17 percent of gross domestic product in 1985.

(2) Total trade of the United States in 1994 was 23 percent of gross domestic product in 1994.

338. From 2004 to 2007, the value of foreign goods consumed annually in the United States increased by what percent?

(1) In both 2004 and 2007, the value of foreign goods consumed constituted 20 percent of the total value of goods consumed in the United States that year.

(2) In 2007 the total value of goods consumed in the United States was 20 percent higher than that in 2004.

339. From May 1 to May 30 in the same year, the balance in a checking account had increased. What was the balance in the checking account on May 30?

(1) If, from May 1 to May 30, the increase in the balance in the checking account had been 12 percent, then the balance in the account on May 30 would have been $ 504.

(2) From May 1 to May 30, the increase in the balance in the checking account was 8 percent.

340. Guy's net income equals his gross income minus his deductions. By what percent did Guy's net income change on January 1, 1989, when both his gross income and his deductions increased?

(1) Guy's gross income increased by 4 percent on January 1, 1989.

(2) Guy's deductions increased by 15 percent on January 1, 1989.

341. How many of the boys in a group of 100 children have brown hair?

(1) Of the children in the group, 60 percent have brown hair.

(2) Of the children in the group, 40 are boys.

342. If Jack's and Kate's annual salaries in 2005 were each 10 percent higher than their respective annual salaries in 2004, what was Jack's annual salary in 2004?

(1) The sum of Jack's and Kate's annual salaries in 2004 was $80,000.

(2) The sum of Jack's and Kate's annual salaries in 2005 was $88,000.

343. If $n > 0$, is 20% of n greater than 10% of the sum of n and 0.5?

(1) $n < 0.1$

(2) $n > 0.01$

344. If p and r are positive, is 25 percent of p equal to 10 percent of r?

(1) r is 300 percent greater than p.

(2) p is 80 percent less than $(r + p)$.

345. If the Lincoln Library's total expenditure for books, periodicals, and newspapers last year was \$35,000, how much of the expenditure was on books?

(1) The expenditures for newspapers were 40 percent greater than the expenditures for periodicals.

(2) The total of the expenditures for periodicals and newspapers was 25 percent less than the expenditures for books.

346. In 1993, Mr. Jacobs paid 4.8 percent of his income in state taxes. In 1994, what percent of Mr. Jacobs' income did he pay in state taxes?

(1) In 1993, Mr. Jacobs' taxable income was \$42,500.

(2) In 1994 Mr. Jacobs paid \$232 more in state tax than he did in 1993.

347. In 2001, Joe paid 5.1 percent of his income in taxes. In 2002, did Joe pay less than 5.1 percent of his income in taxes?

(1) From 2001 to 2002, Joe's income increased by 10 percent.

(2) Taxes paid in 2002 are 3.4 percent of Joe's income in 2001.

348. In 1997, there were 300 female employees at Company C. If the number of female employees at Company C increased by 60 percent from 1977 to 1987, by what percent did the number of female employees at Company C increase from 1987 to 1997?

(1) From 1977 to 1997, the number of female employees increased by 200 percent at Company C.

(2) In 1977, there were 100 female employees at Company C.

349. In June 1989, what was the ratio of the number of sales transactions made by salesperson X to the number of sales transactions made by salesperson Y?

(1) In June 1989, salesperson X made 50 percent more sales transactions than salesperson Y did in May 1989.

(2) In June 1989, salesperson Y made 25 percent more sales transactions than in May 1989.

3.3 Profit & Loss

350. A clothing store acquired an item at a cost of x dollars and sold the item for y dollars. The store's gross profit from the item was what percent of its cost for the item?

(1) $y - x = 20$

(2) $\frac{y}{x} = \frac{5}{4}$

351. A construction company was paid a total of $500,000 for a construction project. The company's only costs for the project were for labor and materials. Was the company's profit from the project greater than $150,000?

(1) The company's total cost was three times its cost for materials

(2) The company's profit was greater than its cost for labor

352. A merchant discounted the sale price of a coat and the sale price of a sweater. Was the discount in dollar on coat greater than that on sweater?

(1) The percent discount on the coat was 2 percentage points greater than the percent discount on the sweater

(2) Before the discounts, the sale price of the coat was $10 less than the sale price of the sweater

353. A store purchased a Brand C computer for the same amount that it paid for a Brand D computer and then sold them both at higher prices. The store's gross profit on the Brand C computer was what percent greater than its gross profit on the Brand D computer?

(1) The price at which the store sold the Brand C computer was 15 percent greater than the price at which the store sold the Brand D computer.

(2) The store's gross profit on the Brand D computer was $300.

354. If the list price of a new car was $12,300, what was the cost of the car to the dealer?

(1) The cost price, when raised by 25 percent was equal to the list price.

(2) The car was sold for $11,070, which was 12.5 percent more than the cost to the dealer.

3.4 Averages (including weighted averages)

355. A total of 20 amounts are entered on a spreadsheet that has 5 rows and 4 columns; each of the 20 positions in the spreadsheet contains one amount. The average (arithmetic mean) of the amounts in row i is $R_i (1 \le i \le 5)$. The average of the amounts in column j is $C_j (1 \le j \le 4)$. What is the average of all 20 amounts on the spreadsheet?

(1) $R_1 + R_2 + R_3 + R_4 + R_5 = 550$

(2) $C_1 + C_2 + C_3 + C_4 = 440$

356. All 48 seniors in a certain high school take one of the two English classes. What is the average (arithmetic mean) height of the seniors in this school?

(1) In the school, the average height of the seniors in the English class with the larger number of students is 70 inches.

(2) In the school, the average height of the seniors in the English class with the smaller number of students is $\frac{4}{5}$ of the average height of the seniors in the other English class.

357. Division R of Company Q has 1,000 employees. What is the average (arithmetic mean) annual salary of the employees at Company Q?

(1) The average annual salary of the employees in Division R is \$30,000

(2) The average annual salary of the employees at Company Q who are <u>not</u> in Division R is \$35,000

358. If every car sold last week at a certain used-car dealership was either a Coupe or a Sedan, what was the average (arithmetic mean) sale price for all the cars that were sold at the dealership last week?

(1) The average sale price for the Sedans that were sold at the dealership last week was \$10,600.

(2) The average sale price for the Coupes that were sold at the dealership last week was \$8,400.

359. If Jill's average (arithmetic mean) score for three games of bowling was 168, what was her lowest score?

(1) Jill's highest score was 204.

(2) The sum of Jill's two highest scores was 364.

360. A group of 20 friends went out for lunch. Five of them spent \$21 each and the rest spent \$$x$ less than the average of all of them. Is the value of the average amount spent by all the friends \$12?

(1) $x = 3$

(2) The total amount spent by all the friends is \$240.

3.5 Ratio & Proportion

361. A department manager distributed a number of pens, pencils, and pads among the staff in the department, with each staff member receiving x pens, y pencils, and z pads. How many staff members were in the department?

(1) The numbers of pens, pencils, and pads that each staff member received were in the ratio $2:3:4$ respectively

(2) The manager distributed a total of 18 pens, 27 pencils, and 36 pads

362. At the beginning of the year, the Finance Committee and the Planning Committee of a certain company each had n members, and no one was a member of both the committees. At the end of the year, 5 members left the Finance Committee and 3 members left the Planning Committee. How many members did the Finance Committee have at the beginning of the year?

(1) The ratio of the total number of members who left at the end of the year to the total number of members at the beginning of the year was $1:6$

(2) At the end of the year, 21 members remained on the Planning Committee

363. Bucket X and bucket Y contain only water and bucket Y was $\frac{1}{2}$ full. If all of the water in bucket X was poured into bucket Y, then what fraction of the capacity of Y was filled with water?

(1) Before the water from X was poured, X was $\frac{1}{3}$ full.

(2) X and Y have the same capacity.

364. Color X ink is created by blending red, blue, green, and yellow inks in the ratio $6:5:2:2$. What is the number of liters of green ink that was used to create a certain batch of color X ink?

(1) The amount of red ink used to create the batch is 2 liters more than the amount of blue ink used to create the batch

(2) The batch consists of 30 liters of color X ink

365. How many liters of apple juice were added to the cranberry juice in a certain container?

(1) The amount of apple juice that was added was $\frac{3}{2}$ times the amount of cranberry juice in the container.

(2) There was 5 liters of cranberry juice in the container.

366. If all the employees of Company K who worked there last January are still there, how many employees does Company K have now?

(1) Last January the ratio of the number of male employees to the number of female employees was 2 to 3.

(2) Since last January, Company K has employed 400 new male employees and no new female employees, raising the ratio of the number of male employees to the number of female employees to 3 to 4.

367. If, on a fishing trip, Jim and Tom each caught some fish, did Jim catch more fish than Tom?

(1) Jim caught $\frac{2}{3}$ of the total number of fish they caught together.

(2) After Tom stopped fishing, Jim continued fishing until he had caught 12 more fish.

368. The ratio of the number of male and female workers in a company in 2002 was 3 : 4. Was the percent increase in the number of men more than that in the number of women from 2002 to 2003?

(1) The ratio of the number of male workers in 2002 to 2003 was 3 : 5.

(2) The ratio of the number of male and female workers in 2003 was 10 : 7.

369. In a certain senior citizens' club, are more than $\frac{1}{4}$ of the members over 75 years of age?

(1) Exactly 60 percent of the female members are over 60 years of age, and, of them, $\frac{1}{3}$ are over 75 years of age.

(2) Exactly 10 male members are over 75 years of age.

370. In a certain professionals' club, are more than $\frac{1}{3}$ of the members mechanical engineers? Only those who are engineers can be mechanical engineers.

(1) Exactly 75 percent of the female members are engineers, and, of them, $\frac{1}{3}$ are mechanical engineers.

(2) Exactly 30 percent of the male members are engineers.

371. What is the length of the line AD?

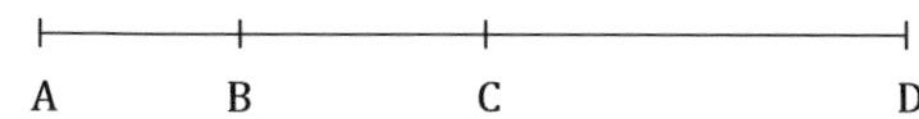

(1) AC = 10, BD = 15

(2) $\frac{AB}{BC} = \frac{BC}{CD}$

3.6 Mixtures

372. Two containers contain milk and water solutions of volume x liters and y liters, respectively. What would be the minimum concentration of milk in either container so that when the entire contents of both containers are mixed, 30 liters of 80 percent milk solution is obtained?

(1) $x = 2y$

(2) $x = y + 10$

373. From a cask containing y liters of milk, x liters of milk is drawn out and z liters of water are then added to the cask. This process is repeated one more time. What is the fraction of milk finally present in the mixture in the cask?

(1) $x = 20, y = 100$

(2) x and z form 20% and 10% of y, respectively

374. Two containers contain milk and water solutions of volume x liters and y liters, respectively. What would be the minimum concentration of milk in either container so that when the entire contents of both containers are mixed, 30 liters of 80 percent milk solution is obtained?

(1) $x = 2y$

(2) $x = y + 10$

375. From a cask containing y liters of milk, x liters of milk is drawn out and z liters of water are then added to the cask. This process is repeated one more time. What is the fraction of milk finally present in the mixture in the cask?

(1) $x = 20, y = 100$

(2) x and z form 20% and 10% of y, respectively

3.7 Speed, Time, & Distance

376. Chan and Mieko drove separate cars along the entire length of a certain route. If Chan made the trip in 15 minutes, how many minutes did it take Mieko to make the same trip?

(1) Mieko's average speed for the trip was $\frac{3}{4}$ of Chan's average speed.

(2) The route is 14 miles long.

377. How many miles long is the route from Houghton to Callahan?

(1) It will take one hour less time to travel the entire route at an average rate of 55 miles per hour than at an average rate of 50 miles per hour.

(2) It will take 11 hours to travel the first half of the route at an average rate of 25 miles per hour.

378. In planning for a trip, Joan estimated both the distance of the trip, in miles, and her average speed, in miles per hour. She accurately divided her estimated distance by her estimated average speed to obtain an estimate for the time, in hours, that the trip would take. Was her estimated time within 0.5 hour of the actual time that the trip took?

(1) Joan's estimate for the distance was within 5 miles of the actual distance.

(2) Joan's estimate for her average speed was within 10 miles per hour of her actual average speed.

379. Is the number of seconds required to travel d feet at r feet per second greater than the number of seconds required to travel D feet at R feet per second?

(1) d is 30 greater than D

(2) r is 30 greater than R

3.8 Time & Work

380. If a certain machine produces screws and bolts at a constant rate, how many seconds will it take the machine to produce 300 bolts?

(1) It takes the machine 56 seconds to produce 40 screws.

(2) It takes the machine 1.5 times more time to produce 1 bolt than to produce one screw.

381. If two copying machines work simultaneously at their respective constant rates, how many copies do they produce in 5 minutes?

(1) One of the machines produces copies at the constant rate of 250 copies per minute.

(2) One of the machines produces copies at twice the constant rate of the other machine.

382. A group of 5 equally efficient skilled workers together take 18 hours to finish a job. How long will it take for a group of 4 skilled workers and 3 apprentices to do the same job, if each skilled worker works at an identical rate and each apprentice works at an identical rate?

(1) An apprentice works at $\frac{2}{3}$ the rate of a skilled worker.

(2) 6 apprentices and 5 skilled workers take 10 hours to complete the same job.

3.9 Computational

383. A certain dealership has a number of cars to be sold by its salespeople. How many cars are to be sold?

(1) If each of the salespeople sells 4 of the cars, 23 cars will remain unsold

(2) If each of the salespeople sells 6 of the cars, 5 cars will remain unsold

384. A certain employee is paid \$9 per hour for an 8-hour workday. If the employee is paid $1\frac{1}{2}$ times this rate for time worked in excess of 8 hours during a single day, how many hours did the employee work today?

(1) The employee was paid \$27 more for the hours worked today than for the hours worked yesterday

(2) Yesterday the employee worked 8 hours

385. A family-size box of cereal contains more cereal and costs more than the regular-size box of cereal. What is the cost per ounce of the family-size box of cereal?

(1) The family-size box of cereal contains 10 ounces more than the regular-size box of cereal.

(2) The family-size box of cereal costs \$5.40.

386. A total of 100 customers purchased books at a certain bookstore last week. If these customers purchased a total of 200 books, how many of the customers purchased only one book each?

(1) None of the customers purchased more than three books

(2) 20 of the customers purchased only two books each

387. At a certain company, 25 percent of the employees are male and 50 percent of the employees are sales staff. What is the number of employees at this company?

(1) Exactly seven of the employees at the company are males who are sales staff.

(2) There are 16 more female employees than male employees at the company.

388. At a fruit stand yesterday, the price of each apple was \$0.10 more than the price of each orange. What was the total revenue from the sale of oranges at the fruit stand yesterday?

(1) The number of oranges sold at the fruit stand yesterday was 5 more than the number of apples.

(2) The total revenue from the sale of apples at the fruit stand yesterday was \$15.00

389. At the beginning of last month, a stationery store had in stock 250 writing pads, which had cost the store \$0.75 each. During the same month, the store made only one purchase of writing pads. What was the total amount of inventory, in dollar, of the writing pads it had in stock at the end of the last month?

(1) Last month, the store purchased 150 writing pads for \$0.80 each.

(2) Last month, the total revenue from the sale of writing pads was \$180

390. Development planners determined the number of new housing units needed in a certain area by using the formula $H = kJ$, where H is the number of new housing units needed in the area, J is the number of new jobs to be created in the area, and k is a constant. How many new housing units did the planners determine were needed?

(1) The number of new jobs to be created was 60,000

(2) According to the formula used by the planners, if 37,500 jobs were to be created, then 7,500 new housing units would be needed

391. During week W, how much did it cost, per mile, for the gasoline used by car X?

(1) During week W, car X used gasoline that cost \$3.10 per gallon.

(2) During week W, car X was driven 270 miles.

392. Each of 20 parents chose one of five days from Monday through Friday to attend parent-teacher conferences. If more parents chose Monday than Tuesday, did at least one of the parents choose Friday?

(1) None of the five days was chosen by more than 5 parents

(2) More parents chose Monday than Wednesday

393.

r	s	t
u	v	w
x	y	z

Each of the letters in the table above represents one of the numbers 1, 2, or 3, and each of these numbers occurs exactly once in each row and exactly once in each column. What is the value of r?

(1) $v + z = 6$

(2) $s + t + u + x = 6$

394. For all integers x and y, the operation $\triangle$ is defined by $x \triangle y = (x+2)^2 + (y+3)^2$. What is the value of integer t?

(1) $t \triangle 2 = 74$

(2) $2 \triangle t = 80$

395. From Leland's gross pay of p dollars last week, t percent was deducted for taxes and then s dollars was deducted for savings. What amount of Leland's gross pay last week remained after these two deductions?

(1) $p - s = 244$

(2) $pt = 7,552$

396. If a certain city loses 12 percent of its daily water supply each day because of water-main breaks, what is the cost in dollars to the city per day for this loss?

(1) The city's daily water supply is 350 million gallons.

(2) The cost to the city for each 12,000 gallons of water loss is \$2.

397. If Ann saves x dollars each week and Beth saves y dollars each week, what is the total amount that they together save per week?

(1) Beth saves $ 5 more per week than Ann saves per week.

(2) It takes Ann six weeks to save the same amount that Beth saves in five weeks.

398. If Antonio bought two half-liter cartons of same ice cream during a special sale, what percent of the total regular price of the two cartons did he save?

(1) Antonio paid the regular price for the first carton and received the second carton for half the regular price.

(2) The regular price of the ice cream Antonio bought was $4.00 per half-liter carton.

399. If the symbol '∇' represents either of addition, subtraction, multiplication or division, what is the value of $6 \nabla 2$?

(1) $10 \nabla 5 = 2$

(2) $4 \nabla 2 = 2$

400. In 2004, Mr. John bought a total of n shares of stock X and Mrs. John bought a total of 300 shares of stock X. If the couple held all of their respective shares throughout 2005, and Mr. John's dividends on his n shares totaled $150 in 2005, what was Mrs. John's total dividend on her 300 shares in 2005?

(1) In 2005, the annual dividend on each share of stock X was $0.75

(2) In 2004, Mr. John bought a total of 200 shares of stock X.

401. In a demographic study, the population and total income of a certain region were estimated, and both estimates had lower and upper limits. At the time of the estimates, was the average income per person for the region greater than $16,500?

(1) The lower limit for the estimate of the population was 330,000 people.

(2) The lower limit for the estimate of the total income was $5,500,000,000.

402.

$$\blacksquare + \triangle = \forall$$

In the addition problem above, each of the symbols ■, △ and ∀ represents a positive digit. If $\blacksquare < \triangle$, what is the value of △?

(1) $\forall = 4$

(2) $\blacksquare = 1$

3.10 Simple Interest

403. A total of \$60,000 was invested for one year. Part of this amount earned simple annual interest at the rate of x percent per year, and the rest earned simple annual interest at the rate of y percent per year. If the total interest earned on investment of \$60,000 for that year was \$4,080, what is the value of x?

(1) $x = \frac{3}{4}y$

(2) The ratio of the amount that earned interest at the rate of x percent per year to the amount that earned interest at the rate of y percent per year was 3 to 2

404. John lent one part of an amount of money at 10 percent rate of simple interest and the remaining at 22 percent rate of simple interest, both for one year. At what rate was the larger part lent?

(1) The total amount lent was \$2400.

(2) The average rate of simple interest he received on the total amount was 15 percent.

3.11 Compound Interest

405. \$10,000 is deposited in a certain account that pays r percent annual interest compounded annually. The amount $D(t)$, in dollars, that the deposit will grow to in t years is given by $D(t) = 10,000\left(1 + \frac{r}{100}\right)^t$. What amount will the deposit grow to in 3 years?

(1) $D(1) = 11,000$

(2) $r = 10$

3.12 Functions

406. For all integers n, the function f is defined by $f(n) = a^n$, where a is a constant. What is the value of $f(1)$?

(1) $f(2) = 100$

(2) $f(3) = -1000$

407. For all numbers x, the function f is defined by $f(x) = 3x + 1$, and the function g is defined by $g(x) = \frac{x-1}{3}$. If c is a positive number, what is the value of $g(c)$?

(1) $f(c) = 13$

(2) $f(1) = c$

408. If f is the function defined by $f(x) = 2x$ for $x \geq 0$ and $f(x) = x^2$ for $x < 0$, what is the value of $f(c)$?

(1) $|c| = 2$

(2) $c < 0$

3.13 Permutation & Combination

409. A box contains 10 light bulbs, fewer than half of which are defective. Two bulbs are to be drawn simultaneously from the box. If n of the bulbs in box are defective, what is the value of n?

(1) The probability that the two bulbs to be drawn will be defective is $\frac{1}{15}$

(2) The probability that one of the bulbs to be drawn will be defective and the other will not be defective is $\frac{7}{15}$

410. A certain jar contains only b black marbles, w white marbles, and r red marbles If one marble is to be chosen at random from the jar, is the probability that the marble chosen will be red greater than the probability that the marble chosen will be white?

(1) $\frac{r}{b+w} > \frac{w}{b+r}$

(2) $b - w > r$

411. In a 21 apartment building, there are in total 12 men and 9 women residing in one apartment each. If a poll taken is to select one of the apartments at random, what is the probability that the resident of the apartment selected will be a woman who is a student?

(1) Of the women, four are students.

(2) Of the women, five are not students.

412. Each of the eggs in a bowl is dyed red, or green, or blue. If one egg is to be removed at random, what is the probability that the egg will be green?

(1) There are 5 red eggs in the bowl.

(2) The probability that the egg will be blue is $\frac{1}{3}$

413. If two different representatives are to be selected at random from a group of 10 employees and if p is the probability that both the representatives selected will be women, is $p > \frac{1}{2}$?

(1) More than half of the 10 employees are women.

(2) The probability that both representatives selected will be men is less than $\frac{1}{10}$.

414. If each of the students in a certain mathematics class is either a junior or a senior, how many students are in the class?

(1) If one student is to be chosen at random from the class to attend a conference, the probability that the student chosen will be a senior is $\frac{4}{7}$.

(2) There are five more seniors in the class than juniors.

3.14 Sets

415. In a school election, if each of the 900 voters voted for either Edith or Jose (but not both), what percent of the female voters in this election voted for Jose?

(1) 80 percent of the female voters voted for Edith.

(2) 60 percent of the male voters voted for Jose.

416. In a survey of 200 college graduates, 30 percent said that they had received student loans during their college careers, and 40 percent said that they had received scholarships. What percent of those surveyed said that they had received neither student loans nor scholarships during their college careers?

(1) 25 percent of those surveyed said that they had received scholarships but no loans.

(2) 50 percent of those surveyed who said that they had received loans also said that they had received scholarships.

417. Is the number of members of Club X greater than the number of members of Club Y?

(1) Of the members of Club X, 20 percent are also members of Club Y.

(2) Of the members of Club Y, 30 percent are also members of Club X.

3.15 Statistics & Data Interpretation

418. A scientist recorded the number of eggs in each of 10 birds' nests. What was the standard deviation of the numbers of eggs in the 10 nests?

(1) The average (arithmetic mean) number of eggs for the 10 nests was 4

(2) Each of the 10 nests contained the same number of eggs

419. Each of the 45 boxes on shelf J weighs less than each of the 44 boxes on shelf K. What is the median weight of the 89 boxes on these shelves?

(1) The heaviest box on shelf J weighs 15 pounds

(2) The lightest box on shelf K weighs 20 pounds

420. If each of the eight employees working on a certain project received an award, was the amount of each award the same?

(1) The standard deviation of the amounts of the eight awards was 0.

(2) The total amount of the eight awards was $ 10,000.

421. If the average (arithmetic mean) of five different numbers is 12, what is the median of the five numbers?

(1) The median of the five numbers is equal to $\frac{1}{3}$ of the sum of the four numbers other than the median.

(2) The sum of the four numbers other than the median is equal to 45.

422. If the average (arithmetic mean) of four different numbers is 30, how many of the numbers are greater than 30?

(1) None of the four numbers is greater than 60.

(2) Two of the four numbers are 9 and 10.

423. If the average (arithmetic mean) of the assessed values of x houses is $ 212,000 and the average of the assessed values of y other houses is $ 194,000, what is the average of the assessed values of the $x + y$ houses?

(1) $x + y = 36$

(2) $x = 2y$

424. Is the standard deviation of the salaries of Company Y's employees greater than the standard deviation of the salaries of Company Z's employees?

(1) The average (arithmetic mean) salary of Company Y's employees is greater than the average salary of Company Z's employees.

(2) The median salary of Company Y's employees is greater than the median salary of Company Z's employees.

3.16 Linear Equations

425. A certain bakery sells rye bread in 16-ounce loaves and 24-ounce loaves, and all loaves of the same size sell for the same price per loaf regardless of the number of loaves purchased. What is the price of a 24-ounce loaf of rye bread?

(1) The total price of a 16-ounce loaf and a 24-ounce loaf of this bread is \$2.40

(2) The total price of two 16-ounce loaves and one 24-ounce loaf of this bread is \$3.40

426. A certain database charges users a registration fee of x dollars, and it charges registered users y dollars per file downloaded. If there are no other charges for users of this database, what is the amount of the registration fee?

(1) The total charge to download 50 files is \$150, including the registration fee.

(2) The total charge to download 100 files is \$225, including the registration fee.

427. A shirt and a pair of gloves cost a total of \$ 41.70. How much does the pair of gloves cost?

(1) The shirt costs twice as much as the gloves

(2) The shirt costs \$27.80

428. A swim club sold only individual and family memberships. It charged \$300 for an individual membership. If the club's total revenue from memberships was \$480,000, what was the charge for a family membership?

(1) The revenue from individual memberships was $\frac{1}{4}$ of the total revenue from memberships

(2) The club sold 1.5 times as many family memberships as individual memberships

429. At a sale, all books were priced equally and all magazines were priced equally. What was the price of 3 books and 4 magazines at the sale?

(1) At the sale, the price of a book was \$1.45 more than the price of a magazine.

(2) At the sale, the price of 6 books and 8 magazines was \$43.70

430. Currently there are 50 picture books on each shelf in the children's section of a library. If these books were to be placed on smaller shelves with 30 picture books on each shelf, how many of the smaller shelves would be needed to hold all of these books?

(1) The number of smaller shelves needed is 6 more than the current number of shelves

(2) Currently there are 9 shelves in the children's section

431. Is $2m - 3n = 0$?

(1) $m \neq 0$

(2) $6m = 9n$

432. Each week John earns x dollars an hour for the first 40 hours he works a week and y dollars for each additional hour. How many dollars an hour does John earn for the first 40 hours?

(1) $y = 1.5x$

(2) If John works 45 hours in a week, he earns a total of \$570 that week.

433. For a convention, a hotel charges a daily room rate of \$120 for one person and x dollars for each additional person. What is the charge for each additional person?

(1) The daily cost per person for 4 people sharing the cost of a room equally is \$45.

(2) The daily cost per person for 2 people sharing the cost of a room equally is \$25 more than the corresponding cost for 4 people.

434. For a recent play performance, the ticket prices were \$25 per adult and \$15 per child. A total of 500 tickets were sold for the performance. How many of the tickets were sold to adults?

(1) Revenue from ticket sales for this performance totaled \$10,500

(2) The average (arithmetic mean) price per ticket sold was \$21

435. For a week Raymond is paid at the rate of x dollars per hour for the first t hours ($t > 4$) he works and \$ 2 per hour for the hours worked in excess of t hours. If x and t are integers, what is the value of t?

(1) If Raymond works $(t - 3)$ hours in one week, he will earn \$14.

(2) If Raymond works $(t + 3)$ hours in one week, he will earn \$23.

436. From May 1, 1980, to May 1, 1995, the closing price of a share of stock X doubled. What was the closing price of a share of stock on May 1, 1980?

(1) From May 1, 1995, to May 1, 2004, the closing price of a share of stock X doubled.

(2) From May 1, 1995, to May 1, 2004, the closing price of a share of stock X increased by \$ 4.50

437. How many books does Ricardo have?

(1) If Ricardo had 15 fewer books, he would have only half as many books as he actually has.

(2) Ricardo has twice as many fiction books as non-fiction books.

438. How many years did Dr. Jones live?

(1) If Dr. Jones had become a doctor 10 years earlier than he actually did, he would have been a doctor for exactly $\frac{2}{3}$ of his life.

(2) If Dr. Jones had become a doctor 10 years later than he actually did, he would have been a doctor for exactly $\frac{1}{3}$ of his life.

439. If $r = \frac{x + y}{2}$ and $s = \frac{x - y}{2}$, what is the value of $(r + s)$?

(1) $y = 4$.

(2) $x = 6$.

440. If $\frac{x}{600} = \frac{y}{300}$, is $y = 1000$?

(1) $x + y = 3000$

(2) $3x = 6000$

441. In what year was Ellen born?

(1) Ellen's brother, Pete, who is 2 years older than Ellen, was born in 1986.

(2) In 2005, Pete turned 18 years old.

3.17 Quadratic Equations & Polynomials

442. How many more men than women are in the room?

(1) There are a total of 20 men and women in the room.

(2) The number of men in the room equals the square of the number of women in the room.

443. If $x^2 + y^2 = 1$, is $(x + y) = 1$?

(1) $xy = 0$.

(2) $y = 0$.

444. If $x \neq y$, is $x + y = xy$?

(1) $(1 - x)(1 - y) = 1$

(2) $x^2 - y^2 = x^2y - xy^2$

445. If $x(x - 5)(x + 2) = 0$, is $x < 0$?

(1) $x^2 - 7x \neq 0$

(2) $x^2 - 2x - 15 \neq 0$

446. If $xy \neq 0$, what is the value of $\left(\frac{1}{x} + \frac{1}{y}\right)$?

(1) $\frac{1}{x + y} = -1$

(2) $xy = 6(x + y)$

447. If $x^2 - y = w$, what is the value of x?

(1) $w + y = 4$

(2) $y = 1$

448. If $(y + 3)(y - 1) - (y - 2)(y - 1) = r(y - 1)$, what is the value of y?

(1) $r^2 = 25$

(2) $r = 5$

449. If b, c and d are constants and $x^2 + bx + c = (x + d)^2$ for all values of x, what is the value of c?

(1) $d = 3$

(2) $b = 6$

450. If $x^2 + 3x + c = (x + a)(x + b)$ for all x, what is the value of c?

(1) $a = 1$

(2) a and b are positive integers.

3.18 Inequalities

451. During a summer vacation, was the average (arithmetic mean) number of books that Carolyn read per week greater than the average number of books that Jacob read per week?

(1) Twice the average number of books that Carolyn read per week was greater than 5 less than twice the average number of books that Jacob read per week.

(2) During the last 5 weeks of the vacation, Carolyn read a total of 3 books more than Jacob.

452. If $\frac{1}{4}$ of the larger of two positive numbers is greater than five times the smaller of the same two numbers, is the smaller number less than four?

(1) The larger number is greater than 70.

(2) The larger number is less than 80.

453. If $xy \neq 0$, is $\frac{x}{y} = 1$?

(1) $x^2 = y^2$

(2) $xy > 0$

454. If $xyz \neq 0$, is $x(y + z) \geq 0$?

(1) $|y + z| = |y| + |z|$

(2) $|x + y| = |x| + |y|$

455. If $R = \frac{P}{Q}$, is $R \leq P$?

(1) $P > 50$

(2) $0 < Q \leq 20$

456. If $s^4v^3x^7 < 0$, is $svx < 0$?

(1) $v < 0$

(2) $x > 0$

457. If $\frac{x}{2} = \frac{3}{y}$, is $x < y$?

(1) $y \geq 3$

(2) $y \leq 4$

458. If $-2x > 3y$, is $x < 0$?

(1) $y > 0$

(2) $2x + 5y - 20 = 0$

459. If a and b are positive, is $(a^{-1} + b^{-1})^{-1} < (a^{-1}b^{-1})^{-1}$?

(1) $a = 2b$

(2) $a + b > 1$

460. If a, b, c and d are positive integers, is $\left(\frac{a}{b}\right) * \left(\frac{c}{d}\right) > \frac{c}{b}$?

(1) $c > b$

(2) $a > d$

461. If w and c are integers, is $w > 0$?

(1) $w + c > 50$

(2) $c > 48$

462. If $wz < 2$, is $z < 1$?

(1) $w > 2$

(2) $z < 2$

463. If $x > 0$, is $x^2 < x$?

(1) $0.1 < x < 0.4$

(2) $x^3 < x^2$

464. If $x > 1$ and $y > 1$, is $x < y$?

(1) $\frac{x^2}{xy + x} < 1$

(2) $\frac{xy}{y^2 - y} < 1$

465. If $x \neq 0$, is $\frac{x^2}{|x|} < 1$?

(1) $x < 1$

(2) $x > -1$

466. If x and y are integers and $y = |x + 3| + |4 - x|$, does y equal 7?

(1) $x < 4$

(2) $x > -3$

467. If x and y are integers and $x > 0$, is $y > 0$?

(1) $7x - 2y > 0$

(2) $- - y < x$

468. If x and y are integers, is $(x + y) > 2$?

(1) $x^2 < 1$

(2) $y < 1$

469. If x and y are positive integers and $y = \sqrt{9 - x}$, what is the value of y?

(1) $x < 8$

(2) $y > 1$

470. If x and y are positive, is $3x > 7y$?

(1) $x > y + 4$

(2) $-5x < -14y$

471. If x and y are positive, is $4x > 3y$?

(1) $x > y - x$

(2) $\frac{x}{y} < 1$

472. If x is a negative integer, is $x < -3$?

(1) $x^2 + 6x < 7$

(2) $x^2 + |x| \le 2$

473. If $x + y > 0$, is $xy < 0$?

(1) $x^{2y} < 1$

(2) $x + 2y < 0$

3.19 Geometry–Lines

474. If $l_1 || l_2$ in the figure given below, is $x = y$?

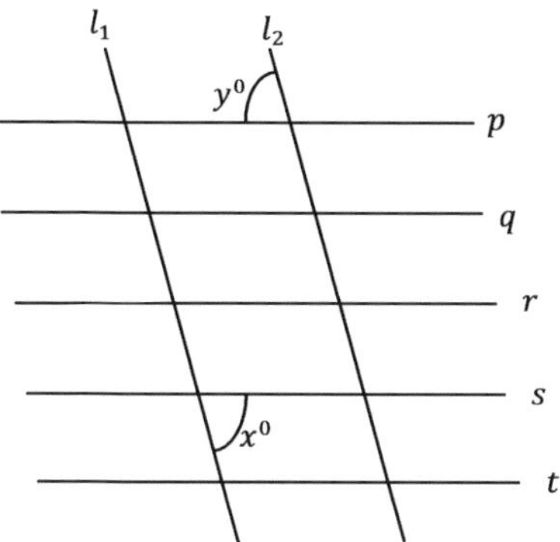

(1) $p || r$ and $r || t$

(2) $q || s$

3.20 Geometry–Triangles

475. In the triangle below, is $x > 90$?

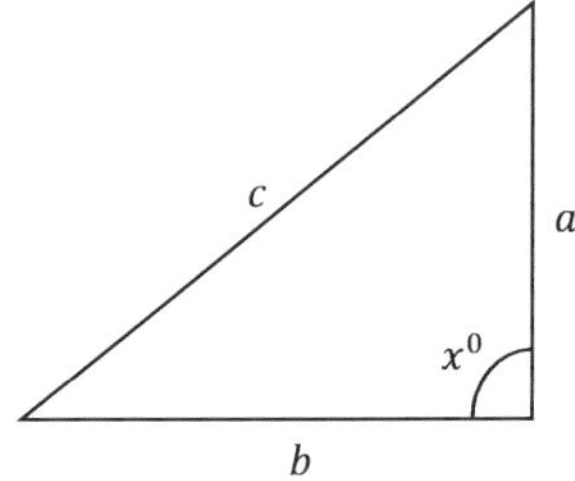

(1) $a^2 + b^2 < 15$

(2) $c > 4$

476. In triangle ABC, point X is the midpoint of side AC and point Y is the midpoint of side BC. If point R is the midpoint of line segment XC and if point S is the midpoint of line segment YC, what is the area of the triangular region CRS ?

(1) The area of the triangular region ABX is 32.

(2) The length of one of the altitudes of triangle ABC is 8.

477. In triangle PQR, the measure of angle P is 30^0 greater than twice the measure of angle Q. What is the measure of angle R?

(1) PQ = QR

(2) The measure of angle P is 78^0.

478. In triangle PQR below, what is the value of y?

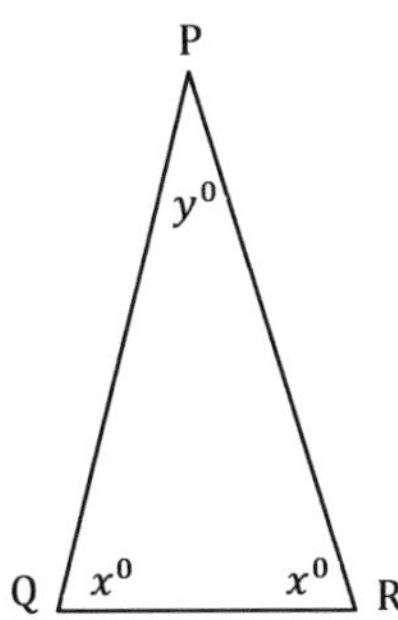

(1) $\frac{3}{2}x = 120$

(2) $x + y = 100$

3.21 Geometry–Circles

479. In the figure shown, triangle ABC is inscribed in the circle. What is the circumference of the circle?

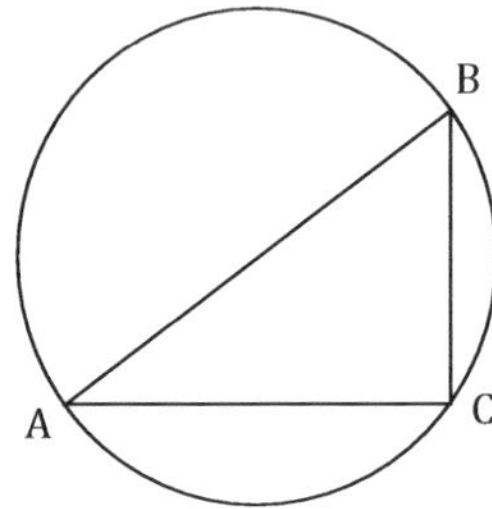

(1) The perimeter of the triangle ABC is 48.

(2) The ratio of the lengths of BC, AC, and AB respectively, is 3 : 4 : 5.

480. In the figure below, ABCD is a rectangle. What is the area of the semi-circular region with centre O and diameter BC?

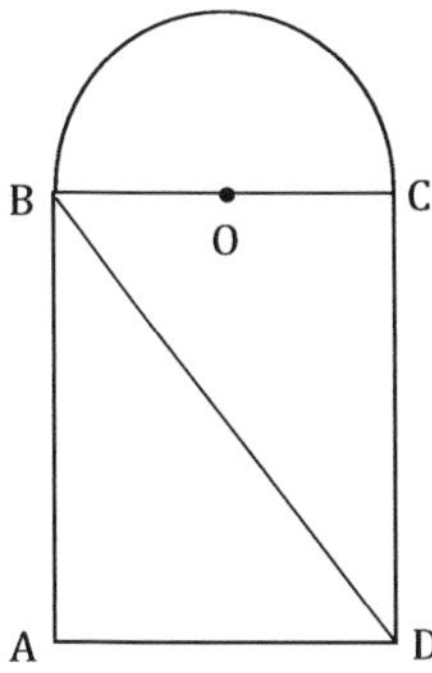

(1) $\frac{BC}{AB} = \frac{3}{4}$

(2) BD = 25

481. In the figure, points A, B, C, D, and E lie on a line. A is the point of contact of the two circles, B is the center of the smaller circle, C is the center of the larger circle, D is a point on the smaller circle, and E is a point on the larger circle. What is the area of the region inside the larger circle but outside the smaller circle?

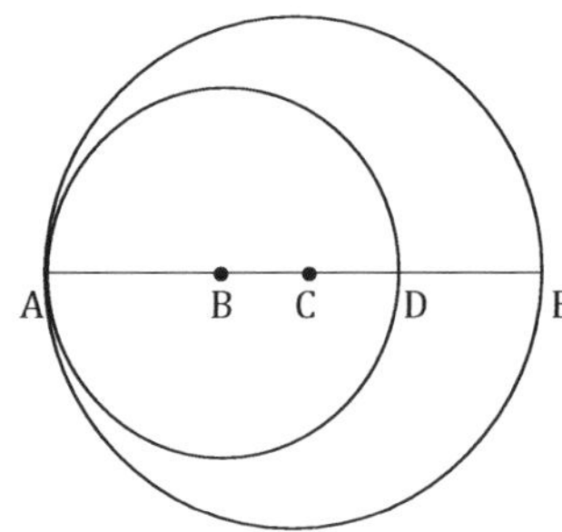

(1) AB = 3 and BC = 2

(2) CD = 1 and DE = 4

3.22 Geometry–Polygon

482. Can a certain rectangular sheet of glass be positioned on a rectangular tabletop so that it covers the entire tabletop and its edges are parallel to the edges of the tabletop?

(1) The tabletop is 36 inches wide by 60 inches long.

(2) The area of one face of the sheet of glass is 2,400 square inches.

483. If the length of a certain rectangle is 2 greater than the width of the rectangle, what is the perimeter of the rectangle?

(1) The length of the diagonal of the rectangle is 10.

(2) The area of the rectangular region is 48.

484. In the figure shown below, the line segment AD is parallel to the line segment BC. Is AC the shortest side of triangle ACD?

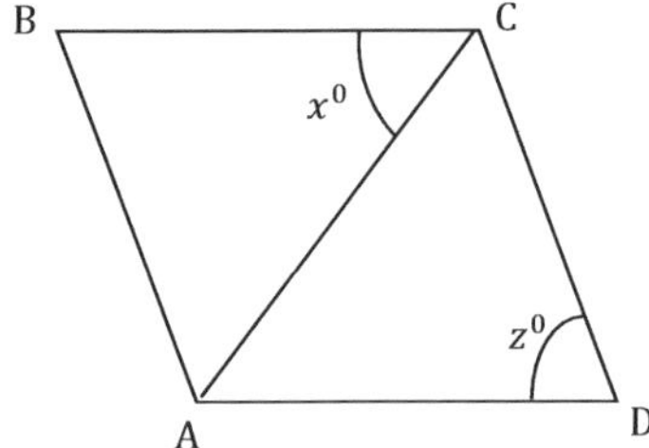

(1) $x = 50$

(2) $z = 70$

485. In the parallelogram shown below, what is the value of x?

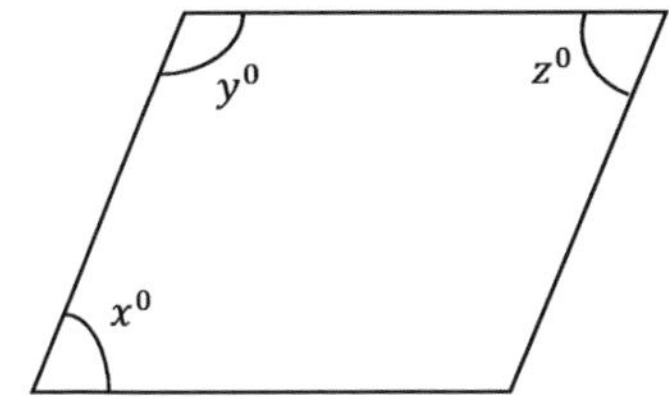

(1) $y = 2x$

(2) $x + z = 120$

3.23 Geometry-3 Dimensional

3.24 Co-ordinate geometry

486. A certain circle in the XY-plane has its center at the origin. If P is a point on the circle, what is the sum of the squares of the coordinates of P?

(1) The radius of the circle is 4.

(2) The sum of the coordinates of P is 0.

487. If line k in the XY-plane has equation $y = mx + b$, where m and b are constants, what is the slope of k?

(1) k is parallel to the line with equation $y = (1 - m)x + b + 1$.

(2) k intersects the line with equation $y = 2x + 3$ at the point (2, 7).

488. In the figure below, ST and TU are parallel to the X-axis and Y-axis respectively. What is the sum of the coordinates of point T?

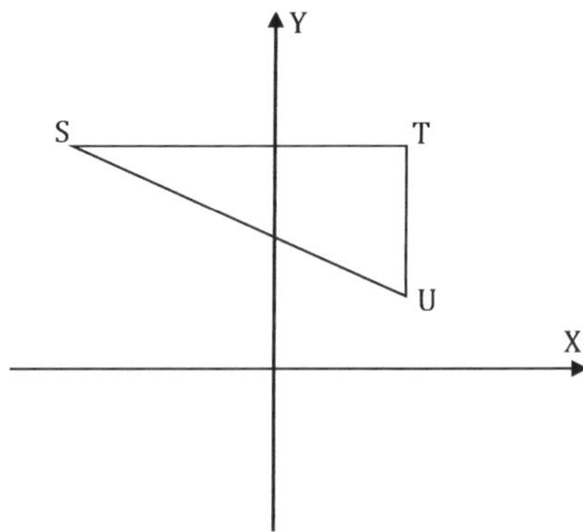

(1) The Y-coordinate of point U is 1.

(2) The X-coordinate of point S is -5.

489. In the figure shown, the circle has center O and radius 50, and point P has coordinates (50, 0). If point Q (not shown) is on the circle, what is the length of line segment PQ?

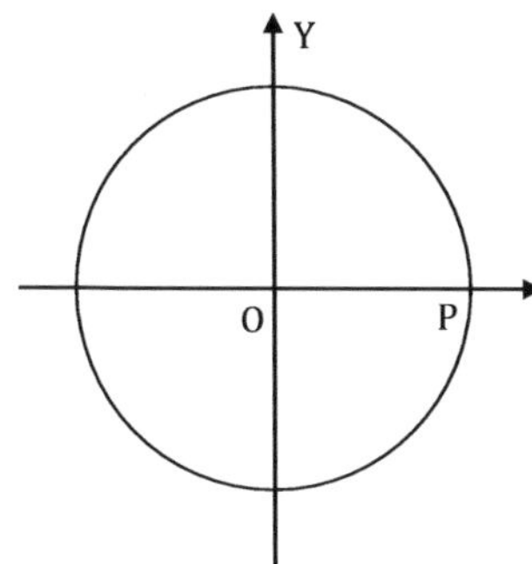

(1) The X-coordinate of point Q is -30.

(2) The Y-coordinate of point Q is -40.

490. In the rectangular coordinate system, are the points (r, s) and (u, v) equidistant from the origin?

(1) $r + s = 1$

(2) $u = 1 - r$ and $v = 1 - s$

491. In the XY-plane, does the point (a, b) lie above the line $y = x$?

(1) $a = 2$

(2) $b = a + 2$

492. In the XY-plane, is the slope of the line k positive?

(1) Line k is perpendicular to the line passing though the points $(1,\ 1)$ and $(-2,\ 5)$.

(2) Line k makes a negative intercept on the X-axis and a positive intercept on the Y-axis.

493. In the XY-plane, lines l and k intersect at the point $\left(\frac{16}{5}, \frac{12}{5}\right)$. What is the slope of line l?

(1) The product of the slopes of lines l and k is -1.

(2) Line k passes through the origin.

494. In the XY-plane, lines a and b are parallel. If the Y-intercept of line a is -1, what is the Y-intercept of line b?

(1) The X-intercept of line a is -1.

(2) Line b passes through the point $(10,\ 20)$.

495. In the XY-plane, the point (r, s) lies on a circle with centre at the origin. What is the value of $(r^2 + s^2)$?

(1) The circle has radius 2.

(2) The point $\left(\sqrt{2},\ -\sqrt{2}\right)$ lies on the circle.

496. In the XY-plane, region R consists of all the points (x, y) such that $2x + 3y \le 6$. Is the point (r, s)in region R?

(1) $3r + 2s = 6$

(2) $r \leq 3$ and $s \leq 2$

497. In the XY-plane, the line k passes through the origin and through the point (a, b), where $ab \neq 0$. Is $b > 0$?

(1) The slope of line k is negative.

(2) $a < b$

498. In the XY-plane, the line with equation $ax + by + c = 0$, where $abc \neq 0$, has slope $\frac{2}{3}$. What is the value of b?

(1) $a = 4$

(2) $c = -6$

499. In the XY-plane, the sides of a certain rectangle are parallel to the X and Y axes. If one of the vertices of the rectangle is $(-1, -2)$, what is the perimeter of the rectangle?

(1) One of the vertices of the rectangle is $(2, -2)$.

(2) One of the vertices of the rectangle is $(2, 3)$.

500. In the XY-plane, what is the slope of line l?

(1) The line l does not intersect with the line having equation $y = 1 - x$

(2) The line l intersects with the line having equation $y = x - 1$

Chapter 4

Answer-key

4.1 Problem Solving Questions

(1) C
(2) C
(3) D
(4) D
(5) E
(6) C
(7) C
(8) D
(9) D
(10) A
(11) D
(12) E
(13) A
(14) C
(15) E
(16) C
(17) C
(18) C
(19) C
(20) B
(21) A
(22) E
(23) C
(24) B
(25) C
(26) D
(27) B
(28) A
(29) D
(30) C
(31) D
(32) D
(33) D
(34) B
(35) D
(36) B
(37) D
(38) D
(39) C
(40) B
(41) B
(42) B
(43) B
(44) B
(45) B
(46) A
(47) A
(48) E
(49) C
(50) D
(51) C
(52) C
(53) E
(54) E
(55) D
(56) D
(57) D
(58) E
(59) A
(60) D
(61) A
(62) C
(63) E
(64) C
(65) E
(66) D
(67) B
(68) D
(69) C
(70) C
(71) C
(72) A
(73) E
(74) A
(75) D
(76) E
(77) E
(78) D
(79) C
(80) B
(81) C
(82) C
(83) A
(84) C
(85) C
(86) C
(87) D
(88) C
(89) B
(90) B
(91) D
(92) B
(93) D
(94) B
(95) E
(96) A
(97) C
(98) B
(99) C
(100) E
(101) A
(102) B
(103) B
(104) D
(105) C
(106) B
(107) C
(108) D
(109) C
(110) C

(111) C	(135) E	(159) C	(183) B	(207) B
(112) C	(136) D	(160) D	(184) B	(208) D
(113) C	(137) D	(161) A	(185) E	(209) C
(114) C	(138) C	(162) E	(186) D	(210) E
(115) A	(139) D	(163) B	(187) C	(211) A
(116) B	(140) C	(164) C	(188) B	(212) A
(117) C	(141) E	(165) E	(189) A	(213) A
(118) D	(142) E	(166) B	(190) B	(214) B
(119) D	(143) E	(167) A	(191) C	(215) D
(120) C	(144) A	(168) C	(192) E	(216) C
(121) D	(145) D	(169) D	(193) C	(217) D
(122) D	(146) D	(170) C	(194) B	(218) C
(123) D	(147) A	(171) C	(195) A	(219) C
(124) B	(148) B	(172) C	(196) B	(220) C
(125) D	(149) D	(173) C	(197) D	(221) E
(126) D	(150) D	(174) D	(198) E	(222) C
(127) C	(151) B	(175) D	(199) B	(223) E
(128) D	(152) B	(176) E	(200) B	(224) D
(129) D	(153) A	(177) D	(201) B	(225) D
(130) E	(154) D	(178) B	(202) D	(226) C
(131) D	(155) D	(179) C	(203) D	(227) D
(132) D	(156) C	(180) C	(204) D	(228) A
(133) D	(157) D	(181) C	(205) C	(229) A
(134) D	(158) D	(182) B	(206) B	(230) B

(231) B	(235) E	(239) B	(243) C	(247) E
(232) C	(236) D	(240) D	(244) A	(248) E
(233) B	(237) C	(241) C	(245) E	(249) C
(234) A	(238) A	(242) E	(246) B	(250) C

4.2 Data Sufficiency Questions

(251) B	(273) A	(295) E	(317) A	(339) C
(252) B	(274) C	(296) D	(318) A	(340) E
(253) C	(275) A	(297) E	(319) C	(341) E
(254) A	(276) D	(298) B	(320) A	(342) E
(255) A	(277) E	(299) D	(321) E	(343) A
(256) C	(278) D	(300) B	(322) B	(344) D
(257) B	(279) B	(301) E	(323) D	(345) B
(258) E	(280) B	(302) A	(324) D	(346) E
(259) A	(281) E	(303) A	(325) C	(347) C
(260) B	(282) B	(304) A	(326) D	(348) D
(261) C	(283) D	(305) A	(327) C	(349) C
(262) C	(284) E	(306) A	(328) C	(350) B
(263) E	(285) D	(307) A	(329) B	(351) C
(264) E	(286) A	(308) B	(330) C	(352) E
(265) B	(287) B	(309) A	(331) A	(353) E
(266) A	(288) B	(310) D	(332) D	(354) D
(267) A	(289) B	(311) D	(333) D	(355) D
(268) E	(290) E	(312) B	(334) D	(356) E
(269) E	(291) A	(313) C	(335) D	(357) C
(270) E	(292) E	(314) A	(336) E	(358) E
(271) B	(293) A	(315) A	(337) E	(359) B
(272) E	(294) C	(316) C	(338) C	(360) D

(361) E	(385) E	(409) D	(433) D	(457) A
(362) D	(386) C	(410) A	(434) D	(458) D
(363) C	(387) B	(411) D	(435) B	(459) B
(364) D	(388) E	(412) E	(436) C	(460) B
(365) C	(389) C	(413) E	(437) A	(461) E
(366) C	(390) C	(414) C	(438) C	(462) A
(367) A	(391) E	(415) A	(439) B	(463) D
(368) B	(392) A	(416) D	(440) D	(464) B
(369) E	(393) D	(417) C	(441) A	(465) C
(370) C	(394) C	(418) B	(442) C	(466) C
(371) C	(395) C	(419) A	(443) E	(467) E
(372) D	(396) C	(420) A	(444) D	(468) C
(373) B	(397) C	(421) D	(445) C	(469) D
(374) D	(398) A	(422) C	(446) B	(470) B
(375) B	(399) A	(423) B	(447) E	(471) E
(376) A	(400) D	(424) E	(448) E	(472) B
(377) D	(401) E	(425) C	(449) D	(473) C
(378) E	(402) A	(426) C	(450) D	(474) E
(379) E	(403) C	(427) D	(451) E	(475) C
(380) C	(404) B	(428) C	(452) B	(476) A
(381) E	(405) D	(429) B	(453) C	(477) D
(382) D	(406) B	(430) D	(454) C	(478) D
(383) C	(407) D	(431) B	(455) E	(479) C
(384) C	(408) A	(432) C	(456) E	(480) C

(481) D	(485) D	(489) A	(493) C	(497) C
(482) E	(486) A	(490) C	(494) C	(498) A
(483) D	(487) A	(491) B	(495) D	(499) B
(484) B	(488) E	(492) D	(496) E	(500) A

Chapter 5

Solutions – Problem Solving Questions

5.1 Number properties

1. Here given expression is in the format $a^2 - b^2 = (a + b)(a - b)$

$=> 99999^2 - 1^2 = (99,999 + 1)(99,999 - 1)$

$=> 100,000 \times (100,000 - 2) = 10^5 \times (10^5 - 2)$

The correct answer is option C.

2. The highest exponent of 3 in $n!$ can be calculated by adding the quotients (integer parts) when n is successively divided by 3:

If $[x]$ denotes the integer part of x, we have:

$$\left[\frac{n}{3}\right] + \left[\frac{\left[\frac{n}{3}\right]}{3}\right] + \cdots = 8$$

Assuming that only $\left[\frac{n}{3}\right]$ equals 8, we have: $n = 3 * 8 = 24$

However, for $n = 24$ the actual value of the exponent of 3 is:

- $\frac{24}{3} = 8$
- $\frac{8}{3} = 2.6 \equiv 2$

The exponent is $8 + 2 = 10$, which is greater by 2 than what was required.

Thus, we need to reduce 24 by 2 multiples of 3 i.e. $2 * 3 = 6$.

Thus, the approximate value of $n = 24 - 6 = 18$.

For $n = 18$, the actual value of the exponent of 3 is:

- $\frac{18}{3} = 6$
- $\frac{6}{3} = 2$

The exponent is $6 + 2 = 8$, which is the exact exponent required.

However, since we need to find the largest value of the highest exponent of 5 in $n!$, we need to check if any higher value of n is possible.

We have obtained the highest exponent of 3 as 8 in 18!

However, we can increase n till a point before the next multiple of 3 gets included.

Thus, we can increase n to20!

Let us verify:

For $n = 20$, the actual value of the exponent of 3 is:

- $\frac{20}{3} = 6.6 \equiv 6$
- $\frac{6}{3} = 2$

Thus the exponent is $6 + 2 = 8$, which is the exact exponent required.

Thus, the maximum value of $n! = 20!$

Thus, for $n = 20$, the value of the highest exponent of 5 is:

- $\frac{20}{5} = 4$

Thus the highest exponent of 5 in 20! is 4.

The correct answer is option C.

3. We have: $0 < r < 1$

Also, $s = r^2$ and $t = \sqrt{r}$

Multiplying both sides of the inequality, $r < 1$, by r (since r is positive, multiplying r will not change the sign of inequality):

$r * r < 1 * r$

$=> r^2 < r$

Thus, we have:

$r > r^2 = s$

Again, since $r < 1$; taking square root on both the sides, we have: $\sqrt{r} < 1$

Multiplying both sides of the above inequality by $\sqrt{r}$, we have:

$\sqrt{r} * \sqrt{r} < \sqrt{r}$

$=> r < \sqrt{r}$

Thus, we have:

$r^2 < r < \sqrt{r}$

$=> s < r < t$

The correct answer is option D.

Alternate approach:

For any number less than 1, its squares, cubes & higher order numbers would be less than the number, and its square roots, cube roots & n^{th} roots would be greater than the number.

Since $r = 0.345 < 1$, this follows that $s < r < t$.

4. Given that,

$s = 100 * 101 * \cdots * 200$

$t = 100 * 101 * \cdots * 200 * 201 = 201 * s$

Thus, we have:

$\frac{1}{s} + \frac{1}{t}$

$= \frac{1}{s} + \frac{1}{201 * s}$

$=> \frac{201 + 1}{201 * s}$

$=> \frac{202}{201 * s}$

$=> \frac{202}{t}$

The correct answer is option D.

5. The sum of all integers from 1 to n is given by $\frac{n(n+1)}{2}$.

Thus, sum of all integers from 1 to 30 = $\frac{30 * 31}{2} = 15 * 31$.

Thus, $s = 15 * 31 = 3 * 5 * 31$

Thus, the prime factors of s are: 3, 5 and 31.

Thus, the factors of s are: 1, 3, 5, 31, 3*5 = 15, 3*31 = 93, 5*31 = 155, and 3*5*31 = 465.

Thus, the sum of all the factors of $s = 1 + 3 + 5 + 31 + 15 + 93 + 155 + 465 = 768$.

The correct answer is option E.

6. $s = \frac{1}{91} + \frac{1}{92} + \cdots + \frac{1}{100}$

Let us try to find the range of values of s.

We know that s is of the sum of 10 terms.

Thus, we can say:

$$s < \frac{1}{91} + \frac{1}{91} + \ldots (10 \text{ times})$$

$$=> s < \frac{10}{91} = \frac{1}{9.1}$$

$$=> s < \frac{1}{9}$$

Again, we have:

$$s > \frac{1}{100} + \frac{1}{100} + \ldots (10 \text{ terms})$$

$$=> s > \frac{10}{100} = \frac{1}{10}$$

Thus, we have:

$$\frac{1}{10} < s < \frac{1}{9}$$

Thus, from the statements I and II, we see that s is less than $\frac{1}{9}$ and hence s is also less than $\frac{1}{8}$ (since $\frac{1}{8} > \frac{1}{9}$).

The correct answer is option C.

7. Since the number is divisible by 36, it is divisible by both 4 and 9.

The number $5m15n$ is divisible by 4, if the last two digits of the number is divisible by 4.

Thus, the number $5n$ is divisible by 4.

This is possible if $n = 2$ or 6 (since both 52 and 56 are divisible by 4).

The number $5m15n$ is divisible by 9, if the sum of the digits of the number is divisible by 9.

The sum of the digits $= 5 + m + 1 + 5 + n = (11 + m + n)$.

Thus, $(11 + m + n)$ should be divisible by 9.

If $n = 2$:

$11 + m + n$

$= 11 + m + 2$

$= 13 + m$.

Thus, $(13 + m)$ is divisible by 9 if $m = 5$ (since $13 + 5 = 18$, which is divisible by 9).

If $n = 6$:

$11 + m + n$

$= 11 + m + 6$

$= 17 + m$.

Thus, $(17 + m)$ is divisible by 9 if $m = 1$ (since $17 + 1 = 18$, which is divisible by 9).

Thus we have two possible situations:

$m = 5, n = 2 => |m - n| = 3$

OR

$m = 1, n = 6 => |m - n| = 5$

Thus, the maximum value of $|m - n| = 5$.

The correct answer is option C.

8. Working with the options one at a time:

- Option A:

$n = 99 = 3^2 * 11$

=> The prime factors of n are 3 and 11

Also, $\sqrt{n} = \sqrt{99}$, which lies between 9 and 10

Product of the prime factors of $n = 3 * 11 = 33 \nless \sqrt{99}$ – Does not satisfy

- Option B:

$n = 98 = 2 * 7^2$

=> The prime factors of n are 2 and 7

Also, $\sqrt{n} = \sqrt{98}$, which lies between 9 and 10

Product of the prime factors of $n = 2 * 7 = 14 \nless \sqrt{98}$ – Does not satisfy

- Option C:

$n = 97$, which is a prime number

=> The prime factor of n is 97

Also, $\sqrt{n} = \sqrt{97}$, which lies between 9 and 10

Product of the prime factors of $n = 97 \nless \sqrt{97}$ – Does not satisfy

- Option D:

$n = 96 = 2^5 * 3$

=> The prime factors of n are 2 and 3

Also, $\sqrt{n} = \sqrt{96}$, which lies between 9 and 10

Product of the prime factors of $n = 2 * 3 = 6 < \sqrt{97}$ – Satisfies

Verifying option E...

- Option E:

$n = 95 = 5 * 19$

=> The prime factors of n are 5 and 19

Also, $\sqrt{n} = \sqrt{95}$, which lies between 9 and 10

Product of the prime factors of $n = 5 * 19 = 95 \nless \sqrt{95}$ – Does not satisfy

The correct answer is option D.

9. According to the problem:

If t is in the set, then $(t + 2)$ is also in the set.

However, it does NOT imply that: If $(t + 2)$ is in the set, then t must be in the set.

What it does imply is that: If $(t + 2)$ is NOT in the set, then t is NOT in the set.

Thus, if we have $t = -1$ as a member of the set, then $(t + 2) = 1$ is a member of the set.

Thus, statement II is correct.

Proceeding in the same way:

Since $t = 1$ is a member of the set, then $(t + 2) = 3$ is a member of the set.

Again, since $t = 3$ is a member of the set, then $(t + 2) = 5$ is a member of the set.

Thus, statement III is correct.

Thus, the correct answer is option D.

10. We have:

$x_1 = 3 = 2^1 + 1 \ldots$ (i)

$x_2 = 2 * x_1 - 1$
$= 2 * (2^1 + 1) - 1$
$= 2 * 2^1 + 2 * 1 - 1$
$= 2^2 + 2 - 1$
$= 2^2 + 1 \ldots$ (ii)

$x_3 = 2 * x_2 - 1$
$= 2 * (2^2 + 1) - 1$
$= 2 * 2^2 + 2 * 1 - 1$
$= 2^3 + 2 - 1$
$= 2^3 + 1 \ldots$ (iii)

Thus, we see that the sequence follows the pattern:

$x_n = 2^n + 1$

$=> x_{20} = 2^{20} + 1$, and $x_{19} = 2^{19} + 1$

$=> x_{20} - x_{19}$

$= (2^{20} + 1) - (2^{19} - 1)$

$= 2^{20} - 2^{19}$

$= 2 * 2^{19} - 2^{19}$

$= 2^{19}(2 - 1)$

$= 2^{19}$

The correct answer is option A.

11. $924 = 2^2 * 3 * 7 * 11$

We see that there is an extra '2' since the exponent of 2 is 2.

This extra '2' can be combined with the other factors to generate different values of z.

Also, keeping the two 2's separate, the other factors may be combined to generate different values of z.

Thus, possible values of w, x, y and z such that $1 < w \le x \le y \le z$, are:

w	x	y	z
3	2 * 2 = 4	7	11
2	2 * 3 = 6	7	**11**
2	3	7	2 * 11 = **22**
2	3	11	2 * 7 = **14**
2	2	7	3 * 11 = **33**
2	2	11	3 * 7 = **21**
2	2	3	7 * 11 = **77**

Thus, there are six possible values of z, which are 11, 14, 21, 22, 33 and 77.

The correct answer is option D.

12. $(\sqrt{x + y - 2\sqrt{xy}}) + (\sqrt{x + y + 2\sqrt{xy}})$

$= \left(\sqrt{(\sqrt{x})^2 + (\sqrt{y})^2 - 2\sqrt{x}\sqrt{y}}\right) + \left(\sqrt{(\sqrt{x})^2 + (\sqrt{y})^2 + 2\sqrt{x}\sqrt{y}}\right)$

Since $y > x$, we have:

$\sqrt{(\sqrt{x})^2 + (\sqrt{y})^2 - 2\sqrt{x}\sqrt{y}}$

$= \sqrt{(\sqrt{y} - \sqrt{x})^2}$

$= \sqrt{y} - \sqrt{x}$

Note: We should not write $(\sqrt{x} - \sqrt{y})$, since this value is negative while the radical sign will only take the positive square root.

Thus, the given expression: $\left(\sqrt{(\sqrt{x})^2 + (\sqrt{y})^2 - 2\sqrt{x}\sqrt{y}}\right) + \left(\sqrt{(\sqrt{x})^2 + (\sqrt{y})^2 + 2\sqrt{x}\sqrt{y}}\right)$

$= (\sqrt{y} - \sqrt{x}) + (\sqrt{y} + \sqrt{x})$

$= 2\sqrt{y}$

The correct answer is option E.

Alternate approach:

Above approach may be time-consuming. We may have an alternate approach for this questions.

We see that in the options, we have to deal with square roots of x & y, thus with the given constraints ($0 < x < 1$ and $y > 1$), we can assume smarter values for x & y.

Say $x = \frac{1}{4}$ & $y = 4$

So, now we have to see what is the value of $(\sqrt{x + y - 2\sqrt{xy}} + \sqrt{x + y + 2\sqrt{xy}})$?

$(\sqrt{x + y - 2\sqrt{xy}} + \sqrt{x + y + 2\sqrt{xy}}) = \left(\sqrt{\frac{1}{4} + 4 - 2\sqrt{\frac{1}{4} * 4}} + \sqrt{\frac{1}{4} + 4 + 2\sqrt{\frac{1}{4} * 4}}\right)$

$=> \left(\sqrt{\frac{1}{4} + 4 - 2\sqrt{1}} + \sqrt{\frac{1}{4} + 4 + 2\sqrt{1}}\right)$

$=> \left(\sqrt{\frac{1}{4} + 2} + \sqrt{\frac{1}{4} + 6}\right)$

$=> \left(\sqrt{\frac{9}{4}} + \sqrt{\frac{25}{4}}\right)$

$=> \left(\frac{3}{2} + \frac{5}{2}\right)$

$=> 4$

Plugging in the value of $x = \frac{1}{4}$ & $y = 4$ in options, we find that the value of only option E equals 4, the correct answer.

13. For $0 < x < 1$, Multiplying x throughout:

$=> 0 < x^2 < x$

Taking square root throughout:

$=> 0 < x < \sqrt{x}$

Thus, we have:

$\sqrt{x} > x$

Taking reciprocal:

$\frac{1}{\sqrt{x}} < \frac{1}{x} \ldots \text{(i)}$

We know that:

$x \geq 0.9$

$=> \frac{1}{x} \leq \frac{1}{0.9} = 1.11 \ldots \text{(ii)}$

Thus, from (i) and (ii), we have:

$\frac{1}{\sqrt{x}} < 1.11$

The correct answer is option A.

Alternate approach:

Say $x = 1$,

$=> \left(\frac{1}{\sqrt{x}}\right) = \left(\frac{1}{\sqrt{1}}\right) = 1$

We see that the value of x increases, the value of $\left(\frac{1}{\sqrt{x}}\right)$ decreases; but we see that no value in the options are less than 1.

Since all the values in options are more than 1, we need to probe further.

If we plug in a value for x, lying between 1 and 0.9, the value of $\left(\frac{1}{\sqrt{x}}\right)$ would be greater 1 However, all the options are greater than 1, so this does not seem to solve the problem, but it is not so.

Since this is a question of MCQ category and only one among five options are correct, at least option A (1.02, least among all the options) must be correct, thus the correct answer.

14. We have: $180x = y^3$

$180 = 2^2 * 3^2 * 5$

Since $180x$ is a perfect cube, we have:

$x = 2 * 3 * 5^2 * k^3$, where k is a positive integer.

In that case, we have:

$180x = 2^3 * 3^3 * 5^3 * k^3$, which is a perfect cube.

Thus, among the statements I, II and III, only those would be an integer where the denominator is a factor of x.

Only in option III, where the denominator is $2 * 3 * 5^2$, x is divisible by the denominator and hence would be an integer.

The correct answer is option C.

15. Given that,

$$\begin{array}{r} A\ B \\ +\ B\ A \\ \hline A\ A\ C \\ \hline \end{array}$$

In the addition in the unit digits, we have:

$B + A = C +$ carry

(Since in the tens position, the same addition results in a different value)

The value of the carry must be 1 (adding 2 digits can result in a maximum carry of 1)

We observe that in the addition of the tens digits, i.e. $(1 + A + B)$, we get a carry to the hundreds' position (since the result is a three-digit number).

Also, we have:

$(1 + A + B)$ results in the digit A in the tens position

$=> (1 + B) = 10$

(Since only $(A + 10)$ would result is the digit A in the tens position)

$=> B = 9$

Since the hundreds' position in the sum comes only from the carry from the tens position, we have:

$A = 1$

Thus, the correct addition is:

$$\begin{array}{r} 19 \\ +\ 91 \\ \hline 110 \end{array}$$

Thus, the value of the unit digit of the integer AAC, i.e. $C = 0$.

Alternate Approach:

As AB and BA are two digit positive integers, we must have:

$AB + BA = AAC < 200$

=> A must be equal to 1

=> $AAC = 11C$, where C is the unit digit

We can write a two digit positive number with digits A and B as:

$AB \equiv 10A + B$

Similarly, we have, the two digit positive number: $BA \equiv 10B + A$

Thus, we have:

$AB + BA \equiv (10A + B) + (10B + A) = 11(A + B)$

We know: $AB + BA = AAC$

=> $AAC = 11C \equiv 11(A + B)$

Thus, AAC is a multiple 11, and also less than 200:

=> $AAC \equiv 110$.

=> $C = 0$

The correct answer is option E.

16. Amount saved by Nancy in the first week = \$1.

Amount saved by Nancy in the second week = \$ (1 + 1) = \$2.

Amount saved by Nancy in the third week = \$ (2 + 1) = \$3.

Thus, we see that the amount saved by Nancy forms an arithmetic progression with first term 1 and constant difference between consecutive terms as 1.

Thus, the amount saved by Nancy in the 52nd week = \$52.

Thus, the average amount saved by Nancy every week

$$= \frac{(\text{Amount saved in the } 1^{st} \text{ week}) + \left(\text{Amount saved in the } 52^{nd} \text{ week}\right)}{2}$$

$$= \$ \left(\frac{1+52}{2}\right) = \$ \left(\frac{53}{2}\right)$$

Thus, total amount saved = (Average amount saved per week) $*$ (Number of weeks)

$$= \$ \left(\frac{53}{2} * 52\right)$$

$$= \$ (53 * 26)$$

$$= \$1378$$

Alternate approach:

Sum of first n natural numbers $= \frac{n * (n+1)}{2}$

Thus, the sum of first 52 natural numbers $= \frac{52 * 53}{2} = 53 * 26 = 1378$

The correct answer is option C.

5.2 Percents

17. The cost of repairing a pair of used shoes so that they last for one year = \$12.5

The cost of a pair of new shoes = \$28.

Since the new shoes last for two years, the average cost per year = $\$\frac{28}{2} = \$14$.

Thus, the required percentage = $\frac{14 - 12.5}{12.5} * 100 = 12\%$.

The correct answer is option C.

18. Let the purchase price of the item be $\$x$.

So tax is applicable on $\$(x - 100)$

Thus, tax paid = 5% of $\$\ (x - 100)$

$=> \$\left(\frac{5}{100} * (x - 100)\right)$

$=> \$\left(\frac{x - 100}{20}\right)$, which is equals to \$4.

Thus, we have:

$\frac{x - 100}{20} = 4$

$=> x = 180$

The correct answer is option C.

19. Tax paid on \$50 = \$0.82

Thus, a tax which thrice as much as the above, would be $\$(0.82 * 3) = \$2.46$ on \$50.

Thus, the new tax on \$100 = 2 * Tax paid on \$50

$=> \$(2.46 * 2) = \$4.92$

Thus, this tax, expressed as a percentage = $\frac{4.92}{100} * 100 = 4.92\%$.

The correct answer is option C.

20. For X, visual range increased from 90 kilometers to 270 kilometers.

Total increase in visual range of X = 270 – 90 = 180 kilometers

Thus, Percentage increase in visual range using X = $\frac{180}{90} * 100 = 200\%$.

For Y, visual range increased from 45 kilometers to 180 kilometers.

Total increase in visual range of X = 180 – 45 = 135 kilometers

Thus, Percentage increase in visual range using Y = $\frac{135}{45} * 100 = 300\%$.

Apparently it seems that the required answer is simply: 300% – 200% = 100%.
However, it is not so since we are here asked to find percent change not absolute change

Here absolute change is 300% – 200% = 100%, which we are going to compare with percent change in X which is 200%.

The required percent = $\frac{100}{200} * 100 = 50\%$.

What this shows us is that the use of telescope Y is 50% more effective than that of telescope X.

The correct answer is option B.

21. Population of country X = 120,108,000 =∼ 120,000,000.
Land area of country X = 2,998,000 square kilometers =∼ 3,000,000 square kilometers.

Thus, population density of country X = $\frac{120000000}{3000000} = 40$.

Population of country Y = 200,323,000 =∼ 200,000,000.
Land area of country Y = 7,899,000 square kilometers =∼ 8,000,000 square kilometers.

Thus, population density of country Y = $\frac{200000000}{8000000} = 25$.

Thus, the percent by which population density of country X is greater than that of country Y $= \left(\frac{40 - 25}{25}\right) * 100$

= 60%.

Note: An exact calculation would lead to:

Population density of country X = $\frac{120108000}{2998000} = 40.06$.

Thus, population density of country Y = $\frac{200323000}{7899000} = 25.36$.

Thus, required percent difference = $\frac{40.06 - 25.36}{25.36} * 100 = 57.96\% =\sim 60\%$.

Thus, the above approximations are justified. The closest option (50%) to 57.96% is too far compared to 60%, thus it cannot be an answer.

In the GMAT, whenever, approximate answer is expected, the options are wide apart from each other.

The correct answer is option A.

22. Since we need to find the overall percent change, we can assume the original price as \$100 (since the overall percent change does not depend on the actual value of the coat).

Price after the price was reduced by 20%

$= (100 - 20)\,\%$ of \$100

$= \$100 * \left(\frac{80}{100}\right)$

$= \$80.$

Price after the new price was increased by 20%

$= (100 + 20)\,\%$ of \$80

$= \$80 * \left(\frac{120}{100}\right)$

$= \$96.$

Thus, the overall percent change $= \frac{\text{Change in value}}{\text{Initial value}} * 100$

$= \frac{100 - 96}{100} * 100$

$= 4\%$

Working with the options one at a time:

- Option A:

$100(1 - 0.2)^2 = 100 * 0.8^2 = 64\%$ - Incorrect

- Option B:

$100(1 - 0.4) = 100 * 0.6 = 60\%$ - Incorrect

- Option C:

$100(1 - 0.4)^2 = 100 * 0.36 = 36\%$ - Incorrect

- Option D:

$100(1 - 0.8) = 100 * 0.2 = 20\%$ – Incorrect

- Option E:

$100(1 - 0.96) = 100 * 0.04 = 4\%$ – Correct

Alternate approach:

We can find the overall percent change using the relation:

$\left(x + y + \frac{xy}{100}\right)\%$, where $x\%$ and $y\%$ represent successive percent changes.

Applying in this problem, we get:

$$\left(20 - 20 - \frac{20 * 20}{100}\right) = -4\%$$

Thus, the overall percent change is 4%.

The correct answer is option E.

23. The prescribed drug dosage for 120 pounds of body weight was 18 cubic centimeters.

The typical drug dosage for every 15 pounds of body weight was 2 cubic centimeters.

Thus, as per the typical dosage, amount of drug required for 120 pounds of body weight $= \frac{2}{15} * 120 = 16$ cubic centimeters.

Thus, the prescribed dosage has to be reduced by $(18 - 16) = 2$ cubic centimeters.

Thus, the percent change in the dosage $= \frac{2}{18} * 100 = \frac{100}{9} = 11.11\%$.

The correct answer is option C.

24. Number of workers who worked for 20 hours in the week = 30% of 100 = 30.

Rate of pay per hour = \$5.

Thus, pay per worker = \$ $(5 * 20)$ = \$100.

Thus, total pay for all 30 workers = \$ $(100 * 30)$ = \$3000 ... (i)

Number of workers who worked for 40 hours in the week = 50% of 100 = 50.

Rate of pay per hour = \$5.

Thus, pay per worker = \$ (5 ∗ 40) = \$200.

Thus, total pay for all 50 workers = \$ (200 ∗ 50) = \$10000 . . . (ii)

Number of workers who worked for 50 hours in the week = 100 − (30 + 50) = 20.

Rate of pay is \$5 per hour for the first 40 hours and $\$\left(5 * 1\frac{1}{2}\right) = \$(5 * \frac{3}{2}) = \$\left(\frac{15}{2}\right)$ per hour for the remaining (50 − 40) = 10 hours.

Thus, pay per worker = $\$\left(5 * 40 + \frac{15}{2} * 10\right) = \$275$.

Thus, total pay for all 20 workers = \$ (275 ∗ 20) = \$5500 . . . (iii)

Thus, total payroll for the entire assembly-line workers
= \$ (3000 + 10000 + 5500) = \$18500.

The correct answer is option B.

25. On the first \$20 million in sales, amount received in royalties = \$3 million

Thus, ratio of royalties to sales = $\frac{3}{20}$.

On the next \$108 million in sales, amount received in royalties = \$9 million

Thus, ratio of royalties to sales = $\frac{9}{108} = \frac{3}{36}$.

Since $\frac{3}{20} > \frac{3}{36}$, there is a decrease in royalties.

Thus, the required percent decrease

$$= \left(\frac{\frac{3}{20} - \frac{3}{36}}{\frac{3}{20}}\right) * 100$$

$= \left(1 - \left(\frac{3}{36} * \frac{20}{3}\right)\right) * 100$; taking $\frac{3}{20}$ common from numerator and canceling it from the denominator

$$= \left(1 - \frac{5}{9}\right) * 100$$

$$= \frac{4}{9} * 100$$

= 44.44% =∼ 44%

The correct answer is option C.

26. Total sales = \$14000.

Thus, commission on the first \$10000 = 6% of \$10000 = $\$\left(\frac{6}{100} * 10000\right) = \$600$.

Total commission received by the salesman = \$920.

Thus, commission received on the remaining sales = \$ (920 − 600) = \$320.

Commission received on the remaining \$ (14000 − 10000) = \$4000 at r%

= r% of \$4000

$= \$\left(\frac{r}{100} * 4000\right)$

= \$40r.

Thus, we have:

$40r = 320$

$=> r = 8$

The correct answer is option D.

27. Total cost of the 1500 heads of cabbage = \$600.

Cost of $\frac{2}{3}$ of the above heads of cabbage = $\$\left(600 * \frac{2}{3}\right) = \$400$.

On first day, these were sold at a 25% higher than the cost price.

Thus, selling price of the above heads of cabbage

= (100 + 25) % of \$400

$= \$\left(\frac{125}{100} * 400\right)$

= \$500 . . . (i)

Cost of the remaining heads of cabbage = \$ (600 − 400) = \$200.

On the second day, these remaining heads of cabbage were sold at a 10% lower than the cost price.

Thus, selling price of the above heads of cabbage on the second day

= (100 − 10) % of \$200

$= \$ \left(\frac{90}{100} * 200\right)$

$= \$180 \ldots \text{(ii)}$

Thus, total selling price = \$ (500 + 180) = \$680.

Thus, percent profit

$= \left(\frac{\text{Selling price} - \text{Cost price}}{\text{Cost price}}\right) * 100$

$= \left(\frac{680 - 600}{600}\right) * 100$

= 13.33%.

Alternate approach:

Percent profit made on $\frac{2}{3}$ of the stock = 25%

Percent profit made on the remaining $\frac{1}{3}$ of the stock = −10% (since price is 10% less)

Thus, overall percent profit

$= \left(\frac{2}{3} * 25 + \frac{1}{3} * (-10)\right)$

$= \frac{50}{3} - \frac{10}{3}$

$= \frac{40}{3}$

= 13.33%.

The correct answer is option B.

28. We know that the price of diesel increased by 25%.

Let the original price of diesel per liter be $\$x$.

Thus, the price of diesel per liter after the price increase

$= \$ (100 + 25)\%$ of $x = \$(125\%$ of $x) = \$ \left(\frac{5x}{4}\right)$.

Number of liters of diesel = $\left(\frac{\text{Total Price}}{\text{Price per liter}}\right)$

Thus, difference in quantity of diesel obtained for \$50

$= \frac{50}{x} - \frac{50}{\frac{5x}{4}} = 10$

$=> \frac{50}{x} - \frac{40}{x} = 10$

$=> \frac{10}{x} = 10$

$=> x = 1$

Thus, the correct answer is option A.

Alternate approach:

If the price of an item goes up/down by x%, the quantity consumed should be reduced/increased by $\left(\frac{100x}{100 \pm x}\right)$% so that the total expenditure remains the same.

Since the price of diesel increased by 25%, the quantity obtained for \$50 would reduce by $100 * \left(\frac{25}{100 + 25}\right) = 20\%$

Thus, 20% of the original quantity = 10 liters

=> Original quantity = $10 * \frac{100}{20} = 50$ liters

Thus, the initial price per liter of diesel = $\left(\frac{\text{Total Initial Price}}{\text{Total Initial number of liters}}\right) = \$\left(\frac{50}{50}\right) = \$1.$

29. Since the problem asks us to find a percent value, we can assume any suitable value of the annual budget for ease of calculation, since the initial value does not affect the final answer.

Since we have the factions $\frac{1}{5}$ and $\frac{1}{8}$, we take the budget to be \$40 (LCM of 5 and 8 = 40).

Thus, amount spent during the first quarter = $\$\left(\frac{1}{5} * 40\right) = \$8.$

Amount of money left = $\$(40 - 8) = \$32.$

Thus, amount spent during the second quarter = $\$\left(\frac{1}{8} * 32\right) = \$4.$

Thus, amount left = $\$(32 - 4) = \$28.$

Total amount spent = $\$(8 + 4) = \$12.$

Thus, the required percent

$= \frac{28 - 12}{12} * 100$

$= \frac{400}{3}\%$

$= 133.33\%$

The correct answer is option D.

30. Amount Dick saved in 2006 = \$3000.

Amount Dick saved in 2007

= 8% more than what he saved in 2006

= (100 + 8) % of what he saved in 2006

$= \$\left(\frac{108}{100} * 3000\right)$

= \$3240

Total amount saved by Dick and Jane in 2007 = \$5000.

Thus, amount saved by Jane in 2007 = \$ (5000 – 3240) = \$1760.

We know that Jane had saved \$3000 in 2006.

Thus, the required percent

$= \frac{(\text{Amount saved by Jane in 2006}) - (\text{Amount saved by Jane in 2007})}{(\text{Amount saved by Jane in 2006})} * 100\%$

$= \frac{3000 - 1760}{3000} * 100\%$

$= \frac{1240}{3000} * 100\%$

$= \frac{124}{3}\%$

$= 41.33\%$

$=\sim 41\%$

The correct answer is option C.

31. It is easier to solve this question can be solved by observing the answer options than by actual solving.

We observe that the options are very large compared to the price change after the first up-down cycle, i.e. \$2.

Let the original price of each share of stock K be $\$x$.

After one up-down cycle, the price of each share reduces by \$2.

Thus, after one up-down cycle, the price per share = $\$(x-2)$.

The next up-down cycle would be calculated on $\$(x-2)$ instead of $\$x$.

However, since 2 is negligible as compared to x, we can say that the reduction in price per share would be very slightly less than \$2.

Thus, the final price $=\sim \ \$\left((x-2)-2\right)=\$(x-4)$.

Thus, we have:

$(x-4) =\sim \ 196.02$

$=> x =\sim \ 200.02$

Thus, the only option that satisfies is 200.

The actual calculation is shown below:

Assuming the initial price of a share to be $\$x$, we have:

$$x-x\left(1+\frac{k}{100}\right)\left(1-\frac{k}{100}\right)=2\ldots\text{(i)}$$

$$x\left(1+\frac{k}{100}\right)\left(1-\frac{k}{100}\right)\left(1+\frac{k}{100}\right)\left(1-\frac{k}{100}\right)=196.02\ldots\text{(ii)}$$

We need to solve for x from the above two equations.

Note: The actual solution is time taking and very involved, and hence, is not suggested.

The correct answer is option D.

32. Cost of planting n trees = $\$p$.

Since the cost increases by 25%, the new cost of planting n trees

$= \$\left((100+25)\%\text{ of }p\right)$

$= \$\left(\frac{125}{100}*p\right)$

$= \$\left(\frac{5p}{4}\right)$

Thus, with a budget of \$ $\left(\frac{5p}{4}\right)$, the orchard grower could plant n trees next year.

Thus, with a budget of \$$(2p)$, the number of trees that can be planted

$= \frac{2p}{\left(\frac{5p}{4}\right)} * n$

$= \frac{8}{5}n$

Thus, percent increase in the number of trees from last year

$= \left(\frac{\frac{8}{5}n - n}{n}\right) * 100$

$= \frac{3}{5} * 100$

= 60%

Thus, there would be a 60% increase in the number of trees that can be planted next year.

The correct answer is option D.

33. Since the question asks about a percent value, we can choose any suitable initial value of the total weight of the tire for ease of calculation, since the initial value will not affect the final answer.

Let the total weight of the tire initially = 100 units.

Thus, weight of tread = 40% of 100 = 40 units.

Weight of the remaining parts of the tire = 100 - 40 = 60 units.

Loss in weight of tread = 50%.

Thus, final weight of tire after a lifetime of use = (100 - 50)% of 40 = 20 units.

Since there is no weight loss in the other parts of the tire, final weight of the tire
= 60 + 20 = 80 units.

Thus, the required percent value = $\left(\frac{\text{Final weight of tread}}{\text{Final weight of tire}}\right) * 100$

$= \frac{20}{80} * 100$

= 25%

The correct answer is option D.

34. Since the question asks about a percent value, we can choose any suitable initial value of the total weight of the mix for ease of calculation, since the initial value will not affect the final answer.

Let the total weight of the mix be 100 units.

Thus, weight of peanuts = 20% of 100 = 20 units.

Weight of cashews = 100 - 20 = 80 units.

Let the price of 100 units (an equal quantity) of peanuts be $\$100x$.

Since the mix costs 10 percent more than the cost of an equal quantity of pure peanuts, the price of 100 units of the mix

$= \$((100 + 10)\,\%\text{ of }100x)$

$= \$110x$

The price of 20 units of peanuts present in the mix $= \$\left(\frac{100x}{100} * 20\right) = \$20x$.

Thus, the price of 80 units of cashews present in the mix $= \$\,(110x - 20x) = \$90x$.

Thus, the price of 100 units of cashews $= \$\left(\frac{90x}{80} * 100\right)$

$= \$\left(90x * \frac{5}{4}\right)$

$= \$112.5x$

Thus, the percent by which cashews are more expensive than peanuts

$= \frac{(\text{price of 100 units of cashews}) - (\text{price of 100 units of peanuts})}{(\text{price of 100 units of peanuts})} * 100$

$= \frac{112.5x - 100x}{100x} * 100$

$= 12.5\%$

The correct answer is option B.

35. Let us assume the number of days in a year to be 365 (it does not matter if one takes 366 for one of the years).

Thus, in a 2-year period, total number of days = 2 * 365 = 730.

We know that senior sales representatives visit the home office once every 30 days and junior sales representatives visit the home office once every 20 days.

Thus, we have:

Number of visits to the home office by senior sales representatives
$= \frac{730}{30}$

$= 24.33 \equiv 24$

Number of visits to the home office by junior sales representatives
$= \frac{730}{20}$

$= 36.5 \equiv 36$

Thus, the required percent difference
$= \frac{\text{(Number of visits by juniors)} - \text{(Number of visits by seniors)}}{\text{(Number of visits by seniors)}} * 100$

$= \frac{36 - 24}{24} * 100$

$= 50\%$

Alternate approach I:

Instead of working with exactly a 2-year period, we may take any suitable period (LCM of 20 and 30) and calculate the answer.

Let us consider a period of 60 days:

Number of visits to the home office by senior sales representatives $= \frac{60}{30} = 2$

Number of visits to the home office by junior sales representatives $= \frac{60}{20} = 3$

Thus, the required percent difference $= \left(\frac{3-2}{2} * 100\right) = 50\%$

Alternate approach II:

We know that senior sales representatives visit the home office once every 30 days and junior sales representatives visit the home office once every 20 days.

Thus, the time gap between 2 consecutive meetings for juniors is $\frac{20}{30} = \frac{2}{3}$ times the corresponding time gap for seniors.

Thus, in the same time period, juniors would make $\left(1 \div \frac{2}{3}\right) = \frac{3}{2} = 1.5$ times as many visits as made by the seniors.

Thus, the number of visits by the juniors is 50% more than that made by the seniors.

The correct answer is option D.

36. Cost of the computer purchased by Anne = \$2000.

Sales tax paid = 5% of \$2000 = $\$\left(\frac{5}{100} * 2000\right) = \$100$.

Thus, total price paid by Anne = \$ (2000 + 100) = \$2100.

Cost of the computer purchased by Henry = \$1800.

Sales tax paid = 12% of \$1800 = $\$\left(\frac{12}{100} * 1800\right) = \$216$.

Thus, total price paid by Henry = \$ (1800 + 216) = \$2016.

Thus, the amount which Henry paid less compared to Anne = \$ (2100 – 2016) = \$84.

Thus, the required % value

$$= \left(\frac{\text{Total price paid by Anne} - \text{Total price paid by Henry}}{\text{Total price paid by Anne}}\right) * 100$$

$$= \left(\frac{84}{2100}\right) * 100$$

= 4%

The correct answer is option B.

37. Let the number of male and female employees be m and f respectively.

Number of male employees who are at least 35 years old = 50% of m

$$= \frac{50}{100} * m$$

$$= \frac{m}{2}$$

Number of female employees who are at least 35 years old

= 40% of f

$$= \frac{40}{100} * f$$

$$= \frac{2f}{5}$$

Thus, total number of employees who are at least 35 years old = $\left(\frac{m}{2} + \frac{2f}{5}\right)$.

Total number of employees = $(m + f)$.

Since 42% of all employees are at least 35 years old, we have:

$$\frac{42}{100} * (m + f) = \frac{m}{2} + \frac{2f}{5}$$

$$=> 21m + 21f = 25m + 20f$$

$$=> f = 4m$$

Thus, fraction of all employees who are female

$$= \frac{f}{m + f}$$

$$= \frac{4m}{m + 4m}$$

$$= \frac{4}{5}$$

Alternate approach:

We can solve the problem using the method of alligation, as shown below:

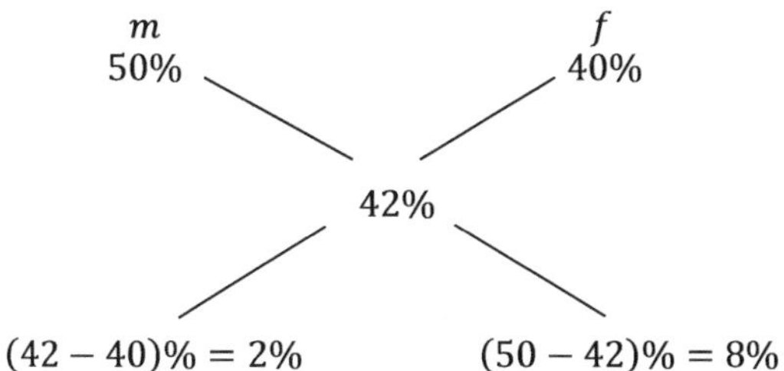

Thus, we have:

$m : f = 2 : 8 = 1 : 4$

$$=> \frac{f}{m+f} = \frac{4}{1+4} = \frac{4}{5}$$

The correct answer is option D.

38. Total number of votes cast = N.

Since 40% of the votes cast were cast by independent voters, percent of votes cast by voters registered with a political party = (100 – 40) = 60%.

Thus, number of votes cast by voters registered with a political party

= 60% of N

= $0.6N$

Of the above, Ms. Robbins received 10% of the votes.

Thus, number of votes received by Ms. Robbins from voters registered with a political party

= 10% of $0.6N$

= $0.06N$

Number of votes received by Ms. Robbins from independent voters = 8000.

Thus, total votes received by Ms. Robbins = $(0.06N + 8000)$.

The correct answer is option D.

39. Since the problem asks about a percent value, we can assume any suitable value of the number of employees in company X for ease of calculation.

Let the number of employees in company X be 100.

Number of employees who live over 10 miles from work = 30% of 100 = 30.

Number of employees who live over 10 miles from work and use car pools

= 60% of 30

= 18

Total number of employees who use car pools = 40% of 100 = 40.

Thus, the number of employees who do not live over 10 miles from work (i.e. live ten miles or less from work) and use car pools

= 40 – 18

= 22

Thus, the percent of the employees of Company X live ten miles or less from work and use car pools

$= \frac{22}{100} * 100$

= 22%

The correct answer is option C.

40. Let the total number of geese in the study = 100 (since the question asks about a ratio, the answer is independent of the initial number chosen, so we choose a suitable number for ease of calculation).

The number of male geese = 30% of 100 = 30.

Thus, the number of female geese = 100 – 30 = 70.

Let the number of geese migrated = x.

Thus, number of male geese migrated = 20% of $x = \frac{20}{100} * x = \frac{x}{5}$

Thus, number of female geese migrated = $\left(x - \frac{x}{5}\right) = \frac{4x}{5}$

Here we know that:

Migration rate for geese of a certain gender $= \frac{\text{Number of geese of that gender migrating}}{\text{Total number of geese of that gender}}$

Thus, the migration rate for the male geese = $\left(\frac{\frac{x}{5}}{30}\right) = \frac{x}{150}$.

Also, the migration rate for the female geese = $\left(\frac{\frac{4x}{5}}{70}\right) = \frac{4x}{350}$.

Thus, the required ratio = $\frac{x}{150} : \frac{4x}{350}$

$= \frac{1}{150} : \frac{4}{350}$

$= \frac{1}{3} : \frac{4}{7}$

$= 7 : 12$

$= \frac{7}{12}$

The correct answer is option B.

41. Since the problem asks us about a percent change, we can assume a suitable initial value of the original purchase price for ease of calculations.

We see that we need to take $\frac{2}{3}$ and $\frac{1}{2}$ or the original purchase price.

So, we should take a value which is a multiple of 6 (LCM of denominators, 2 and 3) for ease of calculations.

Thus, let the original purchase price be \$600.

Thus, the book value in 2006 = $\$\left(\frac{2}{3} * 600\right) = \$400$.

The book value in 2008 = $\$\left(\frac{1}{2} * 600\right) = \$300$.

Thus, the required percent decrease

$= \left(\frac{\text{Change in value}}{\text{Initial value}}\right) *100$

$= \left(\frac{\text{Value in 2006} - \text{Value in 2008}}{\text{Value in 2006}}\right) *100$

$= \frac{400 - 300}{400} * 100$

$= 25\%$

The correct answer is option B.

Alternate approach:

Say the original price be \$1.

Thus, the required percent decrease

$= \left(\frac{\text{Value in 2006} - \text{Value in 2008}}{\text{Value in 2006}}\right) *100$

$= \frac{\frac{2}{3} - \frac{1}{2}}{\frac{2}{3}} * 100$

$$= \frac{\frac{1}{6}}{\frac{2}{3}} * 100$$

$= 25\%$

42. Since the problem asks us about a percent value, we can assume a suitable value of the number of voters for ease of calculations.

Let the number of voters be 100.

Thus, the number of Democrats = 60% of 100 = 60.

Number of Republicans = 100 - 60 = 40.

Number of Democrats who would vote for A = 75% of 60 = $\frac{75}{100} * 60 = 45$.

Number of Republicans who would vote for A = 20% of 40 = $\frac{20}{100} * 40 = 8$.

Thus, total number of expected votes for A = 45 + 8 = 53.

Thus, the required percent = $\frac{53}{100} * 100 = 53\%$.

Alternate approach:

Number of expected votes for A = (75% of 60% of all voters) + (20% of 40% of all voters)

Thus, using weighted average, the expected percent of voters for A

$$= \left(\frac{\frac{75}{100} * 60 + \frac{20}{100} * 40}{60 + 40}\right) * 100$$

$$= \frac{53}{100} * 100$$

$= 53\%$

The correct answer is option B.

43. Number of bank customers in 2005 = 45% of 60 = $\frac{45}{100} * 60 = 27$.

Number of bank customers in 2007 = 25% of 144 = $\frac{25}{100} * 144 = 36$.

Thus, increase in the number of bank customers = 36 – 27 = 9.

Let the simple annual percent growth rate in the number of bank customers be $r\%$.

Thus, in two years (2005 to 2007), increase in the number of bank customers at $r\%$ rate

$$= \left(\frac{27 * r * 2}{100}\right)$$

(The value is calculated on 27 since 27 is the value in the former year)

Thus, we have:

$$\frac{27 * r * 2}{100} = 9$$

$$=> r = \frac{9 * 100}{2 * 27} = 16.6\%$$

The correct answer is option B.

44. Since the problem asks us about a percent change, we can assume a suitable initial value of the original purchase price for ease of calculations.

We see that we need to take $\frac{2}{3}$ and $\frac{1}{2}$ or the original purchase price.

So, we should take a value which is a multiple of 6 for ease of calculations.

Thus, let the original purchase price be \$600.

Thus, the book value in 2006 = $\$\left(\frac{2}{3} * 600\right) = \$400$.

The book value in 2008 = $\$\left(\frac{1}{2} * 600\right) = \$300$.

Thus, the required percent decrease

$$= \left(\frac{\text{Change in value}}{\text{Initial value}}\right) *100$$

$$= \left(\frac{\text{Value in 2006} - \text{Value in 2008}}{\text{Value in 2006}}\right) *100$$

$$= \frac{400 - 300}{400} * 100$$

$$= 25\%$$

The correct answer is option B.

45. Since the problem asks us about a percent value, we can assume a suitable value of the number of voters for ease of calculations.

Let the number of voters be 100.

Thus, the number of Democrats = 60% of 100 = 60.

Number of Republicans = 100 - 60 = 40.

Number of Democrats who would vote for A = 75% of 60 = $\frac{75}{100} * 60 = 45$.

Number of Republicans who would vote for A = 20% of 40 = $\frac{20}{100} * 40 = 8$.

Thus, total number of expected votes for A = 45 + 8 = 53.

Thus, the required percent = $\frac{53}{100} * 100 = 53\%$.

Alternate approach:

Number of expected votes for A = (75% of 60% of all voters) + (20% of 40% of all voters)

Thus, using weighted average, the expected percent of voters for A

$$= \left(\frac{\frac{75}{100} * 60 + \frac{20}{100} * 40}{60 + 40}\right) * 100$$

$$= \frac{53}{100} * 100$$

$$= 53\%$$

The correct answer is option B.

5.3 Profit & Loss

46. Since $\frac{2}{3}$ of the books were sold, the remaining $\left(1 - \frac{2}{3}\right) = \frac{1}{3}$ of the books were not sold.

Thus, $\frac{1}{3}$ of the total books = 36 books.

Thus, $\frac{2}{3}$ of the total books = 2 * 36 = 72 books.

Thus, 72 books were sold each at \$2.50

Thus, total amount received = \$ (72 ∗ 2.50) = \$180.

The correct answer is option A.

47. We know that the farmer produces 750 bushels of a crop at a cost of \$20 per bushel.

Thus, the total cost of crop = \$ (20 ∗ 750) = \$15000.

Selling price of $\left(\frac{2}{3} \text{ of } 750\right)$ or 500 bushels = \$ (2 ∗ 20) = \$40 per bushel.

Thus, selling price of 500 bushels = \$ (40 ∗ 500) = \$20000 . . . (i)

Selling price of (750 − 500) or 250 bushels = \$ ((100 + 25) % of 20) = $\$\left(\frac{125}{100} * 20\right)$ = \$25 per bushel.

Thus, selling price of 250 bushels = \$ (25 ∗ 250) = \$6250 . . . (ii)

Thus, from (i) and (ii):

Total selling price = \$ (20000 + 6250) = \$26250.

Thus, gross profit = Total selling price – Total cost price

= \$ (26250 − 15000) = \$11250.

The correct answer is option A.

48. Selling price of a desk of model A = \$120.

Thus, 30% of the selling price of a desk of model B = \$120.

Thus, selling price of a desk of model B = $\$\left(120 * \frac{100}{30}\right)$ = \$400.

Total number of desks sold by the furniture store = 2000.

Thus, the number of model B desks sold = $\frac{3}{4} * 2000 = 1500$.

Thus, the number of model A desks sold = 2000 - 1500 = 500.

Thus, total revenue from the sale of all desks

= Revenue from model A desks + Revenue from model A desks

= $ (120 ∗ 500) + $ (400 ∗ 1500)

= $ (60000 + 600000)

= $660000

The correct answer is option E.

49. Cost price of the machine = $90.

Percent profit made on the cost = 20%.

Thus, selling price of the machine
= (100 + 20) % of $90

$= \$\left(\frac{120}{100} * 90\right)$

= $108.

This selling price is 10% less than the retail price.

Thus, (100 − 10) % = 90% of the retail price is equal to the selling price of $108.

Thus, the retail price

$= \$\left(108 * \frac{100}{90}\right)$

= $120

The correct answer is option C.

50. Cost of production of each unit = $0.65

Selling price of each unit = $1.20

Thus, profit made on each unit = $ (1.20 − 0.65) = $0.55

Investment made on the equipment = \$9900.

Thus, number of units required to be sold to recover the investment in equipment

$= \frac{9900}{0.55}$

$= \frac{99 * 100}{\frac{55}{100}}$

$= \frac{99 * 100 * 100}{55}$

= 18000

Alternate approach:

Let the number of required units = n.

Thus, total cost = \$ (9900 + 0.65n).

Total selling price = \$1.2n

Thus, we have:

$9900 + 0.65n = 1.2n$

$=> n = 18000$

The correct answer is option D.

51. Initial selling price of the computer

= (100 + 40) % of the cost of the computer

= 140% of the cost of the computer

New selling price of the computer

= (100 + 50) % of the cost of the computer

= 150% of the cost of the computer

Thus, difference between the above two selling prices

= (150% – 140%) of the cost of the computer

= 10% of the cost of the computer

Since the difference between the two selling prices is \$200, we have:

10% of the cost of the computer = \$200

=> Cost of the computer = $\$\left(200 * \frac{100}{10}\right) = \$2000$

Thus, the initial selling price of the computer

= 140% of the cost of the computer

$= \$\left(2000 * \frac{140}{100}\right)$

= \$2800

The correct answer is option C.

52. Total toy trucks produced = 500.

Price of each of the first 100 toy trucks = \$5.00

Thus, total cost of the first 100 toy trucks = $\$ (5 * 100) = \$500$.

Price of each of the remaining 400 toy trucks = \$3.50

Thus, total cost of the remaining 400 toy trucks = $\$ (3.50 * 400) = \$1400$.

Thus, total cost of 500 toy trucks = $\$ (500 + 1400) = \$1900$.

Total selling price of the 500 toy trucks sold at \$10.00 each = $\$ (10 * 500) = \$5000$.

Thus, gross profit = Total selling price – Total cost price

= \$5000 – \$1900

= \$ 3100

The correct answer is option C.

53. Initial selling price of the game = \$44.

Since the initial percent profit was 10% of the cost, we have:

(100 + 10) % of the Cost of the game = \$44

=> Cost of the game = $\$\left(\frac{44}{110} * 100\right) = \$40$

Final selling price of the game = \$46.

Thus, the required percent profit

$$= \left(\frac{\text{Selling price} - \text{Cost price}}{\text{Cost price}}\right) * 100$$

$$= \left(\frac{46 - 40}{40}\right) * 100$$

$$= \frac{6}{40} * 100$$

= 15%

Alternate approach:

Initial percent profit when the selling price was \$44 = 10%.

If the selling price is increased from \$44 to \$46, the corresponding percent increase is (approximately)

$$= \left(\frac{46 - 44}{44}\right) * 100$$

$$= \frac{2}{44} * 100$$

=~ 4.5%

Thus, resultant profit percent (based on the increased selling price) = $10 + 4.5 + \frac{10 * 4.5}{100}$

= 14.5 + 0.45

= 14.95 =~ 15%

The correct answer is option E.

54. The wholesaler has 1200 radios priced at (cost price) \$18 each.

Thus, total cost price = \$ (1200 ∗ 18) = \$21600.

Number of radios sold at \$30 each = 60% of 1200 = $\frac{60}{100} * 1200 = 720$.

Thus, selling price of these 720 radios = \$ (720 ∗ 30) = \$21600.

Number of radios sold at \$15 each = 1200 - 720 = 480.

Thus, selling price of these 480 radios = \$ (480 ∗ 15) = \$7200.

Thus, total selling price of the 1200 radios = \$ (21600 + 7200) = \$28800.

Thus, profit made by selling the 1200 radios = \$ (28800 − 21600) = \$7200.

Thus, average profit made per radio = $\$\left(\frac{7200}{1200}\right) = \$6$.

Alternate approach:

The wholesaler sold 60% of the radios each at a profit of \$ (30 − 18) = \$12.

He sold the remaining 40% of the radios each at a loss of \$ (18 − 15) = \$3.

Thus, his average profit per radio = $\$\left(12 * \frac{60}{100} + (-3) * \frac{40}{100}\right)$

$= \$\ (7.2 - 1.2)$

$= \$6$

The correct answer is option E.

55. Let us understand the problem using the diagram shown below:

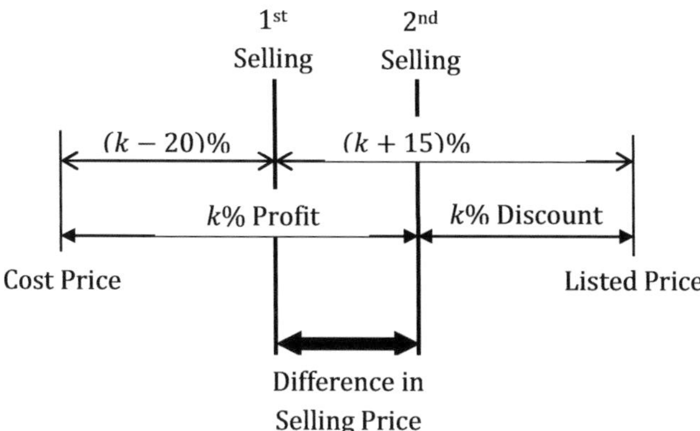

Let us calculate the difference in the two selling prices:

Since in the first case, the profit was $k\%$ and in the second, the profit was $(k-20)\%$, the difference in selling price

$= (k-(k-20))\%$ of Cost Price

$= 20\%$ of Cost price ... (i)

(Since percent profit is calculated on the cost price)

Again, in the first case, the discount was $k\%$ and in the second, the discount was $(k+15)\%$, the difference in selling price

$= ((k+15)-k)\%$ of Listed Price

$= 15\%$ of Listed price ... (ii)

(Since percent discount is calculated on the listed price)

Thus, from (i) and (ii), we have:

20% of Cost price = 15% of Listed price

$$=> \frac{\text{Listed price}}{\text{Cost price}} = \frac{20}{15} = \frac{4}{3}$$

Thus, if no discount were offered (the listed price becomes the selling price), percent profit

$$= \left(\frac{\text{Listed price} - \text{Cost price}}{\text{Cost price}}\right) * 100$$

$$= \left(\frac{\text{Listed price}}{\text{Cost price}} - 1\right) * 100$$

$= \left(\frac{4}{3} - 1\right) * 100$

$= 33.3\%$

The correct answer is option D.

5.4 Averages

56. Number of teachers = $\frac{\text{Total annual salaries}}{\text{Average annual salaries}} = \frac{6760000}{52000} = 130$

=> Number of students = $\frac{11}{1} * 130 = 1430$

The correct answer is option D.

57. Let the number of male and female members be m and f respectively.

Total tickets sold to the male members = $96m$.

Total tickets sold to the female members = $84f$.

Thus, total tickets sold = $(96m + 84f)$.

Thus, average number of tickets sold per member

$$=\left(\frac{\text{Total number of tickets sold}}{\text{Total number of people}}\right) = \left(\frac{96m + 84f}{m + f}\right).$$

Thus, we have:

$$\left(\frac{96m + 84f}{m + f}\right) = 92$$

=> $96m + 84f = 92m + 92f$

=> $4m = 8f$

=> $\frac{m}{f} = \frac{8}{4} = \frac{2}{1}$

Alternate approach:

We can solve the problem by the method of allegation:

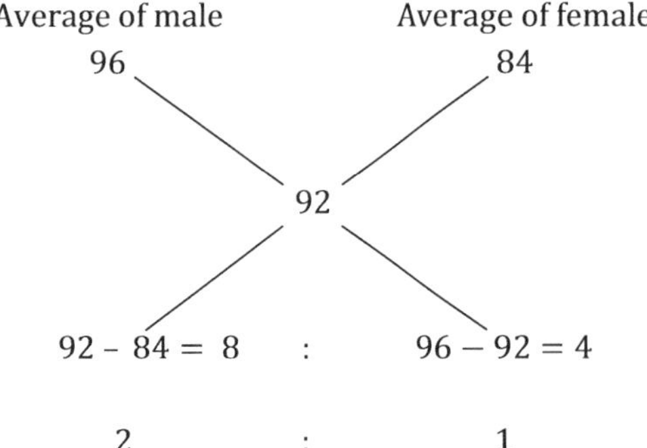

The correct answer is option D.

58. It is given that the total number of students =40.

Let the number of students in section A = n.

Thus, the number of students in section B = $(40 - n)$.

Total score of all students in the two sections combined = $92n + 84\,(40 - n)$.

Thus, average score considering all students

$$= \frac{\text{Total Score}}{\text{Total number of people}} = \frac{92n + 84\,(40 - n)}{40}$$

Thus, we have:

$$\frac{(92n + 84\,(40 - n))}{40} = 89$$

$=> 92n + 3360 - 84n = 3560$

$=> 8n = 200$

$=> n = 25$

Alternate approach:

We can solve this using the method of allegation as shown below:

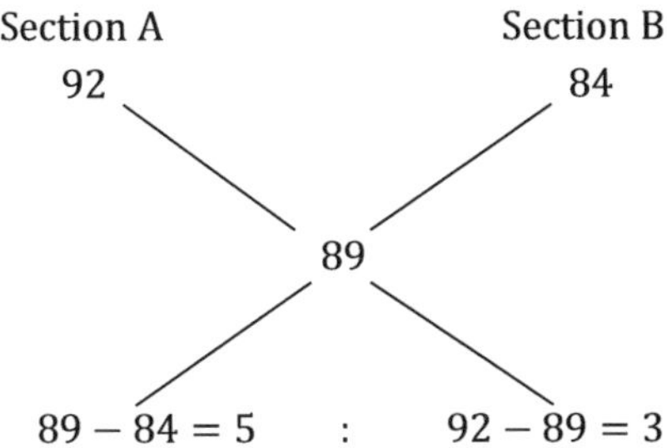

Thus, ratio of the number of students in section A to that in section B = 5 : 3.

Thus, number of students in section A = $\left(\frac{5}{5+3}\right) * 40 = 25$.

The correct answer is option E.

59. The grocer has 400 pounds of 20% decaffeinated coffee and 100 pounds of 60% decaffeinated coffee.

Thus, the grocer has (400 + 100) = 500 pounds of coffee.

Amount of decaffeinated coffee in the first stock = 20% of 400 = 80 pounds.

Amount of decaffeinated coffee in the second stock = 60% of 100 = 60 pounds.

Thus, the total amount of decaffeinated coffee = 80 + 60 = 140 pounds.

Thus, the percent of decaffeinated coffee in the entire stock

$= \frac{140}{500} * 100$

= 28%.

Alternate approach:

The required percent is the weighted average of the percentages of the above two stocks

$$= \left(\frac{\left(400 * \frac{20}{100}\right) + \left(100 * \frac{60}{100}\right)}{400 + 100}\right) * 100$$

$$= \left(\frac{80 + 60}{500}\right) * 100$$

= 28%.

The correct answer is option A.

60. Let the number of students in the sections P, Q, R and S be p, q, r and s, respectively.

Thus, the average weight of all students together in the four sections

$$= \left(\frac{\text{Total weight of all the students combined}}{\text{Total number of students}}\right)$$

$$= \left(\frac{45 * p + 50 * q + 55 * r + 65 * s}{p + q + r + s}\right) \text{lb.}$$

Thus, we have:

$$\left(\frac{45 * p + 50 * q + 55 * r + 65 * s}{p + q + r + s}\right) = 55$$

$=> 45p + 50q + 55r + 65s = 55p + 55q + 55r + 55s$

$=> 10p + 5q = 10s$

$=> 2p + q = 2s$

Since we need to maximize r, we need to find the minimum possible values of p, q and s so that the above equation holds true.

Since the RHS is $2s$, it is even.

Also, in the LHS, $2p$ is even.

Thus, q must be even.

Since the smallest even number that we can consider for q is 2, as we have at least one student in each section. Thus, we have: $q = 2$.

Thus, the equation gets modified to:

$2p + 2 = 2s$

$=> p + 1 = s$

Thus, we use the minimum possible values: $p = 1, s = 2$.

Thus, we have: $p = 1, q = 2$ and $s = 2$.

Since there are a total of 40 students in all sections combined, the maximum value of students in section R $= r = 40 - (p + q + s)$

$= 40 - 5 = 35$

The correct answer is option D.

61. Number of terms in the set S = $(2n + 1)$.

Since the set starts with an odd number and ends with an odd number, number of odd terms is one more than the number of even terms.

Thus, the number of even terms = n

The number of odd terms = $(n + 1)$

We know that the sum (M) of p terms of an arithmetic progression having first term as a and common difference as d is given by:

$$M = \frac{p}{2}(2a + (p - 1) * d)$$

As X is the average of the odd integers in set S and Y is the average of the even integers in set S, we have:

$$X = \frac{(1 + 3 + 5 + \cdots + (2n + 1))}{n + 1} = \frac{\left(\frac{n+1}{2}\right) * (2 * 1 + ((n + 1) - 1) * 2)}{n + 1} = n + 1$$

$$Y = \frac{(2 + 4 + \cdots + 2n)}{n} = \frac{2 * (1 + 2 + \cdots + n)}{n} = \frac{2 * \left(\frac{n(n+1)}{2}\right)}{n} = n + 1$$

Thus, we have:

$$X - Y = (n + 1) - (n + 1) = 0$$

Alternate approach:

Since there is no restriction on n, let us try to find $(X - Y)$ using a few values of n.

If $n = 1$:

S = {1, 2, 3}

$$X = \frac{1 + 3}{2} = 2$$

$$Y = 2$$

$$=> X - Y = 0$$

Again, if $n = 2$:

S = {1, 2, 3, 4, 5}

$$X = \frac{1 + 3 + 5}{3} = 3$$

$Y = \frac{2+4}{2} = 3$

$=> X - Y = 0$

Since $(X - Y) = 0$ for both $n = 1$ and $n = 2$, we can say that the value of $(X - Y)$ would be the same for all values of n, as we have a definite answer among the given answer options.

The correct answer is option A.

62. Let the seven numbers be: a, b, c, d, e, f and g.

Thus, we have:

$\frac{a+b+c+d+e+f+g}{7} = 20$

$=> a+b+c+d+e+f+g = 140 \ldots$(i)

Since the average of the first four numbers is 19, we have:

$\frac{a+b+c+d}{4} = 19$

$=> a+b+c+d = 76 \ldots$(ii)

Since the average of the last four numbers is 24, we have:

$\frac{d+e+f+g}{4} = 24$

$=> d+e+f+g = 96 \ldots$(iii)

Adding (ii) and (iii), we have:

$a+b+c+2d+e+f+g = 172 \ldots$(iv)

Subtracting (i) from (iv), we have:

$d = 172 - 140 = 32$

Thus, the value of the fourth number is 32.

The correct answer is option C.

63. Let the length of each red stick = x inches.

Each red stick is 18 inches less than the average length of the sticks in Box W.

Thus, the average length of sticks in Box W = $(x + 18)$ inches.

Also, each red stick is 6 inches greater than the average length of the sticks in Box V.

Thus, the average length of sticks in Box V = $(x - 6)$ inches.

Thus, the required difference = $((x + 18) - (x - 6)) = 24$ inches.

Note: In this problem, there is a lot of data which has been given to make the question appear complicated. The length of blue sticks is of no consequence. One should carefully read the problem statement and use only the information required to answer the question.

The correct answer is option E.

64. We know that

$$\text{Average salary} = \frac{\text{\# of emp. of group I}*\text{Av. sal.}+\text{\# of emp. of group II}*\text{Av. sal.}+\text{\# of emp. of group III}*\text{Av. sal.}}{\text{Total number of employees}}$$

$$=> \text{Average salary} = \$\left(\frac{10 * 30000 + 30 * 40000 + 20 * 60000}{60}\right)$$

$= \$45000$

The correct answer is option C.

65. Let us use the method of alligation to solve this problem:

Total number of apples and oranges bought = 10.

Price of each apple = 40 cents.

Price of each orange = 60 cents.

Average price of all 10 fruits = 56 cents.

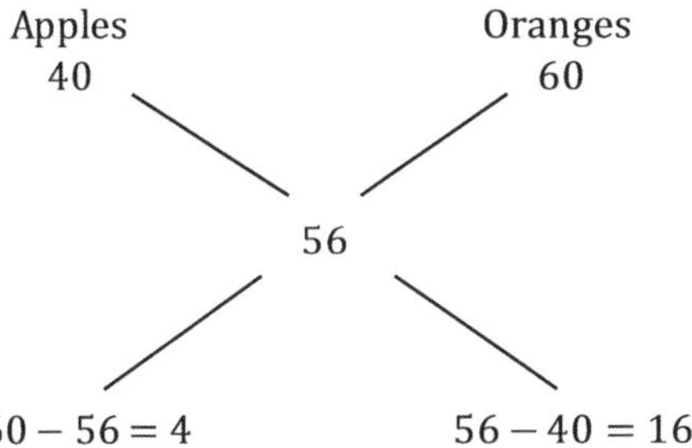

Thus, ratio of the number of apples and the number of oranges = 4 : 16 = 1 : 4.

Since total fruits purchased are 10, we have:

Number of apples = $\left(\left(\frac{1}{1+4}\right) * 10\right) = 2$

Number of oranges = $\left(\left(\frac{4}{1+4}\right) * 10\right) = 8$

We now need to find the number of oranges required to be returned so that the average price falls to 52 cents.

So the situation is this,

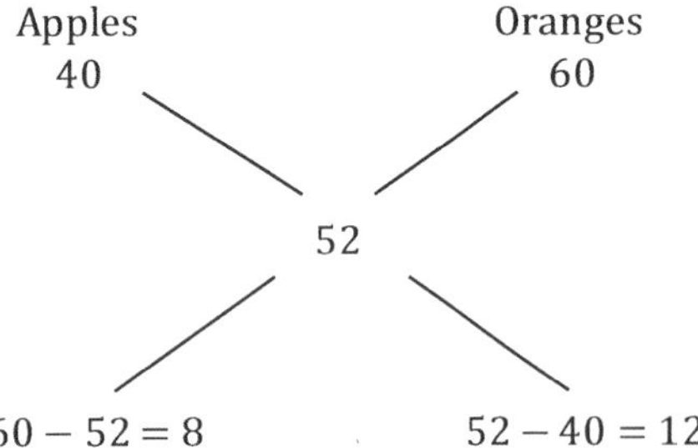

Thus, ratio of the number of apples and the number of oranges now = 8 : 12 = 2 : 3.

Since the number of apples remains the same from the initial situation (only oranges are returned) and we had obtained 2 apples, here too, the number of apples should be 2.

Thus, the number of oranges must be 3 (since the ratio of apples to oranges = 2 : 3).

Since initially, there were 8 oranges, number of oranges returned = 8 − 3 = 5.

Alternate approach I:

Average amount spent for 10 fruits (apples and oranges) = 56 cents.

Total amount spent for 10 fruits = 56 ∗ 10 = 560 cents.

Let us assume that Mary returned x oranges so that the average amount spent is 52 cents.

Thus, total amount spent for $(10 - x)$ fruits = $52 * (10 - x)$ cents.

Thus, price of x oranges returned = $(560 - 52 * (10 - x))$ cents.

Since the price of one orange is 60 cents, we have:

$$60 = \frac{560 - 52 * (10 - x)}{x}$$

=> $60x = 560 - 520 + 52x$

=> $x = 5$

Alternate approach II:

The average price of 10 fruits was 56 cents and after returning some oranges, say x, the average of $(10 - x)$ fruits became 52 cents.

Alternately, we can say that:

The average price of some fruits, say f, was 52 cents and after adding some oranges, say r (at 60 cents each), the average of $(f + r = 10)$ fruits became 56 cents.

Thus, by alligation method:

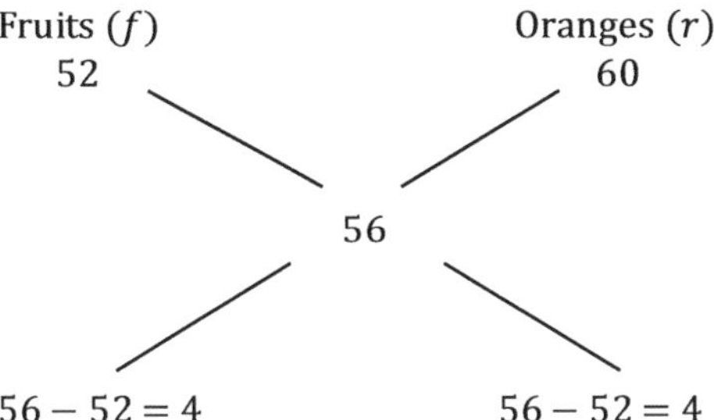

Thus, we have:

$f : r = 1 : 1$

However, we know that:

$f + r = 10$

$=> f = r = \left(\frac{1}{1+1} * 10\right) = 5$

Thus, the number of oranges returned is 5.

Alternate approach III:

We infer the same conclusion as in the previous approach:

The average price of some fruits, say f, was 52 cents and after adding some oranges say r (at 60 cents each), the average of $(f + r = 10)$ fruits became 56 cents.

Thus, the price of each of the f fruits increased by (56 - 52) = 4 cents, resulting in a total increase of $4*f = 4f$ cents.

Also, the price of each of the r oranges reduced by (60 - 56) = 4 cents resulting in a total increase of $4 * r = 4r$ cents.

The increase of $4f$ cents came at the expense of the reduction of $4r$ cents, implying:

$4r = 4f$

$=> r = f$

But, we have:

$f + r = 10$

$=> f = r = \left(\frac{1}{1+1} * 10\right) = 5$

Thus, the number of oranges returned is 5.

The correct answer is option E.

66. We know that the student's average score on four tests is 78.

Thus, his total score on the four tests = 4 * 78 = 312.

Let the score on the 5th test be n.

Thus, his total score on the five tests = $(312 + n)$.

Thus, his average on the 5 tests = $\left(\frac{312 + n}{5}\right)$.

We know that:

The final average increases from the average on 4 tests by an integer

$=> \left(\frac{312 + n}{5} - 78\right)$ is an integer

$=> \left(\frac{312 + n - 390}{5}\right)$ is an integer

$=> \left(\frac{n - 78}{5}\right)$ is an integer

$=> (n - 78)$ is divisible by 5

Working with the options, we see that only option D, i.e. $n = 93$ satisfies since $(93 - 78) = 15$ is divisible by 5.

The correct answer is option D.

67. We know that the ratio of the numbers of students in classes A, B and C was 4 : 6 : 5, respectively.

Let the number of students in classes A, B and C be $4x, 6x$ and $5x$, respectively, where x is a constant of proportionality.

We know that the average scores for the classes A, B and C were 65, 80, and 77, respectively.

Thus, the average score for the three classes combined

$= \left(\frac{65 * 4x + 80 * 6x + 77 * 5x}{4x + 6x + 5x}\right)$

$= \left(\frac{260x + 480x + 385x}{15x}\right)$

$= \left(\frac{1125x}{15x}\right)$

$= 75$

Note: Instead of number of students as $4x, 6x$ and $5x$, the answer will be the same if we consider the number of students as 4, 5 and 6.

Alternate approach:

Let us solve the problem using the concept of assumed mean (deviation method).

We know that the ratio of the numbers of students in the classes A, B and C was 4 : 6 : 5, respectively.

Let the number of students in classes A, B and C be $4x, 6x$ and $5x$, respectively, where x is a constant of proportionality.

We know that the average scores for the classes A, B and C were 65, 80, and 77, respectively.

Let the assumed mean score for the three classes combined = 65.

Thus, the effective scores are: $(65 - 65) = 0$, $(80 - 65) = 15$ and $(77 - 65) = 12$

Thus, we have the average as:

$\left(\frac{0 * 4x + 15 * 6x + 12 * 5x}{4x + 6x + 5x}\right)$

$= \left(\frac{150x}{15x}\right)$

$= 10$

Thus, the actual average $= 10 + 65 = 75$.

Note: This approach leads to lesser calculations than the previous approach.

The correct answer is option B.

68. We know that there are 22 men and 26 women.

Thus, the total number of people = 22 + 26 = 48.

As the average of all 48 people is 35 years, sum of their ages $= 35 * 48 = 1680$

As the average of 22 men is 38 years, sum of their ages $= 38 * 22 = 836$

Thus, the sum of the ages of 26 women $= 1680 - 836 = 844$

Thus, the average age of these 26 women $= \frac{844}{26} = 32.45 \cong 32.5$

Alternate approach I:

Let the average age of the women be x years.

Thus, the total age of all the women = $26x$ years.

Also, the total age of all the men = $22 * 38 = 836$ years.

Thus, average age of all the people = $\left(\frac{836 + 26x}{48}\right)$ years.

Since the above average is given as 35 years, we have:

$\frac{836 + 26x}{48} = 35$

$=> 836 + 26x = 35 * 48$

$=> 26x = 1680 - 836$

$=> x = 32.46 =\sim 32.5$

Alternate approach II:

Here we know that the average age of 48 people = 35 years.

The average age of 22 men = 38

Let us consider the average age of the remaining 26 women = x years.

By the method of alligation:

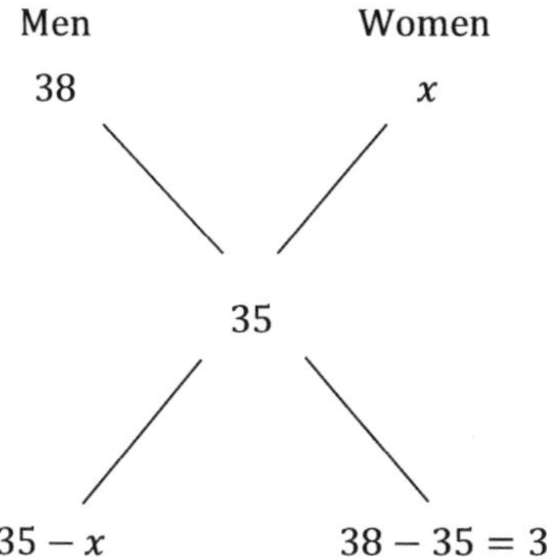

Thus, we have:

$\frac{35-x}{3}=\frac{22}{26}=\frac{11}{13}$

=> $13(35-x)= 11 * 3$

=> $455 - 13x= 33$

=> $422 = 13x$

$x= 32.46$ =~ 32.5 years.

Alternate approach III:

According to the data, we have:

Average age of 22 men is 38 years and the average age of all 48 people is 35 years.

Let us reduce the above averages by 35.

Thus, the modified data is:

Average age of 22 men is 3 years and the average age of all 48 people is 0 years.

Let, in the above situation, the average age of the 26 women be a years.

Thus, we have:

$\frac{22 * 3 + 26a}{48} = 0$

=> $66a + 26a = 0$

=> $a = -\frac{66}{26} = -\frac{33}{13}$ =~ -2.5

To get the actual average age of the women, we must add 35 (which we had subtracted initially).

Thus, the actual average age of the women = $(-2.5) + 35 = 32.5$

Although practically, above approach is not preferred one, for the sake of understanding, you must learn it.

The correct answer is option D.

69. This question is crafted to acknowledge the importance of Alternate Approach 3. While other approaches will certainly consume more time, Alternate Approach 3 would excel.

According to the data, we have:

Average age of 22 men is 69.74 years and the average age of all 48 people is 66.74 years.

Let us reduce the above averages by 66.74

Thus, the modified data is:

Average age of 22 men is 3 years and the average age of all 48 people is 0 years.

Let, in the above situation, the average age of the 26 women be a years.

Thus, we have:

$$\frac{22 * 3 + 26a}{48} = 0$$

$$=> 66a + 26a = 0$$

$$=> a = -\frac{66}{26} = -\frac{33}{13} =\sim -2.5$$

To get the actual average age of the women, we must add 66.74 (which we had subtracted initially).

Thus, the actual average age of the women = $(-2.5) + 66.74 = 64.24$

The correct answer is option C.

5.5 Ratio & Proportion

70. The expense on rent = \$250.

The total expense for 10 guests = \$650.

Thus, the variable component of the total expense for 10 guests = \$ (650 – 250) = \$400.

Thus, variable expense per guest = $\$\frac{400}{10} = \$40$.

Thus, the variable component of the total expense for 20 guests = \$ (40 ∗ 20) = \$800.

The total expense for 20 guests = \$ (250 + 800) = \$1050.

The correct answer is option C.

71. We know that the glass was filled with 10 ounces of water and spirit mixture with the components in the ratio 2 : 3 respectively.

Initial quantity of water = $\left(\frac{2}{2+3}\right) * 10 = 4$ ounces.

Initial quantity of spirit = $\left(\frac{3}{2+3}\right) * 10 = 6$ ounces.

Amount of water evaporated per day = 1% of 4 = 0.04 ounces.

Thus, total amount of water evaporated in 20 days = 0.04 ∗ 20 = 0.8 ounces.

Amount of spirit evaporated per day = 3% of 6 = 0.18 ounces.

Thus, total amount of spirit evaporated in 20 days = 0.18 ∗ 20 = 3.6 ounces.

Thus, total quantity of mixture evaporated in 20 days = 3.6 + 0.8 = 4.4 ounces.

Thus, the percent of the original amount of mixture evaporated

$= \frac{4.4}{10} * 100$

= 44%.

The correct answer is option C.

72. Fraction of total stamps that are Canadian = $\frac{4}{5} \ldots$ (i)

Thus, fraction of total stamps that are not Canadian = $1 - \frac{4}{5} = \frac{1}{5} \ldots$ (ii)

Fraction of Canadian stamps issued before 1940 = $\frac{3}{7}$

Thus, fraction of Canadian stamps issued in 1940 or later = $1 - \frac{3}{7} = \frac{4}{7} \ldots$(iii)

Thus, from (i) and (iii), we have:

Fraction of total stamps that are Canadian and issued in 1940 or later

$= \frac{4}{5} * \frac{4}{7} = \frac{16}{35}$

Thus, we have:

$\frac{16}{35}$ of the total stamps = 192

=> Total stamps = $192 * \frac{35}{16} = 12 * 35 = 420$

Thus, from (ii):

Number of stamps not Canadian = $420 * \frac{1}{5} = 84$

The correct answer is option A.

73. We know that, for a ratio $0 < \frac{x}{y} < 1$, if k is a positive number:

- $0 < \frac{x}{y} < \left(\frac{x+k}{y+k}\right) < 1$ ... (i)
- $0 < \left(\frac{x-k}{y-k}\right) < \frac{x}{y} < 1$ ... (ii)

Also, for a ratio $\frac{x}{y} > 1$, if k is a positive number:

- $1 < \left(\frac{x+k}{y+k}\right) < \frac{x}{y}$ ... (iii)
- $1 < \frac{x}{y} < \left(\frac{x-k}{y-k}\right)$ ... (iv)

In the above problem, we have:

The given ratio of ages of A and B = $\frac{7}{11}$ $(< 1) =\sim 0.63$

Thus, after 5 years, both their ages would increase by 5.

Hence, the final ratio must be greater than $\frac{7}{11}$ (from relation (i) above).

Working with the options, we have:

Option A:

$\frac{1}{3} = 0.3 < 0.63$ – Does not satisfy

Option B:

$\frac{9}{20} = 0.45 < 0.63$ – Does not satisfy

Option C:

$\frac{4}{15} = 0.26 < 0.63$ – Does not satisfy

Option D:

$\frac{3}{5} = 0.6 < 0.63$ – Does not satisfy

Option E:

$\frac{2}{3} = 0.66 > 0.63$ – Satisfies

The correct answer is option E.

74. Since the problem asks us to find a fraction value, we can assume any suitable value of the total number of stereos and the time taken to produce a basic stereo, since the initial value does not affect the final answer.

Let the total number of stereos be 3.

Thus, the number of basic stereos $= \frac{2}{3} * 3 = 2$.

Number of deluxe stereos $= 3 - 2 = 1$.

Let the time taken to produce a basic stereo = 5 hours.

Thus, the time taken to produce a deluxe stereo $= \frac{7}{5} * 5 = 7$ hours.

Thus, total time taken to produce deluxe stereos $= 1 * 7 = 7$ hours.

Total time taken to produce basic stereos $= 2 * 5 = 10$ hours.

Thus, total time taken to produce all the stereos $= 7 + 10 = 17$ hours.

Thus, the required fraction $= \frac{7}{17}$

The correct answer is option A.

75. We have:

$$\frac{\text{Number of second graders}}{\text{Number of fourth graders}} = \frac{8}{5} \ldots \text{(i)}$$

$$\frac{\text{Number of first graders}}{\text{Number of second graders}} = \frac{3}{4} \ldots \text{(ii)}$$

$$\frac{\text{Number of third graders}}{\text{Number of fourth graders}} = \frac{3}{2}\text{; taking reciprocal on both the sides:}$$

$$=> \frac{\text{Number of fourth graders}}{\text{Number of third graders}} = \frac{2}{3} \ldots \text{(iii)}$$

Thus, from the above three equations, we have:

$$\frac{\text{Number of first graders}}{\text{Number of third graders}}$$

$$= \left(\frac{\text{Number of first graders}}{\text{Number of second graders}}\right) \times \left(\frac{\text{Number of second graders}}{\text{Number of fourth graders}}\right) \times \left(\frac{\text{Number of fourth graders}}{\text{Number of third graders}}\right)$$

$$= \frac{3}{4} * \frac{8}{5} * \frac{2}{3}$$

$$= \frac{4}{5}$$

The correct answer is option D.

76. Since the question asks about a fraction value, we can choose any suitable initial value of the total number of attendees for ease of calculation, since the initial value will not affect the final answer.

Let the number of attendees = 100.

Thus, the number of male attendees $= \frac{2}{5} * 100 = 40$.

Number of female attendees = 100 – 40 = 60.

Fraction of male attendees who arrived on time $= \frac{7}{8}$

Thus, the fraction of male attendees who did not arrive on time $= \left(1 - \frac{7}{8}\right) = \frac{1}{8}$

Thus, the number of male attendees who did not arrive on time $= \frac{1}{8} * 40 = 5$.

Fraction of female attendees who arrived on time $= \frac{9}{10}$

Thus, the fraction of female attendees who did not arrive on time $= \left(1 - \frac{9}{10}\right) = \frac{1}{10}$

Thus, the number of female attendees who did not arrive on time = $\frac{1}{10} * 60 = 6$.

Thus, total number of employees who did not arrive on time = $5 + 6 = 11$.

Thus, the required fraction = $\frac{5}{11}$

The correct answer is option E.

77. Total amount to be paid = \$45.

Amount paid by Carol = \$17.

Thus, the amount paid by Ann and Judy = \$ (45 − 17) = \$28.

We know that Ann paid $\frac{2}{5}$ of what Judy paid.

Thus, ratio of the amounts paid by Ann and Judy = 2 : 5

Thus, we need to divide \$28 in the ratio 2 : 5

Thus, amount paid by Judy

$= \$\left(\frac{5}{2+5} * 28\right)$

= \$20

Thus, fraction of the total amount paid by Judy

$= \frac{20}{45}$

$= \frac{4}{9}$

The correct answer is option E.

78. Total number of trucks and cars = n.

We know that the ratio of the number of cars and the number of trucks = 1 : 4

Thus, the number of trucks

$= \left(\frac{4}{4+1}\right) * n$

$= \frac{4n}{5}$

Thus, the number of pickup trucks = $\frac{2}{3}$ of the number of trucks

$= \frac{2}{3} * \frac{4n}{5}$

$= \frac{8n}{15}$

The correct answer is option D.

79. Total weight of the wire = 20 pounds.

We know that the weight (w) of each piece is directly proportional to the square of its length (l).

Weight of the first piece (w_1) which is 36 feet long (l_1) = 16 pounds.

Thus, weight of the other piece (w_2) = 20 - 16 = 4 pounds.

Thus, we have:

$w \propto l^2$

$=> \frac{w_1}{w_2} = \frac{(l_1)^2}{(l_2)^2}$

$=> \frac{16}{4} = \frac{36^2}{(l_2)^2}$

$=> (l_2)^2 = 36^2 * \left(\frac{4}{16}\right)$

$=> (l_2)^2 = \frac{36^2}{4}$

$=> (l_2)^2 = \left(\frac{36}{2}\right)^2$

$=> (l_2)^2 = 18^2$

$=> (l_2)^2 = 18$

Thus, the length of the second piece = 18 feet.

The correct answer is option C.

80. We know that the ratio of shares of John to that of Bob = 5 : 3

Let John's and Bob's share be $\$(5x)$ and $\$(3x)$, respectively, where x is a constant of proportionality.

Thus, the total sum of money = $\$\,(5x + 3x) = \$8x$.

Since John's share exceeded $\frac{5}{9}$ of the total sum of money by \$50, we have:

$5x = \frac{5}{9}(8x) + 50$

$=> 45x = 40x + 450$

$=> x = 90$

Thus, Bob's share

$= \$ (3x) = \$ (3 * 90) = \$270.$

The correct answer is option B.

81. Let T, G and B be the total number of students, the number of girls and the number of boys, respectively

We have:

$\frac{1}{4} * G = \frac{1}{6} * T$

$= > G = \frac{4}{6} * T$

$= > G = \frac{2}{3} * T$

$=> B = \left(1 - \frac{2}{3}\right) * T$

$=> B = \frac{1}{3} * T$

$=> \frac{B}{G} = \frac{\frac{1}{3} * T}{\frac{2}{3} * T}$

$=> \frac{B}{G} = \frac{\frac{1}{3}}{\frac{2}{3}} = \frac{1}{2}$

Thus, the required ratio $= \frac{1}{2}$

The correct answer is option C.

Alternate approach

Let the number of total students be 24 (LCM of 4 and 6)

We know that

$\frac{\text{number of gilrs}}{4} = \frac{\text{Total number of students}}{6}$

$=> \frac{\text{number of gilrs}}{4} = \frac{24}{6} = 4$

=> Number of girls = 16

=> Number of boys = 24 − 16 = 8

$=> \frac{\text{Number of boys}}{\text{number of girls}} = \frac{8}{16} = \frac{1}{2}$

82. Let the number of points for the 1st question = x.

We know that each question is worth 4 points more than the preceding question.

Thus, the worth of each question in points for the 10 questions forms an arithmetic progression with the first term as x and a constant difference between consecutive terms of 4.

The nth term in arithmetic progression = $A + (n - 1) * d$; (A is the first term, and d is the constant difference between consecutive terms)

Thus, the number of points for the 10th question = $x + (10 - 1) * 4 = (x + 36)$.

Since the points for the above questions have a constant difference, the average points per question

$= \left(\frac{\text{First term} + \text{Last term}}{2}\right)$

$= \frac{x + (x + 36)}{2}$

$= (x + 18)$

Thus, the total points for all 10 questions = $10 * (x + 18)$.

Thus, we have:

$10(x + 18) = 360$

$=> x = 18$

Thus, the number of points for the 3rd question = $x + (3 - 1) * 4 = 18 + 8 = 26$.

The correct answer s option C.

83. Let the number of students in the school = x.

Thus, number of students taking a science course = $\left(40 + \frac{x}{3}\right)$.

Thus, the number of students taking physics = $\frac{1}{4}\left(40 + \frac{x}{3}\right)$.

Since $\frac{1}{8}$ of the students are taking physics, we have:

$\frac{1}{4}\left(40 + \frac{x}{3}\right) = \frac{x}{8}$

=> $40 + \frac{x}{3} = \frac{x}{2}$

=> $\frac{x}{2} - \frac{x}{3} = 40$

=> $\frac{x}{6} = 40$

=> $x = 240$

The correct answer is option A.

84. We know that $\frac{1}{3}$ of the boys and $\frac{1}{4}$ of the girls walk to school.

Also, as a fraction, $\frac{1}{3} > \frac{1}{4}$

Thus, we would have the greatest number of students who walk to school, if the number of boys was the maximum possible.

Since $\frac{1}{4}$ of the girls walk to school, the number of girls must be a multiple of 4.

Also, since $\frac{1}{3}$ of the boys walk to school, the number of boys must be a multiple of 3.

Since the number of boys must be the maximum possible, let us work with some values:

- Let the number of boys = 33 (largest number divisible by 3 but less than 36).
  Thus, the number of girls = 36 – 33 = 3 (not divisible by 4) – **Not possible**.

- Let the number of boys = 30.
  Thus, the number of girls = 36 – 30 = 6 (not divisible by 4) – **Not possible**.

- Let the number of boys = 27.
  Thus, the number of girls = 36 – 27 = 9 (not divisible by 4) – **Not possible**.

- Let the number of boys = 24.
  Thus, the number of girls = 36 – 24 = 12 (divisible by 4) – **Possible**.

Thus, to maximize the number of students who walk to school, we must have the number of boys as 24 and the number of girls as 12.

Thus, the number of boys who walk to school = $24 * \frac{1}{3} = 8$.

The number of girls who walk to school = $12 * \frac{1}{4} = 3$.

Thus, the number (maximum) of students who walk to school = 8 + 3 = 11.

Alternate approach:

Let the number of boys = x.

Thus, the number of girls = $(36 - x)$.

Thus, the number of students who walk to school

$= \frac{x}{3} + \frac{36 - x}{4}$

$= \frac{4x + 3(36 - x)}{12}$

$= \frac{x + 108}{12}$

$= \frac{x}{12} + 9$

Thus, to maximize the above value, we must have the largest possible value of x.

Also, since $\frac{x}{12}$ must be an integer, we have to choose $x = 24$ (x cannot be 36, as then there would be no girls at all).

Thus, the required maximum value = $\frac{24}{12} + 9 = 11$

The correct answer is option C.

85. Let T, G and B be the total number of students, the number of girls and the number of boys, respectively

We have:

$\frac{1}{4} * G = \frac{1}{6} * T$

$=> G = \frac{4}{6} * T$

$=> G = \frac{2}{3} * T$

$=> B = \left(1 - \frac{2}{3}\right) * T$

$=> B = \frac{1}{3} * T$

$=> \frac{B}{G} = \frac{\frac{1}{3} * T}{\frac{2}{3} * T}$

$=> \frac{B}{G} = \frac{\frac{1}{3}}{\frac{2}{3}} = \frac{1}{2}$

Thus, the required ratio $= \frac{1}{2}$

The correct answer is option C.

86. Effectively, we have 30 boxes with an average weight 18 pounds, and we need to include, say, x number of 10-pound boxes so that the average weight of the $(30 + x)$ boxes becomes 16 pounds.

Initial total weight of the 30 boxes = 30 ∗ 18 = 540 pounds.

Weight of the extra boxes to be included = $10x$ pounds.

Total weight of the $(30 + x)$ boxes = $(540 + 10x)$ pounds.

Thus, average weight of the $(30 + x)$ boxes = $\left(\frac{540 + 10x}{x + 30}\right)$ pounds.

Thus, we have:

$\left(\frac{540 + 10x}{x + 30}\right) = 16$

$=> 540 + 10x = 16x + 480$

$=> 6x = 60$

$=> x = 10$

The correct answer is option C.

87. We have 90 liters of 20% alcohol solution.

Thus, amount of alcohol = 20% of 90

$= \frac{20}{100} * 90$

= 18 liters

Let x liters of pure alcohol be added.

Thus, the final amount of alcohol = $(x + 18)$ liters.

Total volume of the solution = $(x + 90)$ liters.

Since the final concentration of alcohol is 25%, we have:

$$\frac{x + 18}{x + 90} * 100 = 25$$

$$=> \frac{x + 18}{x + 90} = \frac{25}{100} = \frac{1}{4}$$

$$=> 4x + 72 = x + 90$$

$$=> x = 6$$

Alternate approach:

Amount of water in the initial solution = (100 – 20) % of 90 = 80% of 90 = 72 liters.

Let x liters of pure alcohol be added.

Total volume of the solution = $(x + 90)$ liters.

Final concentration of water = (100 – 25) % = 75%

Since water is not added, the quantity of water remains the same, i.e. 72 liters.

Thus, we have:

$$\frac{72}{x + 90} * 100 = 75$$

$$=> \frac{72}{x + 90} = \frac{75}{100} = \frac{3}{4}$$

$$=> x + 90 = 96$$

$$=> x = 6$$

The correct answer is option D.

5.6 Speed, Time, & Distance

88. T_1 = Time required to travel 450 miles with speed $S = \frac{450}{S}$ hours

S is increased by 5 miles; so new speed = $(S + 5)$ mph

T_2 = Time required to travel 450 miles with speed $(S + 5) = \frac{450}{S + 5}$ hours

Given that the difference between T_1 and T_2 is one hour

$$=> \frac{450}{S} - \frac{450}{S + 5} = 1$$

$$=> 450\left(\frac{1}{S} - \frac{1}{S + 5}\right) = 1$$

$$=> \frac{S + 5 - S}{S\,(S + 5)} = \frac{1}{450}$$

$$=> 5 \times 450 = S^2 + 5S$$

$$=> S^2 + 5S - 2250 = 0$$

Roots of above quadratic equations are '45' and '-50'.

Since speed cannot be negative, -50 is ignored, so $S = 45$ mph.

The correct answer is option C.

89. Car traveled 6 miles less per gallon in city as compared with on highway.

Let's consider if car travels x miles per gallon on highway then car travels $(x - 6)$ miles per gallon in the city.

Capacity of the full tank of gasoline on highway = $\frac{462}{x}$ gallons

Capacity of the full tank of gasoline in the city = $\frac{336}{x - 6}$ gallons

Since the above fractions must be equal, we have:

$$\frac{462}{x} = \frac{336}{x - 6}$$

$$=> \frac{77}{x} = \frac{56}{x - 6}$$

$$=> \frac{11}{x} = \frac{8}{x - 6}$$

$$=> 11x - 66 = 8x$$

=> $3x = 66$

=> $x = 22$

As car travels $(x - 6)$ miles per gallon in the city, required answer is $22 - 6 = 16$.

The correct answer is option B.

90. Time required to travel 1 kilometer with speed 75 kilometers per hour

$= \frac{1}{75}$ hours $= \frac{1}{75} \times 60 \times 60 = \frac{240}{5} = 48$ seconds

Now new time required $= 48 + 2 = 50$ seconds $= \frac{50}{60 \times 60}$ hours.

Speed $= \frac{\text{Distance}}{\text{Time}}$

=> $\frac{\text{1 Kilometer}}{\text{50 Seconds}} = \frac{1}{\frac{50}{60 \times 60}} = \frac{3600}{50} = 72$ kilometers per hour

The correct answer is option B.

91. Speed for first 5-minutes interval= 20 miles per hour

Speed for second 5-minutes interval = 25 miles per hour

Speed for third 5-minute interval = 30 miles per hour

Distance travelled for third 5-minutes interval $= \frac{30}{60} \times 5 = \frac{5}{2}$ miles $= 2.5$ miles

The correct answer is option D.

92. Time taken for the onward journey $= \frac{400}{350} = \frac{8}{7}$ hours.

Time taken for the return journey $= \frac{400}{250} = \frac{8}{5}$ hours.

Thus, total time taken for the round trip $= \frac{8}{7} + \frac{8}{5} = \frac{96}{35}$ hours.

Total distance travelled = 2 * 400 = 800 miles.

Thus, average speed $= \frac{\text{Total distance}}{\text{Total time}} = \frac{800}{\frac{96}{35}} = 800 * \frac{35}{96} = 100 * \frac{35}{12} = 100 * 2.9 = 290$ miles/hr.

Alternate approach:

Since the distance travelled for the onward and the return journey is the same, we have:

Average speed $= \frac{2 * \text{Speed}_1 * \text{Speed}_2}{\text{Speed}_1 + \text{Speed}_2} = \frac{2 * 350 * 250}{350 + 250} = \frac{2 * 350 * 250}{600} = \frac{35 * 25}{3} = 290$ miles/hr.

The correct answer is option B.

93. Average speed of the driver over the first 20 miles is 50 miles per hour.

Thus, time taken to cover the above distance $= \frac{20}{50} = \frac{2}{5}$ hours.

Average speed of the driver over the entire 40 miles is 60 miles per hour.

Thus, time taken to cover the total distance $= \frac{40}{60} = \frac{2}{3}$ hours.

Thus, time taken by the driver to cover the last 20 miles $= \frac{2}{3} - \frac{2}{5} = \frac{4}{15}$ hours.

Thus, average speed of the driver over the last 20 miles $= \frac{20}{\frac{4}{15}} = 75$ miles per hour.

The correct answer is option D.

94. Let the hiker's speed on the first day be x miles per hour.

Thus, the hiker's speed on the second day was $(x + 1)$ miles per hour.

Let the time for which the hiker walked on the first day be t hours.

Thus, the time for which the hiker walked on the second day $= (18 - t)$ hours.

Distance covered by the hiker on the first day $= (x * t)$ miles.

Distance covered by the hiker on the second day $= ((x + 1) * (18 - t))$ miles.

Thus, total distance covered in two days $= (xt + (x + 1)(18 - t))$ miles.

Thus, we have:

$xt + (x + 1)(18 - t) = 64$

$=> xt + 18x - xt + 18 - t = 64$

$=> 18x - t = 46$

Working with the options one at a time:

- Option A:

$x = 2 => t = -10$ – Not possible, since t cannot be negative

• Option B:

$x = 3 => t = 8$ – Possible

Verifying with the other options:

• Option C:

$x = 4 => t = 26$ – Not possible, since t cannot be greater than the total time of 18 hours

Since with $x = 4$, we get a value of t greater than 18, with the options D and E, where x is even greater, the value of t would be even greater and hence would not be possible.

Thus, we have: $x = 3$

Alternate approach:

Average speed of the hiker for the two days $= \left(\frac{\text{Total distance}}{\text{Total time}}\right) = \frac{64}{18} = 3.5$ miles per hour.

If the average speed on the first day be x miles per hour, the average speed on the second day should be $(x + 1)$ miles per hour.

Thus, the average speed of 3.5 miles per hour must lie between the values of the speeds on the two days.

Thus, we have:

$x < 3.5 < x + 1$

Among the options, only $x = 3$ satisfies.

The correct answer is option B.

95. On seeing this question, one would immediately calculate the time taken to meet using the data given.

From there on, one would try to find the distance between them one hour before.

However, such calculations are not necessary.

The question simply asks us: "If two trains traveling at 30 miles per hour and 40 miles per hour need one hour to meet, how far away are they from one another".

Since both trains travel for one hour before they meet, one train travels $30 * 1 = 30$ miles and the other train travels $40 * 1 = 40$ miles.

Thus, together the trains travel $(30 + 40) = 70$ miles before they meet.

Thus, distance between the trains one hour before they meet = 70 miles.

The correct answer is option E.

96. Length of section of the highway = 8 miles.

Original speed limit = 55 miles per hour.

Thus, time taken to cover this distance = $\frac{8}{55}$ hours

New speed limit = 35 miles per hour.

Thus, time taken to cover this distance = $\frac{8}{35}$ hours

Thus, the required difference between the time durations is given = $\left(\frac{8}{35} - \frac{8}{55}\right)$ hours

$= \frac{8}{5}\left(\frac{1}{7} - \frac{1}{11}\right)$ hours

$= \left(\frac{8}{5} * \frac{4}{77}\right)$ hours

$= \frac{8}{5} * \frac{4}{77} * 60$ minutes

$=\sim 5$ minutes

The correct answer is option A.

97. We know that:

Speed of car Y = 50% more than the speed of car X

=> Speed of car Y = (100 + 50)% of the speed of car X

=> Speed of car Y = 150% of the speed of car X

$=> (\text{Speed of car Y}) = \frac{150}{100} * (\text{Speed of car X})$

$=> (\text{Speed of car Y}) = \frac{3}{2} * (\text{Speed of car X})$

$=> \frac{\text{Speed of car Y}}{\text{Speed of car X}} = \frac{3}{2}$

Since time is inversely proportional to speed for a constant distance, we have:

$$\frac{\text{Time taken by car Y to cover a distance}}{\text{Time taken by car X to cover the same distance}} = \frac{1}{\left(\frac{3}{2}\right)} = \frac{2}{3}$$

We know that car X took 2 hours to cover the distance of 80 miles.

Thus, we have:

$$\frac{\text{Time taken by car Y to cover a distance}}{2} = \frac{2}{3}$$

$=>$ Time taken by car Y to cover a distance $= 2*\frac{2}{3} = \frac{4}{3} = 1\frac{1}{3}$ hours

Alternate Approach:

Car X took 2 hours to travel 80 miles.

Thus, the average speed of car X = 40 miles per hour.

Since the average speed of car Y is 50% more than that of car X, we have:

Average speed of car Y = 40 + 50% of 40 = $40 + \frac{1}{2} * 40 = 60$ miles per hour.

Thus, time required to travel 80 miles by car Y

$= \frac{\text{Distance}}{\text{Speed}} = \frac{80}{60} = 1\frac{1}{3}$ hours

The correct answer is option C.

98. Joe's speed = 36 miles per hour.

Thus, distance covered by Joe in 60 minutes = 36 miles.

Thus, distance covered by Joe in 50 minutes $= \frac{36}{60} * 50 = 30$ miles.

This distance of 30 miles is 5 times of what Bob drives in 40 minutes.

Thus, distance covered by Bob in 40 minutes $= \frac{30}{5} = 6$ miles.

Thus, distance covered by Bob in 60 minutes $= \frac{6}{40} * 60 = 9$ miles.

Thus, Bob's speed = 9 miles per hour.

The correct answer is option B.

99. Time taken for the first train to cover the distance between the two stations P & Q = 5 hours.

Time taken for the second train to cover the distance between the two stations P & Q = 3 hours.

Since we need to find the time when the two trains pass one another, the actual length of the distance is not required.

So, we can assume a suitable value of the distance for ease of calculations.

Let the distance between the stations = least common multiple of 5 and 3 = 15 miles.

Thus, speed of the first train = $\frac{15}{5}$ = 3 miles/hour.

Speed of the second train = $\frac{15}{3}$ = 5 miles/hour.

We know that the first train started one hour earlier than when the second train started.

Thus, in 1 hour, the distance covered by the first train = 3 * 1 = 3 miles.

Thus, at 7:00 am, the distance between the two trains = (15 − 3) = 12 miles.

At 7:00 am, both trains approach one another at speeds 3 miles/hour and 5 miles/hour.

Thus, when the trains pass one another, the ratio of the distances covered by the trains would be equal to the ratio of their respective speeds = 3 : 5

Thus, distance covered by the first train = $\left(\frac{3}{3+5}\right) * 12$ = 4.5 miles.

Time taken by the first train to cover 4.5 miles = $\frac{4.5}{3}$ = 1.5 hours = 1 hour, 30 minutes.

Alternately, we can use the concept of relative speed:

Since the trains travel in opposite directions, their relative speed = (3 + 5) = 8 miles/hour.

Thus, time taken to cover 12 miles = $\frac{12}{8}$ = 1.5 hours = 1 hour, 30 minutes.

Thus, the time when the two trains pass one another = 1 hour, 30 minutes past 7:00 am

(since both trains are simultaneously moving towards each other at 7:00am) = 8:30 am.

The correct answer is option C.

5.7 Time & Work

100. Number of units of P produced per hour by the first machine = 1000.

Thus, number of units of P produced per hour by the second machine = 2000
(Since it is twice as efficient as the first machine)

Since the machine works 12 hours a day, number of units produced in a day

= 2000 * 12 = 24000

Thus, number of units produced in seven days = 24000 * 7 = 168000

The correct answer is option E.

101. According to the given data, the pump filled $\left(\frac{3}{4} - \frac{1}{3}\right) = \left(\frac{5}{12}\right)^{\text{th}}$ of the pool in $1\frac{1}{4} = \frac{5}{4}$ hours

Thus, time taken by the pump to fill the entire pool $= \frac{\left(\frac{5}{4}\right)}{\left(\frac{5}{12}\right)} = \frac{5}{4} * \frac{12}{5} = 3$ hours

Thus, the time taken by this same pump to fill a pool twice as large = $(3 * 2) = 6$ hours (since time is directly proportional to the quantity of work)

Since the other pump is thrice as efficient, time taken by the new pump to fill the larger tank = $\frac{6}{3} = 2$ hours (since time is inversely proportional to the efficiency)

The correct answer is option A.

102. Let the volume of the tank = LCM (20, 30) = 60 liters.

The first tap can fill the tank in 20 minutes.
Thus, efficiency of the first tap $= \frac{60}{20} = 3$ liters per minute.

The second tap can fill the tank in 30 minutes.
Thus, efficiency of the second tap $= \frac{60}{30} = 2$ liters per minute.

The first tap was open for the entire 15 minutes in which it filled = $15 * 3 = 45$ liters.

Thus, the remaining $(60 - 45) = 15$ liters were filled by the second tap.

Time taken for the second tap to fill 15 liters $= \frac{15}{2} = 7.5$ minutes.

Thus, of the total 15 minutes, the second tap was open for 7.5 minutes.

Thus, the first tap alone was open for $(15 - 7.5) = 7.5$ minutes.

Thus, $x = 7.5$

The correct answer is option B.

103. The emptying pipe can empty pool which is $\frac{3}{4}$ full in 9 hours.

Thus, time taken to empty the entire pool $= 9 * \frac{4}{3} = 12$ hours.

It is given that capacity of swimming pool is 5760 gallons.

Thus, the rate at which the emptying pipe removes water
$= \frac{5760}{12} = 480$ gallons per hour.

The rate at which the pool can be filled
= 12 gallons per minute

= 12 * 60 = 720 gallons per hour.

Thus, the effective filling rate when both filling and emptying occur simultaneously
= 720 - 480 = 240 gallons per hour.

Since we need to fill only half the pool, the volume required to be filled
$= \frac{5760}{2} = 2880$ gallons.

Thus, time required $= \frac{2880}{240} = 12$ hours.

The correct answer is option B.

104. Machine B produces 100 parts of product X in 40 minutes.

Since machine A produces parts twice as fast as machine B does, time taken by machine A to produce 100 parts of product X
$= \frac{40}{2} = 20$ minutes

Since each part of product Y takes $\frac{3}{2}$ times the time taken to produce each part of product X, the time taken by machine A to produce 100 parts of product Y
$= 20 * \frac{3}{2} = 30$ minutes

Thus, the number of parts of product Y produced by machine A in 30 minutes = 100.

Thus, the number of parts produced in 6 minutes

$= \frac{100}{30} * 6 = 20$

The correct answer is option D.

105. Length of fiber produced by Machine A in 1 hour $= \frac{500}{2}$ feet.

Length of fiber produced by Machine B in 1 hour $= \frac{500}{3}$ feet.

Length of fiber produced by Machine C in 1 hour $= \frac{500}{6}$ feet.

Thus, if all three machines work together, total length of fiber produced in 1 hour

$= \frac{500}{2} + \frac{500}{3} + \frac{500}{6}$

$= 500\left(\frac{1}{2} + \frac{1}{3} + \frac{1}{6}\right)$

$= 500$ feet

Thus, time taken to produce 1000 feet $= \frac{1000}{500} = 2$ hours.

The correct answer is option C.

106. Cost of food consumed by 4 adults in 3 days = \$60

=> Cost of food consumed by 1 adult in 3 days $= \$\left(\frac{60}{4}\right) = \$15$

=> Cost of food consumed by 1 adult in 1 day $= \$\left(\frac{15}{3}\right) = \$5$

We know that one child consumes half the amount of food consumed by an adult in the same time.

Thus, 3 children consume food equivalent to $\frac{3}{2}$ adults in the same time.

Thus, 6 adults and 3 children are equivalent to $\left(6 + \frac{3}{2}\right) = \frac{15}{2}$ adults.

Thus, cost of food consumed by $\frac{15}{2}$ adults in 1 day $= \$\left(5 * \frac{15}{2}\right) = \$\left(\frac{75}{2}\right)$

=> Cost of food consumed by $\frac{15}{2}$ adults in 4 days $= \$\left(\frac{75}{2} * 4\right) = \$150$

The correct answer is option B.

107. Let the time taken by Mark and Kate working together = x hours

Thus, time taken by Mark, working alone = $(x + 12)$ hours

Time taken by Kate, working alone = $(x + 27)$ hours

Let us assume the total work to be 1 unit.

Part of work done by Mark and Kate, working together, in 1 hour = $\left(\frac{1}{x}\right)$

Part of work done by Mark in 1 hour = $\left(\frac{1}{x + 12}\right)$

Part of work done by Kate in 1 hour = $\left(\frac{1}{x + 27}\right)$

Thus, we have:

$$\frac{1}{x} = \frac{1}{x + 12} + \frac{1}{x + 27}$$

$$=> \frac{1}{x} = \frac{(x + 27) + (x + 12)}{(x + 12)(x + 27)}$$

$$=> (x + 12)(x + 27) = x(2x + 39)$$

$$=> x^2 + 39x + 324 = 2x^2 + 39x$$

$$=> x^2 = 324$$

Since x is positive, we have:

$$x = \sqrt{324} = 18$$

Alternate approach:

Work done by Mark and Kate in x hours = Work done by Mark in $(x + 12)$ hours

Cancelling work done by Mark in x hours from both sides:

Work done by Kate in x hours = Work done by Mark in 12 hours

=> Work done by Kate in 1 hour = Work done by Mark in $\left(\frac{12}{x}\right)$ hours . . . (i)

Again, we have:

Work done by Mark and Kate in x hours = Work done by Kate in $(x + 27)$ hours

Cancelling work done by Kate in x hours from both sides:

Work done by Mark in x hours = Work done by Kate in 27 hours

=> Work done by Kate in 27 hours = Work done by Mark in x hours

=> Work done by Kate in 1 hour = Work done by Mark in $\left(\frac{x}{27}\right)$ hours . . . (ii)

Thus, from (i) and (ii), we have:

$$\frac{12}{x} = \frac{x}{27}$$

=> $x^2 = 324$

=> $x = 18$

The correct answer is option C.

5.8 Computational

108. Amount of liquid leaked out in x hours = k liters.

Thus, the amount of liquid leaked out in 1 hour = $\frac{k}{x}$ liters.

Thus, the amount of liquid leaked out in y hours = $\frac{ky}{x}$ liters.

Cost of 1 liter of the liquid = \$6.

Thus, cost of the liquid leaked out in y hours = \$ $\left(6 * \frac{ky}{x}\right)$ = \$ $\left(\frac{6ky}{x}\right)$.

The correct answer is option D.

109. We know that: Measurements on the R-scale of 6 and 24 correspond to measurements on the S-scale of 30 and 60, respectively.

$60 - 30 = 30$ divisions of the S-scale equals $24 - 6 = 18$ divisions of the R-scale

Thus, 1 division of the S-scale equals $\frac{18}{30} = \frac{3}{5}$ divisions of the R-scale.

A measurement of 100 on the S-scale corresponds to $100 - 60 = 40$ divisions above the measurement of 60.

Now, 40 divisions of the S-scale equals $\frac{3}{5} * 40 = 24$ divisions of the R-scale.

Thus, the corresponding measure on the R-scale is 24 divisions above the measurement of 24 (since 60 on the S-scale corresponds to 24 on the R-scale) = $24 + 24 = 48$.

The correct answer is option C.

110. The cost of three hamburgers = \$ $(0.96 * 3)$ = \$2.88

The cost of two milk shakes = \$ $(1.28 * 2)$ = \$2.56

Thus, total cost = \$$(2.88 + 2.56)$ = \$5.44

Thus, Jack has half the above amount = \$ $\left(\frac{5.44}{2}\right)$ = \$2.72

The correct answer is option C.

111. Total increase in population = $378 - 300 = 18$ million

Increase in population per month = 30,000

Thus, increase in population per year = 30,000 * 12 = 360,000 = 0.36 million

Thus, number of years required for the increase = $\frac{18}{0.36}$ = 50 years

Thus, the population would be 378 million in the year $(2012 + 50) = 2,062$

The correct answer is option C.

112. The restaurant uses $\frac{1}{2}$ cup fruit in each serving of its fruit compote.

Since each can has $3\frac{1}{2} = \frac{7}{2}$ cups of fruit, number of servings of fruit compote possible using one can = $\frac{\left(\frac{7}{2}\right)}{\left(\frac{1}{2}\right)} = 7$

Thus, number of cans required for 60 servings of the fruit compote = $\frac{60}{7} = \sim 8.5$

However, the number of cans must be an integer.

Thus, the minimum number of cans required is 9.

The correct answer is option C.

113. We need to minimize the total number of coins such that each pocket has at least 1 coin.

We know that at most 3 pockets can have the same number of coins.

Thus, the number of pockets having the same number of coins may be 2 or 3.

Since we need to minimize the total number of coins, we must have as many pockets having the same number (minimum possible number, i.e. 1 coin) of coins as possible.

Thus, for each of the three pockets containing an equal number of coins, we have 1 coin.

Thus, number of coins in the 3 pockets = 1 * 3 = 3.

Since each of the remaining 4 pockets have a different number of coins, let us use 2, 3, 4 and 5 coins for those pockets.

Thus, the total number of coins = 3 + 2 + 3 + 4 + 5 = 17.

The correct answer is option C.

114. Distance covered by the glacier in 25 days

$= \frac{1}{4}$ mile

$= \frac{1}{4} * 5280$ feet $= 1320$ feet.

Number of hours present in 25 days = $(25 * 24)$ hours.

Thus, time taken by the glacier (in hours) to cover 1 foot

$= \frac{25 * 24}{1320}$

$= \frac{5 * 5 * 24}{11 * 5 * 24}$

$= \frac{5}{11}$

The correct answer is option C.

115. Width of the carpeting = 10 feet.

Rate at which the carpeting moves through the dryer

= 2160 feet per hour

$= \frac{2160}{60 * 60}$ feet per second

= 0.6 feet per second

Thus, area of carpeting that moves through the dryer per second

= 0.6 * 10 square feet

= 6 square feet

Thus, time taken to move 6 square feet of carpeting through the dryer = 1 second.

Thus, time taken to move 1 square feet of carpeting through the dryer = $\frac{1}{6}$ seconds.

The correct answer is option A.

116. We know that for a salary grade s, the hourly wage p, in dollars, is given by:

$p = 950 + 0.25(s - 1)$

Thus, for a salary grade $s = 1$, the corresponding hourly wage p

= \$ (950 + 0.25 (1 − 1))

= \$950

Again, for a salary grade $s = 5$, the corresponding hourly wage p

= \$ (950 + 0.25 (5 − 1))

= \$(950 + 1)

= \$951

Thus, the required difference = \$ (951 − 950) = \$1.

The correct answer is option B.

117. Considering the radios sold:

We know that the price of a particular radio was the 15th highest price as well as the 20th lowest price among the prices of the radios sold.

Thus, the number of radios sold at a price greater than the price of the particular radio = 15 - 1 = 14

Also, the number of radios sold at a price lower than the price of the particular radio = 20 - 1 = 19

Thus, total number of radios sold = 14 + 19 + 1 (including that particular radio) = 34

Considering all the items sold:

We know that the price of a particular DVD player was the 29th highest price as well as the 37th lowest price among the prices of all the items sold.

Thus, the number of items sold at a price greater than the price of the particular item (i.e. DVD player) = 29 - 1 = 28

Also, the number of items sold at a price lower than the price of the particular item (i.e. DVD player) = 37 - 1 = 36.

Thus, total number of items sold = 28 + 36 + 1 (including that particular radio)

= 65

Thus, the number of DVD players sold = 65 - 34 = 31

The correct answer is option C.

118. Royalty received on the first 100,000 copies at the rate of \$0.80 per copy = $\$ (0.80 * 100,000) = \$80,000$

Total royalty received is given as \$260,000.

Thus, royalty received on the additional copies (above 100,000) at \$0.60 per copy $= \$(260,000 - 80,000) = \$180,000$

Thus, number of additional copies sold $= \dfrac{180,000}{0.60}$

$= 300,000$

Thus, total copies sold = Initial 100,000 copies + Additional 300,000 copies

= 400,000 copies

The correct answer is option D.

119. The loss would be minimum if fewer number of \$50 checks were lost as compared to \$10 checks.

Thus, the traveler should have cashed a greater number of \$50 checks than \$10 checks.

We know that the number of \$10 checks cashed was one more or one less than the number of \$50 checks cashed.

Thus, from the above reasoning, we can conclude that the number of \$10 checks was one less than the number of \$50 checks.

Since the total number of checks cashed was 7, from the above information, we have:

Number of \$50 checks cashed = 4
Number of \$10 checks cashed = 3

Alternately:

Let the number of \$10 checks cashed = x

Thus, the number of \$50 checks cashed = $(x + 1)$

Since the total number of checks cashed is 7, we have:

$x + (x + 1) = 7$

$=> x = 3$

Thus, the total value of \$10 checks cashed = $\$ (3 * 10) = \$30$.

The total value of \$50 checks cashed = \$ $(4 * 50)$ = \$200.

Thus, the total value of all the checks cashed = \$ $(30 + 200)$ = \$230.

We know that the total value of all the checks with him was \$1500.

Thus, the total value of all the checks lost = \$ $(1500 - 230)$ = \$1270.

The correct answer is option D.

5.9 Interest

120. Amount after three years = \$1200
Amount after five years = \$1500

Thus, interest accumulated in two years = \$ (1500 – 1200) = \$300

Thus, interest accumulated per year = \$ $\left(\frac{300}{2}\right)$ = \$150 (since under simple interest, interest accumulated every year is constant)

Thus, interest accumulated in the first three years = \$ (150 ∗ 3) = \$450

Thus, principal amount invested = \$ (1200 – 450) = \$750

Thus, on \$750 invested, interest accumulated is \$150 every year.

Thus, rate of interest = $\frac{150}{750} * 100 = 20\%$

The correct answer is option C.

121. Simple interest accumulated after two years = \$180

Thus, simple interest every year = \$ $\left(\frac{180}{2}\right)$ = \$90 (since under simple interest, interest accumulated every year is constant)

Thus, compound interest accumulated after the first year = \$90 (equal to the simple interest accumulated after one year)

Thus, compound interest accumulated in the second year = \$ (90 + 18) = \$108 (since the total compound interest accumulated in two years is \$18 more than that under simple interest)

The higher interest in the second year is due to the additional interest on the interest accumulated after one year.

Thus, we can say that interest on \$90 in one year = \$18

Thus rate of interest = $\frac{18}{90} * 100 = 20\%$

The correct answer is option D.

122. Let the sum borrowed at 4% and 5% rate of interest be \$$x$ each.

Let the time after which he repays the second sum be t years.

Thus, the time after which he repays the first sum is $\left(t - \frac{1}{2}\right)$ years.

Since the amount to be repaid in either case is the same, the interest accumulated is also equal.

Simple Interest $= \left(\frac{PRT}{100}\right)$, where P =Principal, R = Rate of Interest, and T = Time Interval

Hence, we have:

$$\frac{4 * x * \left(t - \frac{1}{2}\right)}{100} = \frac{5 * x * t}{100}$$

$$=> 4\left(t - \frac{1}{2}\right) = 5t$$

$$=> t = 2$$

Since the amount to be repaid is $1100, we have:

Principal amount + Interest accumulated in two years = 1100

$$=> x + \frac{5 * x * 2}{100} = 1100$$

$$=> \frac{11x}{10} = 1100$$

$$=> x = 1000$$

Thus, the total sum borrowed = $x + x = 2x$ = $2000.

The correct answer is option D.

123. Total amount invested = $\$10,000$.

Let $\$x$ be invested at 6% and $\$(10000 - x)$ be invested at 8%

Thus, at the end of 1 year, interest on $\$x$

$$= \$\frac{(x * 6 * 1)}{100} = \$\left(\frac{6x}{100}\right)$$

Also, at the end of 1 year, interest on $\$(10000 - x)$

$$= \$\frac{((10000 - x) * 8 * 1)}{100} = \$\left(\frac{8\,(10000 - x)}{100}\right)$$

Since the total interest is $720, we have:

$$\frac{6x}{100} + \frac{8\,(10000 - x)}{100} = 720$$

$$=> 80000 - 2x = 72000$$

=> $x = 4000$

=> $10000 - x = 6000$

Thus, the fraction of the total invested at the higher rate i.e. 8% $= \frac{6000}{10000} = \frac{3}{5}$

The correct answer is option D.

Alternate approach:

We can use the method of alligation:

Let the amounts invested at 6% and 8% be \$$x$ and \$$y$, respectively.

The total interest on \$10000 is \$720.

Thus, the effective rate of interest as a whole $= \frac{720}{10000} * 100 = 7.2\%$.

Thus, we have:

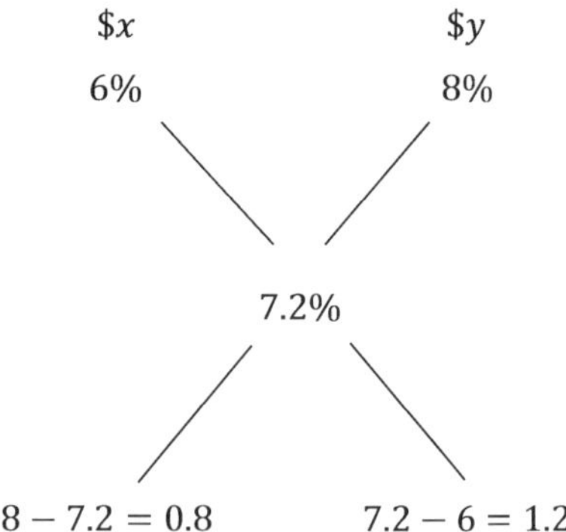

Hence, we have:

$\frac{x}{y} = \frac{0.8}{1.2} = \frac{2}{3}$

Hence, the required fraction = $\frac{3}{2+3} = \frac{3}{5}$

124. Number of bank customers in 2005 = 45% of 60 = $\frac{45}{100} * 60 = 27$

Number of bank customers in 2007 = 25% of 144 = $\frac{25}{100} * 144 = 36$

Thus, increase in the number of bank customers = 36 - 27 = 9

Let the simple annual percent growth rate in the number of bank customers be r%.

Thus, in two years (2005 to 2007), increase in the number of bank customers at r% rate

$= \left(\frac{27 * r * 2}{100}\right)$

(The value is calculated on 27 since 27 is the value in the former year)

Thus, we have:

$\frac{27 * r * 2}{100} = 9$

$=> r = \frac{9 * 100}{2 * 27} = 16.6\%$

The correct answer is option B.

125. Number of ways of selecting 2 apples from 5 apples = $C_2^5 = \frac{5!}{2!\,(5-2)!} = 10$

Number of ways of selecting 2 apples from 4 (Un-spoiled) apples = $C_2^4 = \frac{4!}{2!\,(4-2)!} = 6$

So number of ways of selecting 2 apples from 5 apples such that at least one of them is spoiled

= [Number of ways of selecting 2 apples from 5 apples] – [Number of ways of selecting 2 apples from 4 (non-spoiled) apples]

= 10 – 6 = 4

So required probability $= \frac{\text{Desired outcomes}}{\text{Total outcomes}} = \frac{4}{10} = \frac{2}{5}$

The correct answer is option D.

126. Population at the start of the experiment = x

Increase in population at the end of the 1st month = $2x$

Thus here we can say that, rate of increase $= \left(\frac{2x}{x}\right) * 100 = 200\%$

This 200% increase remains same for each of the next 4 months.

Thus, applying the concept of compounding, we have:

$$x\left(1 + \frac{200}{100}\right)^5 > 1000$$

$$=> x > \frac{1000}{(3)^5}$$

$$=> x > \frac{1000}{243}$$

$$=> x > \left[\frac{1000}{\sim 250} =\sim 4\right]$$

Since we 250 > 243, thus $\frac{1000}{243} > 4 => x > 4$

Since x must be an integer value (it represents the number of organisms), the minimum possible value of $x = 5$.

Alternate approach:

Population at the start of the experiment = x.

Increase in population at the end of the 1st month = $2x$.

Thus, population size at the end of the 1st month = $x + 2x = 3x$.

Increase in population after the 2nd month = $2 * 3x = 6x$.

Thus, population size at the end of the 2nd month = $3x + 6x = 9x$.

Thus, we observe that the population size triples after every month.

Thus, the population size at the end of the 5th month

= 3 * (The population size at the end of the 4th month)

= 3 * 3 * (The population size at the end of the 3rd month)

= 3 * 3 * 3 * (The population size at the end of the 2nd month) = $3^3 * 9x$

= $243x$

Thus, we have:

$243x > 1000$

$=> x > \frac{1000}{243}$

$=> x > 4.1$

Since x must be an integer value (it represents the number of organisms), the minimum possible value of $x = 5$.

The correct answer is option D.

127. The value of the watch increases by $c\%$ every year

The value of the watch on January 1, 1992 = $\$k$

Thus, the value of the watch on January 1, 1994 (i.e. after 2 years) = $\$\left(k * \left(1 + \frac{c}{100}\right)^2\right)$

Since the value of the watch on January 1, 1994 was $\$m$, we have: $k * \left(1 + \frac{c}{100}\right)^2 = m$

$=> \left(1 + \frac{c}{100}\right)^2 = \frac{m}{k}$

$=> \left(1 + \frac{c}{100}\right) = \sqrt{\frac{m}{k}} \ldots \text{(i)}$

Thus, the value of the watch on January 1, 1995 (= $c\%$ higher than that on January 1, 1994)

$= \$\,((100 + c)\%\text{ of } m)$

$= \$\left(\left(\frac{100 + c}{100}\right) * m\right)$

$= \$\left(\left(1 + \frac{c}{100}\right) * m\right)$

Substituting the value of $\left(1 + \frac{c}{100}\right)$ from (i):

$= \$\left(\sqrt{\frac{m}{k}} * m\right)$

$= \$\left(\frac{m\sqrt{m}}{\sqrt{k}}\right)$

The correct answer is option C.

Alternate Approach:

Dealing with three variable, c, k, & m can be taxing; however this questions can be solved through an alternate approach by assuming few smart numbers for the variables.

Say, $c = 10\%$ & $k = \$100$

Thus, the value of the watch on January 1, 1994 (i.e. after 2 years) $= m = \$\left(100\left(1 + \frac{10}{100}\right)^2\right) = 121$.

So the value of the watch on January 1, 1995 $= 121 * (1 + 10\%) = \$133.1$;

So we have the following values for the variables, $c = 10\%$, $k = 100$, & $m = 121$.

By plugging in above values in options, you will find that only option C matches the desired value, \$133.1.

Let us cross check this.

$=> \frac{m\sqrt{m}}{\sqrt{k}} = 121 * \frac{\sqrt{121}}{\sqrt{100}} = \frac{121 * 11}{10} = 133.1$

128. The first $\$x$ deposited in the account earned interest for 2 years while the additional $\$x$ earned interest for only 1 year.

The amount A under compound interest on a sum of money (P) invested at $(r\%)$ rate of interest for (t) years is given by:

$A = P\left(1 + \frac{r}{100}\right)^t$

Thus, the final value after 2 years of the first $\$x$ deposited

$= \$x\left(1 + \frac{8}{100}\right)^2$

$= \$(x * 1.08^2)$

The final value after 1 year of the additional $\$x$ deposited

$= \$x\left(1 + \frac{8}{100}\right)^1$

$= \$1.08x$

Thus, total value of the money present in the account (w)

$= \$\left\{\left(x * 1.08^2\right) + (x * 1.08)\right\}$

$= \$\left(x\left(1.08^2 + 1.08\right)\right)$

Thus, we have:

$w = x\left(1.08^2 + 1.08\right)$

$=> x = \dfrac{w}{\left(1.08^2 + 1.08\right)}$

The correct answer is option D.

129. We need to understand that the interest in the 2nd year and 3rd year is **not** the total interest accumulated in two years and three years respectively.

Thus, we **cannot** use the formula for the interest after t years on a sum of money P at $r\%$ interest $= \left\{P\left(1 + \dfrac{r}{100}\right)^t - P\right\}$

Let us understand the concept of the interest in the nth year with an example:

Let \$100 be invested at 10% rate of interest.

Interest accumulated after one year (or in the **first year**)

$= \$\,(10\% \text{ of } 100) = \$10$

Thus, amount after one year $= \$\,(100 + 10) = \$110$

Thus, interest in the **second year**

$= \$\,(10\% \text{ of } 110) = \$11$ (= 110% of interest in the first year)

Thus, total interest accumulated in two years

= (Interest in the first year + Interest in the second year)

$= \$\,(10 + 11) = \$21$

Thus, amount after two years $= \$\,(100 + 21) = \$121$

Thus, interest in the **third year**

\$ (10% of 121) = \$12.10 (= 110% of interest in the second year)

If we observe the values of the interest in the 1st, 2nd and 3rd years, we observe that:

The interest in the nth year = $(100 + r)$% of (The interest in the $(n-1)^{\text{th}}$ year)

Using the above relation in our problem:

Interest in the 2nd year = \$600

Interest in the 3rd year = \$720

Thus, we have:

$720 = (100 + r)\,\%$ of 600

$=> 720 = \left(\frac{100 + r}{100}\right) * 600$

$=> r = 20$

The correct answer is option D.

5.10 Functions

130. We have:

$f(x) = x^2 + \frac{1}{x^2}$

$=> f\left(-\frac{1}{\sqrt{x}}\right) = \left(-\frac{1}{\sqrt{x}}\right)^2 + \frac{1}{\left(-\frac{1}{\sqrt{x}}\right)^2}$

$= \frac{1}{x} + x$

$=> \left(f\left(-\frac{1}{\sqrt{x}}\right)\right)^2 = \left(\frac{1}{x} + x\right)^2$

$= \frac{1}{x^2} + x^2 + 2 * \frac{1}{x} * x$

$= x^2 + \frac{1}{x^2} + 2 = f(x) + 2$

The correct answer is option E.

131. $f(x) = -\frac{1}{x}$

$=> f(a) = -\frac{1}{a} = -\frac{1}{2}$

$=> a = 2$

Also, we have:

$f(ab) = -\frac{1}{ab} = \frac{1}{6}$

$=> ab = -6$

$=> b = -\frac{6}{a} = -\frac{6}{2}$

$=> b = -3$

The correct answer is option D.

132. $f(x) = \sqrt{x} - 10$

$=> f(t) = \sqrt{t} - 10$

Since $u = f(t)$, we have:

$u = \sqrt{t} - 10$

$=> \sqrt{t} = u + 10$

Squaring both sides, we have:

$=> t = (u + 10)^2$

The correct answer is option D.

133. Let p, q and r be the hundreds', tens and unit digits of m, respectively and a, b and c be the hundreds', tens and unit digits of v, respectively.

Thus, we have:

$f(m) = 2^p 3^q 5^r$

$f(v) = 2^a 3^b 5^c$

Since $f(m) = 9f(v)$, we have:

$2^p 3^q 5^r = 9 * 2^a 3^b 5^c$

$=> 2^p 3^q 5^r = 2^a 3^{b+2} 5^c$

Since p, q, r, a, b, c are integers, comparing coefficients of 2, 3 and 5:

$p = a, q = b + 2$ and $r = c$

Thus, we have:

The three-digit number $v \equiv abc$, where a is the digit in the hundreds' place, b is the digit in the tens place and c is the digit in the tens place

$=> v = 100a + 10b + c$

The three-digit number $m \equiv pqr \equiv a(b+2)c$, where a is the digit in the hundreds' place, $(b + 2)$ is the digit in the tens place and c is the digit in the tens place

$=> m = 100a + 10(b + 2) + c$

$=> m = (100a + 10b + c) + 20$

$=> m = v + 20$

$=> m - v = 20$

The correct answer is option D.

134. Working with the options one at a time:

Option A:

$f(x) = 1 - x$

$=> f(1 - x) = 1 - (1 - x) = x \neq f(x)$ - Incorrect

Option B:

$f(x) = 1 - x^2$

$=> f(1 - x) = 1 - (1 - x)^2 = 1 - (1 - 2x + x^2) = 2x - x^2 \neq f(x)$ - Incorrect

Option C:

$f(x) = x^2 - (1 - x)^2$

$=> f(1 - x) = (1 - x)^2 - (1 - (1 - x))^2 = (1 - x)^2 - x^2 \neq f(x)$ - Incorrect

Option D:

$f(x) = x^2(1 - x)^2$

$=> f(1 - x) = (1 - x)^2(1 - (1 - x))^2 = (1 - x)^2 x^2 = f(x)$ - Correct

Since we already have the answer, we need not check option E.

Verifying option E, we would have had:

$$f(x) = \frac{x}{1 - x}$$

$$=> f(1 - x) = \frac{1 - x}{1 - (1 - x)} = \frac{1 - x}{x} \neq f(x)$$

The correct answer is option D.

135. $f(x) = \dfrac{1}{x}$

$$g(x) = \frac{x}{x^2 + 1}$$

$$=> f(g(x)) = \frac{1}{g(x)} = \frac{1}{\left(\frac{x}{x^2 + 1}\right)}$$

$$= \frac{x^2 + 1}{x}$$

$$= \frac{(x - 1)^2 + 2x}{x}$$

$$= \frac{(x - 1)^2}{x} + 2$$

Since $x > 0$, the minimum value of the above expression will occur when the square term becomes zero (since a square term is always non-negative, the minimum possible value occurs when it is zero).

$=> (x - 1)^2 = 0 => x = 1$

Thus, the minimum value of $f(g(x)) = 0 + 2 = 2$

The correct answer is option E.

136. $P(r) = \frac{8r}{1 - r}$

$=> P(3) = \frac{8 * 3}{1 - 3} = -12$

Thus, we have:

$P(r) = \frac{1}{2} * (-12)$

$=> \frac{8r}{1 - r} = -6$

$=> 8r = -6 + 6r$

$=> r = -3$

The correct answer is option D.

137. We have:
$3f(x) + 2f(-x) = 5x - 10 \ldots$ (i)

Substituting $x = 1$ in equation (i):

$3f(1) + 2f(-1) = 5 - 10$

$=> 3f(1) + 2f(-1) = -5 \ldots$ (ii)

Substituting $x = -1$ in equation (i):

$3f(-1) + 2f(1) = -5 - 10$

$=> 3f(-1) + 2f(1) = -15 \ldots$ (iii)

Equation (ii) * 3 – Equation (iii) * 2:

$5f(1) = -15 - (-30) = 15$

$=> f(1) = 3$

The correct answer is option D.

5.11 Permutation & Combination & Probability

138. Since $C_3^5 = C_x^5$, $x = 3$, but it is given that $x \neq 3$.

We know that $C_n^m = C_{m-n}^m$

$=> C_3^5 = C_x^5 = C_{5-x}^5$

$=> 3 = 5 - x$

$=> x = 2$

The correct answer is option C.

139. This is a question on permutation with undistinguishable objects.

We know that if there are n objects, out of which p objects are undistinguishable, then

Total number of way of arranging them = $\frac{n!}{p!}$

In this question, let's first assume that we use two BLUE and one YELLOW dot, thus,

Total number of way of arranging them = $\frac{3!}{2!} = 3$.

Similarly, let's first assume that we use two YELLOW and one BLUE dot, thus,

Total number of way of arranging them = $\frac{3!}{2!} = 3$.

There can be two more cases where we use all three BLUE or all three YELLOW. (Note: the question does not say that both colors must be used)

Total number of codes = 3 + 3 +2 = 8.

The codes would be: YYB, YBY,YBB, BBY, BYB, BYY, BBB, & YYY.

The correct answer is option D.

140. There are two different sizes and four different colors of notepads.

Packages having the same size and same color of notepads:

Number of ways in which the size can be chosen = $C_1^2 = \frac{2!}{(2-1)! * 1!} = 2$ ways.

Number of ways in which the color can be chosen = $C_1^4 = \frac{4!}{(4-1)! * 1!} = 4$ ways.

Thus, total number of such packages = 2 * 4 = 8.

Packages having the same size and different colors of notepads:

Number of ways in which the size can be chosen = $C_1^2 = \frac{2!}{(2-1)! * 1!} = 2$ ways.

Number of ways in which the three different colors can be chosen = $C_3^4 = \frac{4!}{(4-3)! * 3!} = 4$ ways.

Thus, total number of such packages = 2 * 4 = 8.

Thus, total number of different packages = 8 + 8 = 16.

The correct answer is option C.

141. We know that there are six kinds of cheese and two kinds of fruits for dessert.

Since there are equal number of kinds of cheese and an equal number of kinds of fruit, we have the following two possibilities:

(1) If there is one kind of cheese and one kind of fruit:

Number of ways of selecting one kind of cheese = $C_1^6 = 6$.
Number of ways of selecting one kind of fruit = $C_1^2 = 2$.

Thus, number of desert platters possible = 6 * 2 = 12.

(2) If there are two kinds of cheese and two kinds of fruits:

Number of ways of selecting two kinds of cheese = $C_2^6 = \frac{6!}{4!2!} = 15$.
Number of ways of selecting two kinds of fruits = $C_2^2 = 1$.

Thus, number of desert platters possible = 15 * 1 = 15.

Thus, total possibilities = 12 + 15 = 27.

The correct answer is option E.

142. Using one-letter code, we can uniquely designate 26 stocks (since there are a total of 26 letters).

Using two-letter codes:

The first position can be assigned in 26 ways.

The second position can be assigned again in 26 ways (since the letters may be repeated).

Thus, total two-letter codes possible = 26 * 26 = 676.

Thus, using two-letter codes, we can uniquely designate 676 stocks.

Using three-letter codes:

Each of the three positions can be assigned in 26 ways.

Thus, total three-letter codes possible = 26 * 26 * 26 = 17576.

Thus, using three-letter codes, we can uniquely designate 17576 stocks.

Thus, total number of unique designations possible using one, two or three-letter codes = 26 + 676 + 17576 = 18278.

Alternate approach:

Using one-letter codes: 26 ≡ unit digit is 6.

Using two-letter codes: 26 * 26 ≡ unit digit is 6.

Using three-letter codes: 26 *26 * 26 ≡ unit digit is 6.

Thus, the unit digit of the sum = 6 + 6 + 6 ≡ 8.

Only option E has the unit digit as 8.

Note: This method is not to be used when two or more options are with same unit digit.

The correct answer is option E.

143. We know that no candidate is eligible for a position in both departments.

Here events "Selection of a candidate in Mathematics department" and "Selection of two candidates in Computer Science department" are mutually exclusive or disjoint events.

Number of ways of selecting one candidate from seven candidates = $C_1^7 = 7$

Number of ways of selecting two candidates from ten candidates = $C_2^{10} = \frac{10 * 9}{2 * 1} = 45$.

Thus, total number of ways of filling up the three positions = 7 * 45 = 315.

The correct answer is option E.

144. We need to form a three-digit code using the digits 2, 3, 4, 5, 6, 7, 8, and 9 i.e. 8 possible digits.

Also, it is known that repetition of digits is not allowed.

The hundreds' position of the code can be filled using any of the 8 digits in 8 ways.

The tens position of the code can be filled using any of the remaining 7 digits in 7 ways.

The tens position of the code can be filled using any of the remaining 6 digits in 6 ways.

Thus, the number of distinct codes possible = 8 * 7 * 6 = 336.

Since there are 330 employees, number of unassigned codes = 336 – 330 = 6.

The correct answer is option A.

145. We need to form a four-digit code using the digits 0, 1, 2, 3, 4, 5, 6, 7, 8, and 9 i.e. 10 possible digits.

Also, it is known that repetition of digits is allowed, the code has to be an odd number, and the thousands' position of the code can't be 0.

The thousands' position of the code can be filled using any of the 9 digits (except 0) in 9 ways.

The hundreds' position of the code can be filled using any of the 10 digits (since 0 can now be used and repetition is allowed) in 10 ways.

The tens position of the code can be filled using any of the 10 digits (since 0 can now be used and repetition is allowed) in 10 ways.

The tens position of the code can be filled using any of the 5 odd digits 1, 3, 5, 7, or 9 in 5 ways.

Thus, the number of distinct codes possible = 9 * 10 * 10 * 5 = 4500.

The correct answer is option D.

146. Number of ways of selecting four sites out of six

= (Number of ways in which any four of the six sites are selected without consideration to any constraint) – (Number of ways in which sites both A and B are selected)

Number of ways in which any four of the six sites may be selected without paying consideration to any constraint $= C_4^6$

$= C_{(6-4)}^6 = C_2^6 = \frac{6 * 5}{2 * 1}$

= 15

Number of ways in which four of the six sites may be selected so that both the sites A and B are selected (i.e. two more sites to be selected from the remaining four) $= C_{(4-2)}^{(6-2)}$

$= C_2^4 = \frac{4 * 3}{2 * 1}$

= 6; The above 6 ways do not satisfy the condition given

Thus, the number of ways in which four of the six sites can be selected so that both A and B are not selected simultaneously= $15 - 6 = 9$

The correct answer is option D.

147. In this question, we need to logically decide the positions of the men and manually count the number of possible arrangements.

Randomly checking possible combinations would take a lot of time, so a proper logical approach is necessary.

Let us number the six men using the numbers 1 to 6 in ascending order of height, where 1 represents the shortest man and 6 represents the tallest man.

The positions of the six seats are shown below:

1		
		6

We know that:

(1) The heights of the men within each row must increase from left to right.

(2) Each man in the second row must be taller than the man standing in front of him.

Thus, the top left seat must be occupied by '1' and the bottom right seat must be occupied by '6'.

The bottom left seat may be occupied by '2', '3', or '4'.

Note: '5' cannot be seated in that seat since there would be no one to fill the bottom middle seat (since height increases from left to right).

Similarly, the top right seat may be occupied by '3', '4'or '5'.

Note: '2' cannot be seated in that seat since there would be no one to fill the top middle seat (since height increases from left to right).

Based on this, we list down the possible cases as shown below:

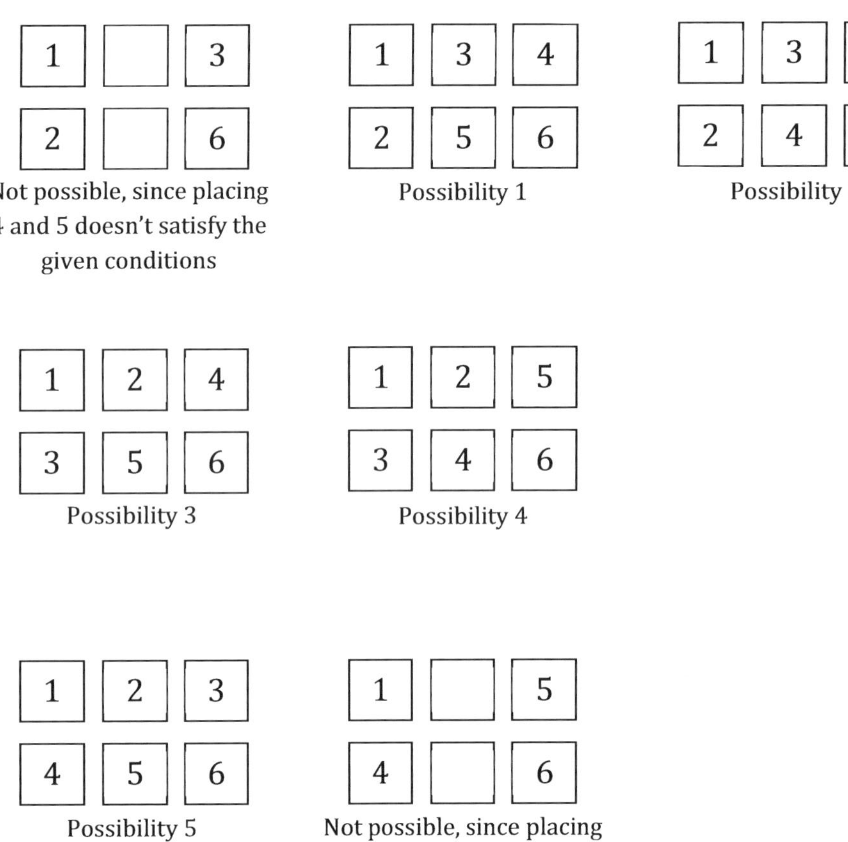

Thus, there are 5 possible ways.

Though this appears to be a straightforward permutation and combination question, it is not so because of the constraints involved.

The correct answer is option A.

148. Let the number of letters to be used be n.

The number of participants who can be identified using a single letter = $C_1^n = n$.

The number of participants who can be identified using two distinct letters = $C_2^n = \frac{n(n-1)}{2}$ (since the letters are to kept in alphabetic order, we do not need to order them)

Thus, total number of participants who can be identified

$= \left(n + \frac{n(n-1)}{2}\right)$

Since we need to have at least 12 identifications, we have:

$n + \frac{n(n-1)}{2} \geq 12$

$=> \frac{2n + n(n-1)}{2} \geq 12$

$=> \frac{n(2 + (n-1))}{2} \geq 12$

$=> \frac{n(n+1)}{2} \geq 12$

$=> n(n+1) \geq 24$

Working with the options and starting with the least value of n, we see that $n = 5$ satisfies the above inequality.

The correct answer is option B.

149. We have to select 1 employee each from Departments A, B, C each having 10 employees and 2 employees from Department D having 20 employees.

Number of ways of selecting 1 employee from Department A = $C_1^{10} = 10$.

Number of ways of selecting 1 employee from Department B = $C_1^{10} = 10$.

Number of ways of selecting 1 employee from Department C = $C_1^{10} = 10$.

Number of ways of selecting 2 employees from Department D = $C_2^{20} = \frac{20 * 19}{2 * 1} = 190$.

As all four events are independent of each other, the number of ways of forming the task force = 10 * 10 * 10 * 190

= 190,000

The correct answer is option D.

150. Total number of stocks available: 5 industrial, 4 transportation, and 3 utility stocks.

Number of stocks to be selected = 3 industrial, 2 transportation, and 2 utility stocks.

Number of ways of selecting 3 out of 5 industrial stocks = $C_3^5 = C_{(5-3)}^5 = C_2^5$

$= \frac{5 * 4}{2 * 1} = 10$

Number of ways of selecting 2 out of 4 transportation stocks = C_2^4

$= \frac{4 * 3}{2 * 1} = 6$

Number of ways of selecting 2 out of 3 utility stocks $= C_2^3$

$= \frac{3 * 2}{2 * 1} = 3$

Thus, the total number of ways of selecting the required number of stocks

= 10 * 6 * 3 (we multiply since the above selections are independent of one another)

= 180

The correct answer is option D.

151. Total number of people present = 3 * 6 = 18.

Number of handshakes if the representatives shook hands with every person other than those from his or her own company

= (Number of handshakes without any constraint) – (Number of handshakes with people from their own company)

Number of handshakes without any constraint $= C_2^{18} = \frac{18 * 17}{2 * 1} = 153$

(Since a handshake requires 2 people, we need to **select** any 2 people from the 18 for a handshake)

Number of handshakes with people from their own company $= 6 * C_2^3 = 6 * \frac{3 * 2}{2 * 1} = 18$

(We need to select any 2 representatives from 3 representatives of the same company, for each of the 6 companies)

Thus, the number of handshakes if the representatives shook hands with every person other than those from his or her own company

= 153 - 18

= 135

The correct answer is option B.

152. We need to select three digits for the code.

The digits to be used are from 0 to 9, thus there are 10 possible digits.

Since the first digit cannot be 0 or 1, number of possibilities for the first digit

$= (10 - 2) = 8.$

Since the second digit can only be 0 or 1, number of possibilities for the second digit = 2.

Let us ignore the restriction for the third digit.

Thus, number of possibilities for the third digit = 10.

Thus, total number of codes possible (ignoring the condition for the third digit) $= 8 * 2 * 10$

$= 160$

In the above cases, there are a few cases which are unacceptable since they violate the condition for the third digit.

The codes which violate the condition for the third digit are of the form $(a00)$, where a is the first digit and both second and third digits are simultaneously 0.

The number of such codes equals the number of possibilities for the first digit, i.e. 8.

Thus, the number of codes possible without violating any of the given conditions $= 160 - 8$

$= 152$

The correct answer is option B.

153. There are total 24 balls, out of which 12 are red.

Probability that both balls will be red $= \frac{\text{Number of ways of drawing both Red balls}}{\text{Number of ways of drawing any two balls}}$

$$=> \frac{C_2^{12}}{C_2^{24}} = \frac{\frac{12 * 11}{1 * 2}}{\frac{24 * 23}{1 * 2}} = \frac{12 * 11}{24 * 23} = \frac{11}{46}$$

The correct answer is option A.

154. In a basket, out of 10 apples, seven are red and three are green.

Number of ways we can select three apples from 10 apples $= C_3^{10} = \frac{10 \times 9 \times 8}{3 \times 2 \times 1} = 120.$

Number of ways of selecting two red apples and one green apple

$$= C_2^7\, C_1^3 = \frac{7 * 6}{1 * 2} \times 3 = 21 \times 3 = 63.$$

So required probability $= \frac{C_2^7\, C_1^3}{C_3^{10}} = \frac{63}{120} = \frac{21}{40}$

The correct answer is option D.

155. We know that the distribution is symmetric about the mean.

Thus, the percent of the distribution equidistant from the mean on either side of it is the same.

Let the percent of the distribution less than $(m + d)$ be x%.

Thus, the percent of the distribution more than $(m + d)$ is also x%.

The situation is shown in the diagram below.

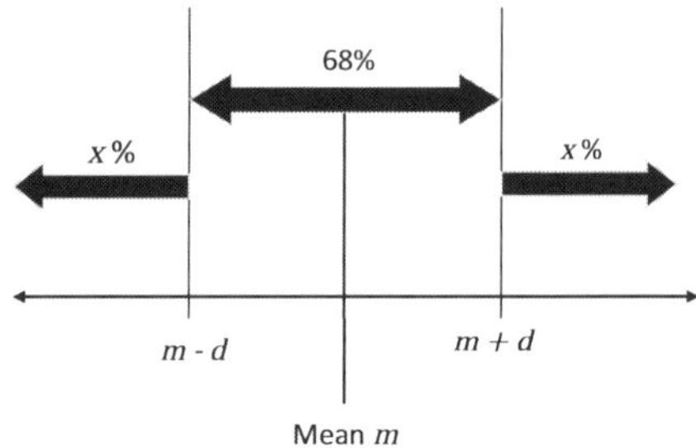

Thus, we have:

$x + 68 + x = 100$

$=> x = 16$

Thus, the percent of the distribution less than $(m + d) = x + 68 = 16 + 68 = 84\%$.

The correct answer is option D.

156. The number of 5-member committees that can be formed from the 20 members $= C_5^{20}$

$= \frac{20 * 19 * 18 * 17 * 16}{5 * 4 * 3 * 2 * 1}$

The number of 4-member committees that can be formed from the 20 members $= C_4^{20}$

$= \frac{20 * 19 * 18 * 17}{4 * 3 * 2 * 1}$

Thus, the required ratio

$$= \frac{\left(\frac{20 * 19 * 18 * 17 * 16}{5 * 4 * 3 * 2 * 1}\right)}{\left(\frac{20 * 19 * 18 * 17}{4 * 3 * 2 * 1}\right)}$$

$= \frac{16}{5} = 16$ to 5

The correct answer is option C.

157. There are two offices to which the three employees need to be assigned.

Thus, the number of options for each employee = 2 (since each employee can be assigned to any of the two offices).

Thus, the total number of ways of assigning the employees = 2*2*2 = 2^3= 8.

Note: For n objects, each with r options, the total number of options= r

The correct answer is option D.

158. We need to select three senior officers from six senior officers.

The number of ways of achieving it = $C_3^6 = \left(\frac{6*5*4}{3*2*1}\right) = 20.$

We also need to select one junior officer from four junior officers.

The number of ways of achieving it = $C_1^4 = 4.$

Thus, the number of ways in which three senior officers and one junior office can be selected = 20*4 = 80.

The correct answer is option D.

159. We see that the quarterly earnings are $1.10 per share, which is more than the expected earnings of $0.80 per share.

Thus, the dividend distributed will be half of $0.80 per share along with an additional payment.

The additional pay is $0.04 per share for each additional $0.10 per share earnings.

The additional earning per share = $ (1.10 – 0.80) = $0.30

Thus, the additional pay in dividend $= \$\left(0.04 * \left(\frac{0.30}{0.10}\right)\right) = \$0.12$

Thus, the total dividend paid per share $= \$\left(\frac{0.80}{2} + 0.12\right) = \$0.52;$

(since the dividend distributed will be half of $0.80 per share, thus it would be $\$\frac{0.80}{2} = \$0.40$)

Thus, total dividend paid to the person having 200 shares = $ (0.52*200) = $104.

The correct answer is option C.

160. Total number of units sold = 800 + 1000 = 1800.

Cost of producing each unit = \$6.

Thus, total cost of producing 1800 units = \$(6*1800) = \$10800.

Selling price of 800 units of the product = \$(800*8) = \$6400.

Selling price of 1000 units of the product = \$(1000*5) = \$5000.

Thus, the total selling price = \$(6400 + 5000) = \$11400.

Thus, profit = \$ (11400 − 10800) = \$600.

The correct answer is option D.

161. Let the car and truck sales in 1996 be c and t respectively.

Thus, the revenue from car sales in 1997 = (100 − 11)% of c = 89% of c = $0.89c$.

Also, the revenue from truck sales in 1997 = (100 + 7)% of c = 107% of c = $1.07c$.

Thus, total revenue in 1996 = $(c + t)$.

Also, total revenue in 1997 = $(0.89c + 1.07t)$.

Thus, we have:

$(0.89c + 1.07t) = (100 + 1)\%$ of $(c + t)$

$=> (0.89c + 1.07t) = 1.01c + 1.01t$

$=> 0.12c = 0.06t$

$=> \frac{c}{t} = \frac{0.06}{0.12} = \frac{1}{2}$

$=> c : t = 1 : 2$

The correct answer is option A.

162. Let the profit of the company in 1995 be \$100 (the assumption of \$100, or any other number does not affect the answer since we have to find the percent change).

Thus, the profit of the company in 1996 = \$((100 + 15)% of 100) = \$115.

Thus, the profit of the company in 1997 = \$((100 + 20)% of 115) = \$138.

Thus, the percent change in profit from 1995 to 1997 = $\frac{138 - 100}{100} * 100 = 38\%$.

Alternate approach:

If the value of a commodity changes by $x\%$ and then by $y\%$ successively, the overall percent change is given by:

$$\left(x + y + \frac{xy}{100}\right)\%$$

Here, we have:

x =Percentage change from 1995 to 1996 = 15 %

y =Percentage change from 1996 to 1997 = 20 %

Thus, the overall percent change

$$= 15 + 20 + \frac{15 * 20}{100}$$

$= 38\%$

The correct answer is option E.

163. We have: $a_1 = a_2 = 1$

We also know that: $a_k = a_{(k-1)} + 2a_{(k-2)}$

Substituting different values of k in the above equation, we have:

At $k = 3 : a_3 = a_{(3-1)} + 2a_{(3-2)}$

$=> a_3 = a_2 + 2a_1$

$=> a_3 = 1 + 2 * 1 = 3$

At $k = 4 : a_4 = a_{(4-1)} + 2a_{(4-2)}$

$=> a_4 = a_3 + 2a_2$

$=> a_4 = 3 + 2 * 1 = 5$

At $k = 5 : a_5 = a_{(5-1)} + 2a_{(5-2)}$

$=> a_5 = a_4 + 2a_3$

$=> a_5 = 5 + 2 * 3 = 11$

At $k = 6 : a_6 = a_{(6-1)} + 2a_{(6-2)}$

=> $a_6 = a_5 + 2a_4$

=> $a_6 = 11 + 2 * 5 = 21$

Finally, at $k = 7 : a_7 = a_{(7-1)} + 2a_{(7-2)}$

=> $a_7 = a_6 + 2a_5$

=> $a_7 = 21 + 2 * 11 = 43$

The correct answer is option B.

164. Given that,

Probability that stock A increases in value = PA = 0.54;

Probability that stock B increases in value = PB = 0.38

Exactly one of the stocks would increase in value if:

Stock A increases AND stock B does not

OR

Stock B increases AND stock A does not

Probability that stock A does not increase in value = $P(\overline{A}) = 1 - 0.54 = 0.46$
Probability that stock B does not increase in value = $P(\overline{B}) = 1 - 0.38 = 0.62$

Thus, the required probability = $P(A) * P\left(\overline{B}\right) + PB * P\left(\overline{A}\right)$

$= 0.54 * 0.62 + 0.38 * 0.46$

$=>\sim 0.5 * 0.6 + 0.4 * 0.5 = 0.30 + 0.20 = 0.50$

Thus, the actual answer would be approximately 0.50.

Note: The actual calculation = $0.54 * 0.62 + 0.38 * 0.46 = 0.5096 =\sim 0.51$

Thus, the above approximations are justified as the options are widely apart.

The correct answer is option C.

165. Since probability of landing on heads or tails is the same, each must be $\frac{1}{2}$ => $P(H) = P(T) = \frac{1}{2}$

Probability that the coin will land on heads at least once on two tosses

$= 1-$ Probability that it will not land on heads at all

$= 1-$ Probability that it will land on tails on both occasions

$= 1-$ (Probability that the first toss will show tails AND the second toss will show tails)

$= 1 - P(T) * P(T)$

$= 1 - \frac{1}{2} * \frac{1}{2}$

$= 1 - \frac{1}{4}$

$= \frac{3}{4}$

The correct answer is option E.

166. Each question has two options of which only one is correct.

Thus, the probability of randomly guessing an answer and getting it correct $= \frac{1}{2}$.

Thus, the probability of randomly guessing answers to all n questions and getting them correct

$= \frac{1}{2} * \frac{1}{2} * \frac{1}{2} * \ldots n$ times

$= \left(\frac{1}{2}\right)^n$

Thus, we have:

$\left(\frac{1}{2}\right)^n < \frac{1}{1000}$

$=> 2^n > 1000$

We observe from the options that $2^{10} = 1024$, which just exceeds 1000.

Thus, the least value of $n = 10$.

The correct answer is option B.

167. We know that the first three gum balls were black.

Thus, there are $(24 - 3) = 21$ gum balls left.

Of these, number of black gum balls $= 12 - 3 = 9$.

We need the next two gum balls to be black.

Thus, we need to select 2 black gum balls from the remaining 9 black gum balls.

Number of ways in which the above case can be achieved (favorable cases)= C_2^9

$= \frac{9 * 8}{2 * 1}$

= 36.

Number of ways in which two gum balls can be selected from the remaining 21 gum balls (total cases) = C_2^{21}

$= \frac{21 * 20}{2 * 1}$

= 210.

Thus, required probability = $\frac{\text{Favorable cases}}{\text{Total cases}}$

$= \frac{36}{210}$

$= \frac{6}{35}$

The correct answer is option A.

168. We need to select two marbles one at a time.

On drawing 2 marbles, one red and one blue can be obtained if:

The first marble is red AND the second marble is blue

OR

The first marble is blue AND the second marble is red

Since the marbles are not replaced after drawing, after the first draw, the total number of marbles would be 1 less than what was present initially, i.e. (16 – 1) = 15.

Thus, the required probability =

p(The first marble is red AND the second marble is blue)

OR

p(The first marble is blue AND the second marble is red)

$= \{p(1^{st} \text{ marble red}) * p(2^{nd} \text{ marble blue})\} + \{p(1^{st} \text{ marble blue}) * p(2^{nd} \text{ marble red})\}$

$$= \left\{\frac{4}{16} * \frac{3}{15}\right\} + \left\{\frac{3}{16} * \frac{4}{15}\right\}$$
$$= \frac{1}{20} + \frac{1}{20}$$
$$= \frac{1}{10}$$

The correct answer is option C.

169. Probability that at least one set is LCD

= 1− Probability that none is LCD

Probability of selecting two television sets such that none is LCD

= Probability of selecting two LED television sets

$$= \left(\frac{\text{Number of ways of selecting 2 LED television sets from 6 sets}}{\text{Number of ways of selecting 2 television sets from 8 sets}}\right)$$
$$= \frac{C_2^6}{C_2^8}$$
$$= \frac{\left(\frac{6*5}{2*1}\right)}{\left(\frac{8*7}{2*1}\right)}$$
$$= \frac{15}{28}$$

Thus, the required probability $= 1 - \frac{15}{28} = \frac{13}{28}$.

The correct answer is option D.

170. Let the number of red cards = r.

Number of blue cards = 9.

Thus, total number of cards = $(r + 9)$.

Thus, probability that both cards would be blue

$$= \left(\frac{\text{Number of ways of selecting 2 blue cards form 9 blue cards}}{\text{Number of ways of selecting 2 cards from } (r+9) \text{ cards}}\right)$$
$$= \frac{C_2^9}{C_2^{(r+9)}}$$
$$= \frac{\frac{9*8}{2*1}}{\frac{(r+9)*(r+9-1)}{2*1}}$$

$= \frac{72}{(r+9)*(r+8)}$

Thus, we have:

$\frac{72}{(r+9)*(r+8)} = \frac{6}{11}$

$=> (r+9)*(r+8) = 132$

$=> r^2 + 17r - 60 = 0$

$=> (r+20)(r-3) = 0$

$=> r = -20$ or 3

Since the number of cards cannot be negative, we have: $r = 3$

Thus, the total number of cards = 3 + 9 = 12.

The correct answer is option C.

171. The probability that a bulb fails = $P(F) = 0.06$
Thus, the probability that a bulb does not fail = $P\left(\overline{F}\right) = 1 - 0.06 = 0.94$
Thus, the probability that none of the 10 bulbs fail = 0.94^{10}
The string will fail if at least one bulb fails.
Thus, the probability that at least one bulb fails = $1 - 0.94^{10}$

The correct answer is option C.

172. Total number of pens = 12.

Number of defective pens = 3.

Thus, the number of non-defective pens = 12 - 3 = 9.

Thus, the customer has to pick 2 pens out of the 9 non-defective pens.

Thus, number of ways (favorable cases)

$= C_2^9 = \frac{9*8}{2*1} = 36.$

Number of ways in which he can pick 2 pens from the 12 pens (total cases)

$= C_2^{12} = \frac{12*11}{2*1} = 66.$

Thus, the required probability

$$= \frac{\text{Favorable cases}}{\text{Total no.of cases}} = \frac{36}{66} = \frac{6}{11}$$

The correct answer is option C.

173. Total number of pens = 12.

Number of defective pens = 3.

Thus, the number of non-defective pens = 12 - 3 = 9.

Thus, the customer has to pick 2 pens out of the 9 non-defective pens.

Thus, number of ways (favorable cases)

$$= C_2^9 = \frac{9 * 8}{2 * 1} = 36.$$

Number of ways in which he can pick 2 pens from the 12 pens (total cases)

$$= C_2^{12} = \frac{12 * 11}{2 * 1} = 66.$$

Thus, the required probability

$$= \frac{\text{Favorable cases}}{\text{Total no.of cases}} = \frac{36}{66} = \frac{6}{11}$$

The correct answer is option C.

5.12 Sets

174. Number of members on the committee M = 8.

As no member of the committee M is on either of the other two committees, the above 8 members belong to only committee M.

However, there may be an overlap with the members of committees S and R.

Number of members on committee S = 12.

Number of members on committee R = 5.

We get the greatest number of members who would not be any of the committees, if there is maximum overlap between the members of committees S and R.

The maximum overlap between the members of committees S and R would be the minimum of the number of members in the two committees i.e. minimum of 5 and 12 = 5.

Thus, we have:

$S \cap R = 5$

Thus, the number of members in the committees S or R = $S + R - S \cap R = 12 + 5 - 5 = 12$

Thus, total number of members belonging to one of more committees = 8 + 12 = 20.

Thus, maximum number of members who don't belong to any committee = 30 - 20 = 10.

The above information can be represented in a Venn-diagram as shown below:

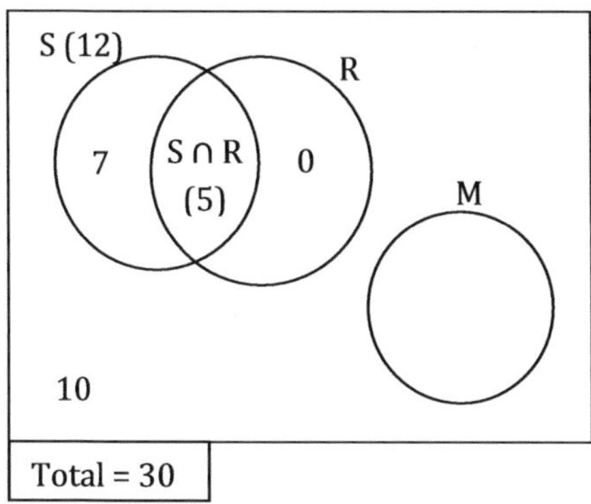

The correct answer is option D.

175. Total number of toys = 100

Number of red toys = 25

Number of blue toys = 75

Number of toys of size A = Number of toys of size B = $\frac{100}{2} = 50$

Number of red toys of size A = 10

Let us represent the above information using a Venn-diagram, as shown below:

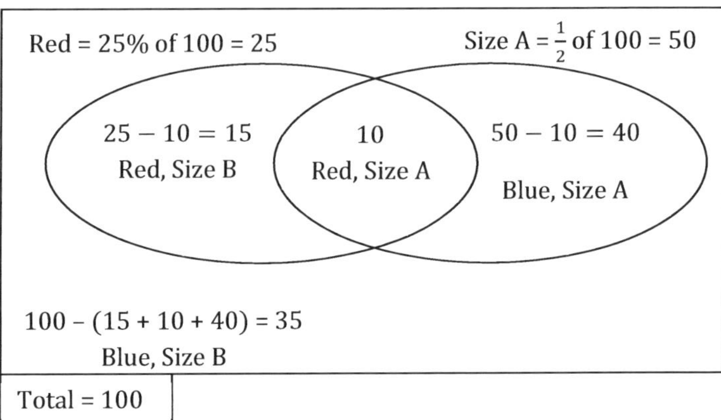

Thus, from the above Venn-diagram, we have:

Number of blue toys of size B = 35

The correct answer is option D.

176. Since the triangle PQR is isosceles, there can be three possible cases:

(1) PQ = PR $\neq$ QR

$=> \angle PQR = \angle PRQ$

We know that: $\angle$QPR =80°

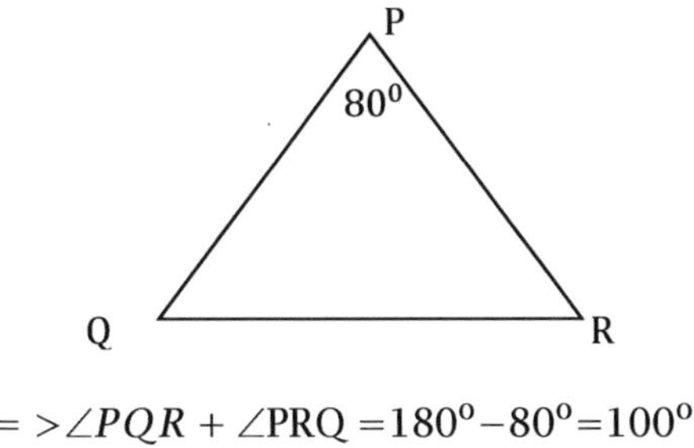

$=> \angle PQR + \angle PRQ = 180^\circ - 80^\circ = 100^\circ$

$=> \angle PRQ = \frac{100^\circ}{2} = 50^\circ$

(2) QP = QR $\neq$ PR

$=> \angle QPR = \angle QRP$

We know that: $\angle QPR = 80^\circ$

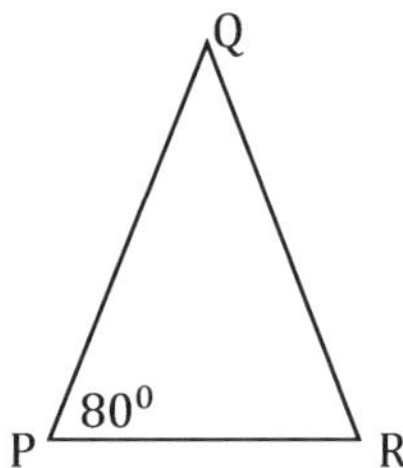

$=> \angle QRP = 80^o$

(3) $RQ = RP \neq QR$

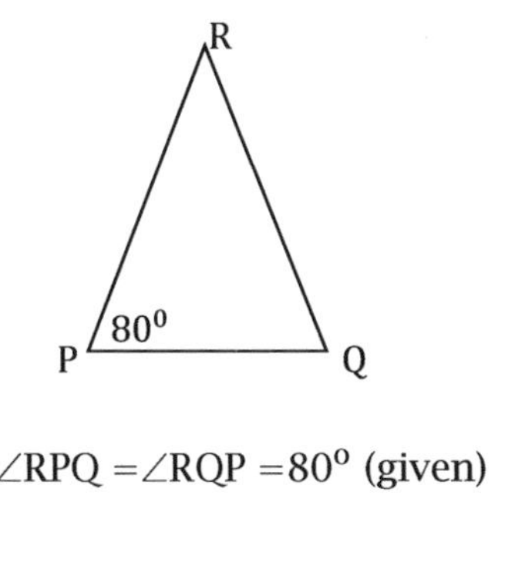

$=> \angle RPQ = \angle RQP = 80^o$ (given)

$=> \angle QRP = 180^o - (80^o + 80^o) = 20^o$

The correct answer is option E.

177. We know that 95 percent teenagers have used a computer to play games or to write reports.

Thus, $(100 - 95) = 5\%$ teenagers have not used a computer for either of these purposes.

Let us represent the above information using a Venn-diagram, as shown below:

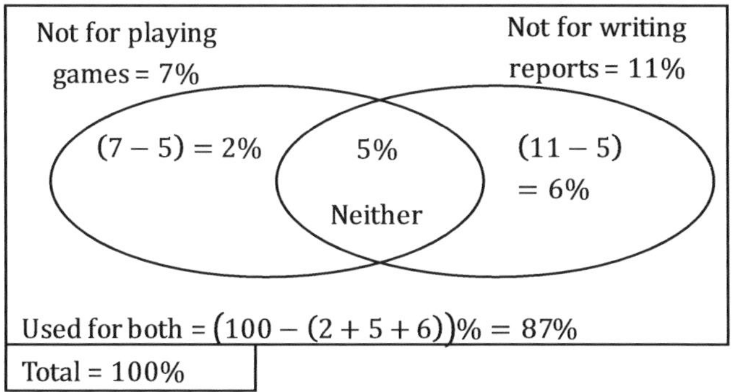

Thus, the percent of teenagers who have used a computer both to play games and to write reports = 87%.

The correct answer is option D.

178. Let us represent the given information using a Venn-diagram, as shown below:

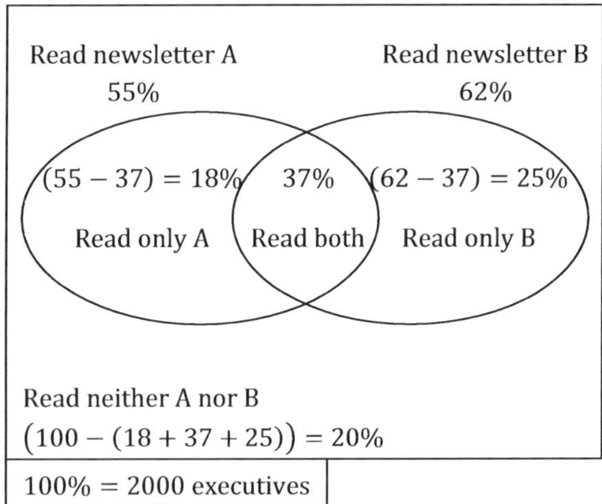

Thus, the number of executives who read at most one among newsletter A and newsletter B

= (Those who read only A) + (Those who read only B) + (Those who read neither A nor B)

= (18 + 25 + 20) % of 2000

= 63% of 2000

$= \frac{63}{100} * 2000$

= 1260

The correct answer is option B.

179. Let us represent the given information using a Venn-diagram, as shown below:

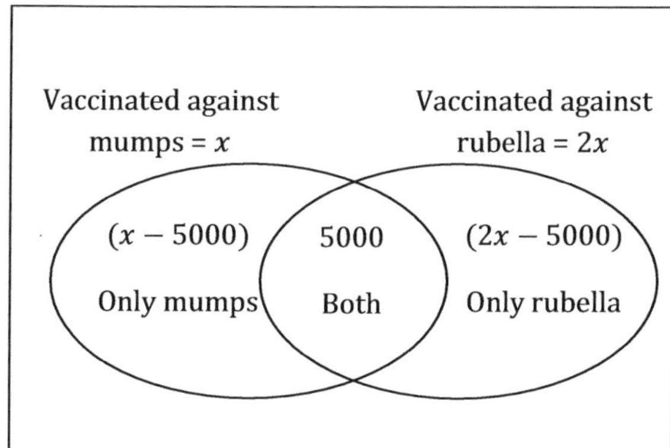

We know that the number of children who have been vaccinated against both is twice the number of children who have been vaccinated only against mumps

Thus, we have:

$5000 = 2\,(x - 5000)$

$=> 2x = 15000$

$=> x = 7500$

Thus, the number of children vaccinated only against rubella $= 2x - 5000$

$= 10000$

The correct answer is option C.

5.13 Statistics & Data Interpretation

180. We know that the median is the middle-most value of any series/data set, but we do not know the value of n, so we cannot calculate exact value of Median; however we can surely find its range.

- Case 1: If n is smallest, the series would be $n, 150,\ 200,\ 250$ and median = average of 150 & 200 = 175—smallest median value.

- Case 2: If n is largest, the series would be $150,\ 200,\ 250, n$ and median= average of 200 & 250 = 225—largest median value.

Thus, the median would lie between 175 & 225, inclusive. Since only options I & II are in the range, option C is correct.

The correct answer is option C.

181. The question asks how many number of scores > (Mean + SD)?

$$\text{Mean} = \frac{40 + 45 + 50 + 55 + 60 + 75 + 75 + 100 + 100 + 100}{10} = 70$$

Mean + SD = 70 + 22.4 = 92.4.

It is clear that three scores (100, 100, and 100) are greater.

The correct answer is option C.

182. Let the sum of the 20 numbers other than n be s.

Thus, we have:

$$n = 4 * \left(\frac{s}{20}\right)$$

$$=> s = 5n$$

Thus, the sum of all 21 numbers in the list = $s + n = 5n + n = 6n$

Thus, the required fraction = $\frac{n}{6n} = \frac{1}{6}$.

The correct answer is option B.

183. We have:

$$w \le \frac{3 + 8 + w}{3} \le 3w$$

$=> 3w \leq 11 + w \leq 9w$

$=> 2w \leq 11 \leq 8w$

$=> 2w \leq 11$ and $8w \geq 11$

$=> w \leq \frac{11}{2} = 5\frac{1}{2}$

and

$=> w \geq \frac{11}{8} = 1\frac{3}{8}$

Since w is an integer, possible values of w are: 2, 3, 4 or 5,

Thus, there are four possible values of w.

The correct answer is option B.

184. Let the five numbers be v, w, x, y and z such that $v > w > x > y > z$.

Thus, we need to find the least possible value of the largest among the five, i.e. v.

Let us assume that $v = w = x = y = z = 10$, because the average is 10.

Now, we reduce z by 2 and increase v by 2.

At the same time, we reduce y by 1 and increase w by 1.

Thus, we get the values:

$v = 12, w = 11, x = 10, y = 9, z = 8$

Thus, the least possible value of the greatest of the five numbers = 12.

The correct answer is option B.

185. We have:

$\frac{x + y + 20}{3} = 10 + \frac{x + y + 20 + 30}{4}$

$=> 4x + 4y + 80 = 120 + 3x + 3y + 150$

$=> x + y = 190$

$=> \frac{x + y}{2} = \frac{190}{2} = 95$

Thus, the average of x and $y = \frac{x + y}{2} = 95$.

The correct answer is option E.

186. If the 15 different integers are arranged in order, the median is the $\left(\frac{15 + 1}{2}\right)^{th} = 8^{th}$ integer.

Thus, the 8th integer is 30.

Since we need to find the maximum possible integer (given a constant range of 30), we need to have the maximum value of the least integer as well.

Since the integers are distinct, we can have the first 8 integers as:

$(30 - 7) = 23$, $(30 - 6) = 24$, $(30 - 5) = 25$, $(30 - 4) = 26$, $(30 - 3) = 27$, $(30 - 2) = 28$, $(30 - 1) = 29$ and 30

Thus, the maximum value of the smallest integer = 23.

Since the range is 30, the value of the greatest integer = 23 + 30 = 53.

The correct answer is option D.

187. We have Mean = $\left(\frac{\text{Sum of the terms}}{\text{Total number of terms}}\right)$

$=> \frac{3 + 2 + 6 + 8 + 5 + x}{6} = \frac{x^2}{2}$

$=> \frac{24 + x}{6} = \frac{x^2}{2}$

$=> 24 + x = 3x^2$

$=> 3x^2 - x - 24 = 0$

$=> (3x + 8)(x - 3) = 0$

$=> x = -\frac{8}{3}$ or 3

Since x is an integer, we have: $x = 3$

Thus, the set of integers = $\{3, 4, 4, 5, 5, 6\}$.

Thus, the range = 6 – 3 = 3.

The correct answer is option C.

188. We know that there are n employees, where n is an odd number.

The median value of n terms, where n is odd, is given by:

Median $= \left(\frac{n+1}{2}\right)^{\text{th}}$ term

Thus, we have:

$\frac{n+1}{2} = 16$

$=> n = 31$

Thus, there are 31 employees in Company A.

Thus, the average salary of the employees in Company A

$= \frac{\text{Total salary}}{\text{Number of employees}}$

$= \$\left(\frac{942400}{31}\right)$

$= \$30400$

The correct answer is option B.

189. Increase in the amount of bacteria from 1:00 pm (10.0 grams) to 4:00 pm (x grams) $= (x - 10)$ grams.

Thus, fractional increase

$= \frac{\text{Increase}}{\text{Original value}}$

$= \left(\frac{x - 10}{10}\right)$

Increase in the amount of bacteria from 4:00 pm (x grams) to 7:00 pm (14.4 grams) $= (14.4 - x)$ grams.

Thus, fractional increase

$= \frac{\text{Increase}}{\text{Original value}}$

$= \left(\frac{14.4 - x}{x}\right)$

Since the fractional increases are the same, we have:

$$\frac{x-10}{10} = \frac{14.4-x}{x}$$

$$=> \frac{x}{10} - 1 = \frac{14.4}{x} - 1$$

$$=> \frac{x}{10} = \frac{14.4}{x}$$

$=> x^2 = 14.4 * 10$

$=> x^2 = 144$

$=> x = 12$

Alternate approach I:

Since the amount of bacteria present increased by the same fraction during each of the two 3-hour periods, we can say that the ratio of the number of bacteria in consecutive intervals would be equal.

Thus we have:

$$\frac{10.0}{x} = \frac{x}{14.4}$$

$=> x^2 = 14.4 * 10.0$

$=> x^2 = 144$

$=> x = 12.0$

Alternate approach II:

Since the fractional increase in each 3-hour period is the same, we can conclude that the percent change in each 3-hour period is also the same.

Let the percent change be p.

Thus, using the concept of compound interest, we have:

$$14.4 = 10 * \left(1 + \frac{p}{100}\right)^2$$

$$=> \left(1 + \frac{p}{100}\right)^2 = 1.44 = 1.2^2$$

$$=> 1 + \frac{p}{100} = 1.2$$

$=> p = 20\%$

$$=> x = 10 * \left(1 + \frac{20}{100}\right)^1 = 12$$

The correct answer is option A.

190. We can make a quick calculation by taking approximate values as shown below:

	Actual Calculation	**Approximate Calculation**	**More Approximation**
Honorary	78	$= \approx 80$	$= \approx 100$
Fellows	9209	$= \approx 9200$	$= \approx 9000$
Members	35509	$= \approx 35500$	$= \approx 36000$
Associate	27909	$= \approx 27900$	$= \approx 28000$
Affiliates	2372	$= \approx 2370$	$= \approx 2400$
Total	75077	75050	75500
fellows (%)	$\frac{9209}{75077} * 100 = 12.26\%$	$\frac{9200}{75050} * 100 = 12.26\%$	$\frac{9000}{75500} * 100 = 11.9\%$

Thus, we can see that even in the case with the most approximation, the answer comes to 11.9% which is enough to mark the correct answer as 12%.

In the GMAT, the options would be sufficiently apart from each other so that reasonable approximations would not deviate the correct answer to a greater degree.

The reason for such large approximations to work is that the total number of members is around 75000 and compared to that, even an error of 500 (in the total) is negligible, in fact, it accounts for $\left(\frac{500}{75000} * 100\right) = 0.66\%$, i.e. not even 1%.

Here, the number of Fellows has been approximated from 9209 to 9000, i.e. only an error of 209.

Such approximations help in increased calculation speed with almost negligible error.

In fact, we could have even made an extreme level of approximation as follows (though, not suggested in every situation):

	Extreme Approximation (easiest calculation)
Honorary	$= \approx 0$
Fellows	$= \approx 9000$
Members	$= \approx 36000$
Associate	$= \approx 28000$
Affiliates	$= \approx 2000$
Total	75000
% of fellows	$\frac{9000}{75000} * 100 = 12\%$

The correct answer is option B.

191. We can calculate the total number of watts of electricity consumed as shown below:

Appliance	Number of hours in use	Number of watts of electricity used per hour	Total number of watts of electricity used
TV	4	145	$4 * 145 = 580$
Computer	3	155	$3 * 155 = 465$
VCR	2	45	$2 * 45 = 90$
Stereo	2	109	$2 * 109 = 218$
Total	$4 + 3 + 2 + 2$ $= 11$ hours		$580 + 465 + 90 + 218$ $= 1353$ watts

Thus, the approximate average number of watts of electricity used per hour per appliance

$= \frac{1353}{11} = 123$ watts.

The correct answer is option C.

5.14 Linear Equations

192. Let us recall the property of two-digit number:

"Difference between the particular two digit number and number obtained by interchanging digits of same two digit number is always 9 times the difference between the digits."

Thus, the difference between actual amount and reversed amount

$= 45 = 9 \times$ difference between digits

=> Difference between digits $= \frac{45}{9} = 5$

The difference between digits of the number, 5, is satisfied only by option E.

The correct answer is option E.

Alternate Approach 1:

If we consider correct amount as $[xy] = 10x + y$, then interchanged amount becomes $[yx] = 10y + x$.

According to the given condition, difference between the new amount and the original amount is 45 cents.

=> $(10x + y) - (10y + x) = 45$

=> $10x - x - 10y + y = 45$

=> $9x - 9y = 45$

On dividing by 9, we have:

$x - y = 5$.

Thus, the difference between the digits is 5, which is satisfied only by option E.

Alternate Approach 2:

Since the cash register contained 45 cents more than it should have as a result of this error, this implies that the tens digit of the correct amount must be greater than its unit digit.

Only three options can qualify. Let us analyze them:

(C) 54: $54 - 45 \neq 45$

(D) 65: $65 - 56 \neq 45$

(E) 83: 83 – 38 = 45; correct answer

193. A certain business produced x rakes per month during November to February.

So total number of rakes produced during this period = $4x$.

Till now, storage cost paid by business = 0.

From next month onwards, that is March till October, business shipped exactly $\frac{x}{2}$ rakes per month.

In the month of March, the business would pay for $4x - \frac{x}{2} = \frac{7x}{2} = 3.5x$ rakes;

Similarly, in the month of April, it would pay for $\frac{7x}{2} - \frac{x}{2} = \frac{6x}{2} = 3x$ rakes;

This way business would pay its last payment in September for $\frac{x}{2} = 0.5x$ rakes.

We see that above is in the form of an Arithmetic Progression, with the first term = $3.5x$, common deference = $-\frac{x}{2}$, and number of terms = 7 (from March to September).

Sum of all the rakes

$$= \frac{\text{Number of months}}{2} \times (\text{Number of rakes in March} + \text{Number of rakes in September})$$

$$=> \frac{7}{2}(3.5x + 0.5x) = 14x$$

Amount paid per un-shipped rake per month = \$0.10

So total amount paid = $14x * 0.10 = 1.4x$

See the following table for a better understanding:

Month	No. of rakes shipped	Un-shipped rakes	Storage amount paid ($)
March	$\frac{x}{2}$	$4x - \frac{x}{2} = \frac{7x}{2}$	$\frac{7x}{2} \times 0.10 = 0.35x$
April	$\frac{x}{2}$	$\frac{7x}{2} - \frac{x}{2} = \frac{6x}{2} = 3x$	$3x \times 0.10 = 0.30x$
May	$\frac{x}{2}$	$3x - \frac{x}{2} = \frac{5x}{2}$	$\frac{5x}{2} \times 0.10 = 0.25x$
June	$\frac{x}{2}$	$\frac{5x}{2} - \frac{x}{2} = \frac{4x}{2} = 2x$	$2x \times 0.10 = 0.20x$
July	$\frac{x}{2}$	$2x - \frac{x}{2} = \frac{3x}{2}$	$\frac{3x}{2} \times 0.10 = 0.15x$
August	$\frac{x}{2}$	$\frac{3x}{2} - \frac{x}{2} = \frac{2x}{2} = x$	$x \times 0.10 = 0.10x$
September	$\frac{x}{2}$	$x - \frac{x}{2} = \frac{x}{2}$	$\frac{x}{2} \times 0.10 = 0.05x$
October	$\frac{x}{2}$	0	0
		Total amount paid	**1.40x**

The correct answer is option C.

Alternatively, we can solve this question by assuming a convenient number; choosing a number is also tricky. The smart number should be divisible by '2' at each stage, thus a number with a higher exponent, such as $2^8 = 256$ can be a good number.

194. Let the number of apples and bananas purchased be a and b, respectively.

Thus, total cost of the fruits = \$ $(0.7a + 0.5b)$

Thus, we have:

$(0.7a + 0.5b) = 6.3$

=> $7a + 5b = 63$

It is clear that a and b are positive integers.

As a starting solution, we can see that 63 is divisible by 7 and hence we take:

$a = 9,\ b = 0$; However this is not possible as the number of bananas > 0.

The other solutions can be obtained by reducing a by the coefficient of b i.e. 5, and increasing b by the coefficient of a i.e. 7.

Thus, we have:

$a = 9 - 5 = 4$
$b = 0 + 7 = 7$

If we apply the same approach again, then the value of a becomes $4 - 5 = -1$ (negative), which is not possible.

Hence, there is only one possible solution to the equation: $a = 4,\ b = 7$

Thus, the total number of fruits purchased = 4 + 7 = 11.

The correct answer is option B.

195. We have:

$x + y + z = 2 \ldots$(i)
$x + 2y + 3z = 6 \ldots$(ii)

Multiplying (i) by 3 and subtracting (ii) from the result:

$3 * (x + y + z = 2) - (x + 2y + 3z = 6)$

=> $2x + y = 0$

=> $2x = -y$

=> $\frac{x}{y} = -\frac{1}{2}$

The correct answer is option A.

196. Let the number pairs of hard contact lenses sold last week be h.

Since the number of pairs of soft contact lenses sold was 5 more than hard contact lenses, the number pairs of soft contact lenses sold last week = $(h + 5)$.

Selling price for each pair of soft contact lens = \$150.

Selling price for each pair of hard contact lens = \$85.

Thus, total selling price obtained = \$ $(85h + 150(h + 5))$.

Thus, we have:

$85h + 150(h + 5) = 1690$

$=> 235h = 1690 - 750$

$=> h = \frac{940}{235} = 4$

Thus, the number of pairs of hard contact lenses sold = 4.

Thus, the number of pairs of soft contact lenses sold = 4 + 5 = 9.

Thus, the total number of pairs of contact lenses sold = 4 + 9 = 13.

Alternate approach:

Number of pairs of soft contact lenses sold is 5 more than the number of pairs of hard contact lenses.

The price of 5 pairs of soft contact lenses = \$ $(150 * 5)$ = \$750.

Removing this from the total, i.e. \$1690, we are left with \$ $(1690 - 750)$ = \$940.

This amount was obtained by selling equal numbers of pairs of soft and hard contact lenses.

Total price of one pair of soft and one pair of hard contact lenses (i.e. 2 pairs of lenses)
= \$ $(150 + 85)$ = \$235.

Thus, number of lenses sold for \$940

$= \frac{940}{235} * 2$

$= 8$

Thus, total number of pairs of lenses sold = 5 + 8 = 13.

The correct answer is option B.

5.15 Quadratic Equations & Polynomials

197. We have:

$x = \sqrt{8xy - 16y^2}$

Squaring both the sides:

$x^2 = 8xy - 16y^2$

$=> x^2 - 8xy + 16y^2 = 0$

$=> (x - 4y)^2 = 0$

$=> x - 4y = 0$

$=> x = 4y$

The correct answer is option D.

198. Given that,

$(x - 2)^2 = 9$

$=> x - 2 = \pm 3$

$=> x = 2 \pm 3$

$=> x = 5 \text{ OR } -1$

Given that,

$(y - 3)^2 = 25$

$=> y - 3 = \pm 5$

$=> y = 3 \pm 5$

$=> y = 8 \text{ OR } -2$

The minimum value of $\left(\frac{x}{y}\right)$ will be that value with the greatest magnitude of x, least magnitude of y and exactly one of x and y being negative in sign.

Thus, we have:

$x = 5, y = -2 => \frac{x}{y} = -\frac{5}{2}$

The maximum value of $\left(\frac{x}{y}\right)$ will be that value with the greatest magnitude of x, least magnitude of y and both x and y being simultaneously positive or negative in sign.

Thus, we have:

$x = 5, y = 8 => \frac{x}{y} = \frac{5}{8}$

OR

$x = -1, y = -2 => \frac{x}{y} = \frac{1}{2}$

Among $\frac{5}{8}$ and $\frac{1}{2}$, the fraction $\frac{5}{8}$ is greater.

Thus, the required difference

$= \frac{5}{8} - \left(-\frac{5}{2}\right)$

$= \frac{5}{8} + \frac{5}{2}$

$= \frac{25}{8}$

The correct answer is option E.

199. Given that,

$2x + 3y + xy = 12$

$=> 2x + 3y + xy + 6 = 12 + 6 = 18$; (adding the product of the coefficients of x and y to both sides)

$=> (2x + 6) + (xy + 3y) = 18$

$=> 2(x + 3) + y(x + 3) = 18$

$=> (x + 3)(y + 2) = 18$

Since x and y are positive integers, we must have:

$x + 3 > 3$, and

$y + 2 > 2$

Possible ways of getting 18 are: 1 * 18, 2 * 9, and 3 * 6

Thus, the only possible solution is:

$x + 3 = 6 => x = 3$, and
$y + 2 = 3 => y = 1$

Thus, we have: $x + y = 3 + 1 = 4$.

The correct answer is option B.

200. We know that:

$h = -16(t - 3)^2 + 150 \ldots$ (i)

We need to find the value of t so that the value of h is maximum.

In the expression for h, we have a term: $-16(t - 3)^2$

We know that: $(t - 3)^2 \geq 0$ for all values of t (since it is a perfect square).

Thus, we have:

$-16(t - 3)^2 \leq 0$ for all values of t (multiplying with a negative reverses the inequality).

Thus, in order that h attains a maximum value, the term $-16(t - 3)^2$ must be 0.

Thus, we have: $-16(t - 3)^2 = 0$

$=> t = 3$

Thus, h attains a maximum value at $t = 3$

Thus, two seconds after the maximum height is attained, i.e. at $t = 3 + 2 = 5$, we have the corresponding value of h (in feet) as:

$-16(5 - 3)^2 + 150$; substituting the value of $t = 5$ in (i)

$= -16 * 4 + 150$

$= 86$

The correct answer is option B.

201. We know that:

$N(t) = -20(t-5)^2 + 500$, where $0 \le t \le 10$

We need to find the value of t so that the value of $N(t)$ is maximum.

In the expression for $N(t)$, we have a term: $-20(t-5)^2$

We know that: $(t-5)^2 \ge 0$ for all values of t (since it is a perfect square).

Thus, we have:

$-20(t-5)^2 \le 0$ for all values of t (multiplying with a negative reverses the inequality).

Thus, in order that $N(t)$ attains a maximum value, the term $-20(t-5)^2$ must be 0.

Thus, we have:

$-20(t-5)^2 = 0$

$\Rightarrow t = 5$

Thus, $N(t)$ attains a maximum value at $t = 5$ i.e. 5 hours past 2:00 am i.e. 7:00 am.

The correct answer is option B.

5.16 Inequalities

202. The possible extreme scenarios are shown in the diagrams below:

(1) Maximum distance away from home:

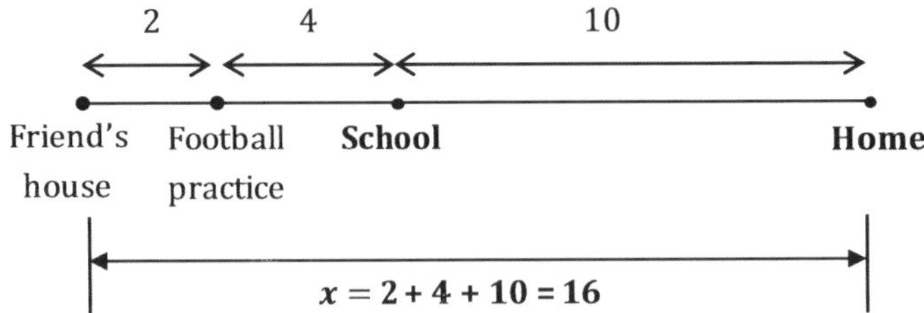

(2) Minimum distance away from home:

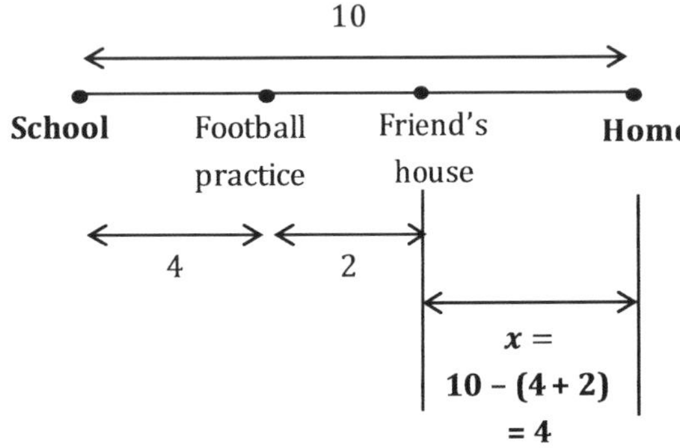

Thus, the maximum value of x is 16 and minimum value of x is 4

$\Rightarrow 4 \le x \le 16$

The correct answer is option D.

203. As per given inequality: $|y| \le 12$, value of 'y' ranges from '-12' to '$+12$'. So by putting these values in first equation: $2x + y = 12$, we can form a table of consistent values of x & y.

x	y
0	12
1	10
2	8
3	6
4	4
5	2
6	0

x	y
Cont...	
7	−2
8	−4
9	−6
10	−8
11	−10
12	−12

So a total 13 ordered pairs are possible.

The correct answer is option D.

Alternate approach:

We see that the value of y ranges from -12 to $+12$; this follows that y can have 25 number of integer values.

Now let us see how many integer values x can have.

$2x + y = 12 => x = \frac{12 - y}{2};$

$=> x = 6 - \frac{y}{2}$

We see that for x to be an integer, $\frac{y}{2}$ must be an integer; this follows that y must be an even number or '0'.

Out of 25 possible values of y, 12 values are even and one value is '0'; so for x to be an integer, the set of arrangement can only have 13 ordered pairs.

204. Let the cost of an egg be $\$x$ and the cost of a sandwich be $\$y$.

Thus, we need to find the range within which $(4x + 3y)$ lies.

We have:

$0.90 < 12x < 1.20$

$=> \frac{0.90}{3} < \frac{12x}{3} < \frac{1.20}{3}$

$=> 0.30 < 4x < 0.40 \ldots$ (i)

Also, we have:

$10 < 5y < 15$

$=> \frac{10}{5} < y < \frac{15}{5}$

$=> 2 < y < 3$

$=> 6 < 3y < 9 \ldots$ (ii)

Adding (i) and (ii):

$6.30 < 4x + 3y < 9.40$

Thus, the correct answer is option D.

205. Working with the options one at a time:

Comparing options A and B:

$(xy)^2 = x^2y^2 < x^2$ (since $0 < y < 1 => y^2$ is a fraction between 0 and 1)

Thus, option B cannot have the greatest value.

Comparing options A and C:

$$\left(\frac{x}{y}\right)^2 = \frac{x^2}{y^2} = x^2 * \left(\frac{1}{y^2}\right) > x^2 \text{ (since } 0 < y < 1 => 0 < y^2 < 1 => \frac{1}{y^2} > 1)$$

Thus, option A cannot have the greatest value.

Comparing options C and D:

$$\frac{x^2}{y} = \frac{x^2}{y^2} * y = \left(\frac{x}{y}\right)^2 * y < \left(\frac{x}{y}\right)^2 \text{ (since } 0 < y < 1 => y \text{ is a fraction between 0 and 1)}$$

Thus, option D cannot have the greatest value.

Comparing options C and E:

$$x^2y = \frac{x^2}{y^2} * y^3 = \left(\frac{x}{y}\right)^2 * y^3 < \left(\frac{x}{y}\right)^2 \text{ (since } 0 < y < 1 => y^3 \text{ is a fraction between 0 and 1)}$$

Thus, option E cannot have the greatest value.

The correct answer is option C.

Alternate Approach:

Since $x < 0$ and $0 < y < 1$ must be true for all the values x & y assumes, let us assume convenient, smart values of x & y.

Say $x = -1$ & $y = \frac{1}{2}$

Let us calculate the values of each option.

(A) $x^2 = (-1)^2 = 1$

(B) $(xy)^2 = \left(-1 * \frac{1}{2}\right)^2 = \frac{1}{4}$

(C) $\left(\frac{x}{y}\right)^2 = \left(\frac{-1}{\frac{1}{2}}\right)^2 = 4$: Maximum

(D) $\frac{x^2}{y} = \frac{(-1)^2}{\frac{1}{2}} = 2$

(E) $x^2y = (-1)^2 * \frac{1}{2} = \frac{1}{2}$

206. Let the distance between the cities A and B be d miles.

Range of speeds of Anne = 25 miles per hour to 45 miles per hour.

Time taken by Anne to cover the distance = 4 hours.

So, the range of distance between cities A and B
= 25 * 4 miles to 45 * 4 miles

= 100 miles to 180 miles

=> $100 < d < 180 \ldots$ (i)

Range of speeds of John = 45 miles per hour to 60 miles per hour.

Time taken by Anne to cover the distance = 2 hours.

So, the range of distance between cities A and B
= 45 * 2 miles to 60 * 2 miles

= 90 miles to 120 miles

=> $90 < d < 120 \ldots$ (ii)

Thus, from (i) and (ii), we have:

Range of distance between cities A and B

= (Higher of the two minimum values) to (Lower of the two maximum values)

= (Higher of 100 and 90) to (Lower of 180 and 120)

= 100 miles to 120 miles

=> $100 < d < 120$

The only option which satisfies is 115 miles.

The correct answer is option B.

5.17 Geometry–Lines & Triangles

207. Working with the statements:

Statement I:

We can have a situation as shown below:

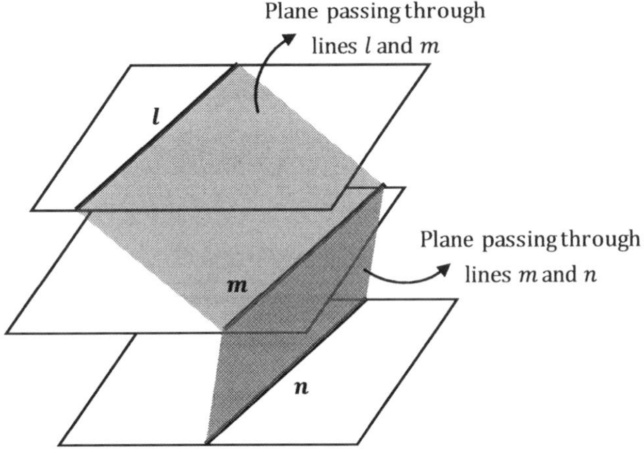

The lines l, m and n are parallel, however, the plane passing through l and m does not pass through n, implying that the lines are in different planes.

Thus, statement I is incorrect.

Statement II:

Since both l and m are separately parallel to n, the lines l and m must be parallel to each other as well.

Thus, statement II is correct.

Statement III:

From the above diagram, it is clear that lines l and m do not need to be the same line.

Thus, statement III is incorrect.

The correct answer is option B.

208. We know that:

$$AB = \frac{1}{2}CD$$

$$=> CD = 2AB \ldots (i)$$

$BD = \frac{3}{2}AC \ldots (ii)$

$BC = 24 \ldots (iii)$

From (ii):

$=> BC + CD = \frac{3}{2}(AB + BC)$

Using (i) and (iii):

$=> 24+2AB = \frac{3}{2}(AB + 24)$

$=> 48 + 4AB = 3AB + 72$

$=> AB = 24$

$=> CD = 2 * 24 = 48$

$=> AD = AB + BC + CD$

$= 24 + 24 + 48$

$= 96$

The correct answer is option D.

209. Since the length of RS > the length of RT, R must be closer to T than to S.

Also, since sum of the lengths of RS and RT is greater than the length of ST, R must line beyond the line segment ST.

The sequence of the points R, S, T and U is shown in the diagram below:

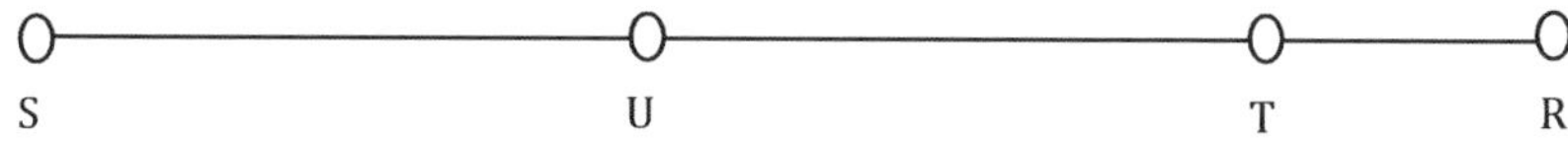

Since U is the midpoint of ST, we have:

$SU = UT = \frac{ST}{2}$

$= \frac{16}{2}$

$= 8$

RU = RT + TU

= 4 + 8

= 12

The correct answer is option C.

210. Here we know that both dressing rooms are equidistant from a cash register and distance between these 2 dressing tables is constant that is 16. So if we join all these 3 places with each other, it will give us an isosceles triangle.

So here property about lengths of sides of triangle is "Sum of any two sides is always greater than third side and positive difference between any two sides is always less than third side."

- Case I – Isosceles triangle is of sides: 6, 6, 16. Here $6 + 6 \not> 16$ so such a triangle does not exist. So this is NOT the possible case.

- Case II – Isosceles triangle is of sides: 12, 12, and 16. This triangle follows above mentioned property. So this is a possible case.

- Case III – Isosceles triangle is of sides: 24, 24, and 16. This triangle follows above mentioned property. So this is a possible case.

The Correct answer is option E.

211. Given that:

$x < y < z$

Since z is the longest side in the right triangle, it must be the hypotenuse.

Also, x and y are the perpendicular legs of this right angled triangle.

Here let us recall formula to find the area of Right Angled Triangle:

$= \frac{1}{2} *$ Product of two legs

Thus, area of the triangle:

$= \frac{1}{2} * x * y = 1$

$=> xy = 2$

If we assume that $x = y$, we have:

$x = y = \sqrt{2}$

However, it is known that $y > x$, we can conclude that $x < \sqrt{2}$ and $y > \sqrt{2}$.

=> $y > \sqrt{2}$

The correct answer is option A.

212. Since z is the longest side in the right triangle, it must be the hypotenuse.

Thus, we have:

$x^2 + y^2 = z^2 \ldots$ (i)

Also, x and y are the perpendicular legs of the triangle.

Thus, area of the triangle:

$= \frac{1}{2} * x * y = 1$

=> $xy = 2 \ldots$ (ii)

From (i), we have:

$z^2 = x^2 + y^2$
$= (x + y)^2 - 2xy$
$= (x + y)^2 - 4$ (since $xy = 2$, from (ii))

Given $xy = 2$, the minimum value of $(x + y)$ occurs if $x = y$.

Let us verify:

Say, $x \neq y$:

$x = 2, y = 1$ => $x + y = 3$

However, if $x = y$:

$x = y = \sqrt{2}$ => $x + y = 2\sqrt{2} \sim 2 * 1.4 = 2.8 < 3$

However, the maximum value of $(x + y)$ is undefined and tends to infinity.

Say, we take $y = 100, x = 0.02$ => $x + y = 100.2$

Thus, the value of $(x + y)$ can be increased to any arbitrarily high value.

Thus, we can see that given $xy = 2$, $(x + y)$ has only a minimum value of $2\sqrt{2}$.

Hence, we have:

$z^2 = (x + y)^2 - 4$

=> The minimum value of z^2 occurs when $(x + y)^2$ is minimum i.e. $(x + y)$ is minimum

=> Minimum value of $z^2 = \left(2\sqrt{2}\right)^2 - 4 = 4$

=> $z > 2$ (the equality does not hold since x and y cannot be equal since $x < y$)

The correct answer is option A.

213. Since DA = DC, triangle DAC is isosceles

=> $\angle DAC = \angle DCA = 30^o$

Since DB = DC, triangle DBC is isosceles

=> $\angle DBC = \angle DCB = 50^o$

Since DA = DB, triangle DAB is isosceles

=> $\angle DBA = \angle DAB = x^o$

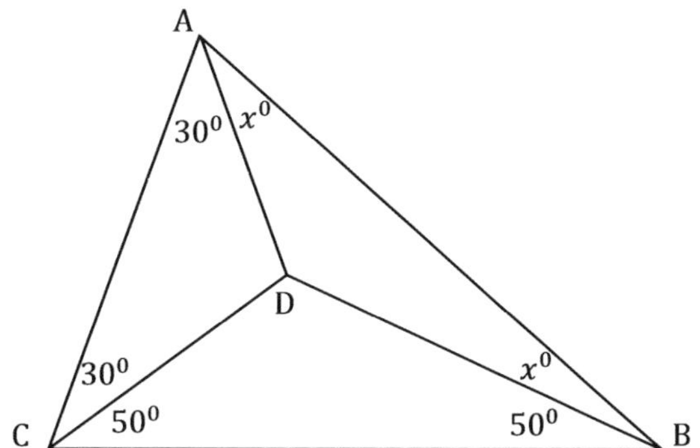

Since sum of the internal angles in a triangle is 180^0, we have:

$(30 + x) + (x + 50) + (50 + 30) = 180$

$\Rightarrow 2x = 20$

$\Rightarrow x = 10$

The correct answer is option A.

214.

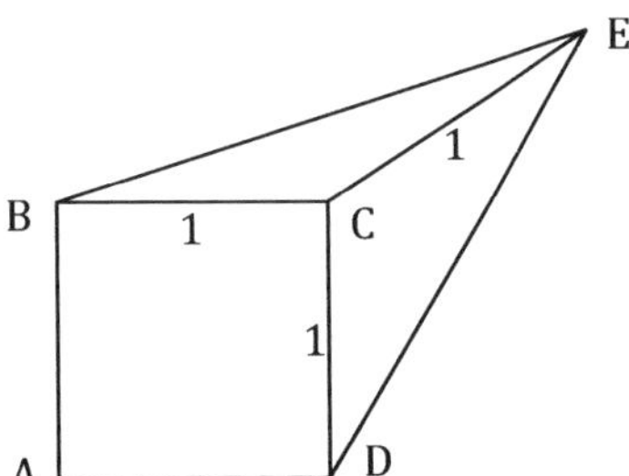

We observe that triangles BCE and DCE are isosceles.

Also, triangle BCE ≅ triangle DCE

(Since CE is common, BC = CD and BE = DE)

Thus, ∠BCE =∠DCE

$=\frac{360^o-90^o}{2} = 135^o$

Considering triangle BCE alone, we have:

In triangle CEF:

∠ECF $=180^o-135^o=45^o$

=> ∠CEF $=180^o-(90^o+45^o) =45^o$

Thus, triangle CEF is isosceles.

Let CF = EF = x

Thus, from Pythagoras' theorem in triangle CEF:

$x^2 + x^2 = 1^2$

=> EF $=x = \frac{1}{\sqrt{2}} = \frac{\sqrt{2}}{2}$

Thus, area of triangle BCE

$= \frac{1}{2} * \text{Base} * \text{Height}$

$= \frac{1}{2} * \text{BC} * \text{EF}$

$= \frac{1}{2} * 1 * \frac{\sqrt{2}}{2}$

$= \frac{\sqrt{2}}{4}$

The correct answer is option B.

Alternate approach:

From symmetry, we can say that EC, when extended would pass through A.

$AC = \sqrt{AB^2 + BC^2} = \sqrt{1+1} = \sqrt{2}$

We know that if the height of two triangles is the same, the ratio of their area equals the ratio of their base.

Thus, we have:

$$\frac{\text{Area of triangle ABC}}{\text{Area of triangle EBC}} = \frac{\text{Base of triangle ABC}}{\text{Base of triangle EBC}}$$

$$= \frac{AC}{CE}$$

$$= \frac{\sqrt{2}}{1}$$

$$\text{Area of triangle ABC} = \frac{\text{Area of square ABCD}}{2}$$

$$\frac{1 * 1}{2} = \frac{1}{2}$$

Thus, we have:

$$\frac{\left(\frac{1}{2}\right)}{\text{Area of triangle EBC}} = \frac{\sqrt{2}}{1}$$

$$\Rightarrow \text{Area of triangle EBC} = \frac{1}{2\sqrt{2}} = \frac{\sqrt{2}}{4}$$

215. Let us bring out the figure.

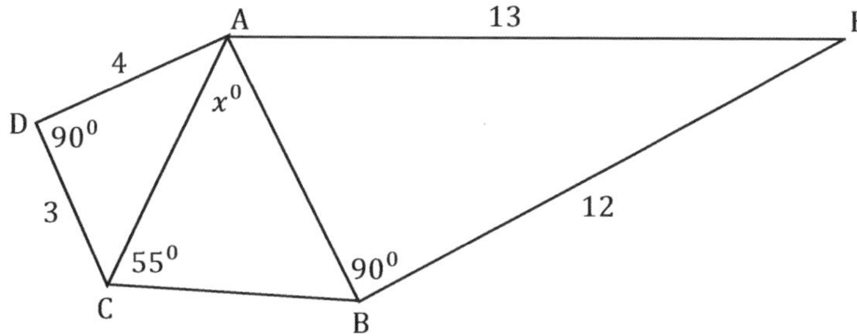

In the right angled triangle ADC, as per Pythagoras theorem, we have:

$AC^2 = AD^2 + CD^2$

=> $AC^2 = 3^2 + 4^2 = 25$

=> $AC = 5$

In the right angled triangle ABE, as per Pythagoras theorem, we have:

$AB^2 = AE^2 - BE^2$

=> $AB^2 = 13^2 - 12^2 = 25$

=> $AB = 5$

Thus, we have:

$AB = AC$

In a triangle, if two sides are equal, angles opposite to them are also equal.

=> $\angle ABC = \angle ACB = 55^o$

=> $\angle BAC = 180^o - (\angle ABC + \angle ACB)$

=> $\angle BAC = 180^o - (55^o + 55^o)$

=> $\angle BAC = 70^o$

=> $x = 70$

The correct answer is option D.

216. Let us bring out the figure.

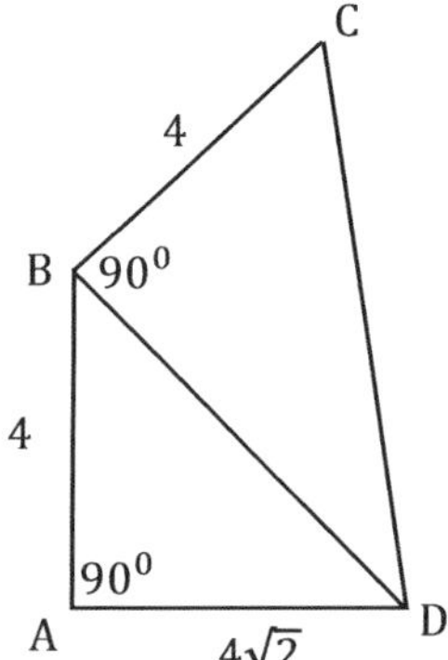

In right angled triangle ABD, as per Pythagoras theorem:

$BD^2 = AB^2 + AD^2$

$=> BD^2 = 16 + 32 = 48$

$=> BD = 4\sqrt{3}$

In right angled triangle CBD, as per Pythagoras theorem:

$CD^2 = CB^2 + BD^2$

$=> CD^2 = 16 + 48 = 64$

$=> CD = 8$

Thus, perimeter of triangle BCD

$= BC + CD + BD$

$= 4 + 8 + 4\sqrt{3}$

$= 12 + 4\sqrt{3}$

The correct answer is option C.

5.18 Geometry–Circles

217. Length of the arc RST (which subtends 60° at the center) $= 2\pi r * \left(\frac{60}{360}\right)$, where r is the radius of the circle.

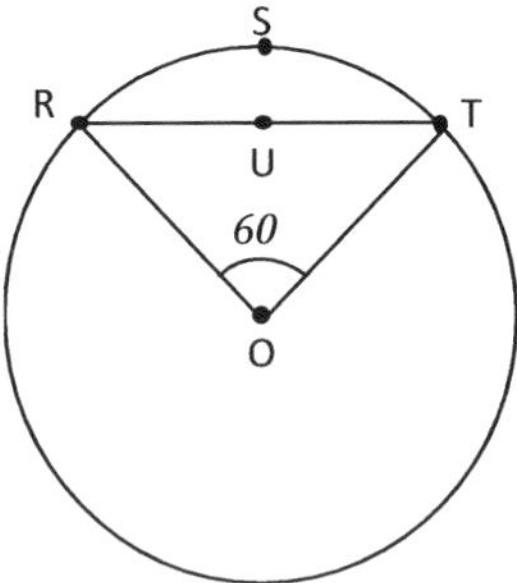

Thus, we have:

$$2\pi r * \left(\frac{60}{360}\right) = 18\pi$$

$$=> r = 54$$

In triangle TOR, we have: RO = TO = radius of the circle

Hence, we have:

$$\angle OTR = \angle ORT = \frac{180^{o} - 60^{o}}{2} = 60^{o}$$

Thus, triangle TOR is equilateral.

Thus, we have: RT = TO = RO = radius of the circle = 54.

Thus, perimeter of the region RSTU $= (18\pi + 54)$.

The correct answer is option D.

218. Let us bring out the figure.

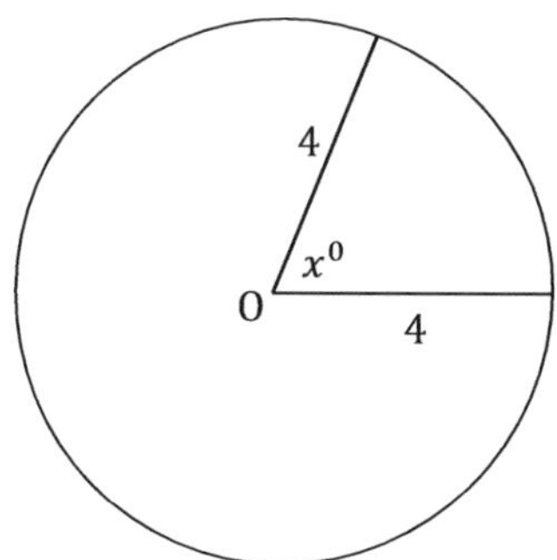

Area of a sector of a circle containing x^0 at the center is given by:

Area $= \pi * (\text{radius})^2 * \left(\frac{x}{360}\right)$

Thus, we have:

$\pi * (4)^2 * \left(\frac{x}{360}\right) = 2\pi$

$=> x = \frac{2 * 360}{16}$

$= 45$

The correct answer is option C.

219. Let us bring out the figure.

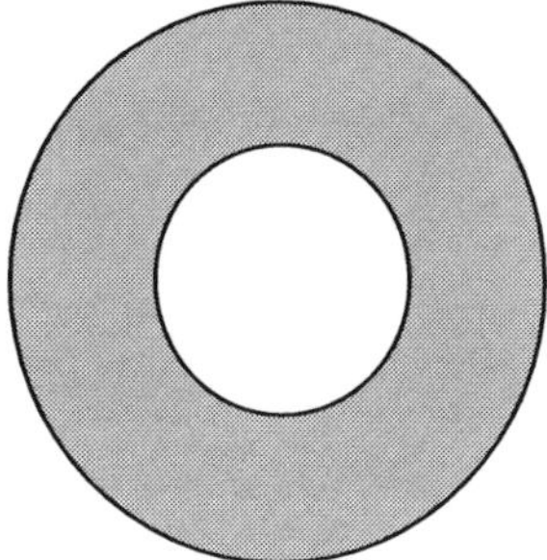

Let the radius of the outer circle be R and the radius of the inner circle be r.

Thus, area of the outer circle $= \pi R^2$

Area of the inner circle $= \pi r^2$

Thus, area of the shaded region $= (\pi R^2 - \pi r^2)$

Since the area of the shaded region is 3 times the area of the smaller circle, we have:

$\pi R^2 - \pi r^2 = 3\pi r^2$

$=> \pi R^2 = 4\pi r^2$

$=> R^2 = 4r^2$

$=> R = 2r$

$=> \frac{R}{r} = 2$

Thus, we have:

$\frac{\text{Circumference of the larger circle}}{\text{Circumference of the smaller circle}}$

$= \frac{2\pi R}{2\pi r} = \frac{R}{r}$

$= 2$

The correct answer is option C.

220.

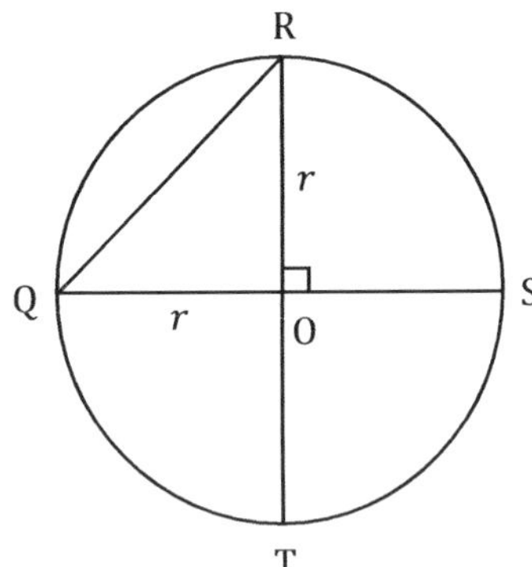

In right angled triangle ROQ, as per Pythagoras theorem, we have:

$=> RQ^2 = RO^2 + QO^2$

Since $RQ = \frac{8}{\sqrt{2}}$ and RO = QO = radius $= r$, we have:

$=> \left(\frac{8}{\sqrt{2}}\right)^2 = r^2 + r^2$

$=> 2r^2 = 32$

$=> r = 4$

Thus, area of the circle

$= \pi r^2$

$= 16\pi$

The correct answer is option C.

221. Let us bring out the figure.

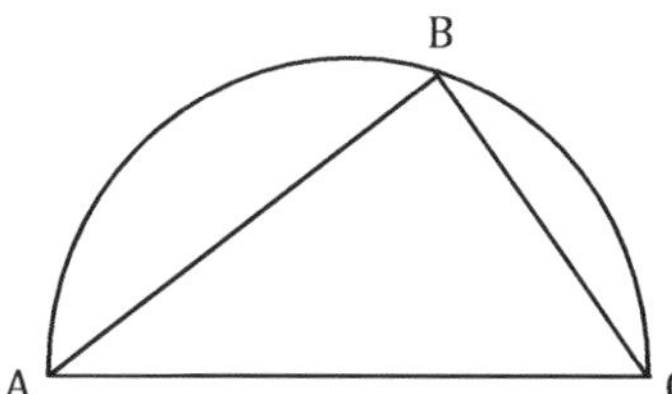

AC is the diameter of the semicircle.

Since the diameter subtends 90° at any point on the circumference, in triangle ABC, we have:

$\angle ABC = 90^o$

Thus, from Pythagoras' theorem, we have:

$AC^2 = AB^2 + BC^2$

$\Rightarrow AC^2 = 8^2 + 6^2$ (it is given that AB = 8 and AC = 6)

$\Rightarrow AC = 10$

$\Rightarrow$ Radius of the semicircle $= \frac{10}{2} = 5$

Thus, length of the arc ABC

$= \pi *$ (radius of the circle)

$= 5\pi$

The correct answer is option E.

222.

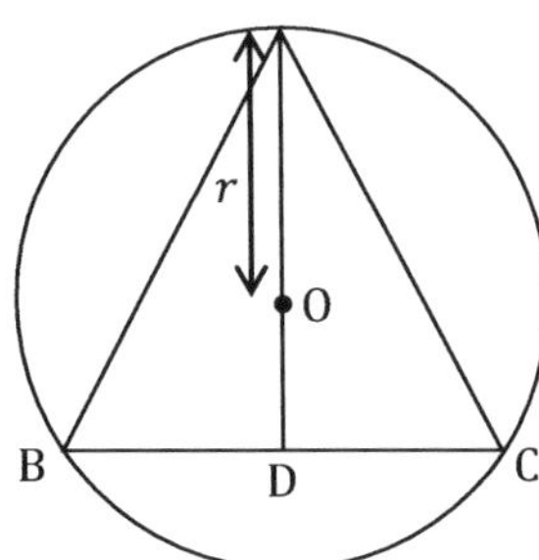

The area of an equilateral triangle = $\frac{\sqrt{3}}{4} * (\text{side})^2 = \frac{\sqrt{3}}{4} * (\text{AB})^2$

Thus, we have:

$\frac{\sqrt{3}}{4} * (\text{AB})^2 = 9\sqrt{3}$

=> AB = 6

Thus, the height (or, the median) of the equilateral triangle (AD)

$= \frac{\sqrt{3}}{2} * (\text{side}) = \frac{\sqrt{3}}{2} * (\text{AB})$

$= \frac{\sqrt{3}}{2} * 6$

$= 3\sqrt{3}$

In an equilateral triangle, the centre of the circumscribing circle is the centroid of the triangle.

Thus, the centre of the circle (O) is the centroid of the equilateral triangle ABC.

The centroid divided the median AD in the ratio 2 : 1.

Thus, we have:

$\text{AO} = \left(\frac{2}{2+1}\right) *\text{AD}$

$= \frac{2}{3} * 3\sqrt{3}$

$= 2\sqrt{3}$

Thus, the radius (r) of the circle = AO = $2\sqrt{3}$

Thus, the area of the circle = πr^2

$= \pi * (2\sqrt{3})^2$

$= 12\pi$

The correct answer is option C.

5.19 Geometry–Polygon

223. The diagram corresponding to the data provided is shown below:

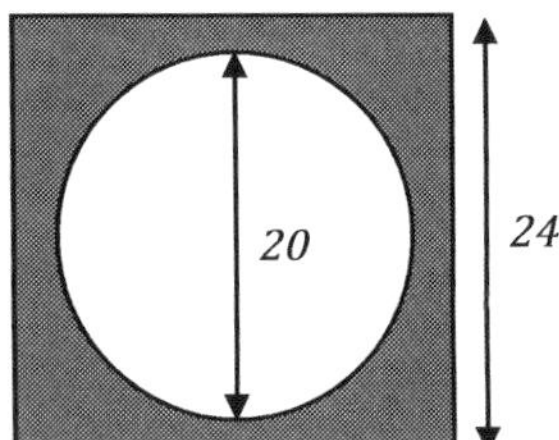

We need to find what fraction the shaded area represents of the area of square table top.

Side of square table top is 24 inches.

Area of the square tabletop = $(\text{Side})^2$

=> $24^2 = 576$ square inches.

Diameter of circular mat is 20 inches.

Area of the circular mat = $\pi(r)^2$

=> $\pi * \left(\frac{20}{2}\right)^2 =\sim 3.14 * 100 = 314$ square inches.

Thus, area of the tabletop not covered by the mat = 576 – 314 = 262 square inches.

Thus, the required fraction = $\frac{\text{area of the tabletop not covered by the mat}}{\text{Area of square table top}}$

=> $\frac{262}{576} = \frac{131}{288}$.

We can see that 131 is less than half of 288 (= 144)

So here option A, B, and C are eliminated.

However, 131 is more than one-fourth of 288 (= 72)

So here option D is eliminated.

Thus, the required fraction must be between 50% (half) and 25% (one-fourth).

The only option satisfying is option E which is $\frac{9}{20} * 100 = 45\%$

The correct answer is option E.

224. Let the length and breadth of the rectangular floors be x meters and y meters, where x and y are integers.

Since the perimeter of all such floors is 16 meters, we have:

$2(x + y) = 16$

$=> x + y = 8$

Thus, the possible cases are:

(1) $(x, y) = (7, 1)$
$=>$ Area of the floor $= 1 * 7 = 7$ square meters
$=>$ Number of carpets required $= \left(\frac{7}{1 * 1}\right) = 7$
$=>$ Total cost of carpeting $= \$ (7 * 6) = \$42$

(2) $(x, y) = (6, 2)$
$=>$ Area of the floor $= 2 * 6 = 12$ square meters
$=>$ Number of carpets required $= \left(\frac{12}{1 * 1}\right) = 12$
$=>$ Total cost of carpeting $= \$ (12 * 6) = \$72$

(3) $(x, y) = (5, 3)$
$=>$ Area of the floor $= 3 * 5 = 15$ square meters
$=>$ Number of carpets required $= \left(\frac{15}{1 * 1}\right) = 15$
$=>$ Total cost of carpeting $= \$ (15 * 6) = \$90$

(4) $(x, y) = (4, 4)$
$=>$ Area of the floor $= 4 * 4 = 16$ square meters
$=>$ Number of carpets required $= \left(\frac{16}{1 * 1}\right) = 16$
$=>$ Total cost of carpeting $= \$ (16 * 6) = \$96$

Note: For a given perimeter, the area is the maximum if the length and breadth are equal.

The correct answer is option D.

225. Let the length and breadth of the photograph be x inches and y inches respectively.

Thus, along with the border of 1 inch, the effective length becomes $(x + 2)$ inches and the effective breadth becomes $(y + 2)$ inches (since the border is along all sides) as shown in the figure below:

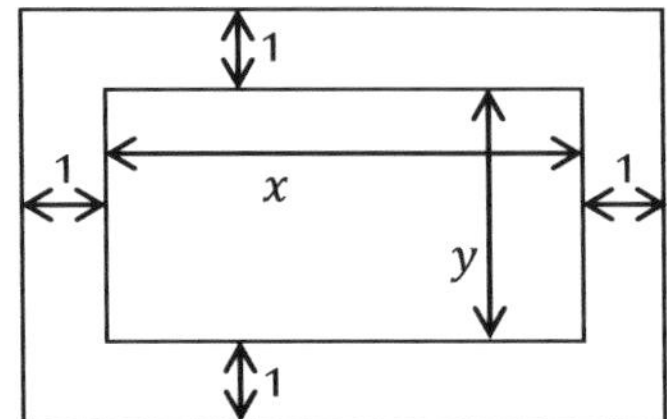

Thus, we have:

$(x + 2)\,(y + 2) = m$

$=> xy + 2\,(x + y) = m - 4 \ldots$ (i)

Again, along with the border of 2 inches, the effective length becomes $(x + 4)$ inches and the effective breadth becomes $(y + 4)$ inches.

Thus, we have:

$(x + 4)\,(y + 4) = m + 52$

$=> xy + 4\,(x + y) = m + 52 - 16$

$=> xy + 4\,(x + y) = m + 36 \ldots$ (ii)

Subtracting (i) from (ii):

$4\,(x + y) - 2\,(x + y) = (m + 36) - (m - 4)$

$=> 2\,(x + y) = 36 - (-4)$

$=> 2\,(x + y) = 40$

=> Perimeter of the photograph = 40 inches.

The correct answer is option D.

226. Let the breadth of the picture without the border be x inches.

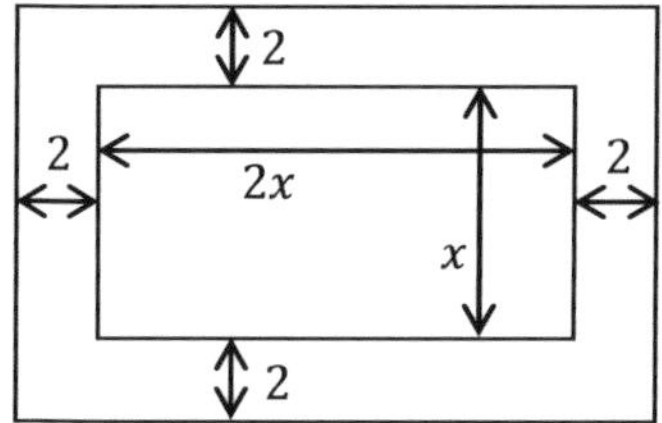

Thus, the length of the picture without the border is $2x$ inches.

Thus, area of the above rectangle without the border = $2x * x = 2x^2$ square inches.

Including the border, the length and breadth are $(2x + 4)$ and $(x + 4)$ inches respectively.

Thus, area of the above rectangle including the border = $(2x + 4)(x + 4)$ square inches.

Thus, the area of the border

= (Area of the outer rectangle) – (Area of the inner rectangle)

$= (2x + 4)(x + 4) - 2x^2$

$= 2x^2 + 12x + 16 - 2x^2$

$= 12x + 16$

Thus, we have:

$12x + 16 = 196$

$=> x = 15$

Thus, the length of the picture without the border = $2x = 30$ inches.

The correct answer is option C.

227. The two possible ways in which the field may be partitioned are shown below:

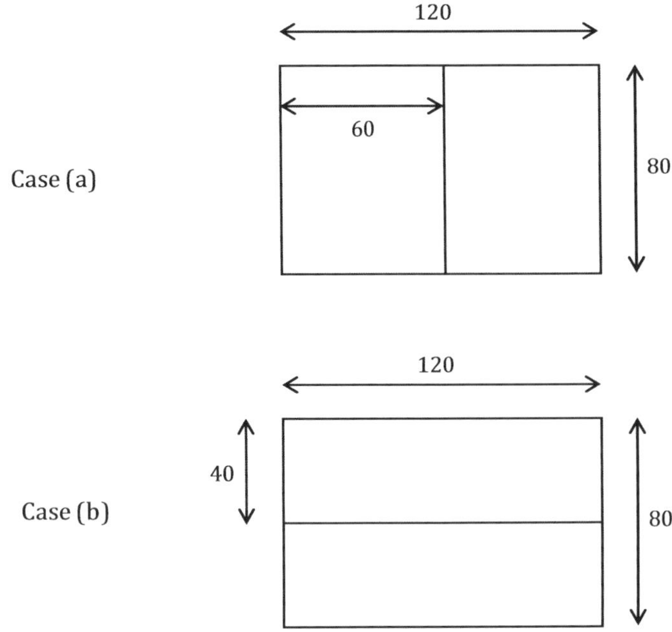

Case A: Perimeter of one half of the field = $2 * (60 + 80) = 280$ feet.

Case B: Perimeter of one half of the field = $2 * (40 + 120) = 320$ feet.

Thus, the perimeter is the minimum in the first case.

Thus, the minimum cost of fencing = $\$ (280 * 2) = \$560$.

The correct answer is option D.

228. We know that the perimeter is 560 feet.

Thus, twice the sum of the length and breadth is 560 feet.

Thus, the sum of the length and breadth is $\frac{560}{2} = 280$ feet.

Let the length of the field = l feet.

Thus, the breadth of the field = $(280 - l)$ feet.

The diagonal of a rectangle is the square-root of the sum of squares of the length and breadth (from Pythagoras' theorem).

Since the diagonal is 200 feet long, we have:

$\sqrt{l^2 + (280 - l)^2} = 200$

$\Rightarrow l^2 + (280 - l)^2 = 200^2$

=> $2l^2 + 280^2 - 560l = 200^2$

=> $2l^2 - 560l + 38400 = 0$

=> $l^2 - 280l + 19200 = 0$

=> $280l - l^2 = 19200$

=> $l * (280 - l) = 19200$

=> Length * Breadth = 19200

Note: We do not need to solve for the length to get the answer.

Thus, area = 19200 square feet.

The correct answer is option A.

Alternate approach:

We know that the perimeter of the rectangle is 560 feet.

Thus, the sum of the length and breadth is $\frac{560}{2} = 280$ feet.

The area of the rectangle would be the maximum if the length and breadth are equal.

In that case, we would have:

Length = Breadth = $\frac{280}{2} = 140$ feet.

Thus, the maximum possible area would be = 140 * 140 = 19600 square feet.

However, in this case, the diagonal would not be 200 feet (since it does not satisfy Pythagoras' theorem).

Thus, the actual area would be less than 19600 square feet.

There is only one option, 19200 square feet which satisfies the above condition.

229. Width of the strip = t inches

= $\left(\frac{t}{12}\right)$ feet

Length of the strip = m miles

= $5280 * m$ feet

Thus, total area of the strip

$$= \left(\frac{t}{12}\right) * (5280 * m)$$

$$= \left(\frac{5280 * m * t}{12}\right) \text{ square feet}$$

Quantity of paint required to paint p square feet = 1 gallon.

Thus, quantity of paint required to paint 1 square foot = $\left(\frac{1}{p}\right)$ gallon.

Thus, quantity of paint required to paint $\left(\frac{5280 * m * t}{12}\right)$ square feet

$$= \left(\frac{1}{p}\right) * \left(\frac{5280 * m * t}{12}\right)$$

$$= \left(\frac{5280 * m * t}{12 * p}\right) \text{ gallons}$$

The correct answer is option A.

230. Let us bring out the figure.

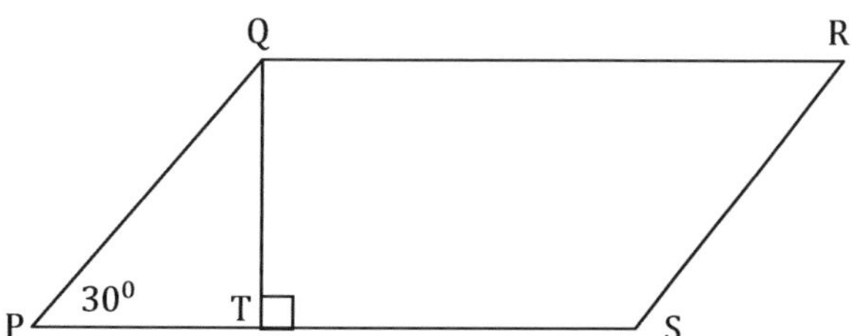

We know that the area of a parallelogram = Base $*$ Height = PS $*$ QT

In triangle PQT, we have:

PQ = 4, and

$\angle QPT = 30^0$

In a 30-60-90 triangle, the ratio of the sides of the triangle is shown below:

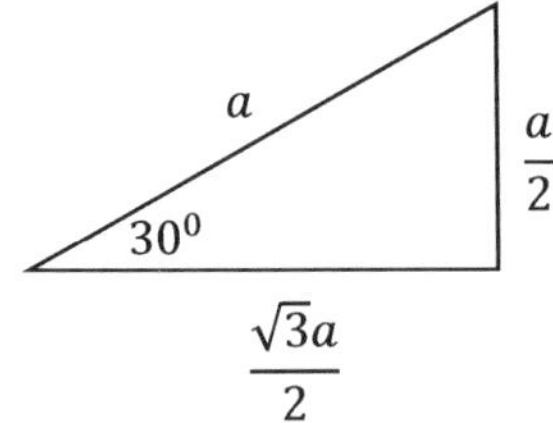

If the hypotenuse is of length a:

(1) The side opposite to 30^0 is $\frac{a}{2}$

(2) The side opposite to 60^0 is $\frac{\sqrt{3}a}{2}$

In the given problem, we have:

PQ = Hypotenuse = 4

=> QT (side opposite to 30^0) = $\frac{4}{2} = 2$

Thus, area of the parallelogram = QT $*$ PS = QT $*$ QR = $2 * 6 = 12$.

The correct answer is option B.

231. Let us bring out the figure.

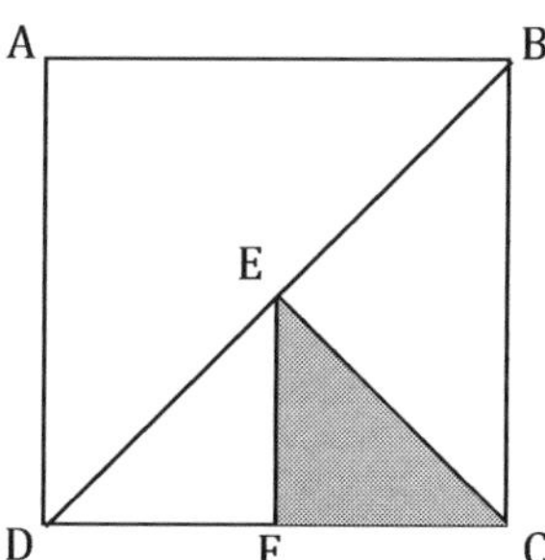

We know that:

E is the mid-point of BD, and

F is the mid-point of DC.

Thus, from intercept theorem, we have: EF ||BC.

Thus, triangle DEF ≅ triangle DBC

The ratio of the corresponding sides of the above two similar triangles

$= \frac{DE}{DB} = \frac{1}{2}$

Thus, ratio of the area of similar triangles DEF and DBC

= (Raio of their corresponding sides)^2

$= \left(\frac{1}{2}\right)^2 = \frac{1}{4}$

Thus, we have:

$\frac{\text{Area of triangle DEF}}{\text{Area of triangle DBC}} = \frac{1}{4}$

Since area of triangle DBC is $\frac{1}{2}$ area of square ABCD, we have:

$=> \frac{\text{Area of triangle DEF}}{\left(\frac{\text{Area of square ABCD}}{2}\right)} = \frac{1}{4}$

$=> 2 * \frac{\text{Area of triangle DEF}}{\text{Area of square ABCD}} = \frac{1}{4}$

$=> \frac{\text{Area of triangle DEF}}{\text{Area of square ABCD}} = \frac{1}{8}$

From the diagram, it is clear that triangles DEF and EFC are congruent and hence, have equal area.

Thus, we have:

$$\frac{\text{Area of triangle EFC}}{\text{Area of square ABCD}} = \frac{1}{8}$$

Alternate approach:

Constructing a few lines (shown below as dotted lines) makes it clear that the shaded part i.e. triangle EFC is 1 out of 8 identical parts in which the square has been divided into.

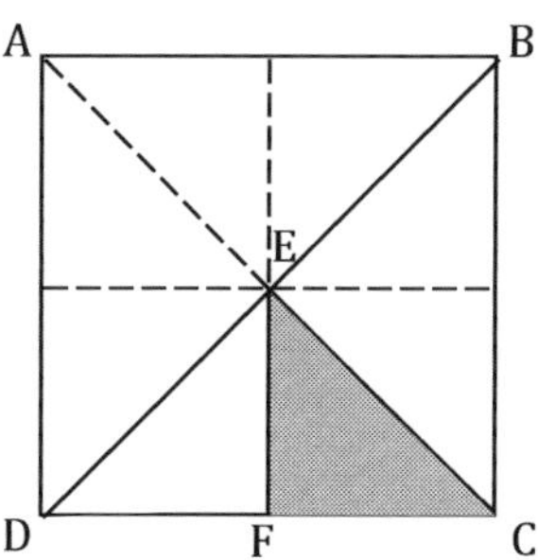

The correct answer is option B.

232. Let us bring out the figure.

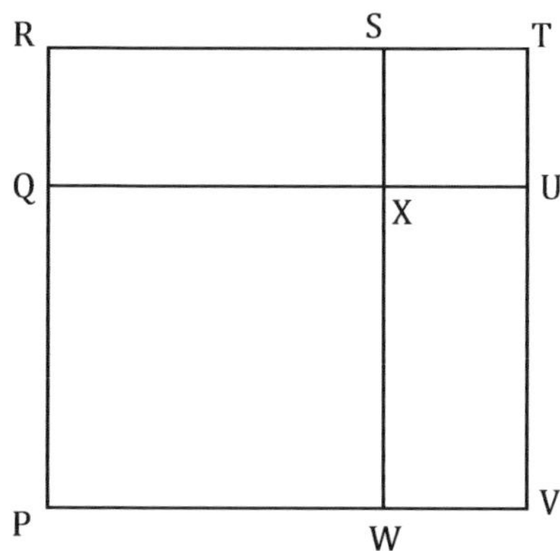

Area of square PRTV = 81

Thus, we have:

$RT^2 = 81$

$\Rightarrow RT = 9 \ldots (i)$

Ratio of the area of square region XSTU to the area of square region PQXW = 1 : 4

$\Rightarrow ST^2 : QX^2 = 1 : 4$

$\Rightarrow ST : QX = 1 : 2$

Since RSXQ is a rectangle, RS = QX

$\Rightarrow ST : RS = 1 : 2 \ldots (ii)$

Thus, from (i) and (ii):

$RS = \left(\frac{2}{1+2}\right) * 9 = 6.$

The correct answer is option C.

233. Let us redraw the figure.

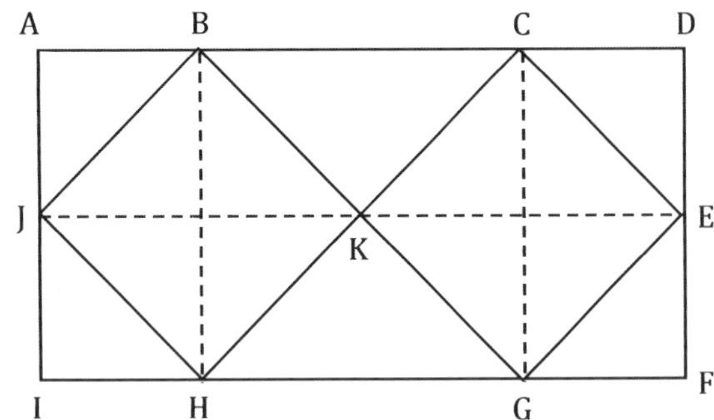

Since BJHK and CKGE are identical squares, we have:

BH = CG = JK = KE (since diagonals of a square are equal)

Thus, we have:

AD = JK + KE

= BH + CG

= AI + AI (since BH = CG = AI)

=> AD = 2 * AI

Since, perimeter of the rectangle is $18\sqrt{2}$, we have:

$2 * (AD + AI) = 18\sqrt{2}$

=> $2 * (2 * AI + AI) = 18\sqrt{2}$

=> $AI = 3\sqrt{2}$

=> Diagonal of each square = $3\sqrt{2}$

If the side of each square be x, then the length of the diagonal = $x\sqrt{2}$

Thus, we have:

$x\sqrt{2} = 3\sqrt{2}$

$=> x = 3$

Thus, perimeter of each square

$= 4x$

$= 4 * 3$

$= 12$

The correct answer is option B.

234. Let the number of desks placed be d and the number of bookshelves placed be b.

Each desk is 2.0 meters long, and each bookshelf is 1.5 meters long.

Thus, the total length covered by d desks and b bookshelves = $(2.0d + 1.5b)$ meters.

We need to find the closest we can take the above value of $(2.0d + 1.5b)$ to 16 (since available space is 16 meters long).

Since we need to maximize the total number of desks and bookshelves, and bookshelves are shorter than desks, we must have a larger number of bookshelves than desks, keeping at least one of each.

Thus, we have:
$(2d + 1.5b) \leq 16$ (Where d and b are positive integers which are not equal to zero)

If we take the maximum value of b to be 10, we have: $1.5b = 1.5 * 10 = 15 < 16$

In the above situation, there is only $(16 - 15) = 1$ meter left which is not sufficient to accommodate a desk.

Checking with the next possible value of $b = 9$, we have: $1.5b = 1.5 * 9 = 13.5 < 16$

Length of space left = $(16 - 13.5) = 2.5$ meters.

Thus, 1 desk (of length 2 meters) can be accommodated in this space.

Thus, space left after accommodating the desk = $(2.5 - 2) = 0.5$ meters.

The correct answer is option A.

235. We know that the radius of the circle formed is r.

Thus, circumference of the circle = $2\pi r$.

Thus, length of wire left to form the square = $(40 - 2\pi r)$.

Thus, length of each side of the square = $\frac{1}{4}(40 - 2\pi r) = \left(10 - \frac{1}{2}\pi r\right)$.

Thus, total area of the circle and the square formed

$= \pi r^2 + \left(10 - \frac{1}{2}\pi r\right)^2$

The correct answer is option E.

5.20 Geometry–3 Dimensional

236. The volume of liquid is the same in both cylinders.

Volume of cylinder = $\pi * r^2 * h$

For first cylinder, we know that $r = 5$ inches and $h = 9$ inches.

Volume of liquid in the first cylinder = $v = \pi * 5^2 * 9 = 225\pi$ cubic inches.

Let the radius of the second cylinder be R inches and height be 4 inches.

Thus, volume of liquid in the second cylinder = $V = \pi * R^2 * 4 = 4R^2\pi$ cubic inches.

As per given data,

$v = V$

Thus, we have:

$4R^2\pi = 225\pi$

$=> R^2 = \frac{225\ \pi}{4\ \pi}$

$=> R = \frac{15}{2} = 7.5$

The correct answer is option D.

237. Diameter of the smaller rim = 28 inches.

Circumference of the smaller rim = Distance covered by smaller ring in one revolution

$=> \ \pi * 28 = 28\pi$ inch.

Number of revolutions made per second by the smaller rim = x.

D_1= distance covered per second by the smaller rim

= No. of revolutions per second × Distance covered by smaller ring in one revolution

$=> 28\pi x$ inch.

Diameter of the larger rim = 35 inch.

Circumference of the larger rim = Distance covered by larger ring in one revolution

=> $\pi * 35 = 35\pi$ inch.

Let the number of revolutions made per second by the larger rim be y.

D_2 = distance covered per sec. by larger rim

= No. of revolutions per sec. × Distance covered by larger ring in one revolution

=> $35\pi y$ inch.

Hence, we have:

$D_1 = D_2$

$28\pi x = 35\pi y$

=> $y = \frac{4x}{5}$

Thus, the number of revolutions made per second by the larger rim = $\frac{4x}{5}$.

Hence, the number of revolutions made per minute by the larger rim = $\frac{4x}{5} * 60 = 48x$.

The correct answer is option C.

238.

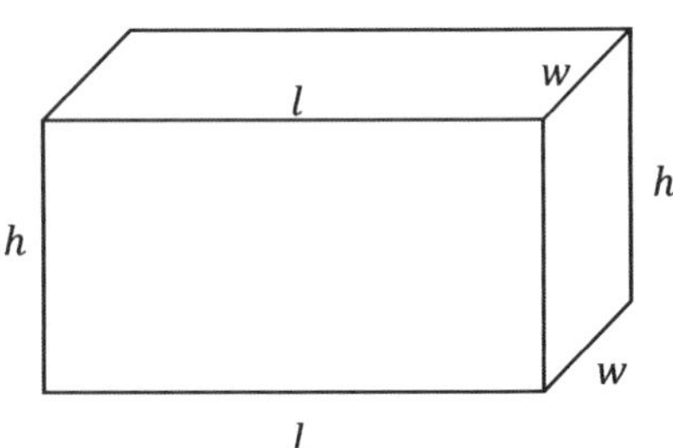

Let the dimensions of the length, width and height be l, w and h respectively.

Since three faces shown have areas 12, 15, and 20, we have:

Top face: $l * w = 12 \ldots$(i)

Front face: $l * h = 15 \ldots$(ii)

Right face: $h * w = 20 \ldots$(iii)

Multiplying the above three equations:

$l^2 * w^2 * h^2 = 12 * 15 * 20 = 3600$

$=> l * w * h = \sqrt{3600} = 60$

Since the volume of the solid is given by $l * w * h$, we have:

Volume of the solid = 60.

The correct answer is option A.

239. Since the ratio of length to width to height is 3 : 2 : 2, we can assume that:

- Length = $3k$
- Width = $2k$
- Height = $2k$

Thus, the volume of the rectangular carton

$= 3k * 2k * 2k$

$= 12k^3$

Thus, we have:

$12k^3 = x$

$=> k^3 = \frac{x}{12}$

$=> k = \sqrt[3]{\frac{x}{12}}$

Thus, the height of the carton

$= 2k$

$= 2 * \sqrt[3]{\frac{x}{12}}$

$= \sqrt[3]{8 * \frac{x}{12}}$

$= \sqrt[3]{\frac{2}{3}x}$

The correct answer is option B.

240. Let the height and radius of can X are h and r, respectively.

Thus, volume of oil in can X = $\pi r^2 h$

Thus, price of oil of quantity $\pi r^2 h$ = \$2 . . . (i)

Height and radius of can Y = $2h$ and $2r$, respectively.

Thus, volume of can Y = $\pi(2r)^2(2h) = 8\pi r^2 h$

Since can Y is filled to half the capacity, volume of oil in can Y = $\frac{1}{2} * 8\pi r^2 h = 4\pi r^2 h$

Thus, from (i), we have:

Price of oil of quantity $4\pi r^2 h$ = \$(4 * 2) = \$8

The correct answer is option D.

241.

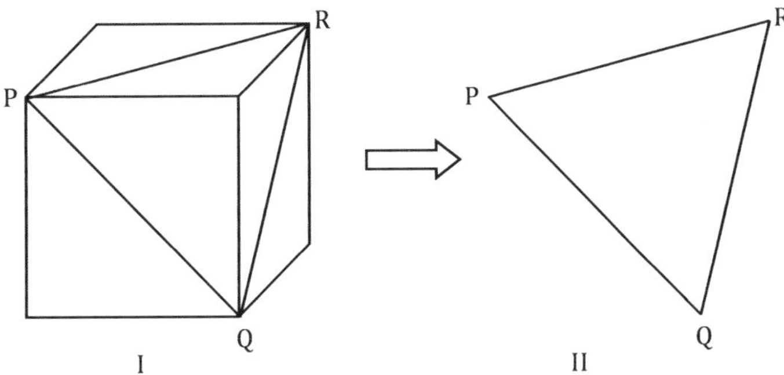

Let us join PR as shown in the figure (I) above.

Let us now remove the edges of the cube from the figure (I) so that only the triangle PQR is left behind as shown in figure (II).

We can see that PR, RQ and PQ are the face diagonals of the cube and hence, are equal to one another.

Thus, triangle PQR is an equilateral triangle.

Thus, $\angle PQR = 60^o$

The correct answer is option C.

242. Let us consider the situation where the largest possible cube (shaded in grey) fits perfectly in a particular cylinder as shown in the diagram below; however, the question does not state that we must fit in a largest possible cube into the cylinder.

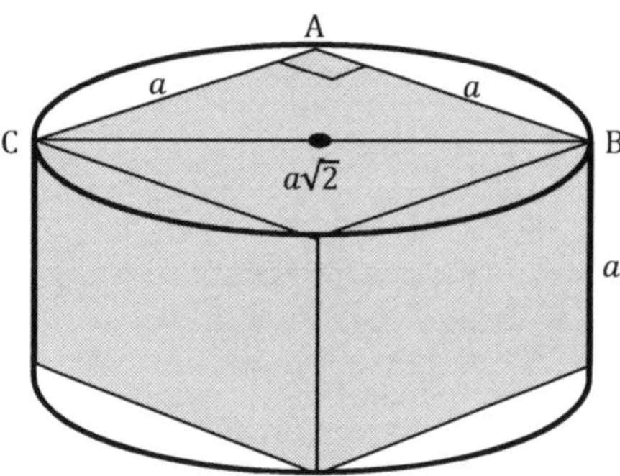

Let the edge of the cube be a.

Since the cube has to have a perfect fit (minimum non-utilization of cylinder space), we must have:

Height of the cylinder = edge of the cube = a

In right angled triangle CAB:

$CB^2 = CA^2 + AB^2 = a^2 + a^2 = 2a^2$

=> $CB = a\sqrt{2}$

Thus, the diameter of the cylinder = $a\sqrt{2}$

=> Radius of the cylinder = $\frac{a\sqrt{2}}{2} = \frac{a}{\sqrt{2}}$

Thus, volume of the cylinder

$= \pi * \text{radius}^2 * \text{height}$

$= \pi * \left(\frac{a}{\sqrt{2}}\right)^2 * a$

$= \frac{\pi a^3}{2}$

$= \frac{3}{2}a^3$

Volume of the cube = a^3

Thus, volume of the cylinder not occupied by the cube

$= \frac{3}{2}a^3 - a^3$

$= \frac{a^3}{2}$

Thus, the required percent

$= \dfrac{\text{Volume of the cylinder not occupied by the cube}}{\text{Volume of the cylinder}} * 100$

$= \dfrac{\left(\dfrac{a^3}{2}\right)}{\left(\dfrac{3}{2}a^3\right)} * 100$

$= 33.3\%$

The above situation depicts the case where minimum volume of the cylinder as a percent of the total volume of the cylinder is unutilized, i.e. not covered by the cube.

Thus, in any other scenario, the required percent value would be either greater than or equal to 33.3%

The only possible value from the answer options is 36%

The correct answer is option E.

5.21 Co-ordinate geometry

243. The length of the line segment between 2 points $(x_1, y_1) = (-3, -6)$ and $(x_2, y_2) = (5, 0)$ is given by:

$L = \sqrt{(x_2 - x_1)^2 + (y_2 - y_1)^2}$

$= \sqrt{(5 - (-3))^2 + (0 - (-6))^2}$

$= \sqrt{8^2 + 6^2}$

$= 10$

Thus, the length of the diameter of the circle = 10.

Thus, the length of the radius of the circle $= \frac{10}{2} = 5$.

Thus, the area of the circle $= \pi * 5^2 = 25\pi$.

The correct answer is option C.

244. Equation of a line is: $y = mx + c$, where m is the slope and c is the Y-intercept.

Thus, we have the equation of the given line as:

$y = 2x + 2$

Let the required point on the above line be: $(a, 500)$.

Thus, we have:

$500 = 2a + 2$

$=> a = 249$

Thus, the required X-coordinate of the point is 249.

The correct answer is option A.

245. Equation of a line passing through a point (p, q) and slope m is given as:

$y - q = m(x - p)$

Thus, the equation of the line n that passes through the origin $(0, 0)$ and has slope 4 is:

$y - 0 = 4(x - 0)$

$=> y = 4x$

Since $(1, c)$ is a point on the line, we have:

$c = 4 * 1$

$=> c = 4 \ldots$ (i)

Since $(d, 2)$ is a point on the line, we have:

$2 = 4 * d$

$=> d = \frac{1}{2} \ldots$ (ii)

Thus, from (i) and (ii), we have:

$\frac{c}{d} = \frac{4}{\left(\frac{1}{2}\right)} = 8$

The correct answer is option E.

246. The equation of a circle having center at (p, q) and radius r is:
$(x - p)^2 + (y - q)^2 = r^2$

Since the center of the circle is at $(-2, -3)$, the equation of the circle is:
$(x - (-2))^2 + (y - (-3))^2 = r^2$

$=> (x + 2)^2 + (y + 3)^2 = r^2$

If a point (m, n) lies inside the circle $(x - p)^2 + (y - q)^2 = r^2$, it must satisfy:

$(m - p)^2 + (n - q)^2 < r^2$

Since $(-2,\ 1)$ lies inside the circle, it must satisfy:
$(-2 + 2)^2 + (1 + 3)^2 < r^2$

$=> r^2 > 16$

$=> r > 4$ OR $r < -4$

Since r must be positive, we have:
$r > 4 \ldots$ (i)

If a point (m, n) lies outside the circle, it must satisfy:

$(m - p)^2 + (n - q)^2 > r^2$

Since (4, −3) lies outside the circle, it must satisfy:
$(4 + 2)^2 + (-3 + 3)^2 > r^2$

$=> r^2 < 36$

$=> -6 < r < 6$

Since r must be positive, we have:
$0 < r < 6 \ldots$ (ii)

Thus, from (i) and (ii), we have:

$r = 5$

The correct answer is option B.

247. The three vertices are: $(c,\ d)$, $(c,\ -d)$ and $(-c, -d)$

We know that $c < 0$ and $d > 0$

$=> -c > 0$ and $- - d < 0$

We can see that the distance of each of the vertices from the origin $(0,\ 0) = \sqrt{c^2 + d^2}$

Thus, the three vertices are equidistant from the origin.

Thus, the centre of the square is at the origin.

Thus, the square would be positioned as shown in the diagram below:

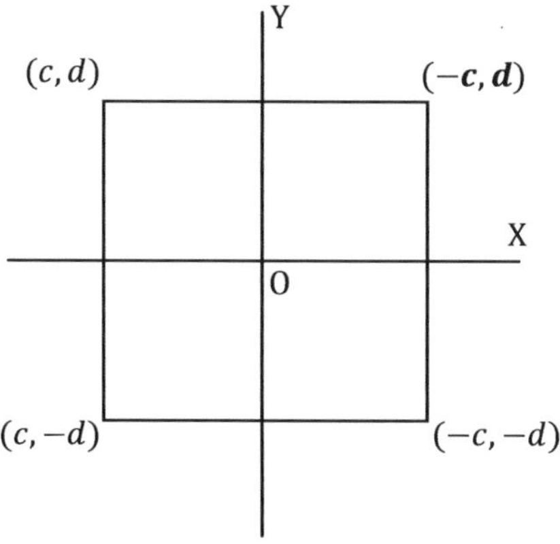

Thus, the fourth vertex would be $(-c, d)$, which lies in the first quadrant.

Thus, the X-coordinate of the fourth vertex is positive and the Y-coordinate of the fourth vertex is also positive.

Thus, the only point which also lies in the same quadrant is (3, 5).

The correct answer is option E.

248. Distance between two points (x_1, y_1) and (x_2, y_2) is given by: $\sqrt{(x_2 - x_1)^2 + (y_2 - y_1)^2}$

Distance between the points (0, 0) and (3, 3)

$= \sqrt{(3-0)^2 + (3-0)^2}$

$= \sqrt{18}$

$= 3\sqrt{2}$

Distance between the points (0, 0) and (7, 0)

$= \sqrt{(7-0)^2 + (0-0)^2}$

$= \sqrt{49}$

$= 7$

Distance between the points (7, 0) and (3, 3)

$= \sqrt{(7-3)^2 + (0-3)^2}$

$= \sqrt{25}$

$= 5$

Thus, the perimeter

$= 3\sqrt{2} + 7 + 5$

$= 12 + 3\sqrt{2}$

The correct answer is option E.

249. Since the points are collinear, their slopes must be equal.

Slope of the line joining two points (x_1, y_1) and (x_2, y_2) is given by: $\left(\frac{x_2 - x_1}{y_2 - y_1}\right)$.

Slope of the line joining the points $(a, 0)$ and $(0, b)$

$$= \frac{b-0}{0-a}$$

$$= -\frac{b}{a}$$

Slope of the line joining the points $(a, 0)$ and $(1,\ 1)$

$$= \frac{1-0}{1-a}$$

$$= \frac{1}{1-a}$$

Thus, we have:

$$-\frac{b}{a} = \frac{1}{1-a}$$

$$=> -b * (1-a) = a$$

$$=> -b + ab = a$$

$$=> b + a = ab$$

$$=> \frac{b+a}{ab} = 1$$

$$=> \frac{b}{ab} + \frac{a}{ab} = 1$$

$$=> \frac{1}{a} + \frac{1}{b} = 1$$

The correct answer is option C.

250. The area of the triangle formed by the line with the two axes

$= \frac{1}{2} *$ (Length of X intercept) $*$ (Length of Y intercept)

We have:

$3y - 4x = 24 \ldots$(i)

The graph of the line and the area of the triangle formed by the line and the axes is shown in the diagram below:

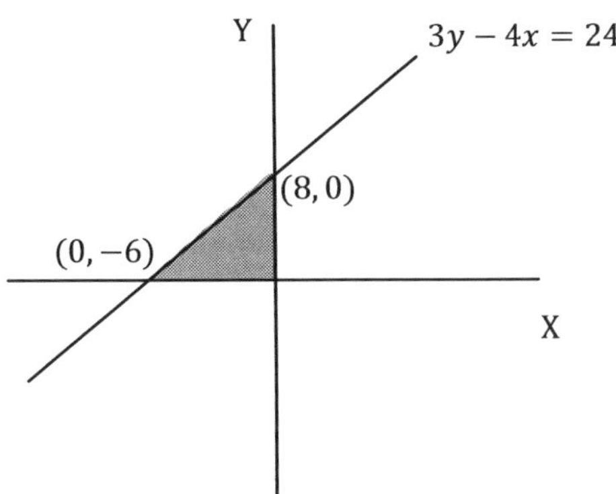

To calculate the X-intercept:

Substituting $y = 0$ in (i):

$$x = -\frac{24}{4} = -6$$

Thus, the length of the X-intercept = 6.

To calculate the Y-intercept:

Substituting $x = 0$ in (i):

$$y = \frac{24}{3} = 8$$

Thus, the length of the Y-intercept = 8.

Thus, required area

$$= \frac{1}{2} * 6 * 8 = 24$$

The correct answer is option C.

Chapter 6

Solutions – Data Sufficiency Questions

6.1 Numbers

251. The 2-height of x is essentially the highest exponent of 2 that perfectly divided x.

For example, if $n = 24 = 2^3 * 3$

The 2-height of 24 is 3 since the highest exponent of 2 that divided 24 perfectly is 3.

From statement 1:

We have: $k > m$.

There are only two possibilities for k, either it is odd or even; likewise, m may either be odd or even.

If k is odd, while m is even:

The 2-height of k will be '0' and hence will be less than that of m.

If both k and m are odd:

The 2-heights of both k and m will be '0', thus equals to heights

If $k = 2m$:

The 2-height of k will be '1' more than that of m (Here, it does not matter whether m is even or odd, either ways, the 2-height of k is greater than that of m).

Hence, there is no definite answer. – Insufficient

From statement 2:

We have: $\frac{k}{m}$ is an even number

=> $k = m *$ (an even number)

=> $k = m * 2^p$; where p is any positive integer

Thus, the 2-height of k will be p greater than that of m. – Sufficient

The correct answer is option B.

252. From statement 1:

We have: $k = 4q + 1$; where q is any positive integer (in this case, the quotient).

Since the value of q is unknown, we cannot determine the value of k. – Insufficient

From statement 2:

We have: $k^{\#} = k^2 + 1$.

$18 \leq k^{\#} \leq 36$

=> $18 \leq k^2 + 1 \leq 36$

=> $17 \leq k^2 \leq 35$

Since k is a positive integer, k^2 must be a perfect square between 17 and 35.
Thus: $k^2 = 25$
$=> k = 5$. – Sufficient

The correct answer is option B.

253. Let the number of biology students in classes K and L be k and l, respectively.

Thus, we have:

$k = 7n$
$l = 6p + 1$

We need to determine the value of l.

From statement 1:

We have: $n = p$

Thus, we have:

$k = 7p$
$l = 6p + 1$

However, there may be many values for p, thus correspondingly many values for l.
Thus, we cannot find the value of l. – Insufficient

From statement 2:

We have: $k = l + 5$

Thus, we have:

$7n = (6p + 1) + 5$
$=> 7n = 6(p + 1)$
$=> \frac{n}{p+1} = \frac{6}{7}$.

There may be many values possible for n and p:

$n = 6,\ p = 6;\ n = 12,\ p = 13$ etc.
Thus, the value of p is not unique.
Hence, $l = 6p + 1$ is also not unique. – Insufficient

Thus, from statements 1 and 2 together:

$\frac{n}{p+1} = \frac{6}{7}$ and $n = p$

Thus, we have:

$\frac{p}{p+1} = \frac{6}{7}$

=> $p = 6$.

Thus: $l = 6p + 1 = 37$. - Sufficient

The correct answer is option C.

254. The number of positive factors of a number N expressed in its prime form as $N = p^x q^y$, where p and q are distinct primes, given by $(x + 1)(y + 1)$.

For example: $24 = 2^3 * 3^1$.

The number of positive factors = $(3 + 1)(1 + 1) = 8$.

The factors of 24 are: 1, 2, 3, 4, 6, 8, 12, 24; i.e. 8 in number.

From statement 1:

$n = a^4 b^3$; where a and b are different prime numbers.

Thus, the number of positive factors = $(4 + 1)(3 + 1) = 20$. - Sufficient

From statement 2:

Here, n can take multiple possible values.

For example, $5 * 7$, $5^2 * 7^3$, $5^4 * 7$ etc. all have 5 and 7 as the only two prime factors.

However, the number of factors of each of the above numbers is different. - Insufficient

The correct answer is option A.

255. Since $\sqrt{x}$ is an integer, x must be a perfect square.

From statement 1:

We have: $11 < x < 17$

The only perfect square between 11 and 17 is 16.

Thus, we have:

$x = 16$.

=> $\sqrt{x} = 4$ ($\sqrt{x}$ only takes the positive square root of x). - Sufficient

From statement 2:

We have: $2 < \sqrt{x} < 5$

The possible values of $\sqrt{x}$ are 3 or 4.

Thus, the value of $\sqrt{x}$ is not unique. – Insufficient

The correct answer is option A.

256. We have:
$xy^{\left(\frac{4}{3}\right)} = \sqrt[3]{432}$

Cubing both sides:

$x^3y^4 = 432 = 3^3 * 2^4$

We need to determine whether $x + y = 5$.

From statement 1:

Nothing is mentioned about x.
For example, two possible solutions are:

If $x = 3,\ y = 2 => x + y = 5$;

OR

if $x = \sqrt[3]{432},\ y = 1 => x + y \neq 5$. – Insufficient

From statement 2:

Nothing is mentioned about y.

For example, two possible solutions are:
If $x = 3,\ y = 2 => x + y = 5$;

OR

If $x = 1,\ y = \sqrt[4]{432} => x + y \neq 5$. – Insufficient

Thus, from statements 1 and 2 together:

Both x and y are integers and $y > 0$.

Thus, the only way in which $x^3y^4 = 432 = 3^3 * 2^4$ is $x = 3,\ y = 2 => x + y = 5$. – Sufficient

The correct answer is option C.

257. From statement 1:

The value of y is not known.

Hence, we cannot determine the value of $\frac{25x^2}{y^2}$ – Insufficient

From statement 2:

$5x - 2y = 0$
$=> 5x = 2y$
$=> \frac{x}{y} = \frac{2}{5}$
$=> \frac{x^2}{y^2} = \left(\frac{2}{5}\right)^2 = \frac{4}{25}$

Thus, we have:

$\frac{25x^2}{y^2} = 25 * \frac{4}{25} = 4$ – Sufficient

The correct answer is option B.

258. $|m + 4| = 2$
$=> m + 4 = \pm 2$
$=> m = -4 \pm 2$
$=> m = -2$ or -6.

From statement 1:

We have: $m < 0$.

Thus, as per the information given in the question $m = -2$ or-6.
Thus, there is no unique value for m. – Insufficient

From statement 2:

$m^2 + 8m + 12 = 0$
$=> (m + 2)(m + 6) = 0$
$=> m = -2$ or -6.

Thus, both values of m are possible. – Insufficient

Thus, from statements 1 and 2 together:

Even after combining both statements, we have:
$m = -2$ or -6. – Insufficient

The correct answer is option E.

259. $|n + 5| = 5$
$\Rightarrow n + 5 = \pm 5$
$\Rightarrow n = -5 \pm 5$
$\Rightarrow n = 0$ or -10.

From statement 1:

We have: $n^2 \neq 0$
$\Rightarrow n \neq 0$

$\Rightarrow n = -10$. – Sufficient

From statement 2:

$n^2 + 10n = 0$
$\Rightarrow n(n + 10) = 0$
$\Rightarrow n = 0$ or -10.

Thus, both values of n are possible, i.e. n is not unique. – Insufficient

The correct answer is option A.

260. For any decimal number, say $a.bcd$, where b, c, d are the digits after the decimal point, the tenth's digit refers to the digit b.

From statement 1:

$d + 0.01 < 2$
$\Rightarrow d < 1.99$
$\Rightarrow 1 < d < 1.99$

Thus, the tenth's digit of d may be 9 (if $d = 1.98$) or less than 9 (if $d = 1.88$). – Insufficient

From statement 2:

$d + 0.05 > 2$
$\Rightarrow d > 1.95$
$\Rightarrow 1.95 < d < 2$.

Thus, the tenth's digit of d must always be 9. – Sufficient

The correct answer is option B.

261. From statement 1:

$3a + 4b$ is even:

For any integer value of b, $4b$ is even, (since (even) $*$ (any integer) = even).

Thus, $3a$ must be even (since (even) + (even) = even).

Hence, a is even.

However, b may be even or odd. – Insufficient

From statement 2:

$3a + 5b$ is even:

Two odd numbers when added result in an even number OR two even numbers when added also result in an even number.

Thus, both $3a$ and $5b$ are odd i.e. both a and b are odd

OR

Both $3a$ and $5b$ are even i.e. both a and b are even

Thus, b may be even or odd. – Insufficient

Thus, from statements 1 and 2 together:

From statement 1: a is even.

Hence, from statement 2: b is even. – Sufficient

The correct answer is option C.

262. From statement 1:

We know that a is a factor of b.
However, we have no information on the exponents k and m, which is likewise important.

For example:

2 is a factor of 6.
Also, 2^3 is a factor of 6^4.

However:

2 is a factor of 6.
But, 2^4 is not a factor of 6^3.

Thus, we need to know whether $k \le m$. – Insufficient

From statement 2:

We know: $k \le m$.

However, there is no information on a and b. – Insufficient

Thus, from statements 1 and 2 together:

a is a factor of b;
$k \le m$

Thus, a^k is a factor of b^m. – Sufficient

The correct answer is option C.

263. From statement 1:

Since the product of the four numbers (10, -2, -8 and 0) is zero, it is immaterial what the fifth integer be; for any value of the fifth integer, the product of five integers would still be '0'. – Insufficient

From statement 2:

The sum of the four integers $= 10 \pm 2 \pm 8 + 0 = 0$.

Since '0' divided by any number is '0', we can only conclude that the fifth integer is not '0', as '0' divided by '0' is not defined; however we cannot determine the value of fifth integer. – Insufficient

Thus, from statements 1 and 2 together:

Even after combining both the statements, we cannot get the value of the fifth integer.

The correct answer is option E.

264. We know that J, S and V lie is a straight line.

However, the order in which they are present is not known and whether they are positive or negative is also not known.

From statement 1:

The distance between J and $S = 20$.

However, the distance between V and either of J or S is not known; neither is the order in which the points are present is known. – Insufficient

From statement 2:

The distance between J and $V = 25$.

However, the distance between S and either of J or V is not known; neither is the order in which the points are present is known. – Insufficient

Thus, from statements 1 and 2 together:

The order in which the points are present is not known.

For example, if the points are as: $J\_\_\ S\_\_\ V$, then the distance between S and V is $=> 25 \; - - 20 \; = \; 5$

However, if the points are as: $S\_\_\ J\_\_\ V$, then the distance between S and V is $=> 25 + 20 = 45$

Thus, the distance between S and V cannot be determined. – Insufficient

The correct answer is option E.

265. The remainder when a number is divided by 10 is the unit's digit of the number.
For example: The remainder when 12 is divided by 10 is 2, which is the unit's digit of 12.

The exponents of 2 follow a cycle for the last digit as shown below (p is a positive integer):

Exponent of 2	Unit's digit
2^{4p+1}	2
2^{4p+2}	4
2^{4p+3}	8
2^{4p}	6

From statement 1:

Since k is divisible by 10, k may or may not be a multiple of 4.

For example, if $k = 20$: Unit's digit of $2^k = 2^{20} \equiv 6$.
Whereas, if $k = 30$: Unit's digit of $2^k = 2^{30} = 2^{(4*7)+2} \equiv 4$.

Thus, we do not have a unique remainder. – Insufficient

From statement 2:

Since k is a multiple of 4, its unit's digit is always 6. – Sufficient

The correct answer is option B.

266. From statement 1:

We know that: k and m are even and p is odd.

Thus, $(k - m - p)$ is
((Even – Even) –Odd) = (Even – Odd) = Odd. – Sufficient

From statement 2:

Since k, m and p are consecutive integers, there are two possibilities:

(1) k = Even, m = Odd, p = Even
=> $(k - m - p)$ is ((Even – Odd) –Even) = (Odd – Even) = Odd.

(2) k = Odd, m = Even, p = Odd
=> $(k - m - p)$ is ((Odd – Even) –Odd) = (Odd – Odd) = Even.

Hence, the nature of value of $(k - m - p)$ is not unique. – Insufficient

The correct answer is option A.

267. $\frac{k}{6} + \frac{m}{4} = \frac{t}{12}$
=> $2k + 3m = t$

From statement 1:

k is a multiple of 3
=> $k = 3u$; where u is an integer.

Thus, we have:

$2k + 3m = t$

=> $6u + 3m = t$

=> $t = 3(2u + m)$

Thus, t is a multiple of 3.

Thus, t and 12 do have a common factor greater than 1. – Sufficient

From statement 2:

m is a multiple of 3

=> $m = 3v$; where v is an integer.

Thus, we have:

$2k + 3m = t$

=> $2k + 9v = t$

Thus, we cannot definitely conclude that t is a multiple of 2 or 3.

Thus, t and 12 may or may not have a common factor greater than 1. – Insufficient

The correct answer is option A.

268. From statement 1:

There is no information about whether m and v are positive.

Hence, there would be different combinations of values of m and v possible, leading to different values of $(m + v)$.

The possible integer values of m and v satisfying the equation $mv = 6$ are:

m	v	$m + v$
1	6	7
2	3	5
3	2	5
6	1	7
-1	-6	-7
-2	-3	-5
-3	-2	-5
-6	-1	-7

Thus, there is no unique value of $(m + v)$. – Insufficient

From statement 2:

$(m + v)^2 = 25$

=> $m + v = \pm 5$

Thus, there is no unique value of $(m + v)$. – Insufficient

Thus, from statements 1 and 2 together:

Even after combining both statements, we have $(m + v) = \pm 5$

Thus, there is no unique value of $(m + v)$. – Insufficient

The correct answer is option E.

269. From statement 1:

In order to check if the number of digits of m^3 is unique, we check with the minimum and maximum values of m.

If $m = 100$ (smallest number with three digits):

$m^3 = 1000000$

=> m^3 has seven digits (minimum).

If $m = 900$ (the largest number with three digits is 999, however, 900 would suffice):

$m^3 = 729000000$

=> m^3 has nine digits (maximum).

Thus, the number of digits of m^3, where m is a three digit number can be seven, eight or nine.

Thus, the number of digits of m^3 is not unique. – Insufficient

From statement 2:

We know that m^2 has five digits.

For example, if $m = 100$ (the smallest three digit number):

$m^2 = 10000$

=> m^2 has five digits.

Here: $m^3 = 1000000$

=> m^3 has seven digits.

However, if $m = 300$ (another three digit number):

$m^2 = 90000$

=> m^2 has five digits as well.

Here: $m^3 = 27000000$

=> m^3 has eight digits.

Thus, the number of digits of m^3 is not unique. – Insufficient

Thus, from statements 1 and 2 together:

Even after combining, the number of digits of m^3 can be seven or eight and hence, is not unique. – Insufficient

The correct answer is option E.

270. The product mpt will be even if at least one among m, p and t is an even integer.

From statement 1:

$t - p = p - m$

=> $m + t = 2p$

Thus, we see that $(m + t)$ is twice of an integer and hence, is even.

However, it may be that m and t are both odd or both even.

Similarly, p may be odd or even.

For example:

$m = 3, t = 19, p = 11$: all are odd, the product mpt is odd.

OR

$m = 3, t = 5, p = 4$: at least one of them is even, the product mpt is even.

Thus, the product mpt may be even or odd. – Insufficient

From statement 2:

$t - m = 16$

Since the difference of t and m is 16 (even), it may be that m and t are both odd or both even.

Also, there is no information on whether p is even.

Thus, the product mpt may be even or odd. – Insufficient

Thus, from statements 1 and 2 together:

Even after combining both statements, we can have all of m, p and t as odd or at least one of them even.

Thus, the product mpt may be even or odd. – Insufficient

The correct answer is option E.

271. We have: $n = 3k$

$=> k = \frac{n}{3}$

Thus, k will be an integer if n is a multiple of '3'.

From statement 1:

We cannot say whether n is a multiple of '3'. – Insufficient

From statement 2:

We have: $\frac{n}{6}$ is an integer

$=> n$ is a multiple of '6'

$=> n$ is a multiple of '3'. – Sufficient

The correct answer is option B.

272. From statement 1:

We have no information on k. – Insufficient

From statement 2:

We have no information on n. – Insufficient

Thus, from statements 1 and 2 together:

n is divisible by 8

$=> n = 8p$, where p is an integer.

k is divisible by 4

$=> k = 4q$, where q is an integer.

Thus, we have:

$\frac{n}{k} = \frac{8p}{4q} = \frac{2p}{q} = 2 * \frac{p}{q}$

If $\frac{p}{q}$ is an integer, then $\frac{n}{k}$ is an even integer.

However, if $\frac{p}{q}$ is not an integer, then $\frac{n}{k}$ is not an even integer. For example, if $\frac{p}{q} = \frac{1}{2} => \frac{n}{k} = 1$; not an even integer. For other non-integer values of $\frac{p}{q}, \frac{n}{q}$ is not an integer at all. Hence, the answer to the question may be 'Yes' or 'No'. – Insufficient

The correct answer is option E.

273. From statement 1:

$n = k(k+1)(k-1)$

This can also be written as: $n = (k-1)k(k+1)$

Thus, n is the product of three consecutive integers $(k-1)$, k and $(k+1)$.

Possible values of k are 1, 2, 3 ...

If $k = 1$:

$n = 0$; which is divisible by 6.

For any other value of k, since n is the product of three consecutive integers, there is at least one even integer and one integer which is a multiple of 3.

Thus, n is divisible by 3*2 = 6.

Hence, n is divisible by 6 for any positive integer value of k. – Sufficient

Alternatively:

Product of 'n' consecutive integers must be divisible by n! thus, product of three consecutive integers must be divisible by 3! i.e. 6. – Sufficient

From statement 2:

There is no information about the relation between k and n. – Insufficient

The correct answer is option A.

274. From statement 1:

2 is not a factor of n

=> n is an odd number.

If $n = 5$:

Remainder (r) when $(n - 1)(n + 1) = n^2 - 1 = 24$ is divided by 24 is '0'.

If $n = 9$:

Remainder (r) when $(n - 1)(n + 1) = n^2 - 1 = 80$ is divided by 24 is '8'.

Thus, the value of r is not unique. – Insufficient

From statement 2:

3 is not a factor of n

=> n is not a multiple of 3.

If $n = 5$:

Remainder (r) when $(n - 1)(n + 1) = n^2 - 1 = 24$ is divided by 24 is '0'.

If $n = 8$:

Remainder (r) when $(n - 1)(n + 1) = n^2 - 1 = 63$ is divided by 24 is '15'.

Thus, the value of r is not unique. – Insufficient

Thus, from statements 1 and 2 together:

n is neither a multiple of 2 nor 3

=> n is not a multiple of 6.

Thus, n when divided by 6 will leave a remainder of either 1 or 5, since it cannot leave remainders 2, or 4 (n is not a multiple of 2) and 3 (n is not a multiple of 3).

Thus, we have:

$n = 6p + 1$ or $n = 6p - 1$, where p is a positive integer.

Thus, we have the following situations:

If **n=6p+1**	If **n=6p−1**
$(n-1)(n+1) = \{(6p+1)-1\}\{(6p+1)+1\}$ $= 6p * (6p+2)$	$(n-1)(n+1) = \{(6p-1)-1\}\{(6p-1)+1\}$ $= (6p-2) * 6p$

Thus, we observe that:

$(n-1)(n+1)$
$= 6p * (6p \pm 2)$
$= 12p * (3p \pm 1)$

Now, we have two situations depending on p as even OR p as odd:

(1) If p is even:
=> $12p(3p \pm 1)$ is a multiple of 24.

(1) If p is odd:
$(3p \pm 1)$ is even

=> $12p(3p + 1)$ is a multiple of 24.

Thus, we see that $(n-1)(n+1)$ is always divisible by 24.

Hence, the remainder (r) when $(n-1)(n+1)$ is divided by 24 is '0'. – Sufficient

The correct answer is option C.

275. From statement 1:

$n = 2k + 1$

Thus, we have:

$n^3 - n$

$= n(n^2 - 1)$

$= n(n-1)(n+1)$

$= (2k+1)(2k)(2k+2)$

$= 4k(2k+1)(k+1)$

=> $(n^3 - n)$ is divisible by 4. - Sufficient

Alternatively:

$n = 2k + 1$

=> n is an odd number.

Thus, $(n - 1)$ and $(n + 1)$ must be even.

Thus, we have:

$n^3 - n$

$= n\,(n^2 - 1) = n * (n - 1)\,(n + 1)$

= odd $*$ even $*$ even, which must be divisible by 4. -Sufficient

From statement 2:

We have: $(n^2 + n)$ is divisible by 6

=> $n(n + 1)$ is divisible by 6.

If $n = 2$:

It satisfies $n(n + 1)$ divisible by 6.

However, $(n^3 - n) = 6$, which is not divisible by 4.

Again, if $n = 3$:

It satisfies $n(n + 1)$ divisible by 6.

However, $(n^3 - n) = 24$, which is divisible by 4.

Hence, we do not have a unique answer. - Insufficient

The correct answer is option A.

276. From statement 1:

We know that $3n$ is odd.

Since n is an integer and '3' is odd, n must be an odd integer (since: odd * odd = odd). - Sufficient

From statement 2:

We know that $(n + 3)$ is odd.

Since '3' is odd, n must be odd (since: odd + odd = even). – Sufficient

The correct answer is option D.

277. From statement 1:

Since n divided by 3 leaves a remainder 2, we have:

$n = 3k + 2$, where k is a positive integer.

However, the value of n cannot be determined as k is unknown. – Insufficient

From statement 2:

We know that n^2 divided by 3 leaves a remainder 1.

We know that any number n divided by 3 leaves a remainder of 0 or 1 or 2.

Thus, n^2 when divided by 3 would leave a remainder $0^2 = 0$ or $1^2 = 1$ or $2^2 = 4 \equiv 1$ (since 4 is greater than 3, we divide 4 by 3 to get the actual remainder as 1).

Thus, n^2 when divided by 3 leaves remainder 0 or 1.

It is obvious that the remainder 0 occurs when the number n is a multiple of 3.

For all other values of n, the remainder would be 1.

Thus, there are infinitely many possible values of n, for example: 4, 5, 7, 8, 10 ...

Thus, we cannot determine any unique value of n. – Insufficient

Thus, from statements 1 and 2 together:

From statement 1, we have:

$n = 3k + 2$

$=> n^2 = 9k^2 + 12k + 4$

$=> n^2 = 3\,(3k^2 + 4k + 1) + 1$

Thus, n^2 when divided by 3 would leave a remainder 1.

However, this is exactly what statement 2 conveys.

Thus, statement 2 provides the same information as statement 1.

Since there is no additional information provided about n, the value of n cannot be determined. – Insufficient

The correct answer is option E.

278. From statement 1:

Since $30^n > 1000$, we have:

$n \geq 3$ (since $30^2 = 900 < 1000$ and $30^3 = 27000 > 1000$).

Since $n \geq 3$, the number of trailing zeroes in 30^n must be at least '3'.

Thus, the hundreds' digit of 30^n is '0'. – Sufficient

From statement 2:

Possible values of n are 3, 6, 9 . . .

If $n = 3$, we have:

$30^n = 30^3 = 27000$.

Thus, when $n = 3$ there are '3' trailing zeroes in 30^n.

For higher values of n, the number of trailing zeroes would be higher.

Thus, the hundred's digit in 30^n is '0'. – Sufficient

The correct answer is option D.

279. From statement 1:

n is a multiple of 36 such that its value is between 100 and 200.

Thus, possible multiples of 36 are: 36*3 = 108, 36*4 = 144, and 36*5 = 180.

Since $\frac{n}{36}$ is an odd integer, possible values of n are $36 * 3 = 108$ or $36 * 5 = 180$.

Thus, the value of n is not unique. – Insufficient

From statement 2:

n is a multiple of 45 such that its value is between 100 and 200.

Thus, possible multiples of 45 are: 45*3 = 135, and 45*4 = 180.

Since $\frac{n}{45}$ is an even integer, the only possible value of n is 45*4 = 180.

Thus, the value of n is unique. - Sufficient

The correct answer is option B.

280. From statement 1:

Factors of 15 are: 1, 3, 5, and 15.

Possible factors of 15 (lying between 2 and 6) are 3 and 5.

Thus, possible values of n are 3 or 5.

Thus, the value of n is not unique. - Insufficient

From statement 2:

Factors of 21 are: 1, 3, 7, and 21.

The only possible factor of 21 (lying between 2 and 6) is 3.

Thus, the only possible value of n is 3.- Sufficient

The correct answer is option B.

281. $x^n - x^{-n} = 0$

$=> x^n - \frac{1}{x^n} = 0$

$=> x^n = \frac{1}{x^n}$

$=> x^n * x^n = 1$

$=> x^{2n} = 1$

Thus, there are two possibilities:

(1) $x = \pm 1$ (here, n can be any number: since '1' raised to any exponent is always '1' and '-1' raised to any even exponent (i.e. 2) is always 1)

OR

(1) $n = 0$ (here, x can be any number: since any non-zero number raised to '0' is always '1')

Thus, we need to use the statements 1 and 2 to decide which of the above cases is possible.

From statement 1:

We only know that x is an integer.

We have no information on whether n is '0'.

Thus, the value of x cannot be determined. – Insufficient

From statement 2:

Since $n \neq 0$, we must have:

$x = \pm 1$

However, we cannot uniquely determine the value of x. – Insufficient

Thus, from statements 1 and 2 together:

Even after combining both statement, we still have $x = \pm 1$.

Thus, the value of x cannot be uniquely determined. – Insufficient

The correct answer is option E.

282. From statement 1:

We know that the sum of the two digits of n is a prime number.

Thus, apart from $n = 11$ (sum of the digits is 2, the only even prime), for all other values of n, one digit of n must be even and the other digit of n must be odd (since the sum of an even and odd number is always odd and all prime numbers above 2 are odd).

Thus, possible values of n could be: 23 (sum of digits = 5, a prime number), 89 (sum of digits = 17, a prime number), etc.

Thus, n may be less than 80 or more than 80. – Insufficient

From statement 2:

We know that each of the two digits of n is a prime number.

In order that $n > 80$ (but less than 99), we need to have a prime number greater than or equal to 8 but less than or equal to 9 in the tens' position of n.

However, this is not possible.

Thus, all possible values of n would have a digit less than 8 in the tens' position.

Possible such digits are: 7, 5, 3, or 2.

Hence, $n < 80$. - Sufficient

The correct answer is option B.

283. $\frac{n}{7}$ will be an integer only if n is a multiple of 7.

From statement 1:

Since $\frac{3n}{7}$ is an integer, we can conclude that $3n$ is divisible by 7.

However, 3 and 7 have no common factors.

Thus, n must be divisible by 7.

Hence, $\frac{n}{7}$ must be an integer. - Sufficient

From statement 2:

Since $\frac{5n}{7}$ is an integer, we can conclude that $5n$ is divisible by 7.

However, 5 and 7 have no common factors.

Thus, n must be divisible by 7.

Hence, $\frac{n}{7}$ must be an integer. - Sufficient

The correct answer is option D.

284. $10^n \le 0.001$

$=> 10^n \le 10^{-3}$

$=> n \le -3$

From statement 1:

Possible values of n are: $-2, -3, -4 \ldots$

Thus, we have:

$n = -2$ ($\nleq -3$)

OR

$n = -3, -4$ etc. (≤ -3).

Thus, we do not have a unique answer to the question. - Insufficient

From statement 2:

Possible values of n are: $-4, -3, -2, -1 \ldots$

Thus, we have:
$n = -4$ or -3 (≤ -3)

OR

$n = -2,\ -1$ etc. ($\nleq -3$)

Thus, we do not have a unique answer to the question. - Insufficient

Thus, from statements 1 and 2 together:

We still have:
$n = -2$ ($\nleq -3$)

OR

$n = -4-$or -3 (≤ -3)

Thus, we do not have a unique answer to the question. - Insufficient

The correct answer is option E.

285. We need to verify whether:

$$\frac{p}{r} = \frac{s}{t}$$

From statement 1:

We have:

$s = 3p \ldots$(i)

$t = 3r \ldots$(ii)

Dividing (i) by (ii)

$\frac{s}{t} = \frac{3p}{3r} = \frac{p}{r}$ - Sufficient

From statement 2:

We have:

$3p = 2r$

$=> \frac{p}{r} = \frac{2}{3} \ldots$(iii)

$3s = 2t$

$=> \frac{s}{t} = \frac{2}{3} \ldots$(iv)

From, (iii) and (iv)

$\frac{p}{r} = \frac{s}{t}$ - Sufficient

The correct answer is option D.

286. From statement 1:

Let us factorize 728:
$728 = 2^3 * 7 * 13.$

Thus, we have:
$p^3st = 2^3 * 7 * 13.$

Since $p, s,$ and t are prime numbers, we have:

$p = 2, s = 7, t = 13$

OR

$p = 2, s = 13, t = 7$

In either case, $p^3s^3t^3 = 2^3 * 7^3 * 13^3$. - Sufficient

From statement 2:

We have no information on p and s. - Insufficient

The correct answer is option A.

287. We have:

x is a multiple of 12

=> x^2 is a multiple of $12^2 = 144 = 2^4 * 3^2$.

Also, y is a multiple of $14 = 2 * 7$.

Or, x^2y is a multiple of $2^5 * 3^2 * 7$

In order that x^2y is a multiple of 216 $(= 2^3 * 3^3)$, we must ensure that there are three 2's and three 3's in x^2y. We see that there are sufficient 2's (five), but deficient by one 3.

From statement 1:

We already know that x^2 is a multiple of 144 i.e. it is a multiple of 8.

Also, we have seen that the maximum exponent of 2 in 216 is 2^3.

Thus, the requirement of three 2's in x^2y is already satisfied.

But, this statement does not provide any information on number of multiples of 3. – Insufficient

From statement 2:

We have: y is a multiple of 6

Also, we know that x^2 is a multiple of 144.

Thus, x^2y is a multiple of 144 * 6 = 864 = 216 * 4.

Thus, x^2y is a multiple of 216. – Sufficient

The correct answer is option B.

288. Since $0 < q < 17$, the remainder (r) when 17 is divided by q can be any of the following:

$r = 0, 1, 2, 3 \ldots 15$ or 16.

From statement 1:

Since $q > 10$, possible values of q are: 11, 12, 13, 14, 15 or 16.

Thus, the corresponding values of r are: 6, 5, 4, 3, 2 or 1.

Thus, the value of r is not unique. – Insufficient

From statement 2:

Since $q = 2^k$ and also less than 17, possible values of q are: $2^1 = 2,\ 2^2 = 4,\ 2^3 = 8$ or $2^4 = 16$.

Thus, the values of the remainder (r) when 17 is divided by 2, 4, 8 or 16 is 1 in each case.

Thus, the value of r is unique. – Sufficient

The correct answer is option B.

289. We have: $r > 0$

We need to determine whether: $rs > 0$

(1) We need to determine whether$s > 0$, since $r > 0$ and, Positive* Positive = Positive
From statement 1:

We have:
$s \leq r$:

If $s = r$:

$rs = s^2 > 0$

If $s < r$:

The value of s may be positive (but less than r) or the value of s may be negative.

If $s < 0$:

$rs < 0$

Thus, there is no unique answer to the question. – Insufficient

From statement 2:

We have: $s \geq r$:

Since $r > 0$

$=> s \geq r > 0$

Since both s and r are positive, we have:

$rs > 0$. – Sufficient

The correct answer is option B.

290. From statement 1:

We have: rs is divisible by 49.

There may be a possibility that both r and s are divisible by 7 and hence, their product is divisible by 49.

However, there is another possibility that s is divisible by 49 and r is not divisible by 7.

Thus, there is no unique answer to the question. – Insufficient

From statement 2:

We have no information about r. – Insufficient

Thus, from statements 1 and 2 together:

Even after combining both statements, we cannot determine whether r is divisible by 7. – Insufficient

The correct answer is option E.

291. From statement 1:

$r - 1 = (s + 1)(s - 1)$

$=> r - 1 = s^2 - 1$

$=> r = s^2$

$=> \frac{r}{s} = s$ (which is given to be an integer). – Sufficient

From statement 2:

We have:
$r - s = 20$

A few possible values of r and s are:

$r = 22,\ s = 2 => \frac{r}{s} = \frac{22}{2} = 11$ (an integer)

$r = 23, s = 3 => \frac{r}{s} = \frac{23}{3}$ (not an integer)

Thus, there is no unique answer to the question. – Insufficient

The correct answer is option A.

292. From statement 1:

We have: $t^{r-1} = 1$

Possible situations are:

(1) $t = 1$ (here r can be any number)
(2) $t = -1$ (here $(r - 1)$ must be an even number)
(3) $r - 1 = 0 => r = 1$ (here t can be any number)

Thus, the value of t cannot be uniquely determined. - Insufficient

From statement 2:

We do not have any information about t. - Insufficient

Thus, from statements 1 and 2 together:

Even after combining both statements, we have:

(1) $t = 1$ (here r can be any number)
(2) $t = -1$ (here $(r - 1)$ must be an even number)

(Note: $t = 1$ is no longer applicable using the information from statement 2)

Thus, the value of t cannot be uniquely determined. - Insufficient

The correct answer is option E.

293. From statement 1:

We have:
$a_{n-1} + a_n = pn(n-1)$

Substituting $n = 30 : a_{29} + a_{30} = p * 30 * 29 \ldots$ (i)
Substituting $n = 31 : a_{30} + a_{31} = p * 31 * 30 \ldots$ (ii)

Thus: (ii) - (i) (since $a_{31} - a_{29}$ is mentioned in the statement 1):

$a_{31} - a_{29} = 30 * (p * 31 - p * 29) = 60p.$

Thus, we have:
$60p = 120$

$=> p = 2.$ - Sufficient

From statement 2:

We have:

$a_{n-1} + a_n = pn(n-1)$

Substituting $n = 2 : a_1 + a_2 = p * 2 * 1 = 2p \ldots$ (iii)

Since $a_2 = 6$, we have:

$a_1 + 6 = 2p$

However, we have no information on the value of a_1, we cannot determine the value of p. – Insufficient

The correct answer is option A.

294. We have find out whether $|R - T| \geq 9$.

From statement 1:

$|R - S| = 50$

$=> R - S = \pm 50 \ldots$ (i)

However, we do not have any information about T. – Insufficient

From statement 2:

$|S - T| = 41$

$=> S - T = \pm 41 \ldots$ (ii)

However we do not have any information about R. – Insufficient

Thus, from statements 1 and 2 together:

Adding (i) and (ii):

$(R - S) + (S - T) = \pm 50 \pm 41$

$= 50 + 41 = 9$

OR

$= 50 - 41 = 9$

OR

$= -50 + 41 = -9$

OR

$= -50 - 41 = -91$

$=> R - T = \pm 91$ OR ± 9

$=> |R - T| = 91$ OR 9

Thus, the value of $|R - T|$ is at least 9. – Sufficient

The correct answer is option C.

295. From statement 1:

We have no information about t. – Insufficient

From statement 1:

We have no information about r. – Insufficient

Thus, from statements 1 and 2 together:

$(r + s) + (s + t) =$ even + even = even

$=> r + 2s + t =$ [even]

$=> r + s + t =$ [even]$-s$

However, s may be even or odd.

Thus, we have:

$r + s + t =$ even – even = even

OR

$r + s + t =$ even – odd = odd

Thus, we cannot determine the nature of $(r + s + t)$. – Insufficient

The correct answer is option E.

296. $w = 60r + 80s$

$\Rightarrow w = 80(r + s) - 20r$

$\Rightarrow w = 80 - 20r$ (since $(r + s) = 1$).

Note: We deliberately took $80(r + s)$ so that we could relate w and r.

We need to determine whether $w > 70$:

$\Rightarrow 80 - 20r > 70$

$\Rightarrow 20r < 10$

$\Rightarrow r < \frac{1}{2}$

From statement 1:

We have: $r > \frac{1}{2}$

This is contrary to what we needed i.e. $r < \frac{1}{2}$

Thus, we have an unique answer 'No'. – Sufficient

From statement 2:

We had obtained: $r < \frac{1}{2}$

Since $r + s = 1$, we have:

$s = 1 - r > 1 - \frac{1}{2}$

$\Rightarrow s > \frac{1}{2}$

$\Rightarrow s > r$.

This is contrary to the information of statement 2 i.e. $r > s$

Thus, we have an unique answer 'No'. – Sufficient

The correct answer is option D.

297. From statement 1:

We can have 10 consecutive integers including -3 in the following ways:

$S = \{-3, -2, -1 \ldots 5,\ 6\}$; (5 is present in S)

OR

$S = \{-5, -4, -3 \ldots 4\}$; (5 is not present in S), etc.

Thus, the integer 5 may be or may not be present in S. - Insufficient

From statement 2:

We can have 10 consecutive integers including 4 in the following ways:

$S = \{4,\ 5,\ 6 \ldots 13\}$; (5 is present in S)

OR

$S = \{-5, -4, \ldots 3,\ 4\}$; (5 is not present in S), etc.

Thus, the integer 5 may be or may not be present in S. - Insufficient

Thus, from statements 1 and 2 together:

We need to have both -3 and 4 in the set S.

We can have the following ways:

$S = \{-5, -4, \ldots 3,\ 4\}$; (5 is not present in S)

OR

$S = \{-4, -3 \ldots\ 4,\ 5\}$; (5 is present in S)

Thus, the integer 5 may be or may not be present in S. - Insufficient

The correct answer is option E.

298. From statement 1:

We know that the 242nd term is -494.

However, the relation between consecutive terms is not known.

Hence, the 243rd term cannot be determined. - Insufficient

From statement 2:

We know that the first term of S is -12 and each term of S after the first term is 2 less than the preceding term.

Thus, if we denote the first term as a, and the difference between two consecutive terms as d, we have:

$a = -12$

$d = -2$

Thus, the second term $t_2 = -12 + 1 * (-2)$

The third term $t_3 = t_2 - 2 = -12 + 2 * (-2)$, etc.

Thus, the nth term is given as:

$t_n = a + (n - 1)d$

Hence, the 243rd term $t_{243} = -12 + (243 - 1) * (-2)$

$= -12 - 484 = -496.$ – Sufficient

The correct answer is option B.

299. From statement 1:

$d < \frac{1}{4}$

$=> d < 0.25$

For all values of $h = 0,\ 1,\ 2,\ 3$ or 4, we have $d < 0.25$

Thus, the value of d rounded to the nearest tenth is:

(1) For $h = 0 : d = 0.206 =\sim 0.2$
(2) For $h = 1 : d = 0.216 =\sim 0.2$
(3) For $h = 2 : d = 0.226 =\sim 0.2$
(4) For $h = 3 : d = 0.236 =\sim 0.2$
(5) For $h = 4 : d = 0.246 =\sim 0.2$

Thus, the value of d to the nearest tenth is 0.2 – Sufficient

From statement 2:

Since $h < 5$, possible values of h are $0,\ 1,\ 2,\ 3$ or 4.

This is the same result as obtained from statement 1. – Sufficient

The correct answer is option D.

300. From statement 1:

Since n has exactly two distinct positive factors, n must be a prime number (the factors of a prime number are 1 and the number itself).

Since 2 is a prime number, we can have $n = 2$.

However, there are other prime numbers greater than 2 as well, for example 3, 5, etc. – Insufficient

From statement 2:

We know that the difference of any two distinct positive factors of n is odd.

This is only possible if one factor is even and the other factor is odd (since the difference between an even and odd number is odd, whereas the difference between any two odd numbers or any two even numbers is even).

Thus, the number must have exactly two factors, one odd (i.e. 1) and the other even (i.e. 2).

Thus, we have: $n = 1 * 2 = 2$. – Sufficient

The correct answer is option B.

301. Possible values of n so that the product of the digits is 12 are: 26, 34, 43 and 62.

From statement 1:

We know that n can be expressed as the sum of perfect squares in only one way.

Let us see for each of the above numbers:

26:

(1) With 1, we have: $1^2 + 5^2 = 26$;
(2) With 2: $2^2 + 22 = 26$; however, 22 is not a perfect square
(3) With 3: $3^2 + 17 = 26$; however, 17 is not a perfect square
(4) With 4: $4^2 + 10 = 26$; however, 10 is not a perfect square

34:

(1) With 1: $1^2 + 33 = 34$; however, 33 is not a perfect square

(2) With 2: $2^2 + 30 = 34$; however, 30 is not a perfect square

(3) With 3: $3^2 + 5^2 = 34$; we see that it can be expressed as the sum of two perfect squares

(4) With 4: $4^2 + 18 = 34$; however, 18 is not a perfect square

Thus, we see that both 26 and 34 can be expressed as the sum of two perfect squares in exactly one way.

Thus, it is enough to observe that statement 1 is not sufficient.

Note: Both 43 and 62 cannot be expressed as the sum of two perfect squares in any way.

Thus, we do not get a unique value of n. – Insufficient

From statement 2:

Since n is smaller than 40, possible values of n are 26 and 34. – Insufficient

Thus, from statements 1 and 2 together:

Even after combining both statements, we still have possible values of n as 26 and 34. – Insufficient

The correct answer is option E.

302. From statement 1:

We know that the sum of three equal integers is even.

Thus, thrice of an integer is even.

Hence, we can conclude that the integer in question is even.

Thus, each of the three equal integers is even.

Thus, their product must be a multiple of 2*2*2 = 8.

Hence, the product of the three integers is a multiple of 4. – Sufficient

From statement 2:

Since the sum of three integers is even, we can say that two of them are odd and the remaining integer is even (since we know that all three integers are not even).

The even integer itself can be a multiple of 4 which would make the product of the three integers a multiple of 4 as well.

However, the even integer may simply be a multiple of 2 (and not higher exponents of 2) which would result in the product of the three integers only a multiple of 2 and not 4.

Thus, we do not have a unique answer. - Insufficient

The correct answer is option A.

303. From statement 1:

We know that the tens digit of k is non-zero.

Thus, in the number $(k + 9)$, the tens digits when added would always lead to a carryover of '1' to the tens' place.

For example:

If the three digit number is 321, where the tens digit is the smallest, i.e. 1, then we have: $321 + 9 = 330$ i.e. the tens' digit has increased by 1.

Again, if the three digit number is 329, where the tens digit is the largest, i.e. 9, then too we have: $329 + 9 = 338$ i.e. the tens' digit has increased by 1.

Since the tens' digit in $(k + 9)$ is 3, the tens' digit in k (i.e. before adding 9) must have been $3 - 1 = 2$ (subtracting the carry of '1').

Thus, the tens' digit in k is 2. - Sufficient

From statement 2:

We know that the tens digit of k is non-zero.

Thus, in the number $(k + 4)$, the tens digits when added may lead to a carryover of '1' to the tens' place if the tens digit in k is 6 or greater; or there may not be any carryover to the tens' place if the tens digit in k is 5 or smaller.

For example:

If the three digit number is 326, where the tens digit is 6, then we have:

$326 + 4 = 330$ i.e. the tens' digit has increased by 1.

Again, if the three digit number is 329, where the tens digit is the largest, i.e. 9, then too we have:

$329 + 4 = 333$ i.e. the tens' digit has increased by 1.

However, if the three digit number is 321, where the tens digit is the smallest, i.e. 1, then we have:

$321 + 4 = 325$ i.e. the tens' digit has not increased by 1.

Again, if the three digit number is 325, where the tens digit is 5, then too we have:

$325 + 4 = 329$ i.e. the tens' digit has not increased by 1.

Thus, if there is a carryover, the tens' digit in k would have been $2 - 1 = 1$.

However, if there is no carryover, the tens' digit in k would have been 2 itself.

Thus, there is no unique answer. – Insufficient

The correct answer is option A.

304. From statement 1:

$vw = v^2$

$=> vw - v^2 = 0$

$=> v(w - v) = 0$

$=> v = 0$ or $w = v$

However, we know that: $w \neq v$, since they are different integers.

Thus, we have: $v = 0$ – Sufficient

From statement 2:

We have no information about v. – Insufficient

The correct answer is option A.

305. We know that: $vmt \neq 0$

=> None among v, m and t is '0'

$v^2m^3t^4$

$= v^2t^4m^2 * m$

We know that $v^2t^4m^2 \geq 0$ (since the exponents are even i.e. the numbers are perfect squares, they must be non-negative).

We need to show that:

$v^2m^3t^4 > 0$
$=> v^2t^4m^2 * m > 0$

As, $v^2t^4m^2 > 0$, thus,

$=> m > 0$ (This is what we need to know to get the answer to the question)

From statement 1:

$m > v^2$

However, $v^2 > 0$

$=> m > 0$

$=> v^2m^3t^4 > 0$ – Sufficient

From statement 2:

$m > t^3$

However, t^3 may be positive or negative depending on the value of t

$=> m$ may be positive or negative.

$=> v^2m^3t^4$ may be positive or negative. – Insufficient

The correct answer is option A.

306. From statement 1:

$2y - x = x^2 - y^2$

$=> 2y + y^2 = x^2 + x$

$=> y(y + 2) = x(x + 1)$

Let us look into two possibilities for x:

(1) If x is odd: $x(x + 1)$ = odd * even = even
(2) If x is even: $x(x + 1)$ = even * odd = even

Thus, we have: $y(y + 2)$ as even.

If y is odd, $(y + 2)$ is also odd

=> $y(y + 2)$ = odd * odd = odd; however, $y(y + 2)$ is even, thus, y cannot be odd.

If y is even, $(y + 2)$ is also even

=> $y(y + 2)$ = even * even = even.

Thus, we have y as even. – Sufficient

From statement 2:

We have no information about y. – Insufficient

The correct answer is option A.

307. From statement 1:

We have: $x^{2y} = 16$

Thus, we have:

$2x^{6y} - 4$

$= 2(x^{2y})^3 - 4$

$= \left(2 * 16^3 - 4\right)$ – Sufficient

Note: We do NOT need to try and get the values of x and y from $x^{2y} = 16$.

From statement 2:

We have: $xy = 4$

Two possible values of $(2x^{6y} - 4)$ depending on the values of x and y are:

(1) $x = 1, y = 4$: $(2x^{6y} - 4) = 2 * 1 - 4 = -2$
(2) $x = 2, y = 2$: $(2x^{6y} - 4) = 2 * 2^{12} - 4$

Thus, there is no unique value. – Insufficient

The correct answer is option A.

308. From statement 1:

Since x is a factor of 54 and is less than half of 54, the possible values of x are: 1, 2, 3, 6, 9 or 18.

Again, we know that 18 is a multiple of xy^2

=> xy^2 is a factor of 18

The factors of 18 are: 1, 2, 3, 6, 9 and 18.

If $x = 1$, the possible values of y are 1 or 3.

Thus, we observe that the value of y cannot be uniquely determined. – Insufficient

From statement 2:

Since xy^2 is a factor of 18, the possible values of xy^2 are: 1, 2, 3, 6, 9 or 18.

Also, we know that: y is a multiple of 3

=> y^2 is a multiple of $3^2 = 9$

Thus, the only possible value of y is 3 (higher multiples of 3 as the value of y would not be possible since xy^2 is a factor of 18). – Sufficient

The correct answer is option B.

309. We have:

$x^y = x^{2y-3}$

=> $x^y = \frac{x^{2y}}{x^3}$

=> $x^{2y-y} = x^3$

=> $x^y = x^3$

=> $y = 3$, for all values of x except 1

OR

y = any positive integer if $x = 1$

Thus, though it appeared that $y = 3$, it is not necessarily so.

Thus, we need to refer to the statements to get the value of y.

From statement 1:

We have: $x = 2$, (i.e. $x \neq 1$)

Thus, $y = 3$

=> $y^x = 3^2 = 9$ – Sufficient

From statement 2:

We have: $x^2 < 9$

=> $0 < x < 3$ (since x is positive)

=> Possible values of x are: 2 or 1.

=> $y = 3$, if $x = 2$

OR

$y =$ any positive integer if $x = 1$

Since the values of x and y cannot be uniquely determined, we cannot determine the unique value of y^x. – Insufficient

The correct answer is option A.

310. We have: $x^{ky} = x^{(ly^2-8)}$

Since $x \neq$, we have:

$ky = ly^2 - 8$

=> $y\,(ly - k) = 8$

From statement 1:

We have: $k = -6$

=> $y\,(ly + 6) = 8$

Possible values of y are: 2 or 4.

If $y = 2$:

$2(2l + 6) = 8$

=> $l = -1$

=> $kl = (-6) * (-1) = 6 > 2$

If $y = 4$:

$4(4l + 6) = 8$

$=> l = -1$

$=> kl = (-6) * (-1) = 6 > 2$

Thus, there is a unique answer and the answer is 'Yes'. - Sufficient

From statement 2:

We have: $3l - k = 3$

We know that: $y\,(ly - k) = 8$

Possible values of y are: 2 or 4.

If $y = 2$:

$2\,(2l - k) = 8$

$=> 2l - k = 4$

$=> (3l - k) - l = 4$

$=> 3 - l = 4$

$=> l = -1$

$=> k = 3l - 3 = -6$ (using the equation: $3l - k = 3$)

$=> kl = (-6) * (-1) = 6 > 2$

If $y = 4$:

$4\,(4l - k) = 8$

$=> 4l - k = 2$

$=> (3l - k) + l = 2$

$=> 3 + l = 2$

$=> l = -1$

$=> k = 3l - 3 = -6$ (using the equation: $3l - k = 3$)

$=> kl = (-6) * (-1) = 6 > 2$

Thus, there is a unique answer and the answer is 'Yes'. – Sufficient

The correct answer is option D.

311. From statement 1:

We have: $|x| + |y| = 5$, where $1 < |x| < y$

Thus, y must be a positive integer (since $y > 1$).

Since $|x| + |y| = 5$, and

$|x| > 1$

$=> |y| < 4$

Thus, possible values of y are: 3, 2 or 1.

If $y = 3 : |x| = 2$; thus $y > |x|$ is satisfied.

Here, $|x| = 2$

$=> x = \pm 2$

However, if $y = 2 : |x| = 3$ i.e. $y \not> |x|$

Also, if $y = 1 : |x| = 4$ i.e. $y \not> |x|$

Thus, the only possible values of x and y are:

$x = 2, y = 3$

OR

$x = -2, y = 3$

Thus, we have:

$x^{2y} - 1 = (\pm 2)^{2*3} - 1 = (\pm 2)^6 = 64$ – Sufficient

From statement 2:

We have: $|x^2 - 4| + |y - 3| = 0$

The sum of two absolute values can be '0' only if each of them is zero.

Thus, we have:

$|x^2 - 4| = 0$

$=> x^2 - 4 = 0$

$=> x = \pm 2$

Also,

$|y - 3| = 0$

$=> y - 3 = 0$

$=> y = 3$

Thus, the only possible values of x and y are:

$x = 2, y = 3$

OR

$x = -2, y = 3$

This is the same result as obtained from statement 1. – Sufficient

The correct answer is option D.

312. The remainder when a number is divided by 10 is essentially the tens digit of the number.

Thus, we need to determine the tens digit of $(3^{4x+2} + y)$.

The tens digit of exponents of 3 follows a cycle as shown below:

(1) $3^{4k+1} \equiv 3$
(2) $3^{4k+2} \equiv 9$
(3) $3^{4k+3} \equiv 7$
(4) $3^{4k} \equiv 1$

Thus, the remainder r is the same as the tens digit of $(3^{4x+2} + y)$, which is the same as the tens digit of $(9 + y)$.

Thus, we need to determine the value of y.

From statement 1:

We have no information about y. – Insufficient

From statement 2:

We have: $y = 1$

Thus, the remainder r = tens digit of $(9 + 1) \equiv 0$ – Sufficient

The correct answer is option B.

313. From statement 1:

We know that:

$x = y - 3$

However, there can be infinitely many positive integer values of x and y satisfying the above equation.

Thus, the value of $(x + y)^2$ cannot be uniquely determined. – Insufficient

From statement 2:

We know that: x and y are prime numbers.

However, there can be infinitely many values of x and y possible.

Thus, the value of $(x + y)^2$ cannot be uniquely determined. – Insufficient

Thus, from statements 1 and 2 together:

We have:

$x = y - 3$, where x and y are prime numbers.

$=> y - x = 3$

Since the difference between two prime numbers is 3 (an odd number), one prime must be even and the other odd.

Thus, one of the prime numbers must be 2 (the only even prime, also the smallest prime number).

Thus, we have: $x = 2$

=> $y - 2 = 3$

=> $y = 5$.

Thus, we have:

$(x + y)^2 = (2 + 5)^2 = 49$ – Sufficient

The correct answer is option C.

314. From statement 1:

We need to find which combination of exponents of 3 and 5 add up to 134.

Since the exponents of 5 would reach 134 faster than the exponents of 3, we need to try with the exponents of 5 so that we can get the answer(s) in the least possible trials.

If $y = 1 : 3^x + 5 = 134$

=> $3^x = 129$

However, 129 cannot be expressed as an exponent of 3 => $y \neq 1$

If $y = 2 : 3^x + 25 = 134$

=> $3^x = 109$

However, 109 cannot be expressed as an exponent of 3 => $y \neq 2$

If $y = 3 : 3^x + 125 = 134$

=> $3^x = 9$

=> $x = 2$

Thus, there is only one solution: $x = 2$ – Sufficient

From statement 2:

There is no information about x. – Insufficient

The correct answer is option A.

315. From statement 1:

$x^2 - 6x + y^2 - 4y = 0$

=> $(x^2 - 6x + 9) + (y^2 - 4y + 4) - 9 - 4 = 0$;; (combining x and y terms separately to form perfect squares)

=> $(x - 3)^2 + (y - 2)^2 = 13$

Thus, we need to add two perfect squares to get 13.

There is only one such combination possible: $2^2 + 3^2 = 13$

Thus, we have two possible situations:

(1) $(x - 3)^2 = 2^2$
=> $x - 3 = \pm 2$

=> $x = 3 \pm 2$

=> $x = 5$ or 1

$(y - 2)^2 = 3^2$

=> $y - 2 = \pm 3$

=> $y = 2 \pm 3$

=> $y = 5$ or -1

=> $y = 5$ (since -1 is not positive)

Thus, we have:

$x = 5, y = 5$ (this is not possible, since x and y are distinct)

Thus,

$x = 1, y = 5$

=> $|x - y| = |1 - 5| = 4$, which is a factor of 12.

(2) $(x - 3)^2 = 3^2$
=> $x - 3 = \pm 3$

=> $x = 3 \pm 3$

=> $x = 6$ or 0

=> $x = 6$ (since 0 is not positive)

$(y-2)^2 = 2^2$

$\Rightarrow y - 2 = \pm 2$

$\Rightarrow y = 2 \pm 2$

$\Rightarrow y = 4$ or 0

$\Rightarrow y = 4$ (since 0 is not positive)

Thus, we have:

$x = 6, y = 4 \Rightarrow |x - y| = |6 - 4| = 2$, which is a factor of 12.

Thus, there is a unique answer 'Yes'. - Sufficient

From statement 2:

There is no information about y. - Insufficient

The correct answer is option A.

316. From statement 1:

$x^2 = 15 + z^2$

$\Rightarrow x^2 - z^2 = 15$

$\Rightarrow (x + z)(x - z) = 15$

Since x and z are positive integers, we have: $x + z > x - z$

Thus, there are two possible cases:

(1) $x + z = 15$, and $x - z = 1$

$\Rightarrow 2x = 16$; (adding the two equations above)

$\Rightarrow x = 8$

$\Rightarrow z = 7$

Thus, at least one among x and z is prime.

(2) $x + z = 5$, and $x - z = 3$

$\Rightarrow 2x = 8$; (adding the two equations above)

=> $x = 4$

=> $z = 1$

Thus, none between x and z is prime.

Thus, there is no unique answer. – Insufficient

From statement 2:

We know: $(x - z)$ is a prime number.

We can have a situation where both x and z are prime, for example: $x = 5,\ z = 3$.

We can also have a situation where none among x and z are prime, for example: $x = 12,\ z = 9$

Thus, there is no unique answer. – Insufficient

Thus, from statements 1 and 2 together:

We have:

$x = 8,\ z = 7$ => $x - z = 1$, which is not a prime

OR

$x = 4,\ z = 1$ => $x - z = 3$, which is a prime.

Thus, the only solution is: $x = 4,\ y = 1$.

Hence, at least one among x and z is prime. – Sufficient

The correct answer is option C.

317. The remainder obtained when a number is divided by 100 is the last two digits of the number.

For example, when 1234 is divided by 100, the remainder obtained is 34, which is the last two digits of the number.

Thus, $(7^x + 1)$ when divided by 100 will leave a remainder having 0 as the tens digit only if $(7^x + 1)$ has 0 as its tens digit as well.

This is possible only if the tens digit of 7^x is 9 (since $9 + 1 = 10 \equiv$ the tens digit is 0)

The tens digit of exponents of 7 follows a cycle as shown below:

(1) $7^{4k+1} \equiv 7$

(2) $7^{4k+2} \equiv 9$

(3) $7^{4k+3} \equiv 3$

(4) $7^{4k} \equiv 1$

Thus, the tens digit of 7^x is 9 only if $x = 4k + 2$ where k is any positive integer.

From statement 1:

We have:

$x = 4n + 2$, where n is a positive integer.

This is exactly the condition as discussed above. – Sufficient

From statement 2:

We have: $x > 5$.

Thus, possible values of x are:

$x = 6$, which is of the form $4n + 2$ – satisfies

$x = 7$, which is not of the form $4n + 2$ – does not satisfy

Thus, we do not have a unique answer. – Insufficient

The correct answer is option A.

318. From statement 1:

$(2xy - x)$ is even

=> $x(2y - 1)$ is even

For any integer value of y, $2y$ is even.

Thus, $(2y - 1) = \text{even} - 1 = \text{odd}$.

Thus, we have: x is even

=> xz is even (since an even number multiplied with any integer is even). – Sufficient

From statement 2:

$(x^2 + xz)$ is even

=> $x(x+z)$ is even

Possible situations are:

(1) x is even, z is even => xz is even

OR

(2) x is even, z is odd => xz is even

OR

(3) x is odd, z is odd => xz is odd

Thus, xz may be even or odd. – Insufficient

The correct answer is option A.

319. From statement 1:

$y^2 = xz$

=> x, y and z form a geometric series

For example:

$x = 1, y = 2, z = 4$: Here, $y > x$ (common ratio of the geometric series is greater than 1)

$x = 4, y = 2, z = 1$: Here, $y \ngtr x$ (common ratio of the geometric series is smaller than 1)

Thus, there is no unique answer. – Insufficient

From statement 2:

There is no information about y. – Insufficient

Thus, from statements 1 and 2 together:

We know that: $z - x > 0$

=> $z > x$

Thus, combining with the information from statement 1, we see that x, y, z form a geometric series with the common ratio greater than 1.

Thus, we have: $y > x$ – Sufficient

The correct answer is option is C.

320. We know that the absolute value of any number is always non-negative.

Thus, we have:
$|x - y| \geq 0$

Here, $|x - y| > 0$ will be satisfied only if $x \neq y$.

From statement 1:

$xy + 2z = z$

$=> xy = -z$

$=> xy < 0$ (since z is positive)

$=> x > 0$ and $y < 0$

OR

$x < 0$ and $y > 0$

Thus, we can conclude that $x \neq y$

$=> |x - y| > 0$ – Sufficient

From statement 2:

$x^2 - 2x = 0$

$=> x(x - 2) = 0$

Since $x \neq 0$, we have: $x = 2$

However, we have no information about y.

If $y = 2$: $|x - y| = |2 - 2| = 0$

If, however $y \neq 2$: $x - y \neq 0 => |x - y| > 0$

Thus, there is no unique answer. – Insufficient

The correct answer is option A.

321. We know that: $y = |x| + x^3$

We need to determine whether:

$y = 0$

$=> |x| + x^3 = 0$

$=> |x| + x^2 * x = 0$

$=> |x| + |x|^2 * x = 0$ (since $|x|^2 = x^2$)

$=> |x|\,(1 + |x| * x) = 0$

$=> |x| = 0 => x = 0$

OR

$(1 + |x| * x) = 0 => |x| * x = -1$

This is possible only if x is negative and its absolute value is 1 i.e. $x = -1$

Thus, we need to determine whether x can take a value only among 0 or -1.

From statement 1:

$x < 0:$

Possible values of x are -1, -2, etc.

Here, x can take values other than only 0 or -1. – Insufficient

From statement 2:

$y < 1:$

$=> |x| + x^3 < 1$

It is best here to try out with some values of x:

(1) For any fractional value of x, i.e. $0 < x < 1$ or $-1 < x < 0$, y can never be an integer.

(2) If $x = 0 : y = |x| + x^3 = 0 => y < 1$
Here, $y = 0$ – satisfies

(3) If $x = -1 : y = |x| + x^3 = 0 => y < 1$
Here, $y = 0$ – satisfies

(4) If $x = -2 : y = |x| + x^3 = 2 - 8 = -6 => y < 1$
Here, $y \neq 0$ – does not satisfy

Thus, there is no unique answer. - Insufficient

Thus, from statements 1 and 2 together:

Even after combining both statements, we still have the following situations:

$x = 0 \Rightarrow y = 0$ - satisfies

OR

$x = -1 \Rightarrow y = 0$ - satisfies

OR

$x = -2 \Rightarrow y \neq 0$ - does not satisfy

Hence, there is no unique answer. - Insufficient

The correct answer is option E.

322. From statement 1:

Since $0 < x < 1$ and $16x$ is an integer, we must have: $x = \left(\frac{\text{An integer less than 16}}{16}\right)$.

(1) If $x = \frac{1}{16}$ (smallest possible value of x): $x = 0.0625 \Rightarrow$ The tenths' digit is zero.

(2) If $x = \frac{15}{16}$ (largest possible value of x): $x = 0.9375 \Rightarrow$ The tenths' digit is non-zero.

Thus, there is no unique answer. - Insufficient

From statement 2:

Since $0 < x < 1$ and $8x$ is an integer, we must have: $x = \left(\frac{\text{An integer less than 8}}{8}\right)$.

If $x = \frac{1}{8}$ (smallest possible value of x):
$x = 0.125 \Rightarrow$ The tenths' digit is non-zero.

Since for the smallest possible value of x, the tenths' digit is non-zero, the tenths' digit will always be non-zero for all higher values of x. - Sufficient

The correct answer is option B.

323. We know that for all n:

$t_{(n+1)} = \frac{t_n}{2}$

Thus, we have:

$t_2 = \frac{t_1}{2}, t_3 = \frac{t_2}{2}, \ldots$

Thus, we see that every number starting from t_2 is half of the previous number.

From statement 1:

$t_3 = \frac{1}{4}$

$=> t_4 = \frac{1}{2} * \frac{1}{4} = \frac{1}{8}$

$=> t_5 = \frac{1}{2} * \frac{1}{8} = \frac{1}{16}$ – Sufficient

From statement 2:

Let $t_5 = x$

$=> t_1 = 2 * t_2$

$= 2^2 * t_3$

$= 2^3 * t_4$

$= 2^4 * t_5$

$= 16x$

$=> t_1 - t_5 = 16x - x = 15x$

$=> 15x = \frac{15}{16}$

$=> x = t_5 = \frac{1}{16}$ – Sufficient

The correct answer is option D.

324. From statement 1:

We have:

$2^{\sqrt{x}} = 8$

$=> 2^{\sqrt{x}} = 2^3$

=> $\sqrt{x} = 3$

=> $x = 3^2 = 9$

=> $2^x = 2^9 = 512 > 100$ - Sufficient

From statement 2:

We have:

$\frac{1}{2^x} < 0.01$

For any value of x, 2^x is positive, also $\frac{1}{0.01}$ is positive. Thus,

=> $2^x > \frac{1}{0.01}$

=> $2^x > 100$ - Sufficient

The correct answer is option D.

325. We need to determine whether:

$|x| < 1$

=> $-1 < x < 1$

From statement 1:

$|x + 1| = 2|x - 1|$

=> $x + 1 = \pm 2(x - 1)$

=> $x + 1 = \pm(2x - 2)$

=> $x + 1 = 2x - 2$

=> $x = 3$ - Does not satisfy the required condition

OR

$x + 1 = -(2x - 2)$

$x = \frac{1}{3}$ - Satisfies the required condition

Thus, there is no unique answer. - Insufficient

From statement 2:

We have:

$|x - 3| \neq 0$

$=> x \neq 3$

However, we do not have any possible values x can take. - Insufficient

Thus, from statements 1 and 2 together:

Combining both statements, we arrive at:

$x = \frac{1}{3}$ - Satisfies the required condition

Thus, we have a unique answer. - Sufficient

The correct answer is option C.

326. We know that the radical sign i.e. $\sqrt{k}$ takes only the positive square root of k.

Thus, we can have the following cases:

(1) $\sqrt{(x-5)^2} = (x-5)$ - Condition: If $x - 5 \geq 0 => x \geq 5$

(2) $\sqrt{(x-5)^2} = \sqrt{(5-x)^2} = (5-x)$ - Condition: If $5 - x \geq 0 => x \leq 5$

For the given condition to be satisfied, x must be ≤ 5

From statement 1:

$-x\,|x| > 0$

We know that $|x| \geq 0$ for all values of x

$=> -x > 0$

$=> x < 0$

Thus, it satisfies the condition that $x < 5$

Thus, we have:

$\sqrt{(x-5)^2} = (5-x)$ - Sufficient

From statement 2:

$5 - x > 0$

$=> x < 5$

$=> \sqrt{(x-5)^2} = (5 - x)$ – Sufficient

The correct answer is option D.

327. $\frac{x}{y} < xy$ is true under the following conditions:

(1) If x is positive, i.e. $x > 0$:

Canceling x from both sides:

$\frac{1}{y} < y$

$=> y > 1$: (Say, $y = 2 => \frac{1}{y} = \frac{1}{2} < 2 = y$)

OR

$-1 < y < 0$: (Say, $y = -\frac{1}{2} => \frac{1}{y} = -2 < -\frac{1}{2} = y$)

(2) If x is negative, i.e. $x < 0$:

Canceling x from both sides and reversing the inequality sign:

$\frac{1}{y} > y$

$=> 0 < y < 1$: (Say, $y = \frac{1}{2} => \frac{1}{y} = 2 > \frac{1}{2} = y$)

OR

$y < -1$: (Say, $y = -2 => \frac{1}{y} = -\frac{1}{2} > -2 = y$)

From statement 1:

We have:

$xy > 0$

$=> x > 0$ and $y > 0$

OR

$x < 0$ and $y < 0$

However, we do not get any of the conditions above. – Insufficient

From statement 2:

We have:

$y < -1$

However, we do not know whether x is positive or negative. – Insufficient

Thus, from statements 1 and 2 together:

We have:

$y < -1$ i.e. y is negative.

Also, since $xy > 0$, we have:

$x < 0$

Thus, we have:

$x < 0$ and $y < -1$

Thus, it satisfies condition (b) above. – Sufficient

The correct answer is option C.

6.2 Percents

328. From statement 1:

We do not have information on the attorney's fees. – Insufficient

From statement 2:

We do not have information on the assessed value of the estate. – Insufficient

Thus, from statements 1 and 2 together:

The required percent $= \frac{2400}{1.2 * 10^6} * 100 = 0.2\%$ – Sufficient

The correct answer is option C.

329. From statement 1:

We have no information on the number of people employed. – Insufficient

From statement 2:

Since 20% (more than 10%) of the men are employed and 10% of the women are employed among the population 65 years old or older, we can definitely say that on an average, more than 10% of that population must be employed (Minimum term Average Maximum term). – Sufficient

The correct answer is option B.

330. From statement 1:

The initial price of the candy bar is not known.
Hence, the percent increase in the price cannot be determined. – Insufficient

From statement 2:

The amount of increase in price of the candy bar is not known.
Hence, the percent increase in the price cannot be determined – Insufficient

Thus, from statements 1 and 2 together:

Increase in price of the candy bar = 5 cents.
Price of the candy bar after increase = 45 cents.

Thus, initial price of the candy bar = (45 – 5) cents = 40 cents.

Hence, the percent increase in the price

$= \frac{5}{40} * 100 = 12.5\%$ – Sufficient

The correct answer is option C.

331. From statement 1:

Payment for the bicycle excluding 10% sales tax = \$ $0.9x$

Thus, payment for the bicycle including sales tax

$= \$(0.9x + 10\% \text{ of } 0.9x)$

$=> \$(0.9x + 0.09x)$

$=> \$\ 0.99x < \$\ x$ – Sufficient

From statement 2:

The value of x is not given, hence a comparison with x is not possible – Insufficient

The correct answer is option A.

332. From statement 1:

Tim's weight is 80 percent of Joe's weight

$=> \frac{\text{Tim's weight}}{\text{Joe's weight}} = \frac{80}{100} = \frac{4}{5}$

=> Joe weighs more than Tim. – Sufficient

From statement 2:

Joe's weight is 125 percent Of Tim's weight

$=> \frac{\text{Joe's weight}}{\text{Tim's weight}} = \frac{125}{100} = \frac{5}{4}$

=> Joe weighs more than Tim. – Sufficient

The correct answer is option D.

333. Let the total sales be \$$x$.

Amount paid to the salesman per week is:
$\$(300 + 5\% \text{ of } (x - 1000))$; provided $(x > 1000)$

OR

\$300; provided ($x \leq 1000$).

From statement 1:

If $x \leq 1000$:
\$300 = 10% of x
$=> x = \$300 * \frac{100}{10} = \$3000$
However, this contradicts our assumption $x \leq 1000$.
Thus, we can conclude that $x \nleq 1000$ i.e. $x > 1000$.

If $x > 1000$:

$\$(300 + 5\% \text{ of } (x - 1000)) = 10\% \text{ of } x$
$=> 300 + \frac{5(x - 1000)}{100} = \frac{10x}{100}$
$=> x = 5000$

Thus, amount paid to the salesman = 10% of \$5000 = \$500 – Sufficient

From statement 2:

Since the total sales of the salesman was \$5000 (> \$1000), the amount paid to him was:
$\$(300 + 5\%\ of\ (5000 - 1000) = \$500$ – Sufficient

The correct answer is option D.

334. Let the total sales be $\$x$.

Amount paid to Connie per week is:

$\$(500 + 20\% \text{ of } (x - 1500))$; provided ($x > 1500$)

OR

\$500; provided ($x \leq 1500$).

From statement 1:

Since Connie's pay exceeds \$500, we can conclude that $x > 1500$.

Thus, we have:
$\$(500 + 20\% \text{ of } (x - 1500)) = 1200 => 500 + \frac{20(x - 1500)}{100} = 1200$

$=> x = 5000$ – Sufficient

From statement 2:

Since Connie received some commission, we can conclude that $x > 1500$.

Thus, we have:

20% of $(x - 1500)) = 1200 => \frac{20\,(x - 1500)}{100} = 1200$

$=> x = 5000$ – Sufficient

The correct answer is option D.

335. Charge for parts excluding sales tax = \$50.00

Sales tax on charge for parts = \$(6% of 50) = \$3.

Thus, charge for parts including sales tax = \$(50 + 3) = \$53.

We need to determine the charge for labor including sales tax to determine the total charge for the repair.

From statement 1:

Sales tax on labor = 6% of the labor charge = \$9.60

Thus, labor charge = $\$9.60 * \frac{100}{6} = \$160.$

Hence, charge for labor including sales tax = \$(160 + 9.60) = \$169.60.

Hence, charge for repair including sales tax = \$(169.60+53) = \$223.20. – Sufficient

From statement 2:

Total sales tax = \$12.60.

Sales tax on charge for parts = \$3.

Thus, tax on charge for labor = \$ (12.60 – 3) = \$9.60.

This is the same information as in statement 1. Subsequent to this, following the calculation as we did in statement 1, we get the answer. – Sufficient

The correct answer is option D.

336. From statement 1:

We have no information on the total number of people tested for the infection. – Insufficient

From statement 2:

Since 90% of the people tested negative, (100 – 10) = 10% of the people tested positive.

However, the specific information about the number of people having the infection among the ones tested positive, and the number of people not having infection among the ones tested negative is not known. For example, it may be that of the 10% who tested positive, not all actually had the infection or that there may be others who had the infection but were tested negative.

The corresponding information on how many actually had the infection is not available.

Hence, the accuracy of the test cannot be determined. – Insufficient

Thus, from statements 1 and 2 together:

We know that of those who tested positive, 8 did not have the infection.

However, we have no information about the number of people who actually had the infection but were tested negative.

Hence, the accuracy of the test cannot be determined. – Insufficient

The correct answer is option E.

337. From statement 1:

We have no information about the trade in 1994.

Hence, the percentage change cannot be determined. – Insufficient

From statement 2:

We have no information about the trade in 1985.

Hence, the percentage change cannot be determined. – Insufficient

Thus, from statements 1 and 2 together:

We have no information on the value of the gross domestic product in 1994 as compared to that in 1985.

Hence, the percentage change cannot be determined. – Insufficient

The correct answer is option E.

338. From statement 1:

We have no information about the total value of goods consumed in the United States in 2007 as compared to 2004.

Hence, the percentage change in the value of foreign goods consumed from 2004 to 2007 cannot be determined. – Insufficient

From statement 2:

We have no information about the value (or proportion) of foreign goods consumed in 2004 and 2007.

Hence, the percentage change in the value of foreign goods consumed from 2004 to 2007 cannot be determined. – Insufficient

Thus, from statements 1 and 2 together:

Let the total value of goods consumed in the United States in 2004 be \$ $100x$.

Thus, the total value of goods consumed in the United States in 2007

$= \$ \ (120\% \text{ of } 100x) = \$ \ 120x.$

The value of foreign goods consumed in the United States in 2004

$= \$ \ (20\% \text{ of } 100x) = \$ \ 20x.$

The value of foreign goods consumed in the United States in 2007

$= \$ \ (20\% \text{ of } 120x) = \$ \ 24x.$

Hence, the percentage change in the value of foreign goods consumed from 2004 to 2007

$$= \frac{24x - 20x}{20x} * 100 = 20\%$$

Since the value of foreign goods consumed forms a constant percentage share of the total value of goods consumed, the percentage change in the value of foreign goods consumed must be the same as the percentage change in the total value of goods consumed, 20%. – Sufficient

The correct answer is option C.

339. From statement 1:

The statement gives us information on the balance on May 30 had the rate been 12%.

This can be used to determine the balance on May 1.

However, since the actual percent increase has not been mentioned, we cannot determine the actual balance on May 30. – Insufficient

From statement 2:

The statement gives us information on the actual percent increase from May 1 to May 30.

However, since the balance on May 1 has not been mentioned, we cannot determine the actual balance on May 30. – Insufficient

Thus, from statements 1 and 2 together:

Let the balance on May 1 be \$ x.

Thus, at 12% increase, the balance on May 30 = \$ (112% of x)

Thus, we have:

$$\frac{112}{100} * x = 504$$
$$=> x = 4500$$

Thus, actual balance on May 30 (at 8% increase) = \$ (108% of 4500) = \$4860. - Sufficient

The correct answer is option C.

340. From statement 1:

There is no information about Guy's deductions. - Insufficient

From statement 2:

There is no information about Guy's gross income. - Insufficient

Thus, from statements 1 and 2 together:

There is no information about Guy's actual gross income and actual deductions or the deductions as a percent of the gross income ratio. - Insufficient

Had the deductions d as a percent of the gross income i been known, say k%, the percent change in net income could have been calculated as follows:

Initial net income: $(100 - k)\%$ of i

Final net income: $(100 - 1.15k)\%$ of $1.04i$; from information provided in statements 1 & 2.

Thus, percent change in net income could have been calculated.

The correct answer is option E.

341. From statement 1:

We know that the number of children with brown hair = $\frac{60}{100} * 100 = 60$.

However, we cannot determine the number of boys with brown hair. - Insufficient

From statement 2:

We only know the number of boys is 40.

However, we cannot determine the number of boys with brown hair. - Insufficient

Thus, from statements 1 and 2 together:

Even after combining the statements, we cannot determine the number of boys with brown hair (since the percent of boys with brown hair is not known: we cannot assume that since 60% of the children have brown hair, 60% of the boys would also have brown hair). – Insufficient

The correct answer is option E.

342. Since each of Jack's and Kate's annual salaries in 2005 were 10% higher than that in 2004, the sum of their salaries in 2005 would also be 10% higher than that in 2004.

From statement 1:

The sum of Jack's and Kate's annual salaries in 2004 = \$ 80,000.

Thus, the sum of Jack's and Kate's annual salaries in 2005 = $\$\ 80,000 * \frac{110}{100} = \$\ 88,000$

However, we cannot determine Jack's individual salary in 2004. – Insufficient

From statement 2:

The sum of Jack's and Kate's annual salaries in 2005 = \$ 88,000.

Thus, the sum of Jack's and Kate's annual salaries in 2004 = $\$\ 88,000 * \frac{100}{110} = \$\ 80,000$

However, we cannot determine Jack's individual salary in 2004. – Insufficient

Thus, from statements 1 and 2 together:

Even after combining both statements, we cannot determine Jack's individual salary in 2004, as we are only aware of the sum of Jack's and Kate's salary, but no individual salary is known. – Insufficient

The correct answer is option E.

343. We need to verify if:

20% of $n > 10\%$ of $(n + 0.5)$

$$=> \frac{20n}{100} > \frac{10\,(n + 0.5)}{100}$$

$$=> \frac{n}{5} > \frac{n + 0.5}{10}$$

$$=> 2n > n + 0.5$$

$$=> n > 0.5$$

From statement 1:

$n < 0.1$

$=> n \ngtr 0.5$

Thus, the answer to the question is 'No'. – Sufficient

From statement 2:

$n > 0.01$

Thus, we may have $n = 0.8(> 0.5)$ or $n = 0.2(\ngtr 0.5)$.

Thus, the answer to the question is not unique. – Insufficient

The correct answer is option A.

344. We need to verify whether:

$$p * \frac{25}{100} = r * \frac{10}{100}$$

$$=> \frac{p}{4} = \frac{r}{10}$$

$$=> p = \frac{2r}{5}$$

From statement 1:

$r = (100 + 300)\,\%$ of p

$=> r = 400\%$ of p

$$=> r = \frac{400}{100} * p$$

$=> r = 4p$

$=> p = \frac{r}{4}$ – the answer is No – Sufficient

From statement 2:

$p = (100 - 80)\,\%$ of $(r + p)$

$=> p = 20\%$ of $(r + p)$

$$=> p = \frac{20}{100} * (r + p)$$

$=> p = \frac{r+p}{5}$

$=> p - \frac{p}{5} = \frac{r}{5}$

$=> \frac{4p}{5} = \frac{r}{5}$

$=> p = \frac{r}{4}$ – the answer is No – Sufficient

The correct answer is option D.

345. Let the expenditures for books, newspapers and periodicals be $\$x$, $\$y$ and $\$z$ respectively.

Thus: $x + y + z = 35000 \ldots$ (i)

From statement 1:

$y = (100 + 40)\%$ of z

$=> y = 1.4z \ldots$ (ii)

The above equation along with equation (i) cannot be used to solve for x since there are three unknowns and only two equations. – Insufficient

From statement 2:

$y + z = (100 - 25)\%$ of x

$=> y + z = \frac{3x}{4} \ldots$ (iii)

Substituting $(y + z)$ above in equation (i):

$x + \frac{3x}{4} = 35000$

$=> \frac{7x}{4} = 35000$

$=> x = 20000$ – Sufficient

The correct answer is option B.

346. From statement 1:

There is no information about the income of or amount of taxes paid by Mr. Jacobs in 1994. – Insufficient

From statement 2:

There is no information about the amount of taxes paid by Mr. Jacobs in 1993.
Hence, the amount of taxes paid in 1994 cannot be determined. – Insufficient

Thus, from statements 1 and 2 together:

Taxes paid in 1993 = \$(4.8% of 42500) = \$2040.
Thus, taxes paid in 1994 = \$(2040 + 232) = \$2272.

However, the taxable income in 1994 is not known.

Thus, the percentage of taxable income paid as taxes cannot be determined. – Insufficient

The correct answer is option E.

347. Let Joe's income in 2001 be \$100

Thus, taxes paid in 2001 = \$(5.1% of 100) = \$5.1

From statement 1:

Joe's income in 2002 = \$\{(100 + 10)% of 100\} = \$110.

However, there is no information about the amount of taxes Joe paid in 2002. – Insufficient

From statement 2:

Taxes paid in 2002 = \$(3.4% of 100) = \$3.4

However, there is no information about Joe's income in 2002. – Insufficient

Thus, from statements 1 and 2 together:

Joe's income in 2002 = \$110.

Taxes paid by Joe in 2002 = \$3.4

Thus, percent of income paid in taxes = $\frac{3.4}{110} * 100 < 5.1$ – Sufficient

Alternate approach:

Since income has increased from 2001 to 2002, while the taxes in 2002 has fallen as a percent of the income in 2001, the percent of income paid in taxes in 2002 would be even lower.

Hence, the answer is 'Yes'. – Sufficient

The correct answer is option C.

348. We know that the number of female employees in 1997 = 300.

Let number of female employees in 1977 be n.

Thus, the number of female employees in 1987 = $(100 + 60)\,\%$ of $n = \frac{160}{100} * n = \frac{8n}{5}$.

From statement 1:

Number of female employees in 1997 = $(100 + 200)\,\%$ of $n = \frac{300}{100} * n = 3n$.

Thus, we have:

$3n = 300$

$=> n = 100$

=> The number of female employees in 1987 = $\frac{8}{5} * 100 = 160$.

Thus, the percent increase in the number of female employees from 1987 to 1997 $= \frac{300 - 160}{160} * 100$

= 87.5% – Sufficient

From statement 2:

We have: $n = 100$

This is the same information as obtained from statement 1. – Sufficient

The correct answer is option D.

349. We need to find the ratio of the number of sales transactions made by X and Y in June 1989.

From statement 1:

The relation between the number of sales transactions made by X in June to the number of sales transactions made by Y in May is given.

However, there is no relation given regarding the number of sales transactions made by Y in June. – Insufficient

From statement 2:

The relation between the number of sales transactions made by Y in June to the number of sales transactions made by Y in May is given.

However, there is no relation given regarding the number of sales transactions made by X in June. - Insufficient

Thus, from statements 1 and 2 together:

Let the number of sales transactions made by Y in May be p.

Thus, the number of sales transactions made by X in June = $(100 + 50)\%$ of $p = \frac{3p}{2}$.

Also, the number of sales transactions made by Y in June = $(100 + 25)\%$ of $x = \frac{5p}{4}$.

Thus, the required ratio = $\frac{3p}{2} : \frac{5p}{4} = 6 : 5$. - Sufficient

The correct answer is option C.

6.3 Profit & Loss

350. Gross profit = $(y - x)$

The gross profit as a percent of the cost = $\left(\frac{y-x}{x}\right) * 100 = (\frac{y}{x} - 1) * 100$.

From statement 1:

$y - x = 20$ However, we have no information on the value of $\left(\frac{y}{x}\right)$. – Insufficient

From statement 2:

$\frac{y}{x} = \frac{5}{4}$.

Thus, the gross profit as a percent of the cost = $\left(\frac{y}{x} - 1\right) * 100$

$= \left(\frac{5}{4} - 1\right) * 100$

= 25%. – Sufficient

The correct answer is option B.

351. Total earning from the project = \$500,000.

Profit = Earning – Cost.

Let the cost for labor = \$$l$.
Let the cost for materials = \$$m$.
Hence, profit = $\$(500000 - (m + l))$.

We need to check if the profit is greater than \$150,000
$=> (500000 - (m + l)) > 150000 => m + l < 350000$.

From statement 1:

$l + m = 3m$
$=> l = 2m$.
We do not have information on the values of l and m – Insufficient

From statement 2:

$500000 - (m + l) > l$
$=> m + 2l < 500000$
We have no information on the value of $(m + l)$ – Insufficient

From statements 1 and 2 together:

We have: $m + 2l < 500000$, and $l = 2m$
$=> m + 2(2m) < 500000$
$=> m < 100000$
$=> l = 2m < 200000$

Thus, we have: $m + l < 100000 + 200000 = 300000$ - Sufficient

The correct answer is option C.

352. From statement 1:

We know that the percentage discount on the coat was 2 percentage points more than that on the sweater.

However, the sale price of the two items of clothing before the discount is not known.

Thus, we cannot determine which item was discounted by a greater amount. - Insufficient

From statement 2:

We know that the sale price of the coat was \$10 less than the sale price of the sweater.
However, we have no information on the discounts offered on the two items.

Thus, we cannot determine which item was discounted by a greater amount. - Insufficient

Thus, from statements 1 and 2 together:

Let the percentage discount on the sweater be s%.
Thus, the percentage discount on the coat = $(s + 2)$%.

Let the sale price of the sweater before the discount be \$ p.
Thus, the sale price of the coat before the discount be \$ $(p - 10)$.

Thus, discount on the coat = $\$\frac{(s+2)(p-10)}{100}$ and the discount on the sweater = $\$\frac{sp}{100}$.

Since the coat has a higher percentage discount on a lower price, we cannot compare which of the two items has a higher discount. - Insufficient

The correct answer is option E.

353. Let the price at which the computers of Brand C and Brand D were purchased by the store be $\$c$ and $\$d$ respectively.

Let the price at which the computers of Brand C and Brand D were sold by the store be $\$x$ and $\$y$ respectively.

Thus, the profit on Brand C $= x - c$ & profit on Brand D $= y - d$

We have to calculate, $\frac{(x-c)-(y-d)}{(y-d)} * 100\%$

From statement 1:

$x = y + 15\%$ of y

$=> x = y\left(1+\frac{15}{100}\right) = 1.15y$

We have no information about the cost of the two computers.

Hence, we cannot determine the answer. – Insufficient

From statement 2:

$y - d = 300$

We have no information about the profit on sale of Brand C.

Hence, we cannot determine the answer. – Insufficient

Hence, from statements 1 and 2 together:

We have no information on the cost of the computer of Brand C.

Hence, we cannot determine the answer. – Insufficient

The correct answer is option E.

354. From statement 1:

List price $= (100 + 25)\%$ of (Cost price)

$=>$ Cost price $=$ (List price) $* \frac{100}{125}$

$= \$12300 * \frac{100}{125}$

$= \$9840$ – Sufficient

From statement 2:

Selling price of the car $= \$11070$.

Thus, we have:

$11070 = (100 + 12.5)\,\%$ of (Cost price)

$=> 11070 = \left(1 + \frac{1}{8}\right) * \text{(Cost price)}$

$=> \text{Cost price} = \$11070 * \frac{8}{9}$

$= \$9840$ – Sufficient

The correct answer is option D.

6.4 Averages (including weighted averages)

355. From statement 1:

R_1 refers to the average of all the amounts in the 1st row.
Similar reasoning is valid for the other rows as well.

Let us take an example:

R_1	1	2	3	6	Average $= \frac{12}{4} = 3$
R_2	4	6	7	7	Average $= \frac{24}{4} = 6$
Average of all the values $= \frac{1+2+3+6+4+6+7+7}{8} = 4.5$					
Average of R_1 and $R_2 = \frac{3+6}{2} = 4.5$					
Thus, average of all the elements is the same as the average of R_1 and R_2					

Thus, we can say that the average of all the 20 elements

$= \frac{R_1 + R_2 + R_3 + R_4 + R_5}{5} = \frac{550}{5} = 110$ – Sufficient

From statement 2:

Similar reasoning is applicable as in statement 1.

Thus, we can say that the average of all the 20 elements

$= \frac{C_1 + C_2 + C_3 + C_4}{4} = \frac{440}{4} = 110$ – Sufficient

The correct answer is option D.

356. From statement 1:

We know that average height of the students in only one class.
Hence, we cannot determine the average height of all the seniors. – Insufficient

From statement 2:

We only know the ratio of the average heights of the seniors in the two classes.

Hence, we cannot determine the average height of all the seniors. – Insufficient

Thus, from statements 1 and 2 together:

Average height of the seniors in the larger class = 70 inches.

Thus, average height of the seniors in the smaller class = $\frac{4}{5} * 70 = 56$ inches.

However, we do not know the number of students in each class, or either the ratio of number of students in each class. If the ratio of larger number of students to smaller number of students is known = $\frac{x}{y}$, then the average would have been = $\frac{70x}{56y}$

Hence, we cannot determine the average height of all the seniors. – Insufficient

The correct answer is option E.

357. From statement 1:

The average annual salary of the employees in Division R is $30,000.

However, we have no information on the employees in any other division in Company Q.

Hence, the average annual salary of the employees at Company Q cannot be determined. – Insufficient

From statement 2:

The average annual salary of the employees not in Division R is $35,000.

However, we have no information on the salary of the employees in Division R in Company Q.

Hence, the average annual salary of the employees at Company Q cannot be determined. – Insufficient

Thus, from statements 1 and 2 together:

We know the average annual salary of the employees in Division R and also the employees not in Division R.

However, we have no information on the ratio of the number of employees in Division R and the number of employees in Division R.

If the ratio $\frac{\text{Number of employees of Division R}}{\text{Number of employees not in division R}} = \frac{x}{y}$,

Then, the average salary of all the employees in Company Q = $(\frac{x * 3000 + y * 3500}{x + y})$

Hence, the average annual salary of the employees at Company Q cannot be determined – Insufficient

The correct answer is option E.

358. From statement 1:

There is no information on the number of Sedans sold, the number of Coupes sold, the average selling price of the Coupes. – Insufficient

From statement 2:

There is no information on the number of Sedans sold, the number of Coupes sold, the average selling price of the Sedans. – Insufficient

Thus, from statements 1 and 2 together:

Let the number of Sedans sold and the number of Coupes be s &c, respectively; thus, the average price for all the cars

$$= \$ \left(\frac{10600s + 8400c}{s + c}\right)$$

However, there is no information about c & s. – Insufficient

The correct answer is option E.

359. Jill's average score for three games $= 168$.

Thus, Jill's total score for three games $= 168 * 3 = 504$.

From statement 1:

Jill's highest score $= 204$.

Thus, sum of Jill's two lowest scores $= 504 - 204 = 300$.

However, we cannot determine Jill's lowest scores. – Insufficient

From statement 2:

Sum of Jill's two highest scores = 364.

Thus, Jill's lowest score = 504 – 364 = 140. – Sufficient

The correct answer is option B.

360. We know that there are 20 friends in all.

Let the average amount spent by each friend = \$$a$.

The amount spent by the first five friends = \$ $(5 * 21)$ = \$105.

The average amount spent by the remaining $(20 - 5) = 15$ friends = \$ $(a - x)$.

Thus, the total amount spent by the 15 friends = \$ $(15 * (a - x))$.

Thus, the total amount spent by all the friends = \$ $\{15 * (a - x) + 105\}$ ...(i)

Thus, the average amount spent by all the friends = \$ $\left(\frac{15 * (a - x) + 105}{20}\right)$.

Thus, we have:

$\frac{15(a - x) + 105}{20} = a$

=> $15(a - x) + 105 = 20a$

=> $3(a - x) + 21 = 4a$

=> $3a - 3x + 21 = 4a$

=> $a + 3x = 21$ ...(ii)

From statement 1:

$x = 3$

Thus, from (ii), we have:

=> $a + 3 * 3 = 21$

=> $a = 12$ – Sufficient

From statement 2:

The total amount spent is \$240.

Thus, from (i), we have:

=> $15 * (a - x) + 105 = 240$

=> $15(a - x) = 135$

$=> a - x = 9$

$=> x = a - 9$

From (ii), we have:

$a + 3(a - 9) = 21$

$=> 4a = 48$

$=> a = 12$ - Sufficient

Alternate Approach:

The total amount spent is \$240, and total friends are 20.

The average amount spent $= \frac{240}{20} = 12$. - Sufficient

The correct answer is option D.

6.5 Ratio & Proportion

361. Let the number of staff members = n.

From statement 1:

$x : y : z = 2 : 3 : 4$
=> $x = 2k,\ y = 3k,\ z = 4k$, where k is a constant of proportionality.

However, we have no information on n. - Insufficient

From statement 2:

$nx = 18,\ ny = 27,\ nz = 36.$

We have no information about x, y, z.
Hence, we cannot determine the value of n. - Insufficient

Thus, from statements 1 and 2 together:

Substituting the values of x or y or z from statement 1 in the information from statement 2, we have:

$nx = 18 = 2k$
$n = \frac{9}{k}$
Since k is unknown, we cannot determine n. - Insufficient

The correct answer is option E.

362. Number of members at the beginning of the year in the Finance and Planning Committees were n each.

Number of members at the end of the year in the Finance and Planning Committees are $(n - 5)$ and $(n - 3)$, respectively.

From statement 1:

Number of members who left at the end of the year = $3 + 5 = 8$.
Thus, number of members at the beginning of the year $\frac{6}{1} * 8 = 48$.

Thus: $2n = 48$
=> $n = 24$ - Sufficient

From statement 2:

Number of members remained in the Planning committee = 21.

Number of members who had left the Planning committee = 3.

Thus, number of members in the Planning committee at the beginning of the year = 21 + 3 = 24.

Thus, $n = 24$ – Sufficient

The correct answer is option D.

363. From statement 1:

Before the water from X was poured, X was $\frac{1}{3}$ full.

However, the capacity of Y in terms of X is not known.

Hence, fraction of water in Y after pouring cannot be determined. – Insufficient

From statement 2:

Let the capacity of X and Y be c units.

Though we know the initial amount of water in $Y = \frac{c}{2}$, we do not know the initial amount of water present in X.

Hence, fraction of water in Y after pouring cannot be determined. – Insufficient

Thus, from statements 1 and 2 together:

The capacity of X and Y is c units.

Initial amount of water in X and $Y = \frac{c}{3}$ and $\frac{c}{2}$ respectively.

Final amount of water in Y when all the water in X is poured in $Y = \frac{c}{2} + \frac{c}{3} = \frac{5c}{6}$.

Hence, fraction of water in Y after pouring $= \frac{5}{6}$ – Sufficient

The correct answer is option C.

364. Ratio in which the inks are blended is given as:

Red : Blue : Green : Yellow = 6 : 5 : 2 : 2.

Thus, we have:

Quantity of red ink = $6k$

Quantity of blue ink = $5k$

Quantity of green ink = $2k$

Quantity of yellow ink = $2k$, where k is the constant of proportionality

We need to determine the quantity of green ink used i.e. $2k$.

From statement 1:

Since quantity of red ink used is 2 liters more than that of blue ink, we have:
$6k = 2 + 5k$

$=> k = 2$

$=>$ The quantity of green ink used $= 2k = 2 * 2 = 4$ liters – Sufficient

From statement 2:

Total volume of color X ink $= 6k + 5k + 2k + 2k = 15k$.

Thus, we have: $15k = 30$

$=> k = 2$

$=>$ The quantity of green ink used $= 2k = 2 * 2 = 4$ liters – Sufficient

The correct answer is option D.

365. From statement 1:

We have the ratio of apple juice and cranberry juice that were mixed.

Since no volume is mentioned, we cannot determine the number of liters of apple juice. – Insufficient

From statement 2:

The volume of cranberry juice is known. However, we cannot determine the number of liters of apple juice. – Insufficient

Thus, from 1 and 2 together:

$$\frac{\text{Apple juice}}{\text{Cranberry juice}} = \frac{3}{2}$$

$$=> \frac{\text{Apple juice}}{5} = \frac{3}{2}$$

$=>$ Apple juice $= 5 * \frac{3}{2} = 7.5$ liters. – Sufficient

The correct answer is option C.

366. From statement 1:

The ratio of the number of male employees to female employees $= 2 : 3$.

There is no information about the present scenario. – Insufficient

From statement 2:

Let the number of male employees last January be m.
Let the number of female employees last January be w.

Thus, the number of male employees at present = $(m + 400)$.
The number of female employees at present = w.

Thus, we have:

$$\frac{m + 400}{w} = \frac{3}{4}$$

There are two unknowns and hence, this equation cannot be solved. – Insufficient

Thus, from statements 1 and 2 together:

$$m : w = 2 : 3$$
$$=> w = \frac{3m}{2}$$

Substituting this in the equation obtained in statement 2, we have:

$$\frac{(m + 400)}{\frac{3m}{2}} = \frac{3}{4}$$
$$=> m = 3200$$

$$=> w = 3 * \frac{3200}{2} = 4800$$

Thus, the number of male employees at present = $(m + 400) = 3600$.

The number of female employees at present = $w = 4800$.

Thus, the total number of employees at present = $3600 + 4800 = 8400$. – Sufficient

The correct answer is option C.

367. From statement 1:

Jim caught $\frac{2}{3}$ of the total fish they caught together.

Thus, Tom caught $\left(1 - \frac{2}{3}\right) = \frac{1}{3}$ of the total fish they caught together.

Thus, Jim caught more fish than Tom did. – Sufficient

From statement 2:

We know that Jim caught 12 more fish than what he had caught till Tom was fishing with him.

However, we have no information on the number of fish either Tom or Jim had actually caught. - Insufficient

The correct answer is option A.

368. We know that:

The ratio of the number of male and female workers in 2002 = 3 : 4.

Let the number of male and female workers in 2002 be $3k$ and $4k$ respectively, where k is a constant of proportionality.

From statement 1:

We know that:

The ratio of the number of male workers in 2002 to 2003 = 3 : 5.

The number of male workers in 2002 = $3k$.
Thus, the number of male workers in 2003 = $\frac{5}{3} * 3k = 5k$.

However, we have no information about the number of female workers in 2003. - Insufficient

From statement 2:

We know that:

The ratio of the number of male and female workers in 2003 = 10 : 7.

Let the number of male and female workers in 2003 be $10l$ and $7l$ respectively where l is another constant of proportionality (not necessarily the same as k).

Percent increase in the number of male workers from 2002 to 2003 = $\left(\frac{10l - 3k}{3k}\right) * 100$

$= \left(\frac{10l}{3k} - 1\right) * 100 = P_m$

Percent increase in the number of female workers from 2002 to 2003 = $\left(\frac{7l - 4k}{4k}\right) * 100$

$= \left(\frac{7l}{4k} - 1\right) * 100 = P_f$

Comparing P_m and P_f, we see that there are two ratios involved: $\left(\frac{10l}{3k}\right)$ and $\left(\frac{7l}{4k}\right)$ respectively.

Comparing the ratios, we see that:

$$\left(\frac{10l}{3k}\right) = \frac{10}{3} * \frac{l}{k} = 3.33 * \frac{l}{k}$$

$$\left(\frac{7l}{4k}\right) = \frac{7}{4} * \frac{l}{k} = 1.75 * \frac{l}{k}$$

As, l and k both are positive thus, ratio $\left(\frac{l}{k}\right)$ must also be positive. Hence, from above equations we can conclude that

Thus, we can say that:

$$\left(\frac{10l}{3k}\right) > \left(\frac{7l}{4k}\right)$$

$=> P_m > P_f$ – Sufficient

The correct answer is option B.

369. From statement 1:

There is no information about the male members in the club. – Insufficient

From statement 2:

There is no information about the female members in the club. – Insufficient

Thus, from statements 1 and 2 together:

We know that 10 male members are over 75 years of age.

However, we cannot find the number of female members over 75 years of age.

Also, the total number of members is not known.

Thus, the answer cannot be determined. – Insufficient

The correct answer is option E.

370. From statement 1:

There is no information about the male members in the club. – Insufficient

From statement 2:

There is no information about the female members in the club. – Insufficient

Thus, from statements 1 and 2 together:

Percent of female members who are mechanical engineers = $\frac{1}{3} * 75\% = 25\%$.

Percent of male members who are engineers = 30%.

Thus, the percent of male members who are mechanical engineers ≤ 30%, (since only engineers can be mechanical engineers).

Since for both male and female members, the fraction of mechanical engineers among them is less than $\frac{1}{3}$ among all members, the fraction of mechanical engineers is definitely not more than $\frac{1}{3}$. - Sufficient

The correct answer is option C.

371. From statement 1:

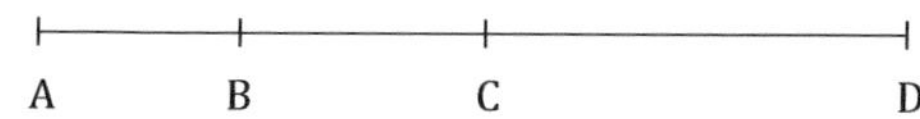

AD = AC + BD - BC

However, the length of BC is not known. - Insufficient

From statement 2:

$BC^2 = AB * CD$

However, none of the lengths are known. - Insufficient

Thus, from statements 1 and 2 together:

Let the length of BC = x.

Thus, from statement 1, we have:

$AB = 10 - x$

$CD = 15 - x$

Thus, from statement 2, we have:

$x^2 = (10 - x)(15 - x)$

$=> x^2 = 150 - 25x + x^2$

$=> 25x = 150$

$=> x = 6$

Thus, we have:

AD = AC + BD - BC

$= 10 + 15 - 6 = 19$ - Sufficient

The correct answer is option C.

6.6 Mixtures

372. We need to find the minimum concentration of milk in any of the two containers so that when mixed they result in 80% milk solution.

Since one container has the minimum milk concentration, the other must have the maximum possible milk concentration, i.e. 100% (this is the limiting case).

Also, in order to find the minimum concentration in one container, we must have 100% concentration of milk in the container having the larger volume so that a large quantity of milk is obtained.

From statement 1:

We have:

$x = 2y$

$=> x > y$

Thus, the container with x liters must be taken to be 100% milk.

Since the entire contents of both containers are mixed to get 30 liters of solution, we have:

$x + y = 30$

$=> 2y + y = 30$

$=> y = 10$

$=> x = 20$

Thus, we have two solutions: 20 liters of 100% concentration of milk and 10 liters of $n\%$ concentration of milk, where $n\%$ represents the minimum concentration of milk.

Thus, equating the final concentration of milk, we have:

$$\frac{20 * \left(\frac{100}{100}\right) + 10 * \left(\frac{n}{100}\right)}{20 + 10} = \frac{80}{100}$$

$$=> 20 + \frac{n}{10} = \frac{4}{5} * 30$$

$$=> 20 + \frac{n}{10} = 24$$

$=> n = 40$ - Sufficient

From statement 2:

We have:

$x = y + 10$

$=> x > y$

Thus, the container with x liters must be taken to be 100% milk.

Since the entire contents of both containers are mixed to get 30 liters of solution, we have:

$x + y = 30$

$=> (y + 10) + y = 30$

$=> y = 10$

$=> x = 20$

This is the same result as obtained from statement 1.

Hence, we would obtain a unique answer. –Sufficient

The correct answer is option D.

373. From statement 1:

We have:

$x = 10$, and

$y = 100$

However, the value of z is not known (we should not assume that $x = z$). – Insufficient

From statement 2:

We have:

$x = 20\%$ of y, and

$z = 10\%$ of y

Since we need the fraction of milk finally present in the mixture, we can assume a suitable value for y for ease of calculations.

Let $y = 100$

Thus, we have:

$x = 20$, and

$z = 10$

Thus, we have:

From 100 liters of milk in a cask, 20 liters are removed and then 10 liters of water are added.

This process is repeated twice.

Thus, in the first cycle, fraction of the total contents of the cask removed $= \frac{20}{100} = \frac{1}{5}$

Thus, fraction of contents left $= 1 - \frac{1}{5} = \frac{4}{5}$

Thus, amount of milk left after the first cycle $= 100 * \frac{4}{5} = 80$ liters.

Now, 10 liters of water are added.

Thus, total contents of the cask $= (80 + 10) = 90$ liters.

Thus, in the second cycle, fraction of the total contents of the cask removed $= \frac{20}{90} = \frac{2}{9}$

Thus, fraction of contents left $= 1 - \frac{2}{9} = \frac{7}{9}$

Thus, amount of milk left after the second cycle $= 80 * \frac{7}{9} = \frac{560}{9}$ liters.

Total volume of cask after removal $= (90 - 20) = 70$ liters.

Now, 10 liters of water are added.

Thus, total contents of the cask $= (70 + 10) = 80$ liters.

Thus, required fraction of milk $= \left(\frac{\frac{560}{9}}{80}\right) = \frac{7}{9}$ - Sufficient

The correct answer is option B.

374. We need to find the minimum concentration of milk in any of the two containers so that when mixed they result in 80% milk solution.

Since one container has the minimum milk concentration, the other must have the maximum possible milk concentration, i.e. 100% (this is the limiting case).

Also, in order to find the minimum concentration in one container, we must have 100% concentration of milk in the container having the larger volume so that a large quantity of milk is obtained.

From statement 1:

We have:

$x = 2y$

$=> x > y$

Thus, the container with x liters must be taken to be 100% milk.

Since the entire contents of both containers are mixed to get 30 liters of solution, we have:

$x + y = 30$

$=> 2y + y = 30$

$=> y = 10$

$=> x = 20$

Thus, we have two solutions: 20 liters of 100% concentration of milk and 10 liters of $n\%$ concentration of milk, where $n\%$ represents the minimum concentration of milk.

Thus, equating the final concentration of milk, we have:

$$\frac{20 * \left(\frac{100}{100}\right) + 10 * \left(\frac{n}{100}\right)}{20 + 10} = \frac{80}{100}$$

$=> 20 + \frac{n}{10} = \frac{4}{5} * 30$

$=> 20 + \frac{n}{10} = 24$

$=> n = 40$ – Sufficient

From statement 2:

We have:

$x = y + 10$

$=> x > y$

Thus, the container with x liters must be taken to be 100% milk.

Since the entire contents of both containers are mixed to get 30 liters of solution, we have:

$x + y = 30$

$=> (y + 10) + y = 30$

$=> y = 10$

$=> x = 20$

This is the same result as obtained from statement 1.

Hence, we would obtain a unique answer. –Sufficient

The correct answer is option D.

375. From statement 1:

We have:

$x = 10$, and

$y = 100$

However, the value of z is not known (we should not assume that $x = z$). – Insufficient

From statement 2:

We have:

$x = 20\%$ of y, and

$z = 10\%$ of y

Since we need the fraction of milk finally present in the mixture, we can assume a suitable value for y for ease of calculations.

Let $y = 100$

Thus, we have:

$x = 20$, and

$z = 10$

Thus, we have:

From 100 liters of milk in a cask, 20 liters are removed and then 10 liters of water are added.

This process is repeated twice.

Thus, in the first cycle, fraction of the total contents of the cask removed $= \frac{20}{100} = \frac{1}{5}$

Thus, fraction of contents left $= 1 - \frac{1}{5} = \frac{4}{5}$

Thus, amount of milk left after the first cycle $= 100 * \frac{4}{5} = 80$ liters.

Now, 10 liters of water are added.

Thus, total contents of the cask $= (80 + 10) = 90$ liters.

Thus, in the second cycle, fraction of the total contents of the cask removed $= \frac{20}{90} = \frac{2}{9}$

Thus, fraction of contents left $= 1 - \frac{2}{9} = \frac{7}{9}$

Thus, amount of milk left after the second cycle $= 80 * \frac{7}{9} = \frac{560}{9}$ liters.

Total volume of cask after removal $= (90 - 20) = 70$ liters.

Now, 10 liters of water are added.

Thus, total contents of the cask $= (70 + 10) = 80$ liters.

Thus, required fraction of milk $= \left(\frac{\frac{560}{9}}{80}\right) = \frac{7}{9}$ - Sufficient

The correct answer is option B.

6.7 Speed, Time, & Distance

376. From statement 1:

Mieko's average speed was $\frac{3}{4}$ of Chan's speed.

Thus, Mieko's travel time

$= \frac{1}{\left(\frac{3}{4}\right)} = \frac{4}{3}$ of Chan's travel time (since for the same distance, time is inversely proportional to speed).

Chan's travel time = 15 minutes.

Thus, Mieko's travel time = $15 * \frac{4}{3} = 20$ minutes – Sufficient

From statement 2:

The length of the route is of no use since actual speeds are not mentioned. – Insufficient

The correct answer is option A.

377. Let the length of the route be d miles.

From statement 1:

Time taken to cover the route at 55 miles per hour is $\frac{d}{55}$ hours.

Time taken to cover the route at 50 miles per hour is $\frac{d}{50}$ hours.

Thus, we have:

$$\frac{d}{55} = \frac{d}{50} - 1$$

=> $d = 550$ miles. – Sufficient

From statement 2:

Speed over the first half of the route = 25 miles per hour.
Time taken to cover the first half of the route = 11 hours.

Hence, length of the first half of the route = 11*25 = 275 miles.

Hence, length of the entire route = 2 * 275 = 550 miles. – Sufficient

The correct answer is option D.

378. From statement 1:

There is no information about Joan's average speed. – Insufficient

From statement 2:

There is no information about the distance. – Insufficient

Thus, from statements 1 and 2 together:

Let the actual distance be d miles.

Thus, Joan's estimate of the distance ranged from $(d + 5)$ miles to $(d - 5)$ miles.

Let Joan's actual average speed be s miles/hour.
Thus, Joan's estimate of her speed ranged from $(s + 10)$ miles to $(s - 10)$ miles/hour.

Thus, actual time $= \frac{d}{s}$ hours.

Maximum value of estimated time $= \left(\frac{d+5}{s-10}\right)$ hours.

Minimum value of estimated time $= \left(\frac{d-5}{s+10}\right)$ hours.

We need to determine whether:

(1) $\left(\frac{d+5}{s-10}\right) - \frac{d}{s} \leq 0.5,$

AND

(2) $\frac{d}{s} - \left(\frac{d-5}{s+10}\right) \leq 0.5$

Since the relation between s and d is not known, we cannot determine the answer.

Let us take some values to verify:

(1) If $d = 20, s = 15$:

Condition (a): $\left(\frac{d+5}{s-10}\right) - \frac{d}{s} = \frac{25}{5} - \frac{20}{15} = 5 - \frac{4}{3} = \frac{11}{3} > 0.5$ – does not satisfy

Condition (b): $\frac{d}{s} - \left(\frac{d-5}{s+10}\right) = \frac{20}{15} - \frac{15}{25} = \frac{4}{3} - \frac{3}{5} = \frac{11}{15} > 0.5$ – does not satisfy

(2) If $d = 60, s = 50$:

Condition (a): $\left(\frac{d+5}{s-10}\right) - \frac{d}{s} = \frac{65}{40} - \frac{60}{50} = \frac{13}{8} - \frac{6}{5} = \frac{17}{40} < 0.5$ – satisfies

Condition (b): $\frac{d}{s} - \left(\frac{d-5}{s+10}\right) = \frac{60}{50} - \frac{55}{60} = \frac{6}{5} - \frac{11}{12} = \frac{17}{60} < 0.5$ – satisfies

Thus, there is no unique answer. – Insufficient

The correct answer is option E.

379. Time (t) taken to travel d feet at r feet per second

$t = \frac{d}{r}$

Time (T) taken to travel D feet at R feet per second

$T = \frac{D}{R}$

From statement 1:

$d = D + 30 \ldots$ (i)

However, there is no information on the values of r and R. – Insufficient

From statement 2:

$r = R + 30 \ldots$ (i)

However, there is no information on the values of d and D. – Insufficient

Thus, from statements 1 and 2 together:

From (i) and (ii), we have:

$$t = \frac{d}{r}$$

$$= \frac{D+30}{R+30}$$

$$= \frac{\left(\frac{D+30}{R}\right)}{\left(\frac{R+30}{R}\right)}$$

$$= \frac{\left(\frac{D}{R} + \frac{30}{R}\right)}{\left(1 + \frac{30}{R}\right)}$$

$$= \frac{\left(T + \frac{30}{R}\right)}{\left(1 + \frac{30}{R}\right)}$$

Let $\frac{30}{R} = k$

Thus, we have:

$$t = \frac{T + k}{1 + k}$$

There are 2 possible cases:

(1) If $T > 1$: $\frac{T + k}{1 + k} < T$; for example:

If $T = 2$ and $k = 1$: $\frac{T + k}{1 + k} = \frac{3}{2} < 2$

=> $t < T$

(2) If $T < 1$: $\frac{T + k}{1 + k} > T$; for example:

If $T = \frac{1}{2}$ and $k = 1$: $\frac{T + k}{1 + k} = \frac{\left(\frac{3}{2}\right)}{2} = \frac{3}{4} > \frac{1}{2}$

=> $t > T$

Thus, there is no unique answer. – Insufficient

The correct answer is option E.

6.8 Time & Work

380. From statement 1:

Time taken to produce 40 screws = 56 seconds.

However, no information is provided about the time taken to produce a bolt. - Insufficient

From statement 2:

Time taken to produce 1 bolt = 1.5 times the time taken to produce one screw.

However, no information is provided about the time taken to produce one screw. - Insufficient

Thus, from statements 1 and 2 together:

Time taken to produce one screw = $\frac{56}{40}$ = 1.4 seconds.
Thus, time taken to produce one bolt = 1.4 * 1.5 = 2.1 seconds.

Thus, time taken to produce 300 bolts = 2.1 * 300 = 630 seconds. - Sufficient

The correct answer is option C.

381. From statement 1:

We have information about only one machine. - Insufficient

From statement 2:

We do not have any information about the actual rate at which the copies are made. - Insufficient

Thus, from statements 1 and 2 together:

We know that one machine produces copies at the rate of 250 copies per minute.

Since one machine is twice as fast as the other machine (we have no information about which machine is twice as efficient), we can have the second machine making copies at the rate of

(1) $\frac{250}{2}$ = 125 copies per minute

OR

(1) 250*2 = 500 copies per minute

Thus, we do not know the actual rate at which the copies are made by the other machine. – Insufficient

The correct answer is option E.

382. Time taken by 5 skilled workers to complete the job = 18 hours.

Thus, time taken by 1 skilled worker to complete the job = 18 * 5 = 90 hours . . . (i)

Also, number of skilled workers required to complete the job in 1 hour = 5 * 18 = 90 . . . (ii)

We need to find the time it takes for a group of 3 skilled workers and 4 apprentices to do the same job.

From statement 1:

Since an apprentice works at $\frac{2}{3}$ the rate of a skilled worker, we can say that 1 apprentice is equivalent to $\frac{2}{3}$ of a skilled worker.

Thus, 3 apprentices are equivalent to $\left(3 * \frac{2}{3}\right) = 2$ skilled workers.

Thus, 4 skilled workers and 3 apprentices are equivalent to $(4 + 2) = 6$ skilled workers.

Thus, from (i), we have:

Time taken by 6 skilled workers to complete the job

$= \frac{90}{6} = 15$ hours – Sufficient

From statement 2:

Time taken by 6 apprentices and 5 skilled workers to complete the job = 10 hours.

Thus, in order to complete the job in 1 hour, number of people required

$= 6 * 10$ apprentices and $5 * 10$ skilled workers

= 60 apprentices and 50 skilled workers

Thus, from (ii), we have:

60 apprentices and 50 skilled workers ≡ 90 skilled workers

=> 60 apprentices ≡ 40 skilled workers

=> 1 apprentice $\equiv \frac{40}{60} = \frac{2}{3}$ skilled worker

This is the same information as in statement 1. – Sufficient

The correct answer is option D.

6.9 Computational

383. Say there are n number of sales people.

Thus from statement 1, total number of cars = $4n + 23$ – Insufficient

Thus from statement 2, total number of cars = $6n + 5$ – Insufficient

Thus from statement 1 & 2 together, $6n + 5 = 4n + 23 \Rightarrow n = 9$ – a unique answer

The correct answer is option C.

384. Let the employee worked for x hours today and for y hours yesterday.

The employee gets paid \$9 per hour for 8 hours i.e. \$72 for a total of 8 hours.

Hence, for an excess of 8 hours, his pay per hour = $\$9 * (1\frac{1}{2}) = \$(9 * \frac{3}{2}) = \$(\frac{27}{2})$.

From statement 1:

Since we have no information on the number of hours the employee worked yesterday, we cannot calculate his yesterday's pay.

Thus, we cannot find his today's pay.

Hence, we cannot determine the number of hours he worked today. – Insufficient

From statement 2:

We have no information on the pay received by the employee today.

Hence, we cannot determine the number of hours he worked today. – Insufficient

From statements 1 and 2 together:

Since the employee worked for 8 hours yesterday, he received \$72 as pay.

Hence, the pay received by the employee today $\$(27 + 72) = \$99$.

For the first 8 hours today, the employee received \$72.

Hence, he received an extra of \$27 today.

For each hour of additional work, the employee receives = $\$\frac{27}{2}$.

Hence, number of hours he worked extra today = $\frac{27}{\frac{27}{2}} = 2$ hours.

Hence, the employee worked for $8 + 2 = 10$ hours today. – Sufficient

The correct answer is option C.

385. Let the regular-size box contain r ounces cereal.

From statement 1:

The family-size box contains $(r + 10)$ ounces cereal.

We cannot determine the cost per ounce since no price is mentioned. – Insufficient

From statement 2:

Cost of the family-size box = \$5.40

We cannot determine the cost per ounce since no quantity is mentioned. – Insufficient

Thus from statements 1 and 2 together:

Cost per ounce of the family-size box = $\$(\frac{5.40}{r+10})$.

We cannot determine the cost per ounce since r is unknown. – Insufficient

The correct answer is option E.

386. From statement 1:

We have no information on how many customers purchased how many books. – Insufficient

From statement 2:

We know that 20 customers purchased two books each.

This accounts for 20*2 = 40 books.

We have no information on the number of books purchased by the others. – Insufficient

Thus, from statements 1 and 2 together:

Let x customers purchased one book each.

Also, 20 customers purchased two books each (from Statement 2).

Thus, the remaining $100 - (x + 20) = (80 - x)$ customers purchased exactly three books each (since no one purchased more than three books (from Statement 1).

Total books purchased = 200.

Thus: $x * 1 + 20 * 2 + (80 - x) * 3 = 200$

$=> x = 40$ – Sufficient

The correct answer is option C.

387. Let the number of employees = x.

Thus, number of males = $x * \frac{25}{100} = \frac{x}{4}$.

Number of sales staff = $x * \frac{50}{100} = \frac{x}{2}$.

From statement 1:

We know that there are seven males who are sales staff.

However, we cannot determine x from this information. – Insufficient

From statement 2:

Number of males = $\frac{x}{4}$.

Thus, number of females = $x - \frac{x}{4} = \frac{3x}{4}$.

Hence, we have: $\frac{3x}{4} - \frac{x}{4} = 16$

=> $x = 32$ – Sufficient

The correct answer is option B.

388. Let the price of each orange yesterday be $\$x$.

Thus, the price of each apple yesterday = $\$(x + 0.10)$

Let the number of apples sold = a

Let the number of oranges sold = r

We have to calculate: Total revenue = $rx + a(x + 0.10)$

From statement 1:

$r = a + 5$.

Since we do not know the actual number of oranges sold, we cannot determine the revenue from the oranges. – Insufficient

From statement 2:

Revenue from apples = $a * (x + 0.10) = 15$.

Since we do not know the number of oranges sold or the price of each orange, we cannot determine the revenue from the oranges – Insufficient

Thus, from statements 1 and 2 together:

Revenue from oranges = $rx = (a + 5)x$; (substituting $r = a + 5$).

We have: $a * (x + 0.10) = 15$;

However, we cannot determine the value of a or x.

Hence, we cannot determine the revenue from the oranges. - Insufficient

The correct answer is option E.

389. Total amount of inventory, in dollar, at the end = Total amount of inventory, in dollar, at the beginning + Total amount of purchases in the month - Total amount of sale in the month

From statement 1:

The store effectively had purchased 250 writing pads at \$0.75 per pad and 150 pads at \$0.80 per pad.

However, the number of pads sold and its price are not known.

Hence, total amount of inventory, in dollar, of stock by the store at the end of last month cannot be determined - Insufficient

From statement 2:

The total revenue from the sale of writing pads = \$180.

However, the number of writing pads purchased by the store and its price in the last month is not known.

Hence, total amount of inventory, in dollar, of stock by the store at the end of last month cannot be determined - Insufficient

Thus, from statements 1 and 2 together:

Total amount of inventory, in dollar, at the end

$= 250 * 0.75 + 150 * 0.80 - 180 = 187.50 + 120 - 180 = 127.50$ - Sufficient

The correct answer is option C.

390. From statement 1:

We have:

$H = kJ$,

$J = 60000$.

However, since k is unknown, we cannot determine the value of H - Insufficient

From statement 2:

We have:

$H = kJ,$
$J = 37500,$

$H = 7500$

Thus,

$$k = \frac{H}{J} = \frac{7500}{37500} = \frac{1}{5}.$$

Thus, we have:

$$H = \frac{J}{5}$$

However, no information is given on the number of jobs to be created i.e. J.

Hence, the value of H cannot be determined – Insufficient

From statements 1 and 2 together:

We know:

$$H = \frac{J}{5},$$

$J = 60000$

Thus, we have:

$$H = \frac{60000}{5} = 12000 \text{ – Sufficient}$$

The correct answer is option C.

391. From statement 1:

We have no information about the distance travelled in one gallon of gasoline.
Hence, the cost of gasoline per mile cannot be determined – Insufficient

From statement 2:

We have no information about the cost of gasoline.
Hence, the cost of gasoline per mile cannot be determined – Insufficient

Thus, from statements 1 and 2 together:

Since we need to find the cost of gasoline per mile, we need to know the total cost of gasoline and the total number of miles travelled.

The cost per gallon of gasoline is known.

Since the number of gallons of gasoline used is not known, we cannot determine the total cost of gasoline.

Hence, the cost of gasoline per mile cannot be determined – Insufficient

The correct answer is option E.

392. Total number of parents = 20.

We also know that more parents chose Monday than Tuesday.

From statement 1:

We know that the maximum number of parents present on any weekday = 5.

If no parent attended on Friday, then 20 parents attended the conference on four days (Monday to Thursday).

This is only possible if on each day, there were $\frac{20}{4} = 5$ parents attending the conference.

However, we know that more parents chose Monday than Tuesday.

Since maximum number of parents on any day can be five, we must have four or less parents on Tuesday.

Thus, 19 parents (five on each of Monday, Wednesday and Thursday and four on Tuesday) have been accounted for.

Thus, the remaining parent must have been present on Friday. – Sufficient

From statement 2:

We have more parents on Monday than both Tuesday and Wednesday.

This does not help in determining the number of parents present on Friday. – Insufficient

The correct answer is option A.

393. From statement 1:

We have: $v + z = 6$

Since none of the numbers are more than ‘3’, the above equation is valid only if $v = z = 3$.

We also know that each of the numbers 1, 2, 3 appear exactly once in each row and column.
Thus, in the first row: $s \neq 3$ (as in column 2 => $v = 3$ is already present) and $t \neq 3$ (as in column 3 => $z = 3$ is already present).

=> $r = 3$ - Sufficient

From statement 2:

Since each of the numbers 1, 2, 3 appear exactly once in each row and column.
Thus, the sum of each row and each column = $1 + 2 + 3 = 6$.

Hence, we have:

$r + s + t = 6$; (considering the first row)

$r + u + x = 6$; (considering the first column)

Adding the above two equations, we have:

$2r + s + t + u + x = 12$.

However, we know: $s + t + u + x = 6$

Hence, $2r = 12 - (s + t + u + x) = 12 - 6 = 6$

=> $r = 3$ - Sufficient

The correct answer is option D.

394. From statement 1:

$t \triangle 2 = 74$

=> $(t + 2)^2 + (2 + 3)^2 = 74$
=> $(t + 2)^2 = 49$
=> $t + 2 = \pm 7$
=> $t = 5$ or -9.

Hence, we do not have a unique value of t. - Insufficient

From statement 2:

$2 \triangle t = 80$

=> $(2 + 2)^2 + (t + 3)^2 = 80$
=> $(t + 3)^2 = 64$
=> $t + 3 = \pm 8$
=> $t = 5$ or -11.

Hence, we do not have a unique value of t. - Insufficient

Thus, from statements 1 and 2 together:

We find that $t = 5$ is common to both statements 1 and 2.
Hence, $t = 5$. - Sufficient

The correct answer is option C.

395. Total deduction = $p * \frac{t}{100} + s = \frac{pt}{100} + s$.

Thus, amount of Leland's payment left = $p - \frac{pt}{100} + s = p - s - \frac{pt}{100}$.

From statement 1:

$p - s = 244$

However, we do not have the value of t. - Insufficient

From statement 2:

$pt = 7552$

However, we do not have the value of s. - Insufficient

Thus, from statements 1 and 2 together:

Amount of payment left = $(p - s) - \frac{pt}{100}$
$= 244 - \frac{7552}{100} = 244 - 75.52 = 168.48$ - Sufficient

The correct answer is option C.

396. Let the daily water supply be x gallons.

Loss in water supply per day = $\frac{12x}{100}$ gallons.

Let the cost to the city for every gallon lost be \$ y.

Thus, we need to determine:

The dollar cost to the city per day for the loss = $\$\left(\frac{12xy}{100}\right)$

From statement 1:

We know $x = 350 * 10^6$gallons.
However, the value of y is unknown.

Hence, the dollar cost to the city per day for the loss cannot be determined. – Insufficient

From statement 2:

The statement gives us the cost to the city for every gallon lost as $y = \$\left(\frac{2}{12000}\right) = \$\left(\frac{1}{6000}\right)$

However, the value of x is unknown.

Hence, the dollar cost to the city per day for the loss cannot be determined. – Insufficient

Thus, from statements 1 and 2 together:

$x = 350 * 10^6$

$y = \$\left(\frac{1}{6000}\right)$

Thus, the dollar cost to the city per day for the loss:

$$= \$\left(\frac{12 * \left(350 * 10^6\right) * \left(\frac{1}{6000}\right)}{100}\right) = \$70000.$$ – Sufficient

The correct answer is option C.

397. From statement 1:

$y = x + 5$

Since the actual values of x and y are unknown, we cannot determine the total amount saved per week i.e. $(x + y)$. – Insufficient

From statement 2:

Amount saved by Ann in six weeks = $\$\ 6x$.
Amount saved by Beth in six weeks = $\$\ 5y$.

Thus, we have:

$6x = 5y$

Since the actual values of x and y are unknown, we cannot determine the total amount saved per week i.e. $(x + y)$. - Insufficient

Thus, from statements 1 and 2 together:

We have:

$6x = 5y$

$=> y = \frac{6x}{5}$

Substituting the value of y from statement 1, in the equation, we have:

$\frac{6x}{5} = x + 5$

$=> x = 25$

$=> y = \frac{6 * 25}{5} = 30$

Thus, the total amount saved per week = \$ $(x + y)$ = \$ 55. - Sufficient

The correct answer is option C.

398. From statement 1:

Let the regular price of the ice cream Antonio bought be \$ x per half-liter carton.

Thus, the price for the second half-liter carton he paid = \$ $\left(\frac{x}{2}\right)$.

Thus, Antonio's savings = \$ $\left(\frac{x}{2}\right)$.

Total regular price (without the discounted offer) = \$ $2x$.

Thus, the percent of the total regular price saved:

$=> \frac{\left(\frac{x}{2}\right)}{2x} * 100 = 25\%$. - Sufficient

From statement 2:

The offered discounted rate is not mentioned.

Hence, the percent of the total regular price saved cannot be determined. - Insufficient

The correct answer is option A.

399. We know that '∇' represents either of addition, subtraction, multiplication or division.

From statement 1:

$10 \nabla 5 = 2$

Checking one at a time:

(1) $10 + 5 = 15 \neq 2$
(2) $10 - 5 = 5 \neq 2$
(3) $10 * 5 = 50 \neq 2$
(4) $10 \div 5 = 2$

Thus, we can say that '∇' represents division.

$=> 6 \nabla 2 = 6 \div 2 = 3$ – Sufficient

From statement 2:

$4 \nabla 2 = 2$

Checking one at a time:

(1) $4 + 2 = 6 \neq 2$
(2) $4 - 2 = 2$
(3) $4 * 2 = 8 \neq 2$
(4) $4 \div 2 = 2$

Thus, we can say that '∇' represents either of subtraction or division.

$=> 6 \nabla 2 = 6 - 2 = 4$

OR

$=> 6 \nabla 2 = 6 \div 2 = 3$

Thus, there is no unique answer. – Insufficient

The correct answer is option A.

400. Number of shares of stock X with Mr. John $= n$.

Dividend earned on the above n shares in 2005 $= \$150$.

Thus, dividend earned per share in 2005 $= \$\left(\frac{150}{n}\right)$.

Number of shares of stock X with Mrs. John $= 300$.

Since the shares are of the same stock X, the dividend earned per share is the same.

Thus, the dividend earned on the above 300 shares in 2005 = $\$\left(\frac{150}{n} * 300\right) = \$\left(\frac{45000}{n}\right)$.

From statement 1:

We have:

$\frac{150}{n} = 0.75$

$=> n = 200$

=> Mrs. John's total dividend on her 300 shares in 2005 = $\$\left(\frac{45000}{n}\right) = \$\left(\frac{45000}{200}\right) = \$225$. – Sufficient

From statement 2:

$n = 200$

This is the same information as obtained from statement 1. – Sufficient

The correct answer is option D.

401. Let the lower limit and upper limit for the population be p and q.

Let the lower limit and upper limit for the total income be i and j.

From statement 1:

There is no information about the total income. – Insufficient

From statement 2:

There is no information about the population. – Insufficient

Thus, from statements 1 and 2 together:

We have:

$p = 330000$

$i = \$5500000000$

Thus, based on the lower estimates, the average income per person

$= \$\left(\frac{5500000000}{330000}\right)$

$= \$16666.7$

$=\sim \$16666 > \$16500$

However, while looking the higher estimates of population and total income, it may be possible that the higher estimate of population was considerably higher than the corresponding lower estimate, whereas, the higher estimate of total income was slightly higher than the corresponding lower estimate. As a result, the average income per person could fall lower than \$16666 and in fact, go on to be lower than \$16500.

For example:

Let the higher estimate of population be 500,000.

Let the higher estimate of total income be \$5,600,000,000.

Thus, based on the higher estimates, the average income per person

$= \$\left(\frac{5600000000}{500000}\right)$

$= \$11200 < \$16500$

Thus, the average income per person may be greater or lesser than \$16500.

Thus, there is no unique answer. – Insufficient

The correct answer is option E.

402. Since ■, △ and ∀ represent positive digits, their values can only be from 1 to 9 (inclusive).

From statement 1:

If ∀ = 4, there is only one possible value of ■ and △ so that ■ < △: ■ = 1, △ = 3. – Sufficient

From statement 2:

If ■ = 1, the possible values of △ are: 2, 3, 4, 5, 6, 7 or 8; since in each case, the addition does not lead to a carry.

Thus, the value of △ cannot be uniquely determined. – Insufficient

The correct answer is option A.

6.10 Simple Interest

403. From statement 1:
We only have information about the ratio of the rates of interest.

However, we have no information on the amounts invested at the given rates $x\%$ and $y\%$.

Thus, we cannot determine the value of x. - Insufficient.

From statement 2:

The amount invested at $x\% = \$\left(\frac{3}{3+2}\right) * 60000 = \$36,000$.
The amount invested at $y\% = \$\left(\frac{2}{3+2}\right) * 60000 = \$24,000$.
However, we have no information on the rates of interest.

Thus, we cannot determine the value of x. - Insufficient

Thus, from statements 1 and 2 together:

We have: $x = \frac{3}{4}y$
$=> y = \frac{4x}{3}$.

Thus, total interest:

$36000 * x\% + 24000 * y\% = 4080$
$36000 * \frac{x}{100} + 24000 * \frac{y}{100} = 4080$
$=> 360x + 240\left(\frac{4x}{3}\right) = 4080$
$=> x = \frac{4080}{680} = 6\%$ - Sufficient

The correct answer is option C.

404. Let John had lent $\$x$ at 10% and $\$y$ at 22%.

From statement 1:

$x + y = 2400$

However, there is no information about the interest received on each amount. - Insufficient

From statement 2:

Since the average rate of interest obtained was 15%, we have:

$$\frac{(x * 10) + (y * 22)}{(x + y)} = 15$$

$$=> 10x + 22y = 15x + 15y$$

$$=> 5x = 7y$$

$$=> \frac{x}{y} = \frac{7}{5}$$

Thus, the higher part is $\$x$ and the lower part is $\$y$

Thus, the higher part was lent at 10% rate of interest. – Sufficient

The correct answer is option B.

6.11 Compound Interest

405. From statement 1:

$D(1) = 11000$

$$=> 10,000\left(1 + \frac{r}{100}\right)^1 = 11000$$
$$=> 1 + \frac{r}{100} = \frac{11000}{10000} = 1.1$$
$$=> \frac{r}{100} = 0.1$$
$$=> r = 10.$$

Amount after three years

$$= D(3) = 10,000\left(1 + \frac{10}{100}\right)^3$$ - Sufficient.

From statement 2:

$r = 10\%$

It is the same information as obtained from statement 1 - Sufficient.

The correct answer is option D.

6.12 Functions

406. From statement 1:

$f(2) = a^2 = 100$
$=> a = \pm 10$

Thus: $f(1) = a^1 = a = \pm 10$.
Hence, we do not have a unique value of a. – Insufficient

From statement 2:

$f(3) = a^3 = -1000$
$=> a = -10$

Thus: $f(1) = a^1 = a = -10$. – Sufficient

The correct answer is option B.

407. From statement 1:

$f(c) = 3c + 1 = 13$
Thus: $3c + 1 = 13$
$=> c = 4$.

Thus, we have: $g(c) = \frac{c-1}{3} = \frac{4-1}{3} = 1$. – Sufficient

From statement 2:

$f(1) = 3 * 1 + 1 = 4$.

Thus, we have: $c = 4$. We can easily find $g(c) = g(4)$ – Sufficient

The correct answer is option D.

408. From statement 1:

$|c| = 2$
$=> c = \pm 2$

If $c = 2$:
$f(c) = f(2) = 2 * 2 = 4$;; (since $c \geq 0$, $f(c) = 2c$)

If $c = -2$:

$f(c) = f(-2) = (-2)^2 = 4$; (since $c < 0$, $f(c) = c^2$)

Thus, we have a unique value of $f(c) = 4$. – Sufficient

From statement 2:

$c < 0$
$\Rightarrow f(c) = c^2$

However, the value of c is not known.

Hence, the value of $f(c)$ cannot be determined. – Insufficient

The correct answer is option A.

6.13 Permutation & Combination

409. We are given that total number of bulbs = 10, and number of defective bulbs $n < 5$.
From statement 1:

We know that

$$\frac{C_2^n}{C_2^{10}} = \frac{1}{15}$$

$$=> \frac{\frac{n.(n-1)}{1.2}}{\frac{10.9}{1.2}} = \frac{1}{15}$$

$$=> n * (n-1) = 6 = 3 * 2$$

Since $n * (n-1)$ is a product of two consecutive integers, which are 3 & 2, thus $n = 3$ –Sufficient.

From statement 2:

We know that $\frac{C_1^n.C_1^{(10-n)}}{C_2^{10}} = \frac{7}{15}$

$$=> \frac{n.(10-n)}{\frac{10.9}{1.2}} = \frac{7}{15}$$

$$=> n.(10-n) = 7 * 3.$$

Thus $n = 7$ or 3. Since $n < 5$, thus $n = 3$ – Sufficient.

The correct answer is option D.

410. Probability that the marble chosen is red $= \frac{r}{b+w+r}$.

Probability that the marble chosen is white $= \frac{w}{b+w+r}$.

From statement 1:

$$\frac{r}{b+w} > \frac{w}{b+r}$$

$$=> 1 + \frac{r}{b+w} > 1 + \frac{w}{b+r} \text{ (adding 1 to both sides)}$$

$$=> \frac{b+w+r}{b+w} > \frac{b+r+w}{b+r}$$

$$=> \frac{1}{b+w} > \frac{1}{b+r}; \text{ (canceling } (b+w+r) \text{ from both sides)}$$

$$=> b+r > b+w$$

$=> r > w$.

Since the number of red marbles is greater than the number of white marbles, the probability that the marble chosen will be red is greater than the probability that the marble chosen will be white. - Sufficient

From statement 2:

$b - w > r$

$=> b > w + r$

We can see that the number of black marbles is the greatest.
However, we have no information on whether $r > w$. - Insufficient

The correct answer is option A.

411. From statement 1:

There are nine women out of which four are students.

Thus, required probability $= \frac{4}{21}$ - Sufficient

From statement 2:

Since five of the nine women are not students, number of women who are students $= 9 - 5 = 4$.

Thus, required probability $= \frac{4}{21}$ - Sufficient

The correct answer is option D.

412. From statement 1:

We have no information on the total number of eggs or on the number of green eggs. - Insufficient

From statement 2:

The probability that the egg will be blue $= \frac{1}{3}$

Thus, the probability that the egg will be red or green $= 1 - \frac{1}{3} = \frac{2}{3}$

Since we do not know the probability of the egg being red, we cannot determine the probability of the egg being green. - Insufficient

Thus, from statements 1 and 2 together:

Since we do not know the total number of eggs, we cannot determine the probability of the egg being red.

Hence, we cannot determine the probability of the egg being green. – Insufficient

The correct answer is option E.

413. Let the number of women be w.

Thus, we have:

$$p = \frac{C_2^w}{C_2^{10}}$$

We need to determine whether $p > \frac{1}{2}$.

From statement 1:

Number of women, $w > \frac{10}{2} = 5$.

If $w = 6$:

$$p = \frac{C_2^w}{C_2^{10}} = \frac{C_2^6}{C_2^{10}} = \frac{15}{45} = \frac{1}{3} \not> \frac{1}{2}.$$

Thus, if $w \geq 6 : 1 \geq p \geq \frac{1}{3}$.

Thus, the value of p can be less than $\frac{1}{2}$ or even be more than $\frac{1}{2}$ (for example, if $w = 10$, then $p = 1$).

Thus, the answer cannot be uniquely determined. – Insufficient

From statement 2:

Number of men $= (10 - w)$.

We know that the probability that both representatives are men is less than $\frac{1}{10}$.

Thus, we have:

$$\frac{C_2^{(10-w)}}{C_2^{10}} < \frac{1}{10}.$$

Rather than solving, it is best to put a few values of w.

Since the probability $\frac{1}{10}$ is very small, possible values of w would be on the higher side, but less than or equal to '8' (since there are at least two men):

$$w = 8: \frac{C_2^{(10-w)}}{C_2^{10}} = \frac{C_2^2}{C_2^{10}} = \frac{1}{45} < \frac{1}{10}; \text{(satisfies)}$$

$$w = 7: \frac{C_2^{(10-w)}}{C_2^{10}} = \frac{C_2^3}{C_2^{10}} = \frac{3}{45} = \frac{1}{15} < \frac{1}{10}; \text{(satisfies)}$$

$$w = 6: \frac{C_2^{(10-w)}}{C_2^{10}} = \frac{C_2^4}{C_2^{10}} = \frac{6}{45} = \frac{2}{15} \not< \frac{1}{10}; \text{(does not satisfy)}$$

Thus, possible values of w are 7 or 8.

Let us now calculate the probability that both representatives are women i.e. p.

At $w = 7: \; p = \frac{C_2^w}{C_2^{10}} = \frac{C_2^7}{C_2^{10}} = \frac{21}{45} \not> \frac{1}{2}$

At $w = 8: \; p = \frac{C_2^w}{C_2^{10}} = \frac{C_2^8}{C_2^{10}} = \frac{28}{45} > \frac{1}{2}$

Thus, the answer cannot be uniquely determined. - Insufficient

Thus, statements 1 and 2 together:

Even after combining both statements, p may be more than $\frac{1}{2}$ or less than $\frac{1}{2}$. - Insufficient

The correct answer is option E.

414. Let the number of seniors and the number of juniors be s and j, respectively.

We need to determine the value of $(s + j)$.

From statement 1:

The probability of selecting a senior $= \left(\frac{s}{s+j}\right)$.

Thus, we have:

$$\frac{s}{s+j} = \frac{4}{7}$$

$$=> s = \frac{4j}{3}$$

Since the exact values of s and j are not known, we cannot determine the value of $(s + j)$. - Insufficient

From statement 2:

$s = j + 5$

Since the exact values of s and j are not known, we cannot determine the value of $(s + j)$. – Insufficient

Thus, from statements 1 and 2 together:

Substituting the value of $s = \frac{4j}{3}$ in the equation from statement 2, we have:

$\frac{4j}{3} = j + 5$

$=> j = 15$

$=> s = j + 5 = 20$

$=> s + j = 35$. – Sufficient

The correct answer is option C.

6.14 Sets

415. From statement 1:

It is known that each of the voters voted for exactly one candidate.

We also know that 80 percent of the female voters voted for Edith.

Thus, the remaining $(100 - 80)\% = 20\%$ of the female voters voted for Jose. – Sufficient

From statement 2:

There is no information about the female voters. – Insufficient

The correct answer is option A.

416. Let us draw the corresponding Venn-diagram:

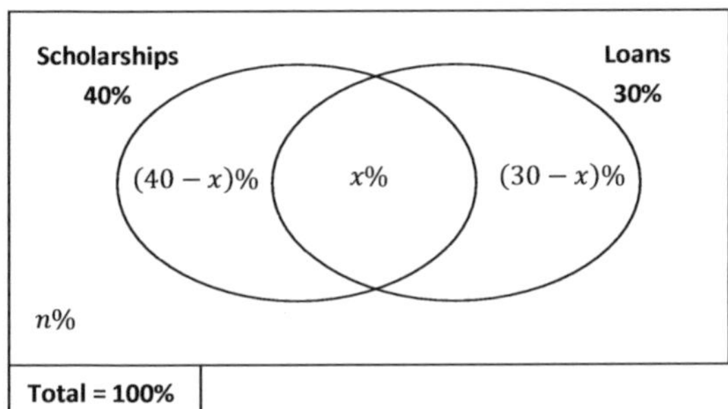

We need to determine the value of n.

From statement 1:

We have:

$(40 - x)\% = 25\%$

$=> x = 15\%$

Thus, the percent of students who received scholarships or loans

$= (40 + 30 - x)\%$

$= 55\%$

Thus, the percent of students who received neither student loans nor scholarships ($n\%$)

$= (100 - 55)\%$

$= 45\%$ – Sufficient

From statement 2:

Percent of students who received loans = 30%.

Thus, percent of students who received loans as well as scholarships ($x\%$)

= 50% of 30%

$= \frac{50}{100} * 30\%$

$= 15\%$

This is the same information as obtained from statement 1. – Sufficient

The correct answer is option D.

417. Let us refer to the Venn-diagram shown below:

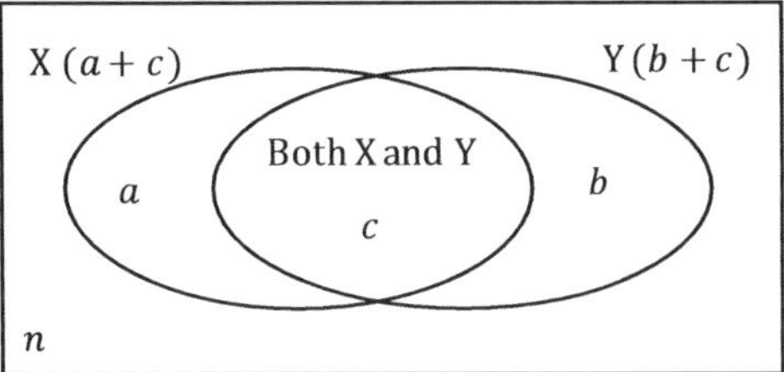

From statement 1:

$c = 20\%$ of $(a+c)$

$=> c = \frac{a+c}{5}$

$=> 5c = a + c$

$=> a = 4c \ldots$ (i)

However, there is no information on the value of b. – Insufficient

From statement 2:

$c = 30\%$ of $(b+c)$

$=> c = \frac{3}{10}(b+c)$

$=> b = \frac{7c}{3} =\sim\ 2.3c \ldots$ (ii)

However, there is no information on the value of b. – Insufficient

Thus, from statements 1 and 2 together:

From (i) and (ii):

$a > b$

$=> a + c > b + c$

=> The number of members of Club X is greater than that of Club Y. – Sufficient

Alternately, we have:

20% of X = 30% of Y

$=> \frac{X}{Y} = \frac{30}{20} > 1$

=> X > Y

=> The number of members of Club X is greater than that of Club Y. – Sufficient

The correct answer is option C.

6.15 Statistics & Data Interpretation

418. Standard deviation (SD) is a measure of deviation of items in a set w.r.t their arithmetic mean (average). Closer are the items to the mean value, lesser is the value of SD, and vice versa; thus, it follows that if a set has all equal items, its SD = 0.

Statement 1 is clearly insufficient as we do not know how many numbers of eggs are there in each nest; merely knowing the mean value is insufficient.

Statement 2 is clearly sufficient. As discussed above since each set has an equal number of eggs, their mean = number of eggs in each set, so SD = 0—no deviation at all!

The correct answer is option B.

419. The median weight of 89 boxes would be the weight of the $\left(\frac{89+1}{2}\right)^{th} = 45^{th}$ box after the boxes have been arranged in increasing order of weight (the boxes may be arranged in decreasing order of weight as well).

Since each of the 45 boxes on shelf J weighs less than each of the 44 boxes on shelf K, the median weight will be the weight of the heaviest box on shelf J.

From statement 1:

The heaviest box on shelf J weighs 15 pounds.
Hence, the median weight of 89 boxes = 15 pounds. - Sufficient

From statement 2:

The lightest box on shelf K weighs 20 pounds.
However, we need information on the heaviest box on shelf J. - Insufficient

The correct answer is option A.

420. From statement 1:

Standard deviation (SD) is a measure of deviation of items in a set with respect to their arithmetic mean (average). Closer are the items to the mean value, lesser is the value of SD, and vice versa.

Thus, it follows that if a set has all equal items, its SD = 0.

Since the SD of the amounts of the eight awards is the same, the amount for each award must have been the same. - Sufficient

From statement 2:

The total amount of the eight awards will not help us to determine whether the amount for each award was the same. – Insufficient

The correct answer is option A.

421. Let the five numbers be a, b, c, d and e (where $a > b > c > d > e$).

Thus, we have:

$$\frac{a+b+c+d+e}{5} = 12$$

$$=> a+b+c+d+e = 60$$

We need to determine the median of the five numbers.

It is clear that the median is one of the five numbers.

Since we have assumed $a > b > c > d > e$, the median must be c.

From statement 1:

Thus, we have:

$$c = \frac{1}{3}(a+b+d+e)$$

$$=> c = \frac{1}{3}\{(a+b+c+d+e) - c\}$$

$$=> c = \frac{1}{3}(60 - c)$$

$$=> 3c = 60 - c$$

$$=> c = 15$$

Thus, the median is 15. – Sufficient

From statement 2:

It is clear that the median is one of the five numbers.

Since we have assumed $a > b > c > d > e$, the median must be c.

Thus, we have:

$$a+b+d+e = 45$$

However, we have:

$a + b + c + d + e = 60$

$=> c = 60 - 45 = 15$

Thus, the median is 15. – Sufficient

The correct answer is option D.

422. Let the four numbers be a, b, c and d.

Thus, we have:

$\frac{a + b + c + d}{4} = 30$

$=> a + b + c + d = 120$

From statement 1:

We know that none of the four numbers is greater than 60.

However, it may be that only one number is greater than 30 or three numbers are greater than 30 as shown below:

(1) 27, 28, 29, 36: Average is 30; only one number greater than 30
(2) 28, 29, 31, 32: Average is 30; two numbers greater than 30
(3) 24, 31, 32, 33: Average is 30; three numbers greater than 30

Hence, we cannot determine the answer. – Insufficient

From statement 2:

We know that two of the numbers are 9 and 10.

Without loss of generality, we can assume that:

$a = 9$
$b = 10$

$a + b + c + d = 120$

$=> 9 + 10 + c + d = 120$

$=> c + d = 101$

Thus, it may be that:

Both c and d are more than 30, for example: $a = 50, b = 51$

OR

Only one among them is more than 30, for example: $a = 80, b = 21$

Hence, we cannot determine the answer. – Insufficient

Thus, from statements 1 and 2 together:

We know that none of the numbers is greater than 60.

Also, we have: $c + d = 101$.

Thus, maximum value of either c or d is 60.

Hence, the value of the other number $= 101 - 60 = 41$.

Thus, we can see that two of the numbers are greater than 30. – Sufficient

The correct answer is option C.

423. The average of the assessed values of x houses = \$ 212,000.

Thus, the total of the assessed values of x houses = \$ 212,000x.

The average of the assessed values of y houses = \$ 194,000.

Thus, the total of the assessed values of y houses = \$ 194,000y.

Thus, the total of the assessed values of $x + y$ houses = \$ $(212000x + 194000y)$.

Thus, the average of the assessed values of $x + y$ houses = \$ $\left(\frac{212000x + 194000y}{x + y}\right)$.

From statement 1:

We only know the value of $(x + y)$ and not the relation between x and y.

Hence, the average of the assessed values of $(x + y)$ houses cannot be determined. – Insufficient

From statement 2:

We have: $x = 2y$.

Thus, the average of the assessed values of $x + y$ houses

$$= \$ \left(\frac{212000x + 194000y}{x + y}\right)$$

$$= \$ \left(\frac{212000 * 2y + 194000y}{2y + y}\right)$$

$= \$\ 206000.$ - Sufficient

The correct answer is option B.

424. Standard deviation (SD) is a measure of deviation of items in a set with respect to their arithmetic mean (average). Closer are the items to the mean value, lesser is the value of SD, and vice versa; this follows that if a set has all equal items, its SD = 0.

From statement 1:

We know that the average salary of Company Y's employees is greater than the average salary of Company Z's employees.

However, we have no information about the deviation of the actual salaries of the employees about the mean.

Hence, we cannot compare the standard deviations. - Insufficient

From statement 2:

We know that the median salary of Company Y's employees is greater than the median salary of Company Z's employees.

However, we have no information about the deviation of the actual salaries of the employees about the mean.

Hence, we cannot compare the standard deviations. - Insufficient

Thus, from statements 1 and 2 together:

Even after combining the two statements we cannot determine the deviation of the actual salaries of the employees about the mean. - Insufficient

The correct answer is option E.

6.16 Linear Equations

425. From statement 1:

Let the price of a 16-ounce loaf be \$$x$ and that of a 24-ounce loaf be \$$y$.
We need to find the value of y.

Thus: $x + y = 2.40$ – Insufficient

From statement 2:

Let the price of a 16-ounce loaf be \$$x$ and that of a 24-ounce loaf be \$$y$.
We need to find the value of y.

Thus: $2x + y = 3.40$ – Insufficient

Thus, from statements 1 and 2 together: we can solve for y: $(x + y = 3.40) - (x + y = 2.40) = x = 1 => y = 1.40$ – Sufficient

The correct answer is option C.

426. We need to find the value of x.

From statement 1:

$x + 50y = 150$ – Insufficient

From statement 2:

$x + 100y = 225$ – Insufficient

Thus, from statements 1 and 2 together:

$(x + 100y = 225) - (x + 50y = 150\ ) => y = \frac{3}{2}$

$=> x = 75$ – Sufficient

The correct answer is option C.

427. Let the price of the shirt be \$ s and the price of the pair of gloves be \$ g.

Thus, we have: $s + g = 41.70$.

From statement 1:

$s = 2g$.

Thus: $s + g = 41.70$
=> $2g + g = 41.70$
=> $g = \$\ 13.90$ - Sufficient

From statement 2:

$s = 27.80$.

Thus: $g = 41.70 - s = 41.70 - 27.80$
=> $g = \$\ 13.90$ - Sufficient

The correct answer is option D.

428. Let the charge of a family membership be $\$f$.
The charge of an individual membership = \$300.
Let the number of family and number of individual memberships be x and y, respectively.

Thus, revenue from family and revenue from individual memberships are $\$xf$ and $\$300y$, respectively.

Thus: $xf + 300y = 480000$.

We need to determine the value of f.

From statement 1:

$300y = \frac{1}{4}(480000)$
=> $y = 400$
We have no information on x.

Hence, we cannot determine f. - Insufficient

From statement 2:

$x = 1.5y$
We have no information about the value of $x\ and\ y$.
Hence, we cannot determine f. - Insufficient

From statements 1 and 2 together:

$xf + 300y = 480000$
=> $1.5yf + 300y = 480000$; (Substituting $x = 1.5y$ from Statement 2)
=> $1.5 * 400f + 300 * 400 = 480000$ (Substituting $y = 400$ from Statement 1)

=> $f = 600$. - Sufficient

The correct answer is option C.

429. Let the price of each book and each magazine be $\$b$ and $\$m$ respectively.

We need to find: $3b + 4m = ?$

From statement 1:

$b = m + 1.45.$

We do not know the actual value of m and b.

Hence, we cannot determine the answer - Insufficient

From statement 2:

$6b + 8m = 43.70$

=> $2(3b + 4m) = 43.70$

=> $3b + 4m = \frac{43.70}{2} = 21.85$ - Sufficient

The correct answer is option B.

430. From statement 1:

Let the number of smaller shelves (holding 30books each) required be x.
Number of smaller shelves is six more than those currently present.

Thus, the number of shelves present currently (holding 50 books each) = $(x - 6)$.

Thus, equating the total number of picture books:

$50(x - 6) = 30x$
=> $20x = 300$
=> $x = 15$ - Sufficient

From statement 2:

Number of shelves present currently (holding 50 books each) = 9.
Thus, total number of picture books = 9*50 = 450.

Each smaller shelf can hold 30 books.

Thus, the number of smaller shelves required $= \frac{450}{30} = 15$ – Sufficient

The correct answer is option D.

431. From statement 1:

We have no information on n - Insufficient

From statement 2:

$6m = 9n$

$=> 2m = 3n$; (canceling 3 from both the sides)
$=> 2m - 3n = 0$ – Sufficient

The correct answer is option B.

432. Let John work for t hours.

If $t \leq 40$: John's earnings $= \$\ xt$
If $t > 40$: John's earnings $= \$\ (40x + (t - 40)\,y)$

From statement 1:

$y = 1.5x$

Since x is unknown, we cannot determine the value of y. – Insufficient

From statement 2:

John's earnings for 45 hours $= \$\ (40x + (45 - 40)\,y) = 570 => 40x + 5y = 570$.

There are two unknowns, hence we cannot determine the value of y. – Insufficient

Thus, from statements 1 and 2 together:

Substituting $y = 1.5x$ in the equation: $40x + (t - 40)\,y = 570$

$40x + 5 * 1.5x = 570$
$=> 47.5x = 570$
$=> x = \frac{570}{47.5} = 12$
$=> y = 12 * 1.5 = 18.$ – Sufficient

The correct answer is option C.

433. Let the number of additional people be p.

Thus, total daily cost for all $(p + 1)$ people = $\$(120 + xp)$.
We need to calculate the value of x.

From statement 1:

Total daily cost for 4 people (i.e. 3 additional people) = $\$(120 + 3x)$.

Thus, average daily cost for 4 people = $\$\frac{(120 + 3x)}{4}$.

Thus, we have: $\frac{120 + 3x}{4} = 45$

=> $x = 20$. – Sufficient

From statement 2:

Total daily cost for 2 people (i.e. 1 additional person) = $\$(120 + x)$.

Thus, average daily cost for 2 people = $\$\frac{(120 + x)}{2}$.

Similarly, average daily cost for 4 people = $\$\frac{(120 + 3x)}{4}$; (from statement 1).

Thus, we have: $\frac{(120 + x)}{2} - \frac{(120 + 3x)}{4} = 25$

=> $\frac{120 - x}{4} = 25$

=> $x = 20$. – Sufficient

The correct answer is option D.

434. Total tickets sold = 500
Let the number of tickets sold to adults = x.
Thus, the number of tickets sold to children = $(500 - x)$

From statement 1:

Revenue from ticket sales = $\$\,(25x + 15\,(500 - x))$

Thus, we have:
$25x + 15\,(500 - x) = 10500$
=> $x = 300$ – Sufficient

From statement 2:

Revenue from ticket sales = $\$\,(25x + 15\,(500 - x))$

Thus, average price per ticket sold = \$ $\left(\frac{25x + 15(500 - x)}{500}\right)$

Thus, we have:

$$\frac{25x + 15(500 - x)}{500} = 21$$

=> $25x + 15(500 - x) = 10500$.
This is the same as the information in statement 1. – Sufficient

The correct answer is option D.

435. Let the number of hours worked in a week be w.

If $w \le t$: Raymond's earnings = \$ xw.
If $w > t$: Raymond's earnings = \$ $(xt + 2(w - t))$.

From statement 1:

We have: $w = (t - 3)$; i.e. $w < t$.
Raymond's earnings = \$ $(x(t - 3))$.
Thus, we have: $x(t - 3) = 14$

Possible values of x and t are:

(1) $x = 14; t - 3 = 1 => t = 4$: not possible since $t > 4$
(2) $x = 7; t - 3 = 2 => t = 5$: possible
(3) $x = 2; t - 3 = 7 => t = 10$: possible
(4) $x = 1; t - 3 = 14 => t = 17$: possible

There are multiple possible values of t possible, hence we cannot determine the value of t. – Insufficient

From statement 2:

We have: $w = (t + 3)$; i.e. $w > t$.
Raymond's earnings = \$ $(xt + 2((t + 3) - t))$ = \$ $(xt + 6)$.
Thus, we have: $xt + 6 = 23$
=> $xt = 17$.

Possible values of x and t are:

(1) $x = 17; t = 1$: not possible since $t > 4$
(2) $x = 1; t = 17$: possible

Thus, we have a unique value of t. – Sufficient

The correct answer is option B.

436. The price of a share on May 1, 1980 was half the price of a share on May 1, 1995.

We need to determine the price of a share on May 1, 1980.

From statement 1:

There is no information regarding the price of a share on May 1, 1995. – Insufficient

From statement 2:

There is no information regarding the actual price of a share on May 1, 2004. – Insufficient

Thus, from statements 1 and 2 together:

Let the price of a share on May 1, 1980 be \$ x.
Thus, the price of a share on May 1, 1995 = \$ $2x$.

Hence, the price of a share on May 1, 2004 = \$ $(2 * 2x)$ = \$ $4x$.
Thus, increase in price of a share from May 1, 1995 to May 1, 2004 = \$ $2x$.

Thus, we have:

$2x = 4.50$
$=> x = 2.25$. – Sufficient

The correct answer is option C.

437. Let the number of books with Ricardo be n.

From statement 1:

$$n - 15 = \frac{n}{2}$$

$=> n = 30$. – Sufficient

From statement 2:

This statement gives us information on the ratio of types of books with Ricardo and not the total number of books. – Insufficient

The correct answer is option A.

438. Let the number of years for which Dr. Jones lived be x.

From statement 1:

Let the number of years for which Dr. Jones had been a doctor be y.

Thus, we have:

$y + 10 = \frac{2x}{3} \ldots \text{(i)}$

We cannot determine x from this equation since there are two unknowns. – Insufficient

From statement 2:

Let the number of years for which Dr. Jones had been a doctor be y.

Thus, we have:

$y - 10 = \frac{x}{3} \ldots \text{(ii)}$

We cannot determine x from this equation since there are two unknowns. – Insufficient

Thus, from statements 1 and 2 together:

Subtracting equations (i) and (ii):

$20 = \frac{x}{3}$

$x = 60$. – Sufficient

The correct answer is option C.

439. We have:

$r = \frac{x + y}{2}$ & $s = \frac{x - y}{2}$

$\Rightarrow r + s = \frac{(x + y) + (x - y)}{2} = x$.

Now, in order to find $(r + s)$, we need to find x.

From statement 1:

We do not have the value of x. – Insufficient

From statement 2:

$r + s = x = 6$. – Sufficient

The correct answer is option B.

440. We have:

$$\frac{x}{600} = \frac{y}{300}$$

$=> x = 2y.$

From statement 1:

$x + y = 3000$
$=> 2y + y = 3000;$ (substituting $x = 2y$)
$=> y = 1000.$ – Sufficient

From statement 2:

$3x = 6000$
$=> x = 2000$
$=> 2y = 2000;$ (substituting $x = 2y$)
$=> y = 1000.$ – Sufficient

The correct answer is option D.

441. From statement 1:

Pete was born in 1986 and is 2 years older than Ellen.

Thus, Ellen must have been born 2 years after Pete was born, i.e. in the year

$1986 + 2 \;=\; 1986$ – Sufficient

From statement 2:

We have no information on Ellen. – Insufficient

The correct answer is option A.

6.17 Quadratic Equations & Polynomials

442. Let the number of men and women be m and w respectively.

We need to determine the value of $(m - w)$.

From statement 1:

We have:
$m + w = 20$.

We cannot determine $(m - w)$ from this information. - Insufficient

From statement 2:

We have:
$m = w^2$.

We cannot determine $(m - w)$ from this information. - Insufficient

Thus, from statements 1 and 2 together:

$m = w^2$ and $m + w = 20$:
$w^2 + w = 20$
$w(w + 1) = 20$
$=> w = 4$
$=> m = 4^2 = 16$
$=> m - w = 16 - 4 = 12$. - Sufficient

The correct answer is option C.

443. $(x + y)^2 = x^2 + y^2 + 2xy$

$=> (x + y) = \pm\sqrt{(x^2 + y^2 + 2xy)}$.

From statement 1:

$(x + y) = \pm\sqrt{(x^2 + y^2) + 2xy}$

$=> (x + y) = \pm\sqrt{1 + 0} = \pm 1$.

Thus, the value of $(x + y)$ may be or may not be '1'. - Insufficient

From statement 2:

$(x + y) = \pm\sqrt{(x^2 + y^2) + 2xy}$

$=> (x + y) = \pm\sqrt{1 + 2x * 0} = \pm 1.$

Thus, the value of $(x + y)$ may be or may not be '1'. - Insufficient

Thus, from statements1 and 2 together:

Even after combining, we still get the same solution: $(x + y) = \pm 1$. - Insufficient

The correct answer is option E.

444. From statement 1:

$(1 - x)(1 - y) = 1$

$=> 1 - x - y + xy = 1$

$=> x + y = xy$. - Sufficient

From statement 2:

$x^2 - y^2 = x^2y - xy^2$

$=> (x + y)(x - y) = xy(x - y)$

We know:

$x \neq y$ i.e. $(x - y) \neq 0$ and hence it can be cancelled from both sides.

$=> x + y = xy$ - Sufficient

The correct answer is option D.

445. $x(x - 5)(x + 2) = 0$
$=> x = 0, 5$ or -2.

From statement 1:

$x^2 - 7x \neq 0$
$=> x(x - 7) \neq 0$
$=> x \neq 0$ and $x \neq 7$.

However, from the question statement, we can still have: $x = 5$ $(\nless 0)$ or $x = -2(< 0)$. - Insufficient

From statement 2:

$x^2 - 2x - 15 \neq 0$
$=> (x - 5)(x + 3) \neq 0$
$=> x \neq 5$ and $x \neq -3$.

However, from the main question, we can still have: $x = 0\ (\nless 0)$ or $x = -2(< 0)$. - Insufficient

Thus, from statements 1 and 2 together:

$x \neq -3$ and $x \neq 0$ and $x \neq 5$ and $x \neq 7$.
Thus, from the main question, we have: $x = -2\,(< 0)$. - Sufficient

The correct answer is option C.

446. $\frac{1}{x} + \frac{1}{y} = \frac{x + y}{xy}$

From statement 1:

The value of xy is not known.

Hence, the value of $\left(\frac{1}{x} + \frac{1}{y}\right)$ cannot be determined. - Insufficient

From statement 2:

$xy = 6\,(x + y)$
$=> \frac{x + y}{xy} = \frac{1}{6} => \frac{1}{x} + \frac{1}{y} = \frac{1}{6}$. - Sufficient

The correct answer is option B.

447. $x^2 - y = w$
$=> x^2 = w + y$.

From statement 1:

$w + y = 4$

Thus: $x^2 = w + y = 4$
$=> x = \pm 2$

Thus, the value of x is not unique. - Insufficient

From statement 2:

The value of w is unknown.

Hence, the value of x cannot be determined. – Insufficient

Thus, from statements 1 and 2 together:

Even after combining both statements, we cannot determine a unique value of x. – Insufficient

The correct answer is option E.

448. $(y+3)(y-1)-(y-2)(y-1)=r(y-1)$

$=> (y+3)(y-1)-(y-2)(y-1)-r(y-1)=0$

$=> (y-1)((y+3)-(y-2)-r)=0$

$=> (y-1)(5-r)=0$

$=> y=1$ or $r=5$

Looking at the results, it seems that the question is sufficient in itself and not even a single statement is needed as it yields $y=1$; however it is not so. The meaning of $y=1$ or $r=5$ is that if $r \neq 5$, then $y=1$, else not!

Moreover, if $r=5$, y may have any value under the sun!

So the question boils down to the either the determination of value of y or the determination whether $r \neq 5$.

From statement 1:

$r^2 = 25$

$=> r = \pm 5$

If $r=5$, y can take any value.

If $r=-5\ (\neq 5)$, then $y=1$.

Thus, the unique value of y cannot be determined. – Insufficient.

From statement 2:

If $r=5$, y can take any value.

Thus, the unique value of y cannot be determined. – Insufficient.

Thus, from statements 1 and 2 together:

Even after combining both statements, we cannot determine the unique value of y. – Insufficient

The correct answer is option E.

449. We have:

$x^2 + bx + c = (x + d)^2$

$=> x^2 + bx + c = x^2 + 2dx + d^2$

Since this is true for all values of x, we can compare the coefficients of x and the constant terms on either side:

$b = 2d;$
$c = d^2$

From statement 1:

$c = d^2 = 3^2 = 9$. – Sufficient

From statement 2:

$b = 2d$
$=> 6 = 2d$
$=> d = 3$

$=> c = d^2 = 9$. – Sufficient

The correct answer is option D.

450. Since the equation $x^2 + 3x + c = x^2 + x(a + b) + ab$ is valid for all values of x, we have (equating the coefficients of x and constants):

$a + b = 3 \ldots$(i)
$ab = c \ldots$(ii)

From statement 1:

We have: $a = 1$

Thus, from (i), we have:
$b = 2$

Thus, from (ii), we have:
$c = 1 * 2 = 2$ – Sufficient

From statement 2:

We know that: $a + b = 3$

Since a and b are positive integers, possible solutions are:

$a = 1, b = 2$

OR

$a = 2, b = 1$

In either of the two cases: $c = ab = 1 * 2 = 2$ – Sufficient

The correct answer is option D.

6.18 Inequalities

451. Let the average number of books that Carolyn read per week = c, and the average number of books that Jacob read per week = j.

We need to determine whether $c > j$.

From statement 1:

$2c > 2j - 5$

$=> 2j - 2c < 5$

$=> c > j - \frac{5}{2}$

However, we cannot determine whether $c > j$, since c is greater than a quantity j, which is reduced by a certain amount, $\frac{5}{2}$ - Insufficient

From statement 2:

We only have information about the last five weeks of the vacation.

We have no information about the situation during the remaining part of the vacation; also we do not know vacation is for how many weeks.

Hence, we cannot determine whether $c > j$ - Insufficient

Thus, from statements 1 and 2 together:

Even after combining the statements, we do not get any concrete information - Insufficient

The correct answer is option E.

452. Let the larger and the smaller numbers be l and s respectively.

Thus, we have:

$\frac{l}{4} > 5s$

$=> s < \frac{l}{20}$

We need to determine if:

$s < 4$

$=> l < 80.$

From statement 1:

We have: $l > 70$

We may have $l < 80$ (say, if $l = 75$) OR $l \nless 80$ (say, if $l = 85$). – Insufficient

From statement 2:

We have: $l < 80$. – Sufficient

The correct answer is option B.

453. We have: $xy \neq 0$
=> None of x or y is '0'.

From statement 1:

$x^2 = y^2$
$=> x = \pm y$
$=> \frac{x}{y} = \pm 1$
Thus, $\frac{x}{y}$ may or may not be equal to 1. – Insufficient

From statement 2:

$xy > 0$

$=> x > 0$ and $y > 0$

OR

$x < 0$ and $y < 0$.

However, we cannot determine whether $x = y$ or $\frac{x}{y} = 1$. – Insufficient

Thus, from statements 1 and 2 together:

We have: $x > 0$ and $y > 0$

OR

$x < 0$ and $y < 0$

$=> \frac{x}{y} > 0$
From statement 1 we had: $\frac{x}{y} = \pm 1$
Thus, we can conclude: $\frac{x}{y} \neq -1$, (since $\frac{x}{y} > 0$)

=> $\frac{x}{y} = 1$. - Sufficient

The correct answer is option C.

454. We have: $xyz \neq 0$

=> None of x, y or z is '0'.

$x(y+z) \geq 0$

=> $x \geq 0$ and $(y+z) \geq 0$

OR

$x \leq 0$ and $(y+z) \leq 0$.

From statement 1:

$|y+z| = |y| + |z|$

=> y and z are of the same sign i.e. $y \geq 0$ and $z \geq 0$

OR

$y \leq 0$ and $z \leq 0$.

However, there is no information on x. - Insufficient

From statement 2:

$|x+y| = |x| + |y|$

=> x and y are of the same sign i.e. $x \geq 0$ and $y \geq 0$

OR

$x \leq 0$ and $y \leq 0$.

However, there is no information on y. - Insufficient

Thus, from statements 1 and 2 together:

We have two possibilities:

(1) $x \geq 0,\ y \geq 0,\ z \geq 0$ => $x \geq 0$ and $(y+z) \geq 0$

(2) $x \leq 0,\ y \leq 0,\ z \leq 0$ => $x \leq 0$ and $(y+z) \leq 0$

In both the cases, we have: $x\,(y + z) \geq 0$. – Sufficient

The correct answer is option C.

455. We have:

$$R = \frac{P}{Q}$$

Thus, for $R \leq P$, we have:

$Q \geq 1$ if $(R \geq 0$ and $P \geq 0)$

OR

$Q < 0$ if $(R \leq 0$ and $P \geq 0)$

From statement 1:

$P > 50$
Since no information on Q is provided, we cannot determine if $R \leq P$. – Insufficient

From statement 2:

$0 < Q \leq 20$.
Since no information on P is provided, we cannot determine if $R \leq P$. – Insufficient

Thus, from statements 1 and 2 together:

We find that both P and Q are positive, thus R is also positive.
However, $Q \geq 1$ or $0 < Q \leq 1$ is possible.

$Q \geq 1 => R \leq P$
Whereas, $0 < Q \leq 1 => R \geq P$ – Insufficient

The correct answer is option E.

456. $s^4v^3x^7 < 0$

$=> (s^4v^2x^6)\,(vx) < 0$

$=> vx < 0$; since $(s^4v^2x^6) > 0$ being a perfect square.

We need to determine whether $svx < 0$.

If $svx < 0$, then we have:

$s > 0$, (since $vx < 0$)

Thus, we need to determine whether $s > 0$.

From statement 1:

There is no information on s. – Insufficient

From statement 2:

There is no information on s. – Insufficient

Thus, from statements 1 and 2 together:

There is still no information on s. – Insufficient

The correct answer is option E.

457. $\frac{x}{2} = \frac{3}{y}$
$=> xy = 6$.

From statement 1:

$y \geq 3$.

Since we want to know whether $x < y$, we must test the inequality for minimum possible value of y against the maximum possible value of x.

The minimum value of y results in the maximum value of x since xy is constant.

Minimum value of $y = 3$.

Thus, we have the maximum value of $x = \frac{6}{3} = 2$.

Since the maximum value of x is less than the minimum value of y, we have: $x < y$. – Sufficient

From statement 2:

$y \leq 4$.

We know that the maximum value of y results in the minimum value of x since xy is constant.

Maximum value of $y = 4$.

Thus, we have the minimum value of $x = \frac{6}{4} = \frac{3}{2}$.

However, x can attain values higher than $\frac{3}{2}$ while y can attain values lower than 4.

For example: if $y = 4$

$=> x = \frac{6}{4} = \frac{3}{2}$ i.e. $x < y$.

However, if $y = 1$

$=> x = \frac{6}{1} = 6$ i.e. $x > y$.

Thus, there is no unique answer. – Insufficient

The correct answer is option A.

458. $-2x > 3y$

$=> 2x < -3y$

$=> x < -\frac{3y}{2}$

If y is positive, the answer is Yes, else No.

From statement 1:

$y > 0$

$=> -\frac{3y}{2} < 0$

Thus, we have:

$x < -\frac{3y}{2} < 0$. – Sufficient

From statement 2:

$2x + 5y - 20 = 0$

$=> 2x + 5y = 20 \ldots$ (i)

We know: $-2x > 3y$

$=> -2x - 3y > 0 \ldots$ (ii)

Adding (i) and (ii), we get:

$-3y + 5y > 20$

$=> y > 10$

$=> y > 0$.

This is the same as in statement 1. – Sufficient

The correct answer is option D.

459. We need to determine whether:

$(a^{-1}+b^{-1})^{-1} < (a^{-1}b^{-1})^{-1}$

$=> \frac{1}{\frac{1}{a}+\frac{1}{b}} < \frac{1}{\frac{1}{ab}}$

$=> \frac{ab}{a+b} < ab$

$=> \frac{1}{a+b} < 1$ (canceling (ab), since $a > 0,\ b>0$)

$=> a+b > 1$ (the inequality does not change while taking reciprocal since $a > 0,\ b > 0$)

From statement 1:

$a = 2b$

However, we cannot determine whether $a+b > 1$. - Insufficient

From statement 2:

$a+b > 1$. - Sufficient

The correct answer is option B.

460. We need to determine whether:

$\frac{a}{b} * \frac{c}{d} > \frac{c}{b}$

$=> \frac{a}{d} * \frac{c}{b} > \frac{c}{b}$(rearranging terms)

Since a, b, c and d are positive, we can cancel out $\frac{c}{b}$ from both sides, it implies that:

$=> \frac{a}{d} > 1$

$=> a > d$

From statement 1:

We have: $c > b$

However, there is no comparison between a and d. - Insufficient

From statement 2:

We have: $a > d$ - Sufficient

The correct answer is option B.

461. From statement 1:

$w + c > 50$

Since w and c are any integers, we can have a situation where:

(1) $w = 0$ and $c = 51 \Rightarrow w + c = 51 > 50$

(2) $w = 3$ and $c = 50 \Rightarrow w + c = 53 > 50$

(3) $w = -2$ and $c = 56 \Rightarrow w + c = 54 > 50$

Thus, w may be greater than '0' or equal to '0' or less than '0'. – Insufficient

From statement 2:

There is no information about w. – Insufficient

Thus, from statements 1 and 2 together:

Even after combining the statements, we can still have all the situations shown for statement 1. – Insufficient

The correct answer is option E.

462. From statement 1:

We have:

$wz < 2$, and $w > 2$

Since the product wz is smaller than 2 with w itself being greater than 2, we must have z as either a fraction between '0' and '1' or a number less than or equal to '0'

For example:

(1) $w = 3, wz = 1$
$\Rightarrow z = \frac{1}{3} < 1$

(2) $w = 3, wz = -1$
$\Rightarrow z = -\frac{1}{3} < 1$

Thus, we have:

$z < 1$ – Sufficient

From statement 2:

We have:

$wz < 2$, and $z < 2$

Since the product wz is smaller than 2 with z itself being smaller than 2, z can take any value depending on the value assigned to w.

For example:

(1) If $z > 1$
$z = \frac{3}{2}, w = 1$
$=> wz < 2$

(2) If $z < 1$
$z = \frac{1}{2}, w = 2$
$=> wz < 2$

Thus, there is no unique answer. – Insufficient

The correct answer is option A.

463. We know that $x > 0$.

There are two possibilities:

(1) $0 < x < 1$: Here, x is a proper fraction.

Thus, higher the exponent of x, smaller is the value of (since the denominator is greater than the numerator).

$x^4 < x^3 < x^2 < x$

For example: $x = 0.2$
$=> x^2 = 0.04 < 0.2 = x$

(2) $x > 1$:

Here, higher the exponent of x, higher is the value (since the numerator is greater than the denominator).

For example: $x = 2$
$=> x^2 = 4 > 2 = x$

From statement 1:

We have:

$0.1 < x < 0.4$

$=> 0 < x < 1$

$=> x^2 < x$ - Sufficient

From statement 2:

We have:

$x^3 < x^2$

As, $x > 0$ canceling x^2 from both sides:

$x < 1$

$=> 0 < x < 1$

$=> x^2 < x$ - Sufficient

The correct answer is option D.

464. From statement 1:

$\frac{x^2}{xy + x} < 1$

$=> x^2 < xy + x$ (since both x and y are positive, $(xy + x)$ is positive and hence can be cross-multiplied without reversing the inequality)

$=> x^2 < x(y + 1)$

$=> x < y + 1$ (since x is positive, we can cancel x from both sides without reversing the inequality)

However, we cannot determine whether $x < y$ - Insufficient

From statement 2:

$\frac{xy}{y^2 - y} < 1$

$=> \frac{xy}{y(y - 1)} < 1$

$=> \frac{x}{y - 1} < 1$

=> $x < y - 1$ (since $y > 1$ => $y - 1 > 0$, we can cross-multiply $(y - 1)$ without reversing the inequality)

=> $x + 1 < y$

Thus, we can definitely say that: $x < y$ - Sufficient

The correct answer is option B.

465. We need to determine whether:

$\frac{x^2}{|x|} < 1$

=> $\frac{|x|^2}{|x|} < 1$, as $x^2 = |x|^2$

=> $|x| < 1$

=> $-1 < x < 1$

From statement 1:

We know: $x < 1$

However, we do not have the lower bound. – Insufficient

From statement 2:

We know: $x > -1$

However, we do not have the higher bound. – Insufficient

Thus, from statements 1 and 2 together:

We have: $-1 < x < 1$; which is the required condition. – Sufficient

The correct answer is option C.

466. Let us understand the concept of the modulus (or the absolute value):

$|x - a|$ refers to the distance of the point x from the point a on either side of .

Thus: $|x - a| = b$ implies that the distance of the point x from the point a on either side of a is b units.

We have: $y = |x + 3| + |4 - x|$

=> $y = |x - (-3)| + |x - 4|$

We need to determine whether $y = 7$

Let us see the different possibilities shown on the number line below:

(1) If $x < -3$:

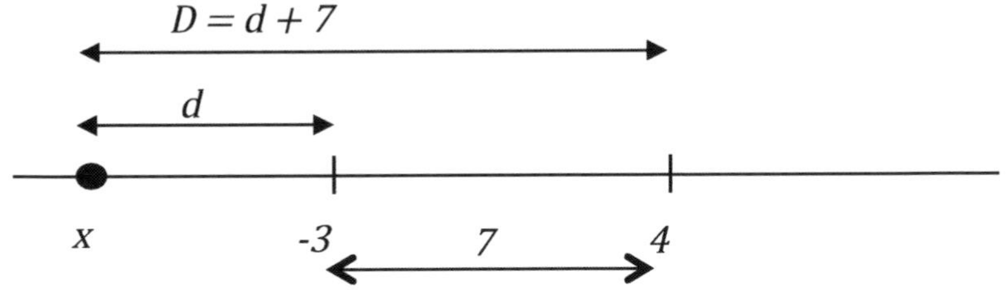

We have: $d + d + 7 = 7$ => $d = 0$
=> $x = -3$

(2) If $x > 4$:

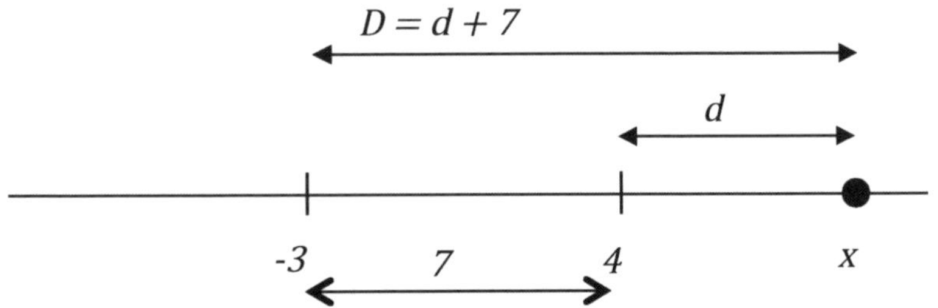

We have: $d + d + 7 = 7$ => $d = 0$
=> $x = 4$

(3) If $-3 < x < 4$:

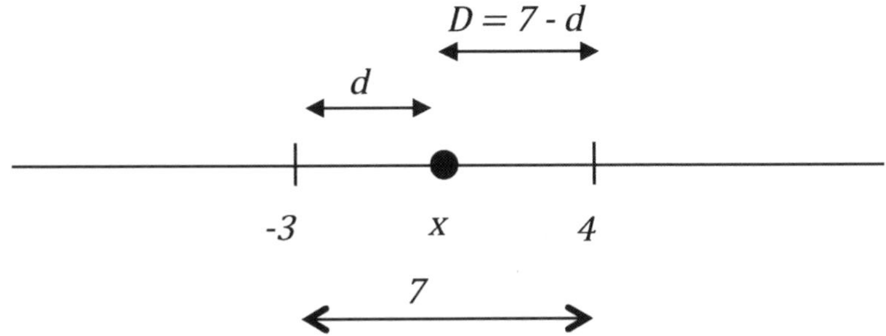

We have: $d + 7 - d = 7$, which is true for all x from -3 to 4.

In short, we can see that if x is to the left of -3 OR to the right of 4, the sum of the distances of x from the points -3 and 4 is greater than 7.

However, if x lies between -3 and 4 (both inclusive), the sum of the distances of x from the points -3 and 4 is equal to 7.

Thus, we have:

$y = 7 => -3 < x < 4$

From statement 1:

We know: $x < 4$

However, we do not have the lower bound. - Insufficient

From statement 2:

We know: $x > -3$

However, we do not have the higher bound. - Insufficient

Thus, from statements 1 and 2 together:

We have: $-3 < x < 4$; which is the required condition. - Sufficient

Alternate approach:

We know that:

$|a| + |b| = |a + b|$ holds true only if:

(1) a and b are both positive

OR

(2) a and b are both negative

Thus, we have to determine if:

$y = |x + 3| + |4 - x| = 7 = |(x + 3) + (4 - x)|$

This would hold true if:

(1) $x + 3 > 0 => x > -3$ AND $4 - x > 0 => x < 4 => -3 < x < 4$

OR

(2) $x + 3 < 0 => x < -3$ AND $4 - x < 0 => x > 4$, which is not possible.

Thus, we have the required condition by combining the statements.

The correct answer is option C.

467. From statement 1:

$7x - 2y > 0$

$=> 2y < 7x$

$=> y < \frac{7x}{2}$

Thus, we see that y is smaller than a positive quantity i.e. $\left(\frac{7x}{2}\right)$.
Thus, the value of y may be positive, may be zero or may even be negative. – Insufficient

From statement 2:

$-y < x$

$=> y > -x$

Thus, we see that y is greater than a negative quantity i.e. $(-x)$.

For example:

If $x = 5$:

$-x = -5$,

$=> y > -5$

Thus, the value of y may be positive, may be zero or may even be negative. – Insufficient

Thus, from statements 1 and 2 together:

$-x < y < \frac{7x}{2}$

Like the previous example, if $x = 5$

$-5 < y < \frac{7 * 5}{2}$

Thus, depending on the value of x, the value of y may be positive, may be zero or may even be negative. – Insufficient

The correct answer is option E.

468. From statement 1:

$x^2 < 1$

$=> -1 < x < 1$

Since x is an integer, $x = 0$

However, we have no information about y. – Insufficient

From statement 2:

We have: $y < 1$

y may be positive or negative or zero.

Also, we have no information about x. – Insufficient

Thus, from statements 1 and 2 together:

We have:

$x = 0$, and

$y < 1$

Thus, we have:

$x + y < 0 + 1$

$=> x + y < 2$ – Sufficient

The correct answer is option C.

469. Since $y = \sqrt{9 - x}$; in order that y can be a positive integer (a real number), we must have:

$9 - x > 0$

$=> x < 9$

From statement 1:

We have: $x < 8$:

Possible values of x are: 1, 2, 3, 4, 5, 6 or 7.

The only value of x for which y is an integer is: $x = 5$

Thus, we have:

$y = \sqrt{9-5} = \sqrt{4} = 2$

Note: The radical sign i.e. $\sqrt{n}$, by definition, only taken the positive square root of n.

Thus, we have a unique value of y. – Sufficient

From statement 2:

We have: $y > 1$

We have already established that: $x < 9$

Thus, possible values of x are: 1, 2, 3, 4, 5, 6, 7 or 8.

The possible values of x for which y is an integer are: $x = 5$ or 8

If $x = 5$: $y = \sqrt{9-5} = 2 > 1$

If $x = 8$: $y = \sqrt{9-8} = 1 \not> 1$

Thus, there is only possible value of $y = 2$ – Sufficient

The correct answer is option D.

470. From statement 1:

$x > y + 4$

$\Rightarrow 3x > 3y + 12$

However, there is no relation between $(3y + 12)$ and $7y$ since y can be any positive number.

Thus, we cannot conclude that $3x > 7y$. – Insufficient

From statement 2:

$-5x < -14y$

$\Rightarrow x > \left(\frac{-14}{-5}\right) y$

$\Rightarrow x > 2.8y$

=> $3x > 8.4y$

Since $y > 0$, we have:

$8.4y > 7y$

=> $3x > 7y$ - Sufficient

The correct answer is option B.

471. From statement 1:

$x > y - x$

=> $2x > y$

=> $4x > 2y$

Thus, $4x$ may be greater than $3y$ or be equal to $3y$ or even be smaller than $3y$.

For example:

If $y = 2 : 4x > 2y$

=> $4x > 4$

=> Possible values of $4x$ may be anything more than 4, say 5, 6, 10, etc.

Here, $3y = 6$.

If $4x = 5 : 4x < 3y$

If $4x = 6 : \ 4x = 3y$

If $4x = 10 : 4x > 3y$

Hence, there is no unique answer. - Insufficient

From statement 2:

$\frac{x}{y} < 1$

=> $x < y$ (since x and y are positive, we can cross-multiply without reversing the inequality)

=> $4x < 4y$

Thus, $4x$ may be greater than $3y$ or be equal to $3y$ or even be smaller than $3y$.

Hence, there is no unique answer. – Insufficient

Thus, from statements 1 and 2 together:

We have:

$4x > 2y$, and

$4x < 4y$

=> $2y < 4x < 4y$

Thus, possible values of $4x$ may be equal to $3.5y$, $3y$ or $2.5y$

Thus, $4x$ may be greater than $3y$ or be equal to $3y$ or even be smaller than $3y$.

Hence, there is no unique answer. – Insufficient

The correct answer is option E.

472. From statement 1:

$x^2 + 6x < 7$

=> $x^2 + 6x + 9 < 16$ (in order to convert the quadratic equation to a perfect square)

=> $(x + 3)^2 < 16$

=> $-4 < x + 3 < 4$

=> $-7 < x < 1$

But, we know that $x < 0$.

Thus, possible values of x are: $-1, -2, -3, -4, -5$ or -6.

Thus, x may be greater than -3 or equal to -3 or even smaller than -3. – Insufficient

From statement 2:

$x^2 + |x| \leq 2$

We know that both x^2 and $|x|$ are non-negative.

Also, $x^2 + |x|$ must be an integer since x is a negative integer.

Thus, we have:

(1) $x^2 + |x| = 2$

This is only possible if each of x^2 and $|x|$ are 1

$=> x^2 = |x| = 1$

$=> x = -1$, which is not less than -3

(2) $x^2 + |x| = 0$

$=> x = 0$, which is not negative, hence not valid.

Thus, we only have $x = -1 \not< -3$.

Thus, we have a unique answer 'No'. – Sufficient

The correct answer is option B.

473. We have:
$x + y > 0 => x > -y \ldots$(i)

From statement 1:

$x^{2y} < 1 => (x^2)^y < 1$

We know that $x^2 \geq 0$ for all values of x.

The above inequality can be satisfied in any of the following situations:

(1) $x > 1$ and $y < 0$, for example:

$x = 2$ and $y = -1$ (satisfying $x + y > 0$)

$=> x^{2y} = 2^{-2} = \frac{1}{4} < 1$

$=> xy = 2 * (-1) = -2 < 0$

(2) $0 < |x| < 1$ and $y > 1$, for example:

$x = \pm\frac{1}{2}$ and $y = 2$ (satisfying $x + y > 0$)

$=> x^{2y} = \left(\frac{1}{2}\right)^4 = \frac{1}{16} < 1$

$=> xy = \left(\frac{1}{2}\right) * 2 = 1 > 0$

OR

$xy = \left(-\frac{1}{2}\right) * 2 = -1 < 0$

(3) $|x| = 0$ and y is any number except 0, where $x^{2y} = 0$ and $xy = 0$

Thus, xy may be positive, negative or zero. – Insufficient

From statement 2:

$x + 2y < 0$
$=> x < -2y \ldots$(ii)

Thus, combining (i) with (ii), we have: $-y < x < -2y$

Thus, we have: $-y < -2y$

$=> y > 2y$

$=> y < 0$

Thus, y is negative.

Hence, $-y$ and $-2y$ are both positive.

Thus, x lies between two positive numbers, implying x is positive.

Thus, we have: $x > 0$ and $y < 0 => xy < 0$ – Sufficient

The correct answer is option C.

6.19 Geometry-Lines

474. Let us reproduce the figure, assigning names for intersection points

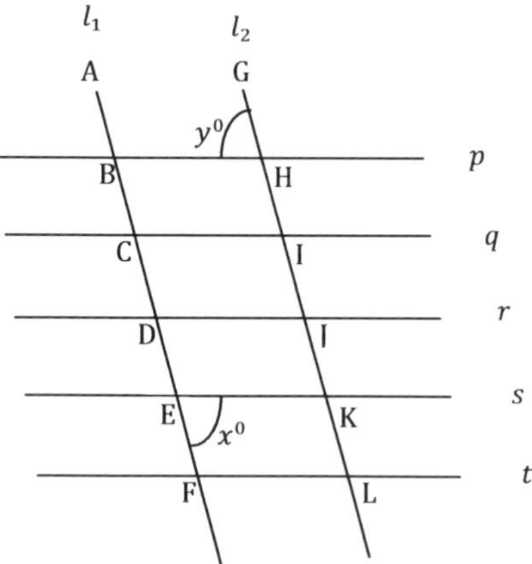

From statement 1:

Since $p||r$, we have $\angle$GHB $=\angle$GJD $= y^0$ (corresponding angles).

Since $r||t$, we have $\angle$GJD $=\angle$GLF $= y^0$ (corresponding angles).

Since it is not given that $t||s$, we cannot relate $\angle$FEK and $\angle$GHB.

The above diagram may be as following.

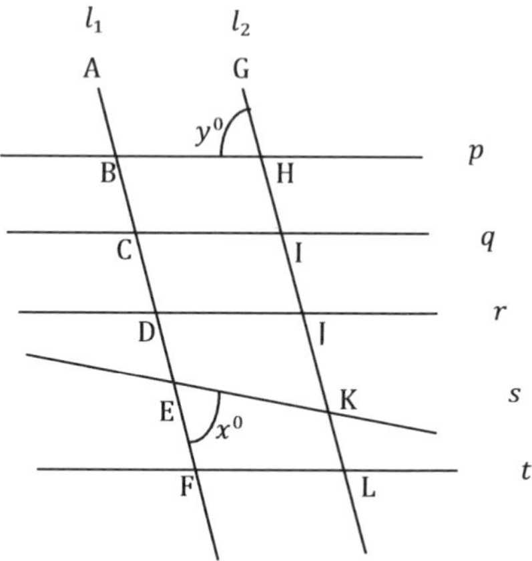

Note: If it were known that $t||s$, since $p||r$ and $r||t$, we would have $s||p$.

In that case, we would have:

$\angle$JKE $= x^0 = \angle$FEK (alternate angles) and $\angle$GHB $= y^0 = \angle$JKE (corresponding angles).

Thus, we would have had $x = y$.

Hence, we cannot conclude that $x = y$ - Insufficient

From statement 2:

Since $q||s$, we have $\angle$FCI =$\angle$FEK =x^0 (corresponding angles).

Since it is not given that $q||p$, we cannot relate $\angle$FEK and $\angle$GHB.

Note: If it were known that $q||p$, since $q||s$, we would have $s||p$.

Thus, following the reasoning presented in statement 1, we would have had $x = y$.

Hence, we cannot conclude that $x = y$ - Insufficient

Thus, from statements 1 and 2 together:

Even after combining both statements, we cannot relate $\angle$FEK and $\angle$GHB.

Hence, we cannot conclude that $x = y$ - Insufficient

The correct answer is option E.

6.20 Geometry–Triangles

475. We need to determine if $x > 90$:

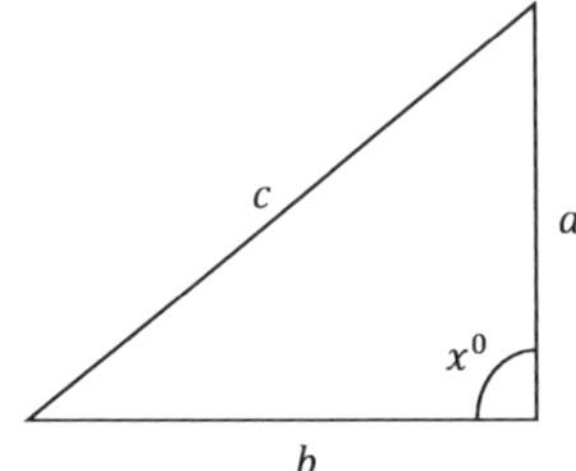

If c is the longest side of the triangle then,

(1) If $x = 90$, we have: $c^2 = a^2 + b^2$
(2) If $x < 90$, we have: $c^2 < a^2 + b^2$
(3) If $x > 90$, we have: $c^2 > a^2 + b^2$

Thus, we need to check which of the above three conditions is true.

From statement 1:

We have no information about c. - Insufficient

From statement 2:

We have no information about a and b. - Insufficient

Thus, from statements 1 and 2 together:

We know that:

$a^2 + b^2 < 15$

Also, we know that:

$c > 4$

$=> c^2 > 16$

Thus, we see that:

$c^2 > a^2 + b^2$

$=> x > 90$ - Sufficient

The correct answer is option C.

476. The figure depicting the information in the problem is shown below:

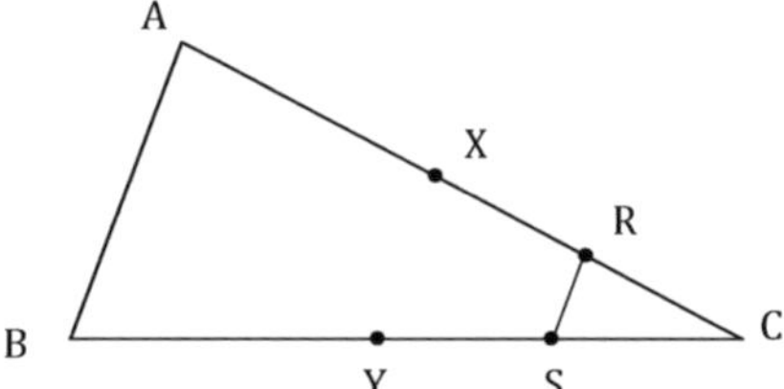

We know that:

AX = CX . . . (i)

RX = RC . . . (ii)

BY = CY . . . (iii)

YS = SC . . . (iv)

We have:

$$\frac{CR}{CA} = \frac{CR}{2 * CX} = \frac{CR}{2 * 2 * CR} = \frac{1}{4}$$

Also, we have:

$$\frac{CS}{CB} = \frac{CS}{2 * CY} = \frac{CS}{2 * 2 * CS} = \frac{1}{4}$$

Thus, triangle CRS is similar to triangle CAB since:

$\frac{CR}{CA} = \frac{CS}{CB}$, and $\angle RCS = \angle ACB$ (included angle)

Thus, ratio of the corresponding sides of the above two similar triangles $= \frac{CR}{CA} = \frac{CS}{CB} = \frac{1}{4}$

Thus, ratio of the areas of the above two similar triangles

$$= \frac{\text{Area of triangle CRS}}{\text{Area of triangle CAB}} = \text{(Ratio of their corresponding sides)}^2 = \left(\frac{1}{4}\right)^2 = \frac{1}{16} \ldots \text{(i)}$$

From statement 1:

Area of triangle ABX = 32

We know that a line drawn from the vertex which divides the base in the ratio 1 : 1, also divides the area in the same ratio i.e. 1 : 1.

Since AX = CX, we have:

Area of triangle BCX = Area of triangle ABX = 32.

Thus, area of triangle CAB = 32 + 32 = 64.

Thus, from (i):

$$\frac{\text{Area of triangle CRS}}{64} = \frac{1}{16}$$

=> Area of triangle CRS $= \frac{64}{16} = 4$ - Sufficient

From statement 2:

We only know the length of an altitude of triangle ABC.

However, the length of the corresponding base of the triangle ABC is not known.

Hence, the area of triangle ABC cannot be determined.

Hence, the area of triangle CRS cannot be determined either. - Insufficient

The correct answer is option A.

477. The figure depicting the information in the problem is shown below:

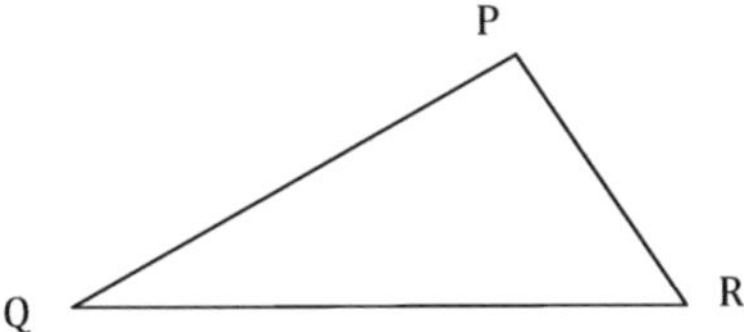

We know that:

$\angle P = 30^0 + 2 * \angle Q \ldots (i)$

Also, in triangle PQR:

$\angle P + \angle Q + \angle R = 180^0$

$=> \left(30^0 + 2 * \angle Q\right) + \angle Q + \angle R = 180$

$=> 3 * \angle Q + \angle R = 150^0 \ldots (ii)$

From statement 1:

Since PQ = QR, we have:

$\angle P = \angle R$

Thus, from (i), we have:

$\angle R = 30^0 + 2 * \angle Q \ldots (iii)$

From (ii) and (iii), we have:

$3 * \angle Q + (30^0 + 2 * \angle Q) = 150^0$

$=> 5 * \angle Q = 120^0$

$=> \angle Q = 24^0$

Thus, from (iii)

$=> \angle R = 30^0 + 2 * \angle Q$

$= 30^0 + 2 * 24^0$

$= 78^0$ – Sufficient

From statement 2:

We have:

$\angle P = 78^0$

Thus, from (i), we have:

$78^0 = 30^0 + 2 * \angle Q$

$=> \angle Q = 24^0$

Thus, from (ii), we have:

$3 * 24^0 + \angle R = 150^0$

$=> \angle R = 150^0 - 72^0$

$= 78^0$ - Sufficient

The correct answer is option D.

478. Let us bring out the figure.

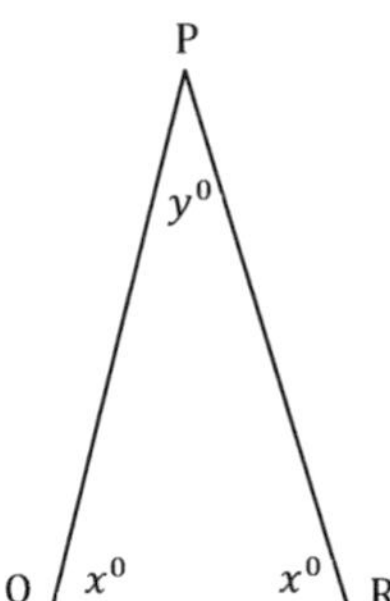

We know that the sum of the angles in a triangle is 180^0

$=> 2x + y = 180 \ldots$ (i)

From statement 1:

$\frac{3}{2}x = 120$

$=> x = 120 * \frac{2}{3} = 80$

Thus, from (i), we have:

$2 * 80 + y = 180$

$=> y = 20$ – Sufficient

From statement 2:

$x + y = 100$

$=> x = 100 - y$

Thus, from (i), we have:

$=> 2(100 - y) + y = 180$

$=> 200 - y = 180$

$=> y = 20$ – Sufficient

The correct answer is option D.

6.21 Geometry–Circles

479. From statement 1:

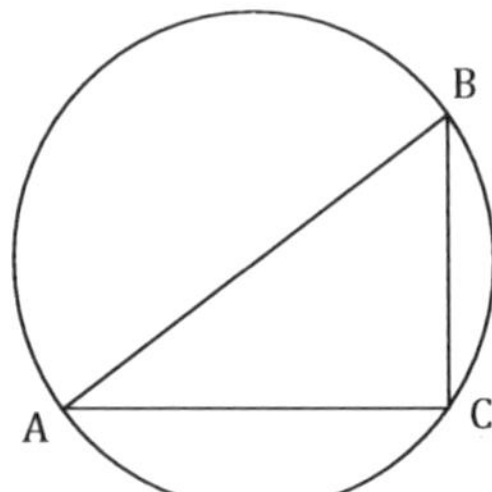

Since we have no information about the nature of the triangle ABC, we cannot determine the sides of the triangle.

Hence, we cannot determine the radius of the circle.

Hence, we cannot determine the circumference of the circle. – Insufficient

From statement 2:

Let the length of the sides BC, AC and AB respectively be $3x, 4x$ and $5x$, where x is a constant of proportionality.

We see that: $(5x)^2 = (3x^2) + (4x)^2$

=> Triangle ABC is right-angled at C.

=> AB is the diameter of the circle (since the diameter subtends 90^0 at the circumference).

However, the exact lengths are not known.

Hence, we cannot determine the radius of the circle.

Hence, we cannot determine the circumference of the circle. – Insufficient

Thus, from statements 1 and 2 together:

Sum of the three sides = $3x + 4x + 5x = 12x$.

Thus, we have:

$12x = 48$

=> $x = 4$

=> Diameter of the circle = AB = $5x = 20$

=> Radius of the circle = $\frac{20}{2} = 10$

=> Circumference of the circle = $2\pi * 10 = 20\pi$ – Sufficient

The correct answer is option C.

480. Area of a semi-circle = $\frac{\pi r^2}{2}$, where r is the radius of the semi-circle.

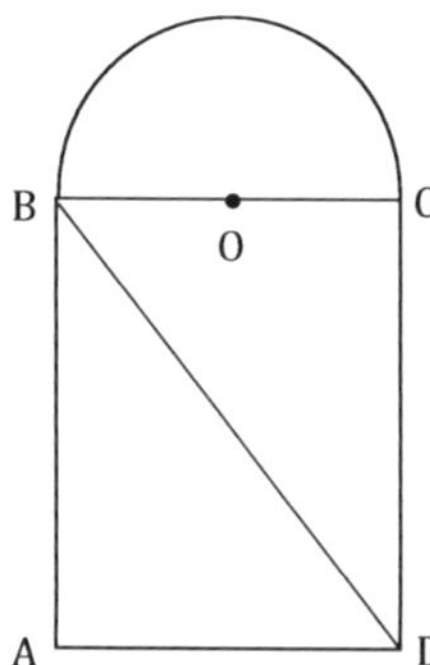

Thus, to determine the area, we need to determine the radius using the relation: BC = $2r$.

From statement 1:

We only know the ratio of the sides of the rectangle.

We have no information about any actual dimensions. – Insufficient

From statement 2:

We know: BD = 25

From Pythagoras' theorem:

$AB^2+BC^2=BD^2$

=> $AB^2+BC^2=25^2$

However, we cannot determine BC since both BC and AB are unknowns. – Insufficient

Thus, from statements 1 and 2 together:

$\frac{BC}{AB}=\frac{3}{4}$

=> Let BC = $3x$ and AB = $4x$, where x is a constant of proportionality.

Thus, we have:

$AB^2+BC^2=25^2$

=> $(4x)^2 + (3x)^2 = 25^2$

=> $x^2 = 25$

=> $x = 5$ (x cannot be -5 since lengths must be positive)

=> $BC = 3x = 15$

=> Radius of the semi-circle = $\frac{15}{2}$. – Sufficient

The correct answer is option C.

481. Required area = (Area of bigger circle with centre C) – (Area of smaller circle with centre B)

$= \pi * AC^2 - \pi * AB^2$

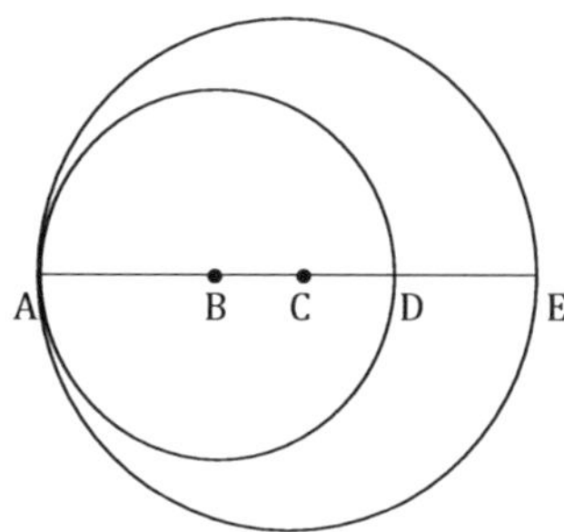

From statement 1:

We know:

AB = 3 and BC = 2

=> AC = AB + BC = 3 + 2 = 5

Thus, required area

$= \pi * AC^2 - \pi * AB^2$

$= \pi\ (5^2 - 3^2)$

$= 16\pi$ – Sufficient

From statement 2:

We know:

CD = 1 and DE = 4

=> CE = 1 + 4 = 5

=> AC = CE = 5

Also, we have:

AD = AE – DE

= 2* AC – DE

= 10 – 4 = 6

=> AB + BD = 6

=> 2* AB = 6

=> AB = 3

Thus, we have: AC = 5 and AB = 3, which is the same result as obtained from statement 1. – Sufficient

The correct answer is option D.

6.22 Geometry–Polygon

482. We need to check if the rectangular glass sheet covers the entire tabletop.

From statement 1:

We only have information on the dimensions of the tabletop.
However, we have no information on the rectangular glass sheet. – Insufficient

From statement 2:

We only have information on the area of the glass sheet.
However, we have no information on the tabletop. – Insufficient

Thus, from statements 1 and 2 together:

Combining both statements we can see:
The area of the glass sheet = 2,400 square inches
The area of the table top = 36*60 = 2160 square inches
Thus, the area of the glass sheet is more than that of the tabletop.

However, it is not sufficient to determine if the glass sheet can cover the table top entirely.

Say, for example, if the glass sheet is 40 inches by 60 inches, i.e. both the length and breadth are more than or equal to the corresponding dimensions of the tabletop, the glass sheet will cover the tabletop entirely.

However, if the glass sheet is 30 inches by 80 inches, i.e. both the length and breadth are **not** more than or equal to the corresponding dimensions of the tabletop, the glass sheet will not cover the tabletop entirely.

Hence, we cannot determine if the glass sheet covers the entire tabletop. – Insufficient

The correct answer is option E.

483. Let the width of the rectangle be x units.

Thus, the length of the rectangle = $(x + 2)$ units.

Hence, the perimeter = $2\,(x + (x + 2)) = (4x + 4)$ units.

From statement 1:

Diagonal of the rectangle = $\sqrt{x^2 + (x + 2)^2}$

Thus, we have:

$\sqrt{x^2 + (x + 2)^2} = 10$

$=> x^2 + (x + 2)^2 = 100$

$=> 2x^2 + 4x - 96 = 0$

$=> x^2 + 2x - 48 = 0$

$=> (x + 8)(x - 6) = 0$

$=> x = 6$ or -8

However, the width cannot be negative.

Hence, $x = 6$

Thus, the perimeter $= 4x + 4 = 28$ units. – Sufficient

From statement 2:

Area of the rectangle $= x(x + 2)$ square units.

Thus, we have:

$x(x + 2) = 48$

$=> x^2 + 2x - 48 = 0$

This is the same as the result obtained from statement 1. – Sufficient

The correct answer is option D.

484. We know that in a triangle, the longest side is opposite to the largest angle and the shortest side is opposite to the smallest angle.

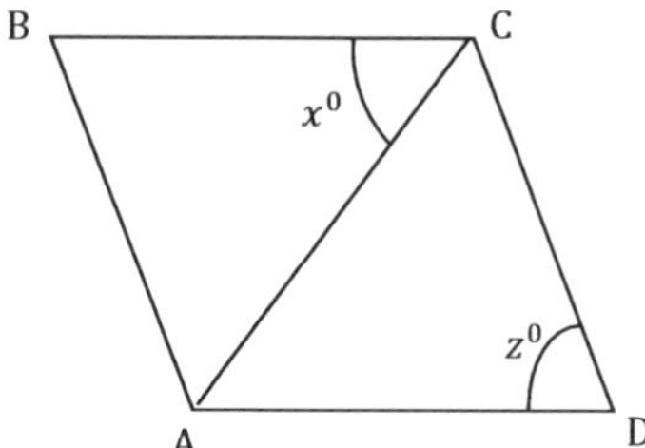

From statement 1:

Since BC ||AD, we have:

$\angle BCA = \angle CAD = x^0 = 50^0$ (alternate angles)

Thus, the sum of the other two angles in triangle ACD = $180^0 - 50^0 = 130^0$.

If CD has to be the shortest side, $\angle CAD$ must be the smallest angle.

However, since the other two angles in triangle ACD are not known, we can have:

(1) $\angle ACD = 20^0$, $\angle CDA = 110^0$
=> $\angle ACD$ is the smallest angle
=> AD is the shortest side
=> AC is not the shortest side.

(2) $\angle ACD = 110^0$, $\angle CDA = 20^0$
=> $\angle CDA$ is the smallest angle
=> AC is the shortest side.

Thus, we cannot uniquely determine whether AC is the shortest side of the triangle. – Insufficient

From statement 2:

We have:

$\angle CDA = z^0 = 70^0$

Thus, the sum of the other two angles in triangle ACD = $180^0 - 70^0 = 110^0$.

If AC is the shortest side, then $\angle CDA$ should be the smallest angle.
It follows that the other two angles of the triangle ACD must be more than 70^0.
In such an event, the sum of those two angles should be more than 140^0, which is not possible.

Thus, $\angle CDA$ is not the smallest angle
=> AC is not the shortest side. – Sufficient

The correct answer is option B.

485. In the parallelogram above, we have:

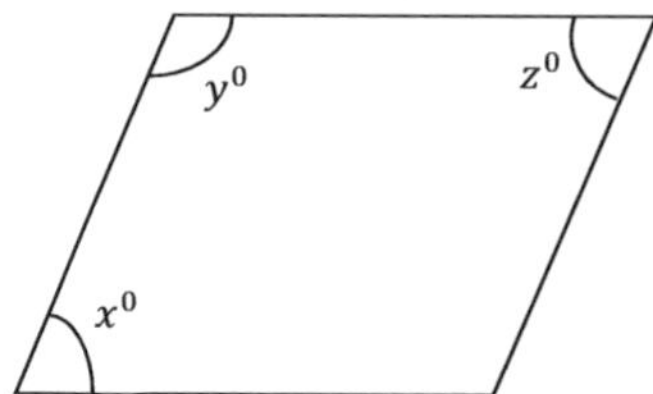

$x = z$; (angles at opposite vertices are equal) ... (i)

$x + y = y + z = 180$; (angles at adjacent vertices are supplementary) ... (ii)

From statement 1:

We know:

$y = 2x$

Substituting the above value of y in (ii), we have:

$x + y = 180$

$=> x + 2x = 180$

$=> x = 60$ – Sufficient

From statement 2:

We know:

$x + z = 120$

Using relation (i) along with the equation above, we have:

$x = z = \frac{120}{2} = 60$ – Sufficient

The correct answer is option D.

6.23 Geometry–3 Dimensional

6.24 Co-ordinate geometry

486. The equation of a circle in the XY-plane with its centre at the origin is given by: $x^2 + y^2 = r^2$, where r is the radius of the circle and (x, y) are the coordinates of any point on the circle.

From statement 1:

$x^2 + y^2 = 4^2 = 16$.

Thus, sum of the squares of the coordinates of any point P on the circle is 16 – Sufficient

From statement 2:

$x + y = 0$
$=> (x + y)^2 = 0$
$=> x^2 + y^2 = -2xy$.

Since we do not know the values of x and y, we cannot determine the answer – Insufficient

The correct answer is option A.

487. $y = mx + b$

We need to determine the slope of the above line i.e. the value of m.

From statement 1:

We know that:

$y = (1 - m)x + (b + 1)$ and $y = mx + b$ are parallel.

Thus, their slopes should be same.

Thus, we have:

$(1 - m) = m$

$=> m = \frac{1}{2}$. – Sufficient

From statement 2:

We know that:

$y = mx + b$ and $y = 2x + 3$ intersect at (2, 7).

Substituting $x = 2, y = 7$ in $y = mx + b$, we have:

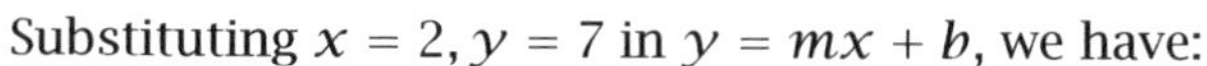

$7 = 2m + b$

Since there are two unknowns, we cannot determine the value of m. - Insufficient

The correct answer is option A.

488. Let the coordinates of S be (a, b).

Let the coordinates of U be (c, d).

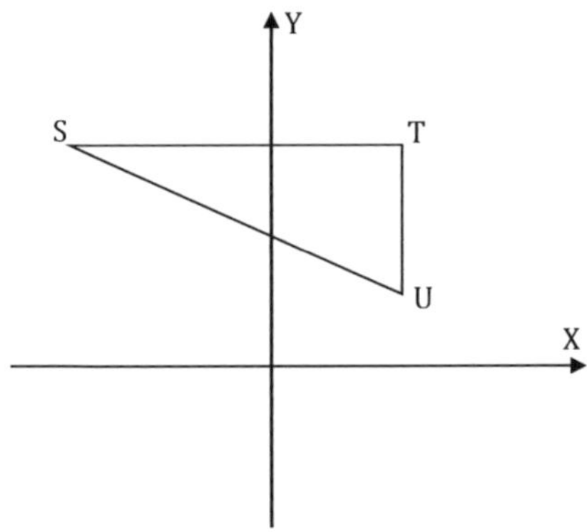

Thus, the coordinates of T = (c, b), since S and T have the same Y-coordinate (ST parallel to X-axis, also, U and T have the same X-coordinate (UT parallel to the Y-axis).

From statement 1:

We have: $d = 1$.

However, we cannot determine the values of c or b. – Insufficient

From statement 2:

We have: $a = -5$.

However, we cannot determine the values of c or b. – Insufficient

Thus, from statements 1 and 2 together:

We have: $a = -5, d = 1$.

However, we still cannot determine the values of c or b. – Insufficient

The correct answer is option E.

489. The equation of the above circle having centre at the origin and radius 50, is:

$x^2 + y^2 = 50^2$

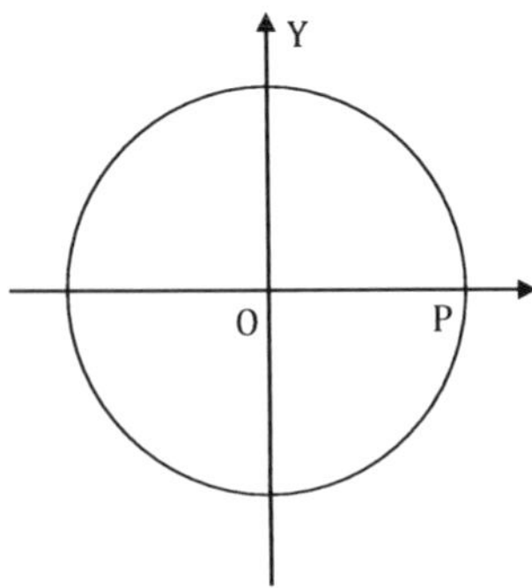

From statement 1:

Let the coordinates of point Q be $(-30, a)$.

Since Q is on the circle, it must satisfy the equation of the circle. Thus:

$(-30)^2 + a^2 = 50^2$

$=> a^2 = 1600$

$=> a = \pm 40$

Thus, the length of PQ $= \sqrt{(50 - (-30))^2 + (0 - a)^2}$

$= \sqrt{(50 - (-30))^2 + (0 - (\pm 40))^2}$

$= \sqrt{80^2 + 40^2}$

$= \sqrt{8000}$

$= 40\sqrt{5}$ - Sufficient

From statement 2:

Let the coordinates of point Q be $(b, -40)$.

Since Q is on the circle, it must satisfy the equation of the circle. Thus:

$b^2 + (-40)^2 = 50^2$

$=> b^2 = 900$

$=> b = \pm 30$

Thus, the length of PQ $= \sqrt{(50 - (\pm 30))^2 + (0 - (-40))^2}$

$= \sqrt{(50 \mp 30)^2 + (40)^2}$

$= \sqrt{20^2 + 40^2}$ OR $\sqrt{80^2 + 40^2}$

$= \sqrt{2000}$ OR $\sqrt{8000}$

$= 20\sqrt{5}$ OR $40\sqrt{5}$

Thus, there is no unique answer. – Insufficient

The correct answer is option A.

490. The points (r, s) and (u, v) would be equidistant from the origin $(0, 0)$ if:

$\sqrt{(r-0)^2 + (s-0)^2} = \sqrt{(u-0)^2 + (v-0)^2}$

$\Rightarrow r^2 + s^2 = u^2 + v^2$; (this is the condition we need to verify).

From statement 1:

We have no information about u and v. – Insufficient

From statement 2:

We have:

$u = 1 - r$ and $v = 1 - s$

$\Rightarrow u^2 + v^2$

$= (1-r)^2 + (1-s)^2$

$= 2 + r^2 + s^2 - 2(r+s)$

We do not know the value of $(r+s)$. – Insufficient

Thus, from statements 1 and 2 together:

$u^2 + v^2$

$= 2 + r^2 + s^2 - 2\,(r+s)$

$= 2 + r^2 + s^2 - 2$ (since $r + s = 1$)

$= r^2 + s^2$ – Sufficient

The correct answer is option C.

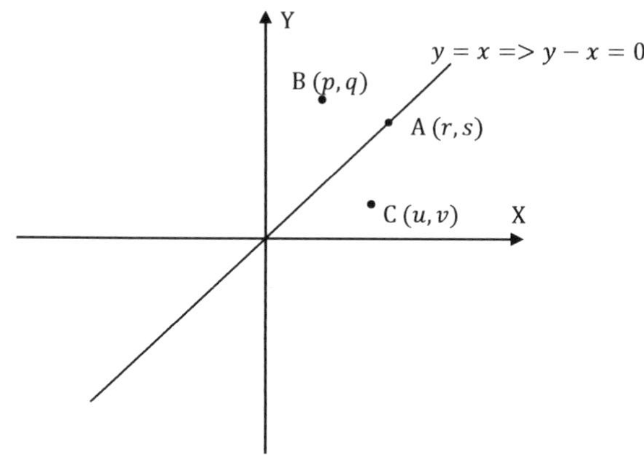

Let us refer to the figure above:

(1) For a point A on the line, it must satisfy the equation of the line. Thus, we have:

$y - x = 0$
$\Rightarrow s - r = 0$
$\Rightarrow s = r$

(2) For a point B above the line, we have:

$y - x > 0$ (it can be observed that the value of the Y-coordinate is greater than the value of the X-coordinate)
$\Rightarrow q - p > 0$
$\Rightarrow q > p$

(3) For a point C below the line, we have:

$y - x < 0$ (it can be observed that the value of the Y-coordinate is smaller than the value of the X-coordinate)
$\Rightarrow v - u < 0$
$\Rightarrow v < u$

Thus, we need to determine which of the above cases is true.

From statement 1:

491. There is no information about b. - Insufficient

From statement 2:

We have:

$b = a + 2$

=> $b - a = 2$

=> $b - a > 0$ (i.e. it satisfies $y - x > 0$)

=> The point is above the line $y = x$ - Sufficient

The correct answer is option B.

492. Form statement 1:

Slope of the line joining $(1,\ 1)$ and $(-2,\ 5)$

$= \frac{5 - 1}{-2 - 1}$

$= -\frac{4}{3}$

Since the line k is perpendicular to the above line, product of slopes of the above line and the slope of the line k is -1.

Thus, slope of line $k = \frac{3}{4}$ - Sufficient

From statement 2:

It is clear that the line must be oriented as shown in the diagram below:

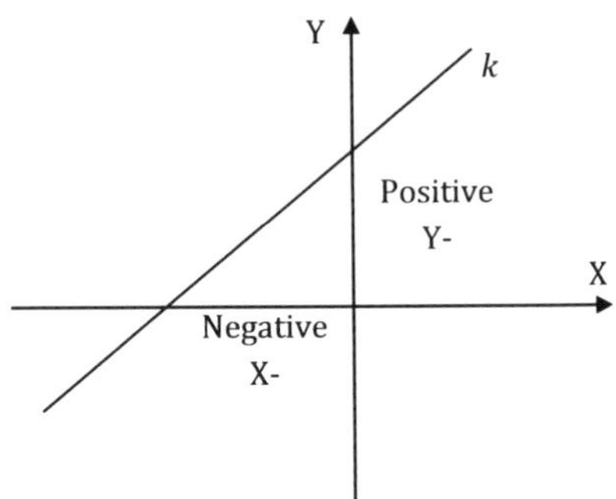

If a line is increasing towards right hand side, the slope is positive.

If line is parallel to x- axis, the slope is 0.

And, if the line is decreasing towards the right hand side, the slope is negative.

Thus, we see that the line k has a positive slope. - Sufficient

The correct answer is option D.

493. From statement 1:

We have no information about the value of the slope of line k. - Insufficient

From statement 2:

We have no information about the line l. - Insufficient

Thus, from statements 1 and 2 together:

We can see that line k passes through the points (0, 0) and $\left(\frac{16}{5}, \frac{12}{5}\right)$.

Thus, slope of line $k = \left(\frac{\frac{12}{5} - 0}{\frac{16}{5} - 0}\right) = \frac{3}{4}$.

Since the product of the slopes of lines l and k is -1, slope of line $l = -\left(\frac{1}{\frac{3}{4}}\right) = -\frac{4}{3}$. - Sufficient

The correct answer is option C.

494. If a line intersects the X-axis at $(p, 0)$ and the Y-axis at $(0, q)$, the slope of the line $= \frac{q - 0}{0 - p}$

$= -\frac{q}{p}$

$= -\left(\frac{\text{Y intercept}}{\text{X intercept}}\right)$

Let line b intersect the X-axis and Y-axis at points $(m, 0)$ and $(0, n)$ respectively.

We need to determine the value of n.

From statement 1:

Slope of line a

$= -\left(\frac{-1}{-1}\right) = -1$

Since lines a and b are parallel, slope of line b is -1.

Thus, for line b, we have:

$-\left(\frac{n}{m}\right) = -1$

$=> n = m.$

We cannot determine the value of n since m is not known. – Insufficient

From statement 2:

We see that line b passes through the point (10, 20) and the points $(m, 0)$ and $(0, n)$ as assumed earlier.

We cannot determine the value of n, since we do not know the slope of line b. – Insufficient

Thus, from statements 1 and 2 together:

We see that line b passes through the point (10, 20) and the point $(0, n)$ and also has a slope of -1.

Thus, we have:

$\frac{20 - n}{10 - 0} = -1$

$=> 20 - n = -10$

$=> n = 30$ – Sufficient

The correct answer is option C.

495. The equation of a circle with centre at the origin and radius c is given by:

$x^2 + y^2 = c^2$

Since (r, s) lies on the circle, it must satisfy the equation of the circle.

Thus, we have:
$r^2 + s^2 = c^2$

From statement 1:

$c = 2$

$=> r^2 + s^2 = c^2 = 4$ - Sufficient

From statement 2:

Since the point $\left(\sqrt{2}, -\sqrt{2}\right)$ lies on the circle, it must satisfy the equation of the circle.

Thus, we have:

$\left(\sqrt{2}\right)^2 + \left(-\sqrt{2}\right)^2 = c^2$

$=> c^2 = 4$

$=> r^2 + s^2 = 4$ - Sufficient

The correct answer is option D.

496. The point (r, s) would lie in region R if it satisfies the condition: $2x + 3y \leq 6$.

Thus, we have:

$2r + 3s \leq 6 \ldots$ (i)

From statement 1:

We have:

$3r + 2s = 6$

$=> (2r + 3s) + (r - s) = 6$

$=> 2r + 3s = 6 + (s - r) \ldots$ (ii)

Comparing (i) and (ii), we have:

$6 + (s - r) \leq 6$

$=> s - r \leq 0$

$=> s \leq r$

Thus, the point (r, s) would lie in region R if:

$s \leq r$

However, such a condition has not been stated in the problem.

Hence, the answer cannot be determined. – Insufficient

From statement 2:

We have:

$r \leq 3$

$=> 2r \leq 6 \ldots$ (iii), and

$s \leq 2$

$=> 3s \leq 6 \ldots$ (iv)

Thus, from (iii) and (iv):

$2r + 3s \leq 6 + 6$

$=> 2r + 3s \leq 12 \ldots$ (v)

Thus, we may have:

(a) $2r + 3s \leq 6$

OR

(b) $6 \leq 2r + 3s \leq 12$

Thus, the answer cannot be uniquely determined. – Insufficient

Thus, from statements 1 and 2 together:

We have from statement 2:

$r \leq 3 => 3r \leq 9$, and

$s \leq 2 \Rightarrow 2s \leq 4$

Thus, we have:

$3r + 2s \leq 9 + 4$

$\Rightarrow 3r + 2s \leq 13$

However, we also have from statement 1:

$3r + 2s = 6$

We cannot determine the value of $(2r + 3s)$ from the above two relations. – Insufficient

Alternate approach:

Let us try with some values:

Statement 1:

$3r + 2s = 6$:

(1) $r = 2,\ s = 0$: $2x + 3y \equiv 2r + 3s = 4 \leq 6$ – Satisfies

(2) $r = \frac{2}{3},\ s = 2$: $2x + 3y \equiv 2r + 3s = \frac{4}{3} + 6 \nleq 6$ – Does not satisfy

Thus, statement 1 is not sufficient.

Statement 2:

$r \leq 3,\ s \leq 2$:

(1) $r = 2,\ s = 0$: $2x + 3y \equiv 2r + 3s = 4 \leq 6$ – Satisfies

(2) $r = \frac{2}{3},\ s = 2$: $2x + 3y \equiv 2r + 3s = \frac{4}{3} + 6 \nleq 6$ – Does not satisfy

Thus, statement 2 is not sufficient.

Combining statements 1 and 2:

We can still have the same above values of r and s.

Thus, even combining the statements is not sufficient.

The correct answer is option E.

497. From statement 1:

Slope (m) of the line k passing through $(0,\ 0)$ and (a, b) is:

$$m = \frac{b-0}{a-0} = \frac{b}{a}$$

Thus, we have:

$$\frac{b}{a} < 0$$

Thus, the possible cases are:

(1) $a > 0$ and $b < 0$

OR

(2) $a < 0$ and $b > 0$

Thus, there is no unique answer. – Insufficient

From statement 2:

We know that: $a < b$

However, it is not sufficient to determine the answer, whether $b > 0$. – Insufficient

Thus, from statements 1 and 2 together:

From statement 1, we had:

(1) $a > 0$ and $b < 0 \Rightarrow a > b$ – Does not satisfy the condition of statement 2
(2) $a < 0$ and $b > 0 \Rightarrow a < b$ – Satisfies the condition of statement 2

Thus, combining the statements, we can conclude that: $b > 0$. – Sufficient

The correct answer is option C.

498. $ax + by + c = 0$

$\Rightarrow by = -ax - c$

$\Rightarrow y = \left(-\frac{a}{b}\right)x - \frac{c}{b}$

$\Rightarrow$ The slope of the line $= \left(-\frac{a}{b}\right)$

$=> -\frac{a}{b} = \frac{2}{3}$

$=> \frac{a}{b} = -\frac{2}{3}$

$=> b = -\frac{3a}{2}$

From statement 1:

$a = 4$

$=> b = -\frac{3 * 4}{2} = -6$ - Sufficient

From statement 2:

The value of c cannot be used to determine the value of b, as we are not aware of the value of the Y-intercept.

If Y-intercept would have been given it would be $-\frac{c}{b}$, and then we would have been able to find the value of b. - Insufficient

The correct answer is option A.

499. From statement 1:

The figure depicting the two vertices of the rectangle $(-1, -2)$ and $(2, -2)$ is shown below:

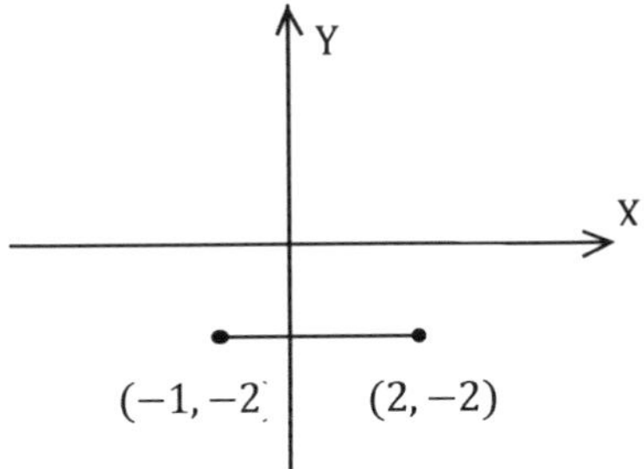

Thus, we know that the length of the rectangle is the difference between the X values of the coordinates of the two points (since the length is parallel to the X axis).

Thus, the length of the rectangle

$= 2 - (-1) = 3$

However, we do not know the width of the rectangle and hence, the perimeter cannot be determined. - Insufficient

From statement 2:

The figure depicting the two vertices of the rectangle $(-1, -2)$ and $(2, 3)$ is shown below:

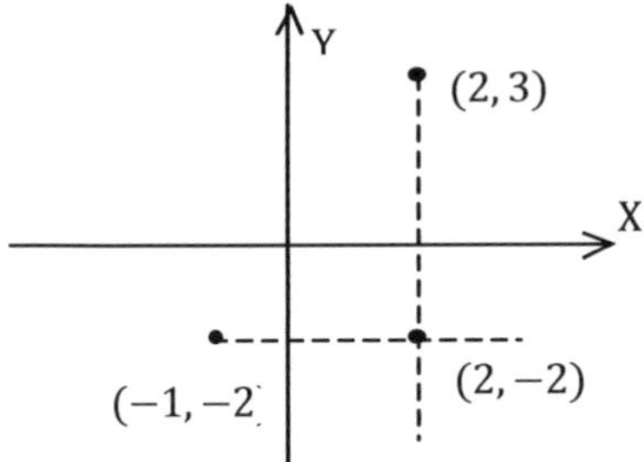

Since the length and width of the rectangle are parallel to the X and Y axes, the dotted lines shown in the figure above must denote the length and width of the rectangle.

Thus, the third vertex must be the point of intersection of the dotted lines i.e. $(2, -2)$.

Thus, we know that the length of the rectangle is the difference between the X values of the coordinates of the two points (since the length is parallel to the X axis).

Thus, the length of the rectangle

$= 2 - (-1) = 3$

Also, the width of the rectangle is the difference between the Y values of the coordinates of the two points (since the width is parallel to the Y axis).

Thus, the width of the rectangle

$= 3 - (-2) = 5$

Thus, the perimeter of the rectangle

$= 2 * (\text{Length} + \text{Width})$

$= 2 * (3 + 5)$

$= 16$ - Sufficient

The correct answer is option B.

500. From statement 1:

Since the line l does not intersect with $y = 1 - x$, these lines are parallel.

Thus, their slopes are the same.

We have:

$y = 1 - x$

=> $y = -x + 1$

=> Slope of the line is -1

Thus, slope of the line l is -1 - Sufficient

From statement 2:

Since the line l intersects with $y = x - 1$, these lines are not parallel.

However, we do not know the angle at which the lines intersect.

Hence, we cannot determine the slope of the line l. - Insufficient

The correct answer is option A.

Chapter 7

Speak to Us

Have a Question?

Please email your questions to info@manhattanreview.com. We will be happy to answer you. You questions can be related to a concept, an application of a concept, an explanation of a question, a suggestion for an alternate approach, or anything else you wish to ask regarding the GMAT.
Please mention the page number when quoting from the book.

31477023R00306

Made in the USA
Middletown, DE
02 May 2016